W9-APF-559

fP

ALSO BY ELIOT A. COHEN

Supreme Command:
Soldiers, Statesmen, and Leadership in Wartime

MILITARY MISFORTUNES

The Anatomy of Failure in War

Eliot A. Cohen

John Gooch

FREE PRESS

New York   London   Toronto   Sydney

FREE PRESS
A Division of Simon & Schuster, Inc.
1230 Avenue of the Americas
New York, NY 10020

Copyright © 1990 by The Free Press

All rights reserved,
including the right of reproduction
in whole or in part in any form.

First Free Press paperback edition 2006

FREE PRESS and colophon are trademarks
of Simon & Schuster, Inc.

For information regarding special
discounts for bulk purchases,
please contact Simon & Schuster Special Sales:
1-800-456-6798 or business@simonandschuster.com.

Manufactured in the United States of America

7   9   10   8   6

Library of Congress Cataloging-in-Publication Data
Cohen, Eliot A.
Military misfortunes : the anatomy of failure in war / Eliot A. Cohen, John Gooch.
p. cm.
"Originally published in hardcover by The Free Press . . . New York, 1990"—T.p. verso.
1. Military art and science—History—20th century. 2. Military history, Modern—20th
century. I. Gooch, John. II. Title.
[U42.C56 1991]
355.4'8'0904—dc20   90-50491

ISBN-13: 978-0-02-906060-5
ISBN-10:   0-02-906060-5
ISBN-13: 978-0-7432-8082-2 (Pbk)
ISBN-10:   0-7432-8082-2 (Pbk)

Contents

Preface

A BOOK ABOUT MISFORTUNE has emerged from what was, for us, a stroke of good fortune. In the autumn of 1985 we met as visiting faculty members in the Strategy Department of the U.S. Naval War College in Newport, Rhode Island. Following one of many heated but friendly informal debates about strategy and military history in Hewitt wardroom—the immediate subject was the Dardanelles campaign, about which see chapter 6—we decided to teach a seminar together on operational failure in war. More specifically, we decided to examine a dozen cases of what we label here "misfortunes"—that is, failures attributable neither to gross disproportions in odds nor to egregious incompetence on the part of the victim nor yet to extraordinary skill on the part of the victor. In short, we asked, Why do competent military organizations fail? After the seminar we came to the conclusion (endorsed by our students) that this question deserved book-length treatment.

Although we chose cases sufficiently close to our time to be recognizably "modern," we quite deliberately refrained from including one from Vietnam. (To discuss that misfortune, we are more-than-ever convinced, would require not a chapter but a separate book.) We chose to look at the experiences of Western democracies, believing that the nature of a country's regime shapes its military organizations in important ways. The origins and nature of (not to mention the penalties for) failure in, say, Sadam Hussein's Iraq or Stalin's Russia are very different from those one sees in free states; for in many, though not all, respects, military organizations reflect the societies for which they fight. To strike a balance between a narrow focus and a broader scope, we have looked at the experiences of four nations over a period of nearly sixty years. We considered and rejected many more cases than we include, for a variety of reasons. In some instances we concluded, upon reflection, that we were indeed dealing with failures born of incompetence rather than "misfortunes"; in others, we found that the evidence available was too scanty to permit a sober judgment.

We have divided our work evenly, Gooch writing the first drafts of chapters 2, 6, 8, and 9 and Cohen tackling 3, 4, 5, and 7. Chapters 2 and 3 and the last chapter, which are broader in scope than the intervening five case studies, underwent extensive rewriting, so that the result is very much a joint product. Unless otherwise noted, all translations from the French, German, and Hebrew are by us.

We have had the assistance and advice of many people, whose help we would like to acknowledge. We begin with our students Edward Colonna, William Dalecky, James Hagen, Joseph King, James Lasswell, David Lindauer, Patrick Saxon, Peter Scofield, Drake Trumpe, Anthony Veiga, and Stanley Winarsky. As is so often the case at the Naval War College, these officers from the U.S. Navy, Army, Marine Corps, and Air Force (and in this case a civil servant as well) had much to teach their nominal teachers. This would not be the same book without the benefit of their professional experience and judgment as well as their enthusiasm and insight; individually and collectively they demonstrated the high worth of the ethic of responsibility that we discuss in chapter 3.

Our research took us to a number of libraries and archives, and we are grateful for the aid we got there. In particular, we would like to acknowledge our debts to the resources of the Naval War College Library, Newport, R.I. (Robert Schnare); the Naval War College Historical Collection, Newport, R.I. (Evelyn Cherpak); Harvard's Widener Library; the Public Record Office, London; the University of London Library; the Liddell Hart Center for Military Archives, King's College, London (Patricia Methven); the Imperial War Museum, London (R. W. Suddaby); the Jaffee Center for Strategic Studies, Tel Aviv; the Modern Military Records branch of the National Archives, Washington, D.C. (John Taylor and Richard Boylan); the MacArthur Memorial, Norfolk, Va. (Edward J. Boone); the U.S. Navy Operational Archives, Washington, D.C. (Dean Allard and Bernard Cavalcante); the U.S. Marine Corps Historical Center, Washington, D.C. (H. I. Shaw); the U.S. Army Center for Military History, Washington, D.C. (Alexander Cochrane); and the U.S. Army Military History Institute, Carlisle, Pa. (Richard Somers and John Slonaker). In addition, Eliot Cohen had generous and frank interviews with a number of senior Israeli officials for his research on chapter 5, most notably Major Generals Aharon Yariv, Shlomo Gazit, and Israel Tal. Many others gave of their time, memories, and views but have requested anonymity, which in no way lessens our debt to them.

Colleagues and friends were generous in their comments on various chapters of the draft manuscript of the book. We would like to thank, in particular, Marino Bartolomei, Philip Bell, Richard Betts, Joseph Bower, Donald Disney, Zeev Eytan, William Fuller, Michael Handel, Samuel Huntington, Robert Jervis, Ephraim Kam, Ephraim Karsh, Bradford Lee, Ariel Levite, Andrew Marshall, Williamson Murray, Charles Perrow, Juergen Rohwer, Stephen Rosen, David Rosenberg, Steven Ross, Zeev Schiff, Gary Schmitt, Abram Shulsky, Doug Smith, Frank Snyder, Brian Sullivan, Arthur Waldron, and Barry Watts. More broadly, we owe a debt to all of our colleagues in the Strategy Department of the Naval War College for their collegial interest and aid and to Tim Somes of the Operations Department for his encouragement. Robert Watts of the Naval War College and later of the Naval War College Foundation was a great help to us and made many administrative impediments vanish, for which we are grateful. The research was facilitated as well by John Mojdehi's logistical support, and we received financial assistance from the Olin, Smith Richardson, and Naval War College foundations for which we are very grateful. Barbara Atkins was indispensable in the preparation of the manuscript; she brought not only promptness and accuracy to her work but her special good humor as well. Edward Rothstein introduced us to The Free Press, and our editor there, Robert Wallace, has been most helpful over the last few years. Ann Gooch and Judy Cohen provided gracious hospitality to one another's partners during our trans-Atlantic consultations, wise criticism in the interim, and when the occasion demanded it, invaluable albeit gentle prodding to get on with it.

We owe a particular debt to those who have made the Naval War College an incomparable place to study strategy. Rear Admirals (as they then were) James Service, Ronald Marryott, John Baldwin, and Ronald Kurth have each, as presidents of that institution, renewed its commitment to unfettered scholarship. Secretary of the Navy John Lehman, who believed deeply in the importance of liberal education for the profession of arms, created the Secretary of the Navy Senior Research Fellowships at Newport, positions both of us have held, which enabled us to pursue some of the themes herein described. But above all, we want to thank Alvin Bernstein, the chairman of the Strategy Department at the Naval War College who brought both of us to Newport and who has made that department such a source of intellectual stimulation on the one hand and conviviality on the other. His many virtues, rooted in the best of mid-twentieth-century Brooklyn and ancient Rome, are well known to his friends, among whom we are proud to number ourselves. We dedicate this book to him, with affection.

MILITARY MISFORTUNES

The
Anatomy
of
Failure
in
War

1

Why Misfortune?

THIS BOOK IS ABOUT a particular kind of failure—failure in battle. Much of the literature dealing with this subject has tended to oversimplify what is in reality a complex and complicated phenomenon. Therefore, to explain how and why such failures occur we must begin by questioning some popular and much-cherished misconceptions.

"All battles," John Keegan has remarked, "are in some degree . . . disasters."[1] It is certainly true that every battle, and particularly every lost battle, looks like a disaster; but *disaster* is not a term that translates easily from the civil world to the military one. For one thing, it overlooks the fact that men in uniform are trained to function efficiently and effectively in an environment marked by danger and the imminent prospect of death—that is to say, to do their job in exactly those conditions that characterize civil disasters. Everyone in uniform lives with what has perceptively been called "the knowable possibility of disaster."[2]

So we do not expect sudden shocks to have the same paralyzing effect in the world of the soldier as they do in the world of the civilian. More important, war is a contest between two sides, and once a battle begins each party will do its level best to make a disaster occur by breaking the enemy's physical strength and destroying his mental resilience. Thus in every military setback or defeat there is an interplay between adversaries that is never present in the world of civil disasters. A fire will not "react" to the actions of the men who are trying to put it out in a way that makes their task more difficult. An enemy will do exactly that. This makes war a very special kind of "disaster environment."

1

At a superficial level, military setbacks do seem to bear comparison with civil disasters insofar as they come in different shapes and sizes and have consequences of different magnitudes. An operation may fail with small loss of life and be only a minor setback, as with the abortive Dakar expedition undertaken by de Gaulle's Free French forces in 1940. On the other hand, an operation may fail with relatively small loss and yet represent a major setback, as happened in the summer of 1940 when Britain lost the campaign in Norway. At a higher level of magnitude, the surrender of Singapore in February 1942 was both a big loss and a major setback—as was General Friedrich von Paulus's surrender of the German Sixth Army at Stalingrad a year later. And, on an altogether different plane, the fall of France in June 1940 was nothing less than a catastrophe.

Thinking this way, it is all too easy to perceive military setbacks as part of a progression from minor embarrassment to mortal failure. However, regarding the problem as a matter of degree is of no help in explaining why these setbacks occur. It could be that the size of the setback is a function of the aggregation of adverse factors: The more that goes wrong, the greater the degree of failure. But we could just as well assume that major failures are born of major errors: The bigger the stumble, the harder the fall. Rough-and-ready categorizing of this sort, which differentiates defeats according to their magnitude, reflects their consequences but does nothing to explain their causes.

The very notion of defeat—ostensibly the touchstone of failure—can be just as big an obstacle to understanding as disaster. For one thing, as the above examples suggest, the only feature many defeats have in common is their outcome. Also, defeat is not the only alternative to victory. Between these two poles lies the middle ground of missed opportunity—what Field Marshal Erich von Manstein called the "lost victories."[3] By making the concept of failure our central concern, we can incorporate into our analysis not merely battles lost but also battles that were not won. Understanding these is every bit as important to any military organization as understanding its defeats.

Although military failure commonly results in defeat, not all defeats are equally worthy of study. Some are evidently the consequence of facing overwhelming odds; in such circumstances the only thing to be done is to try to exercise some form of damage limitation. Others can be the result of a stroke of blind chance. Carl von Clausewitz acknowledged this possibility in his classic work *On War*. "No other human activity," he declared, "is so continuously or universally bound up with chance."[4] Others again may be the inescapable consequence of straightforward incompetence. The historian Guy Chapman found plenty of that in his inquiry into the causes of the fall of France in 1940: "There was hesitation, there was indecision, there was sheer bloody funk at the highest level, among ministers, politicians, generals, civil service chiefs."[5] Once we have identified the battles that fall into these categories, little benefit is to be gained from further study—they have yielded up their secret, such as it is.

However, not all military failures fall into these convenient categories. Some are defeats, and others are the "lost victories" to which we have referred. They seem to share certain common characteristics that raise important questions about the nature and causes of military failure. Most striking is the fact that when they occur, no one individual is obviously to blame. Field Marshal Joseph Joffre was fond of saying that he did not know whether he was responsible for the victory on the Marne in September 1914, but he knew one thing—if the battle had been lost, it would have been he who lost it.[6] True military "misfortunes"—as we define them—can never be justly laid at the door of any one commander. They are failures of the organization, not of the individual.

The other thing the failures we shall examine have in common is their apparently puzzling nature. Although something has clearly gone wrong, it is hard to see what; rather, it seems that fortune—evenly balanced between both sides at the outset—has turned against one side and favored the other. These are the occasions when it seems that the outcome of the battle depended at least as much on one side's mishandling of the situation as on the other's skill in exploiting a position of superiority. Competent professionals have failed in their task, for reasons that are not immediately apparent. In truth, this is another side of the same coin: The causes of organizational failure in the military world are not easy to discern.

Our choice of terminology, then, is both an indication of the complexity of military failure and an echo of the cry of bewilderment that so often greets it. It is a cry uttered as often by civilians as by soldiers. "What has happened at Chernobyl," *Pravda* remarked three weeks after the double steam-hydrogen explosion at the Soviet nuclear reactor in May 1986, "is of course a great misfortune."[7]

2

Understanding Disaster

INTRODUCTION

WE SHALL BEGIN OUR EXPLORATION of military misfortune by looking at the five explanations most commonly offered by historians trying to account for defeat and disaster on the field of battle. As we look at each one in turn, we shall see that its deficiencies outweigh its merits—often considerably. First, to illustrate the difficulties that have beset attempts to find convincing general explanations for major setbacks in the world of arms, we shall look at one of the greatest military conundrums of the twentieth century: the failure of Allied—especially British—commanders to achieve victory on the Western Front between 1915 and 1917, despite their prodigal expenditure of manpower and munitions.

Following this, we shall turn aside briefly from battles and battlefields to look at general explanations that have been offered to account for civil disasters and business failures. Analysts of civil—as opposed to military—failures have recently begun to look at their subject from a new perspective: how organizations can misfunction in unintended and unexpected ways. With this new perspective in mind, the final section of this chapter will develop a general theory of military misfortune and lay out a taxonomy of five types of military failure.

EXPLANATIONS AND MISAPPREHENSIONS

"The Man in the Dock"

The temptation to explain military failure in terms of human error is a characteristic feature of much of the literature of defeat in battle. According to this view, catastrophe occurs because one man—almost invariably the commander—commits unpardonable errors of judgment. At first sight, the idea that a solitary, highly placed individual can, by his own incompetence and stupidity, create a military disaster is deceptively attractive. It is at one with the traditional idea that a commander carries the responsibility for everything that happens in—and therefore to—his command; it is the counterpart to the picture of the heroic leader, handsomely rewarded for ushering his forces to victory; and it can be legitimated by appealing to history. The most superficial acquaintance with the past quickly yields a rich crop of professional incompetents who led or ordered their followers into the jaws of disaster in pursuit of what hindsight shows to have been an unlikely success, or who simply lacked the intellectual grasp to understand the true nature of their situation.

In the age of heroic leaders, any individual commander—combining, as he often did, both military and political authority—was in an ideal position to bring about a military disaster entirely unaided. In 1302 Robert of Courtrai's stupidity in ordering a cavalry charge across entirely unsuitable ground at the Battle of Courtrai met the fate it richly deserved; and when King Henry VI of France, lured into attacking the English at Agincourt in 1415, launched his heavily armored men-at-arms in tight-packed formations, they were unable to fight properly and fell easy victims to their more mobile opponents.[1] Later leaders failed just as dismally. When Doctor William Brydon rode into Jalalabad in 1842, the lone survivor of a force of 4,500 fighting men and 12,000 camp followers who had begun the retreat from Kabul in Afghanistan, his lucky escape simply magnified the extent of General John Elphinstone's inadequacies.[2] Major General Sir Hugh Wheeler, cautiously trying not to provoke sepoy mutineers who had occupied Cawnpore in 1857, gave them time and opportunity to massacre the white women and children they held captive; and in 1879 General Lord Chelmsford, rather too casual in his attitude to the Zulus, crashed to defeat at Isandhlwana.[3] Only three years earlier, George Armstrong Custer's decision to attack the Sioux encampment on the Little Big Horn had induced a disaster of cinematic proportions.

Misfortunes of this kind, which occur at the tactical level and are localized in scope, may often properly be laid at the door of individuals. But

there is a very great difference between the degree of con[ ]
by a Napoleon, who could oversee a whole battlefield and [ ]
ence what was happening on it, and a modern military lea... ....
of a campaign, much farther from events and vulnerable to more varied
forces as his command undertakes a great and protracted effort. In a
word, the modern commander's world is far more complex than that of
his dashing predecessor. His decisions are affected by the perceptions,
demands, and requirements of others, and his actions do little more than
shape the tasks to be carried out by his many subordinates.[4]

Since 1870 a commander has seldom if ever been able to survey a
whole battlefield from a single spot; and in any case he has had little
opportunity—although sometimes a considerable inclination—to try. For
the modern commander is much more akin to the managing director of
a large conglomerate enterprise than ever he is to the warrior chief of old.
He has become the head of a complex military organization, whose many
branches he must oversee and on whose cooperation, assistance, and support he depends for his success. As the size and complexity of military
forces have increased, the business of war has developed an organizational
dimension that can make a mighty contribution to triumph—or to tragedy. Hitherto, the role of this organizational dimension of war in explaining military performance has been strangely neglected. We shall return to
it later—indeed, it will form one of the major themes of this book. For
now we simply need to note its looming presence.

And yet the urge to find, excoriate, judge, and sentence culpable individuals has led contemporaries as well as historians to blame men for very
much more than the loss of a battle over which they exercised a tolerable
degree of control. When a royal commission was convened in 1917 to
explain the failure of the Gallipoli campaign two years earlier, Field Marshal Lord Kitchener, who had been secretary of state for war at the time,
was dead. A bevy of soldiers and politicians appeared for questioning, and
almost to a man they blamed Kitchener for having made the decision to
undertake the campaign in the first place—thereby conveniently forget-
ting that it had been a communal choice.[5] Some years later, the congressional inquiry into the disaster at Pearl Harbor in December 1941 put
the men on the spot—Admiral Husband E. Kimmel and Lieutenant General Walter C. Short—in the dock. Recently an attempt has been made
to get both men off the hook by hanging two more admirals—Harold R.
Stark and Richmond Kelly Turner—on it.[6] The urge to blame military
misfortunes on individuals runs as deep as the inclination to blame human
error for civil disasters.

"Criminalizing" military misfortune in this way by arraigning a guilty party serves an important military function; but as an explanation of failure it is really little more than a concealed confession of perplexity. Yet even those who have perceived its limitations have not been able to replace it with any more sophisticated explanation. Indeed, they have been unable to go much beyond postulating the existence of "a fatal conjunction of circumstances; a devil's brew of incompetence, unpreparedness, mistaken and inappropriate tactics, a brash underestimating of the enemy, a difficult terrain, raw recruits, treacherous opponents, diplomatic hindrance and bone-headed leadership."[7] This is no more than a cry of despair masquerading as an explanation.

"The Man on the Couch"

Are the grievous faults that soldiers sometimes exhibit due to something more—and more complex—than individual incompetence and dimwittedness? Are the causes of military misfortune to be found in some collective way of thinking, which all generals share and for which they cannot be held to blame? This is certainly the opinion of the psychologist Norman Dixon. "Stupidity does not explain the behavior of these generals," he writes of Field Marshal Douglas Haig and his subordinates in World War I.

> So great was their fear of loss of self-esteem, and so imperative their need for social approval, that they could resort to tactics beyond the reach of any self-respecting "donkey." From their shameless self-interest, lack of loyalty to their subordinates and apparent indifference to the verdict of posterity, a picture emerges of personalities deficient in something other than intellectual acumen.[8]

Casting his eye over a formidable collection of military incompetents, Dixon finds that the generals who fail all exhibit the same psychological characteristics. They are passive and courteous, obstinate and rigid, ambitious and insensitive. In short, they are all psychological cripples—walking wounded who bear no visible scars.

If such men were distributed at random across the command posts of the military world, disaster would be likely enough for us to shudder in apprehension. But things are much worse than that. The people who get to the top do so because they possess certain institutionally desirable characteristics: They are cautious, they adhere to rules and regulations, they respect and accept authority, they obey their superiors, and they regard discipline and submission to authority as the highest virtues. Twenty-five or thirty years spent gaining promotion simply accentuate these characteristics, so that by the time a soldier reaches the top of the tree he lacks the very qualities of flexibility, imaginativeness, and adventurousness he needs in order to exercise command effectively.

Here, then, lies the heart of the problem, the inevitability of disaster: "Authoritarianism, itself so damaging to military endeavour, *will actually predispose an individual towards entering upon the very career wherein his restricted personalty can wreak the most havoc.* [Dixon's italics]."[9] It is, as Dixon says, like learning that only people with Parkinson's disease decide to become eye surgeons.

It remains only for Dixon to fit the last piece of the jigsaw into place. The soldier who has reached the top is anal-retentive. The evidence for this lies not merely in associated traits of character and their ineluctable consequences, such as slowness to accept unexpected information and difficulty in controlling aggressive impulses, but in the world the anal-obsessive general creates.

> Whether by accident or design, the events of Third Ypres [in 1917]—the enormous release of destructive energy, the churning up of ground until the overlapping craters coalesced into one great reeking swamp, and the expulsion into this mass of more and yet more "faecal" bodies—constitutes the acting out of an anal fantasy of impressive proportions.[10]

It should therefore come as no surprise that the top brass regularly mess things up.

It would be easy to dismiss Dixon's theorizing as simply the kind of thing that gets psychoanalysis a bad name. In fact, a little reflection on the reality of military history provides ample refutation for his theories. Though many of the personality traits he identifies do seem to be present in some of the more notable cases of failure, it is by no means obvious that, by the same token, they are not also among the mental baggage of history's successful generals. Many great commanders have had their share of obsessional jealousy, mental rigidity, and authoritarianism; and at least one—Eisenhower—has been accused of having exactly the opposite caste of mind.[11]

Even more perplexing if we hold to the "man on the couch" theory of military misfortune is the case of the commander who fails at one time but creates a remarkable victory at another. The Douglas MacArthur who so utterly misjudged the likelihood and imminence of China's entry into the Korean War was, after all, the same Douglas MacArthur who first conceived and then implemented the Inchon landing in the teeth of strong opposition from his subordinates. Was he struck by a sudden attack of anal-retentiveness sometime between June and October 1950? It seems unlikely.

If Dixon's theory were true, we would see much more evidence of incompetence—and therefore of failure—in the military world than in business, industry, or any other activity that involves controlling substantial numbers of human beings. Observation and experience suggest that competence and incompetence are much more evenly spread among those in and out of uniform than such theories would suggest.

Military disaster would also be much more common than it is, and our problem would lie in explaining military success. Because this is not the case we have to explain why some military actions fail and others do not. The mental characteristics of individual commanders are of only limited use in this.

Collective Incompetence and the "Military Mind"

Somewhere between the "man in the dock" and the "man on the couch" stands the idea of straightforward collective military incompetence. To move from blaming a particular individual for disaster to claiming that all senior soldiers are more or less equally likely to fail the test of professional competence is not to take a big step. According to this theory, any individual could count himself unfortunate to be in the dock when the generally low level of professional ability would permit few of his contemporaries to avoid similar accusations if put to the test. General Ambrose Burnside's stubborn persistence in attacking the Confederate army at Fredericksburg in 1864, long after it was apparent that the effort was fruitless, has placed him securely within the cohort of military incompetents. But was he any less capable than most of his brother officers? The question is impossible to answer, but the temptation is to guess that he was not. Forced to offer an explanation as to why this should be so, Charles Fair could only claim that "the man who is by temperament and physique close to the going tribal norms tends to rise no matter how stupid he is."[12] At this point we may as well give up all hope, for if Fair is correct mankind is clearly doomed to interminable military disasters!

Compared with this theory, the idea that the "military mind" is the cause of all military misfortune seems complex and sophisticated. The idea that simply living in and serving a hierarchical institution such as an army encourages and intensifies potentially disastrous habits of mind, regardless of their supposed psychological origins, has found fertile soil—and nowhere more so than in the history of the First World War. Its generals seem condemned without prospect of reprieve by the hell of the

Western Front, where hundreds of thousands of humble combatants were condemned to death by generals who concealed behind luxuriant mustaches and lantern jaws their complete incomprehension of modern war.[13]

The Conundrum of World War I

By far the most powerful—and most damning—portrait of the military mind is to be found in C. S. Forester's novel *The General*. Narrowly schooled, unflinchingly devoted to their duty, and unmoved in the face of difficulty, the generals of the First World War were "single-minded and . . . simple-minded," as indeed they had to be: "Men without imagination were necessary to execute a military policy devoid of imagination, devised by a man without imagination."[14] In their care, armies died in an uncomplaining spirit of self-sacrifice:

> It occurred to no-one that they had to die in that fashion because the men responsible for their training had never learned any lessons from history, had never realized what resources modern invention had opened to them, with the consequence that men had to do at the cost of their lives the work which could have been done with one-quarter the losses and at one-tenth the risk of defeat if they had been adequately armed and equipped.[15]

Forester's damning indictment of the military profession was a novelist's reaction to the enormity of the human price paid in the course of the First World War—a slaughter so unparalleled that it has been termed "the cruelest scourge that Europe had suffered since the Black Death."[16] In all, some ten million fell in battle during the four years it took for all sides to exhaust themselves—and one another. The seemingly endless casualty lists published in British newspapers during the war provided unmistakable evidence of the cost of British strategy on the Western Front. The official justification was that attrition was costing the enemy even more dearly, so that the process of wearing down Germany's reserves of military manpower would lead inexorably to victory. The publication of the official *Statistics of the Military Effort of the British Empire during the Great War* in 1922 revealed that the strategy of Haig's campaigns on the Somme in 1916 and at Passchendaele in 1917 had probably cost the Allies more than the Germans. It began a battle of statistics that has continued more or less ever since.

The Great War was not long over before men began to weigh the cost of Haig's great offensives against the outcomes. In the case of the Somme, a campaign that began on July 1 with sixty thousand British casualties ended with ten times that number, expended for a strip of ground some 30 miles long and 7 miles deep. It was not long before the accusing finger began to point at the leaders. Winston Churchill, with some sense of the complexities of the war and of the advantages of hindsight, pointed out that Haig and Foch "had year after year conducted with obstinacy and serene confidence offensives which we now know to have been as hopeless as they were disastrous."[17] Lloyd George categorized Passchendaele in his *Memoirs* as a needless bloodbath. But it was H. G. Wells, in his *Outline of History*, who extended the responsibility for the failure on the Western Front to the military as a whole. The war, he declared, was "a hopelessly professional war; from first to last it was impossible to get it out of the hands of the regular generals." Herein lay the true cause of disaster, for "the professional military mind is by necessity an inferior and unimaginative mind; no man of high intellectual quality would willingly imprison his gifts in such a calling. . . ."[18]

During the 1920s and 1930s, Haig was singled out as almost criminally responsible for the apparently meaningless slaughter his strategy had engendered, "an unfeeling, stupid and ignorant blimp who sent men to futile death in fighting conditions he knew nothing of."[19] Narrowly educated, unimaginative, rigid, and remote, he became the exemplar of his profession, a man who both encapsulated and imposed the mental limitations of his kind. His professional mentality was so deeply rooted in the cavalry ethos of the late nineteenth century that he was quite unable to understand the technological revolution in warfare that had taken place by 1916.[20] An attempt in 1963 to get Haig out of the dock went too far in the opposite direction by trying to prove that his intellectual powers were far greater than anyone had given him credit for—an argument that failed to convince.[21]

It is possible, however, to take a more sympathetic view of Haig and his fellow generals, and of the very considerable and perplexing difficulties they found themselves facing, when we acknowledge the frightful novelty of the military situation in which they were called upon to wage successful war. No army was adequately prepared for the trench warfare that became the dominant feature of war on the Western Front and elsewhere after Christmas 1914. The technical problems it presented—chiefly those of achieving surprise, carrying the first line of enemy trenches against the defensive power of rifle and machine gun, and then pushing on into the enemy's rear across ground churned into an almost impassable morass by heavy artillery—would have taxed the mental resources of Napoleon himself.[22] Gradually, as the war went on, a younger generation of middle-ranking commanders applied their minds to the problem, aided by the advent of such new weapons as the tank and the airplane. The answer to the conundrum of the Western Front, in purely military terms, did not lie just with new instruments of war, however; it entailed developing new techniques for combining artillery, infantry, tanks, and airplanes and developing a doctrine that emphasized flexibility over rigidity and innovation over obedience to long-established "principles."[23] For the generals, the First World War was a long and costly learning process.

Not only was the high command confronted by a novel environment; it was also imprisoned in a system that made it well-nigh impossible to meet the challenges of trench warfare. The submissive obedience of Haig's subordinates, which Forester took for blinkered ignorance and whole-hearted support, was in reality the unavoidable consequence of the way in which the army high command functioned as an organization under its commander in chief. A personalized promotion system, built on the bedrock of favoritism and personal rivalry that had characterized the pre-1914 army, ensured that middle-ranking officers undertook offensives of no tactical or strategical use whether they believed in them or not: If they obeyed orders, they could hope for promotion, but if they did anything else they faced the certainty of removal and disgrace. The way Haig ran his headquarters, preserving an Olympian detachment, tolerating no criticism, and accepting precious little advice, reinforced the rigidity of the system.[24] That system was itself a product of a different age and a different army, and was no longer appropriate to the circumstances. But rather than change it, Haig and his fellow commanders preferred to rely on the traditional tools of the general—men and guns—in ever-larger quantities. In Tim Travers's words:

> The British army's reaction to the emergence of modern warfare was therefore a conservative reflex, perhaps because full accommodation to machine warfare would have required social and hierarchical changes with unforeseen consequences.[25]

Our excursion into the controversy over the talents—or otherwise—of the First World War generals shows very clearly that the most promising line of inquiry into the roots of military misfortune is not to issue imprecise blanket condemnations of the supposed deficiencies of the "military mind," but to look more closely at the organizational systems within which such minds have to operate. Leveling the same charge at quite different men, operating in differing circumstances, and at different times, is not an aid to analysis but a barrier against it. Indeed, the essential uselessness of the concept of the "military mind" for our purposes is evident in the fact that it is rarely offered as the reason behind the setbacks of World War II, whereas the opposite is the case with the war of 1914–18. If any further proof were needed that this is not the answer, it surely lies in the fact that generals such as Pétain, Foch, and even Haig performed much better in 1917–18 than they did in the earlier years of the war. They could not have done so had they been encumbered with permanent mental blinkers.

Institutional Failure

Sometimes, in cases in which it is self-evidently absurd to pin the blame for military failure on a single individual, entire institutions have been held responsible. Thus the United States Navy as a whole has been blamed for its failure to adopt the practice of convoying in 1942, and the whole French army indicted for the collapse of France in 1940. At first glance, this looks like another cry of analytical despair: If no one can be blamed, everyone must be at fault. But nevertheless something useful can be gleaned from this approach, for it seeks to explain failure in collective rather than in individual terms. However, the difficulty of attempting to explain military misfortune by putting an entire institution in the dock can be clearly illustrated by looking briefly at the case of the French army at the outbreak of the First World War.

Operating according to a tactical doctrine developed by General Ferdinand Foch, who believed that morale was stronger than firepower, the French army went to war in 1914 believing that charges by massed ranks of infantry with artillery support could overwhelm the defensive power of magazine rifles and machine guns. The result was a disaster, and the French lost some five hundred thousand casualties during August 1914 in the process of discovering that their cherished tactical doctrine was fatally flawed.

What is the explanation for this failure, in which many parties were involved? One historian has claimed that the fatal disregard of firepower was the expression of "a long tradition of French intellectual arrogance."[26] Another has discovered a collective lack of brains, arguing that the intellectual quality of the whole French officer corps was in decline from the close of the nineteenth century, thereby rendering it liable to faulty decision making.[27] More recently a third has suggested that the French army adopted the offensive with such enthusiasm because it conformed to organizational ideology and institutional aims. Belief in the offensive protected the standing regular army and created suspicion and doubt about the capabilities of reserve forces composed of civilians who had undergone only brief periods of military instruction and were held to be incapable of the disciplined tactical maneuvers necessary to carry out successful attacks.[28]

All these arguments collapse when a comparative dimension is added to the inquiry. In 1914 all major armies believed more or less equally in the efficacy—and necessity—of the tactical offensive, regardless of whether they were composed largely of conscripts, like the Russian army, or entirely of regulars, like the British; and of whether they believed in the strategic offensive, like the Germans; or the strategic defensive, like the Italians.[29] This being so, we cannot really accuse the French of being more arrogant or more stupid than anyone else.

Paradoxically, the idea of institutional failure draws some strength from its counterpart, the study of institutional success. Here, the imagination of historians has been transfixed by the competence of the German army. Ignoring the unfortunate outcome of both World Wars (from the German point of view), many writers have probed for the secret of German success on the field of battle. Some have found the answer in the higher direction of the German army, and in particular in the excellence of the German general staff system.[30] Others believe that it lies in less-elevated strata, and that a greater spirit of professional dedication among junior officers, more rigorous and effective training, a closer attention to tactical doctrine, a high degree of institutional integration, and a willingness to subject both successes and failures to close critical examination have been the real sources of German fighting power.[31] There are many possible explanations for the tactical and operational virtuosity of the Germans in the first half of the twentieth century, but (perhaps for that very reason) no consensus exists as to which ones were the most significant.

This kind of analysis is more fruitful than the traditional pastime of garlanding heroes and castigating villains. Nevertheless, looking at military forces as institutions is not entirely helpful in explaining why some of them sometimes fail because it directs us toward their distinctive social characteristics and seeks to identify special features or traits that make one army—or navy, or air force—different from another. Even supposing that we can identify these qualities correctly (which is difficult), and that they are truly unique (which is often not the case), this does not mean that we have found the cause of misfortune. For though we may now know what the institution *is*, we do not know how it *works*. To do this, we must think of armed forces not as institutions but as organizations.

Cultural Failure

One more form of blanket condemnation remains to be considered: putting a whole nation, rather than its army, navy, or air force, in the dock. This kind of national character assassination has been justified on the grounds that "certain qualities of intellect and character occur more frequently and are more frequently valued in one nation than in another."[32] Finding a firm analytical basis for such prejudices is well-nigh impossible.[33] For one thing, no one has yet succeeded in setting out supposed national characteristics in anything like a sophisticated and acceptable form. For another, this kind of activity ignores the fact that the laurels of success are not selectively conferred by some celestial divinity on a favored people or peoples. Disaster is not the inescapable fate of any nation. If anything can be said about the importance of cultural stereotypes, so far it does not amount to much more than the injunction not to underrate your enemy.[34]

LESSONS FROM CIVILIAN LIFE

Disaster Theory

Failure is by no means a monopoly of the military. Since the Second World War, a good deal of effort and energy has been expended in analyzing civil disasters; and these related studies have much to tell us about how to tackle our problem.

Disaster study really began in the years following 1945. It was heavily funded by the American federal government, in the hope that it would be able to come up with ways to minimize the effects of a nuclear strike on the civil population. Teams of sociologists went to work to generate the necessary data, and their field studies generally consisted of a detailed examination and analysis of what was involved in the task of clearing up after disaster had struck.[35] This concentration on practical matters contrasted with a general dearth of broad covering explanations about why disasters happen in the first place. The early literature virtually ignored this problem, and a rare foray into the question of causation concluded that it was impossible to construct a single theory of disaster that could encompass all the many sociopoliticopsychological variables involved.[36] However, an important step forward occurred when theories of cognition began to be incorporated into disaster study—although contemporary analysts did not realize their true significance. Armed with the blessings of hindsight, it is fairly easy to see in civil disasters chains of cause and effect (invisible to contemporaries) whose interruption would have prevented disaster occurring at all. Thus, "disaster-provoking events tend to accumulate because they have been overlooked or misinterpreted as a result of false assumptions, poor communications, cultural lag and misplaced optimism."[37] As we shall see, a direct parallel exists in the military world, where failure can arise from inadequate or imperfect anticipation of an enemy's actions.

The lack of any general theory of disaster has not meant that accidents and catastrophes have remained puzzlingly inexplicable, for an easily identifiable culprit is always around to take the blame: human error. It would be foolish to deny that human error is clearly a major ingredient in the making of many disasters. Only human beings make decisions, and wrong decisions can easily result in misfortune. But the more one unravels the causes of disaster, the less satisfactory an explanation human error turns out to be—at least in the simple and straightforward sense of pinning the blame on someone.

An example of where the hunt for human error can lead was the debate over the cause of the racetrack accident at Le Mans in June 1955, in which seventy-seven people died. The disaster occurred when one driver sheered into the crowd after being overtaken by another. At first the drivers were blamed. Then the mechanical features of the fatal car were the subject of critical scrutiny. From there the debate widened to take in the characteristics of the different nationalities whose representatives were most directly involved in the crash, the construction of the track, the organization of that particular race, the rules governing all motor racing, and finally the rationale of racing in general.[38] By concentrating on human error, this inquiry into the causes of a particular disaster lost itself in an inescapable maze of unanswerable questions.

What the Le Mans inquiry reveals—although it may have gone too far down this path—is that "operator error" may not be the sole or even the prime cause of disaster. To illustrate this, we can cite the Chernobyl incident, which took place on April 26, 1986. Although the plant's operators had repeatedly violated established safety procedures, at least two other factors contributed to the genesis of disaster. Soviet reactor design depended to a large extent on written instructions to the operators to ensure that the reactor remained in a safe condition, rather than on built-in engineering safeguards; and it was readily possible to carry out tests without proper authorization and supervision.[39] Clearly errors had been made at a number of levels. But things can sometimes go badly wrong in circumstances where there has been no obvious operator error.

At 4:00 A.M. on March 28, 1979, a serious malfunction in the nonnuclear part of the Three Mile Island nuclear reactor triggered a series of automated responses in the cooling system. During this process, a relief valve on the top of a pressurizer became jammed open. For over two and a quarter hours—abetted by an inadequate warning system that failed to register that the valve was stuck open and instead signaled that a switch had been thrown that ought to have closed it—operators misread the symptoms, turning off an automatic cooling system and thereby allowing the reactor core to become partially uncovered. Another twelve hours passed before plant crew and service engineers agreed on an effective course of action to overcome the results of these errors. Meltdown was avoided when an operator joining the emergency team correctly deduced that the pressurizer relief valve had jammed open. At that moment disaster was only sixty minutes away.

The independent investigatory commission that examined the Three Mile Island incident found many areas of human error that had contributed to creating a "disaster environment":

> Licensing procedures were not entirely adequate, giving rise to some
> deficiencies in plant designs. Operator training was totally inadequate
> for emergencies, and poorly monitored. Control rooms were often
> designed with precious little attention to the operator's needs. The
> lessons learned from malfunctions and mistakes at nuclear plants both
> here and abroad were never effectively shared within the industry.[40]

Once the incident had begun, design failure and psychological predisposition combined to make things worse: Operators elected to believe the misleading indicator light but disbelieved a series of ominous readings from other instruments that indicated that something was going badly wrong.

From this brief account it is obvious that Three Mile Island was anything but a straightforward case of operator error. Rather, it was a complex accident in which a number of factors combined in unforeseen and unexpected ways. The Nuclear Regulatory Commission's report acknowledged this complexity. "While there is no question that operators erred . . .," it concluded, "we believe there were a number of important factors not within the operators' control that contributed to this human failure. These include inadequate training, poor operator procedures, a lack of diagnostic skill on the part of the entire site management group, misleading instrumentation, plant deficiencies, and poor control room design."[41]

These examples are important to our inquiry in two respects. First, they confirm the wisdom of our earlier rejection of the "man in the dock" theory as an explanation of military misfortune. Second, they emphasize the fact that—in peace and in war—men operate in environments in which events are only partly the result of controlled decisions taken by the person "in charge." To go beyond this, and penetrate further into the complex world of misfortune and disaster, we must turn elsewhere for guidance.

Failure in Business

Like their military counterparts, businessmen, professors of business administration, and their students do not appear to enjoy discussing failure.[42] Like *their* counterparts, business journalists relish the opportunity to tell the tale of how greed and ineptitude lead businesses to produce products that do not sell, to undertake projects that cannot work, to pile up debts that cannot be repaid. A few authors, however, have produced a literature on business failure that repays some attention.[43]

Most business failures take the form of the collapse of small, young companies—the equivalent of the explainable military failures we discussed in the previous chapter. There are other cases, however, which closely approximate military misfortunes: a spectacular failure of a large and competent organization in a major undertaking—the business equivalent of a military campaign. One particularly good example of this is the story of the Edsel, the car introduced by Ford with much fanfare in 1957, which failed miserably and was withdrawn from the market within two years.[44] As usually told, the story of the Edsel is that of an organization that deceived itself through the use of pseudoscientific public opinion surveys, making a mockery of the techniques of market research and itself in the process.

The case of the Edsel, however, becomes far more puzzling (and interesting) when placed in the larger context of the Ford Corporation's performance since World War II. After its initial glorious period under its founder, Henry Ford, whose Model T became synonymous with the popularly owned automobile, Ford underwent a long period of decline, during which it was outstripped by its major American competitors. It was only after World War II that its recovery began—a recovery under way at the time of the Edsel fiasco. Indeed, after the bruising experience of the Edsel (which some estimate cost Ford as much as $350 million, although that figure is probably too high) Ford produced one of its most successful cars ever, the Thunderbird.

The more careful studies of the Edsel failure reveal that its sources lay in the confluence of several different kinds of factors. One set of problems involved particular tactical choices made by different managers: a confused pricing policy, a publicity campaign that created excessive expectations, and a design that was not terribly alluring. Another set of problems stemmed from erratic quality control—a deeper-seated problem in Ford cars that plagued the company for some years; many of the first Edsels had defects (most of them minor) that contrasted sharply with the image created by the public relations men. Tactics was not the problem here; organization of production was. Another organizational problem was the company's decision to create a completely new division to handle the Edsel, a division immediately thrust into competition with the other Ford divisions for resources and outlets, as well as with the divisions of other American car manufacturers.

Finally, and perhaps most seriously of all, the strategic environment in which Ford operated had changed. One environmental change was the recession of 1958, which temporarily depressed the demand for cars. More important, however, was a change in the very understanding of what cars were. Ford, like most of the American public, had hitherto thought of cars in terms of price (low, medium, and high), and the Edsel was Ford's opportunity to break into the medium-price bracket. Until then Ford managers had complained that they were simply grooming customers for General Motors, the assumption being that customers went from low-priced Fords to the more expensive models offered by GM. In fact, the car industry was in the middle of a shift to categories defined more by "life-style" than by price—and the Thunderbird would capture the "life-style" aspirations of many Americans quite nicely.

This thumbnail sketch of a "business misfortune" has a number of instructive points. First, it is striking that no one attributes the Edsel fiasco exclusively or even primarily to the decisions of the president of Ford Motor Company, Henry Ford II. As important as Ford was in the history of the company, the responsibility for failure was shared by a number of the members of the management team at Ford: There is, in other words, no "man in the dock." Instead, students of the Edsel failure focus on particular components of the Ford organization, and in particular the Special Products Division, which later took over the Edsel operation. Second, it becomes clear from the Edsel story that three kinds of forces produced failure: what one might call "command decisions" by particular managers (on, for example, the peculiar grille of the car), organizational deficiencies (the quality control problems referred to above), and changes in the environment. The first could easily have been changed; the second might have been corrected but with great difficulty; the last was virtually unalterable.

This tripartite division of cause is useful as well in understanding military failure, in which all three kinds of forces are often lumped together. Finally, the story of the Edsel reminds us of the importance of the political psychology of failure—the role of the expectations built up by those undertaking a venture. Numerous models of new cars fail to make it in the marketplace; not all reverberate as widely as the Edsel. Had Ford not convinced itself and the attentive public (particularly automotive journalists) that the Edsel would be an extraordinary success, its failure, though still painful, would have been far less of a humiliation.

Students of corporate failure point out that when it is triggered by normal business hazards, such as recession, the critical question becomes how a corporation found itself in an inherently fragile position.[45] Rather than suggesting that a business organization can foresee environmental change or predict the precise actions of its competitors—the equivalent of surprise attack theory—they concentrate on the ability of corporations to adapt to change and uncertainty. And when they do this they frequently turn to a study of corporate culture—the norms and "way of life" of an organization. This in turn leads to an understanding that failure is frequently directly and paradoxically connected with success, in the same way that a species' biological adaptation to one set of circumstances can leave it acutely vulnerable in others.[46]

Men, Organizations, and Systems

Although it has been brief, our inspection of the world of civil disasters and business failures has something important to tell us. Apart from proving that putting the operator in the dock—the equivalent of blaming the commander—is often quite valueless as a way of discovering what went wrong in a particular operation, it also suggests that we need to look at the military world in a new way. Instead of testing men and institutions, we must examine the structures through which they work and explore how those structures stand up to the stresses they encounter.

Wherever people come together to carry out purposeful activity, organizations spring into being. The more complex and demanding the task, the more ordered and integrated the organization. How organizations work is a complicated and difficult matter, and different schools of thought put different emphasis on the roles of leadership and motivation, the significance of information inputs and decision making, and the degree to which function shapes and influences structure. Without entering into these disputes, we should note an important assumption all organization theory holds in common. In Charles Perrow's words: "One cannot explain organizations by explaining the attitudes and behavior of individuals or even small groups within them. We learn a great deal about psychology and social psychology but little about organizations per se in this fashion."[47]

As an antidote to Dixon's psychoanalytical theories of individual responsibility, this is both refreshing and analytically valuable. We cannot and should not push the individual into the wings in our analysis of the causes of military misfortune; but we must take account of the fact that all organizations—not least military organizations—have characteristics that can determine how tasks are approached, shape decisions, and affect the management of disaster.

Military organizations present us with special problems, for while on the one hand they are especially rigidly ordered and hierarchical, they are also designed to function in situations where chains of authority may break down or where higher direction may be temporarily intermittent or non-existent. There may be something about all military organizations that makes them behave in a similar fashion in some situations regardless of their nationality: For example, they have been regarded as being particularly prone to resist innovation.[48] However, it is probably more important to take account of the fact that a particular organization may function in a special way at a particular moment in its history. We have already seen that this was the case with Douglas Haig's headquarters in France during the First World War. Later we shall examine particular military organizations in more detail as part of our explanation of different types of military misfortune. For now we need note only the general point that some military organizations may be more susceptible to misfortune than others, regardless of whether or not they are led by anal-retentive commanders, simply because they are the kind of organizations that they are.

Men form organizations, but they also work with systems. Whenever technological components are linked together in order to carry out a particular scientific or technological activity, the possibility exists that the normal sequence of events the system has been designed to carry out may go awry when failures in two or more components interact in an unexpected way. Once this begins to happen—as it did at Three Mile Island—the operators lose control of the system. Charles Perrow has christened such incidents "normal accidents," to distinguish them from "true" or "random" ones. These are the disasters that lurk within all complex systems, simply waiting to happen and beyond the control of man. "The odd term *normal accident*," writes Perrow, "is meant to signal that, given the system characteristics, multiple and unexpected interactions of failures are inevitable."[49]

According to Perrow, systems are characterized by linear or complex interaction and by tight or loose coupling. Linear interaction connects the links in a system along a single invariable path, whereas complex interactions "are those of unfamiliar sequences, or unplanned and unexpected sequences, and either not visible or not immediately comprehensible."[50] Loose coupling allows the sequence of a set of components to be changed, making alternatives available; while tight coupling connects a sequence that is fast moving, allows no by-passes or alternative channels, and will only work in one fixed order. Armed with these important conceptual distinctions, Perrow distinguishes between component accident failures in which one or more things go wrong and are linked in an anticipated sequence (as when a wing comes off an airplane) and systems accidents. Such systems accidents occur in tight-coupled, complex systems such as petrochemical plants, space rockets, and nuclear reactors.

Perrow specifically excludes what he calls "military adventures" from the category of disasters that can be explained by using his theory.[51] But nonetheless we shall gain much from thinking in terms of systems as well as organizations. For Perrow tells us that some events can be connected in unexpected and even unforeseeable ways to create the conditions in which disaster can occur and that failure at one level can have immediate and adverse repercussions at another. Tracing these interconnections, which we shall call "Pathways to Misfortune," will be the task of our detailed case analyses. For now we need to note only that they exist, that they help to explain how military misfortune comes about, and that—if we look carefully enough—they can always be found.

A THEORY OF MILITARY MISFORTUNE

Simplicity and Complexity

In the age of the heroic leader, a lone individual could justly be awarded the victor's trophies or suffer the ignominy of defeat. But modern war—like modern life—is a complex business. The commander no longer has a free hand to do whatever he likes. How soldiers fight is their business, and they may be either good or bad at it. Why they fight, when they fight, and very often where they fight are the decisions over which they usually have little control, for they lie in the province of politics. The modern general is the servant of his government, and its decisions may present the most able commander with an incipient disaster; or such a general may find himself the heir of decisions taken by politicians now out of office or predecessors presently basking in retirement, which threaten to pull misfortune down about his ears.

Because strategic decision making is a fusionist process that involves a variety of groups and individuals, it has been suggested that military incompetence "is no longer the sole property of generals, but results from the combined efforts of inept strategists, in and out of uniform."[52] Attractive as this explanation of military misfortune may be, a closer inspection reveals that it does not provide us with the comprehensive answer we seek. For although soldiers may be bound by decisions over which they are unable to exercise any control, they are not bound hand and foot. Their options may be limited, but opportunities still remain for them to outthink, outsmart, or outfight their opponent—or at least to put up a good enough show to salvage honor and reputation. In other words, failure lurks at many levels. It will be our task to locate and identify those levels, and to explore the links that can bind together actions and decisions taken at different times and in different places that, considered individually, do not seem to invite disaster but interreact to generate military misfortune.

Military misfortunes—like natural or human-made disasters—come in many different kinds. Any explanation of their causes must find a balance between the emotional urge to simplify and the intellectual acknowledgement of complexity. Even Clausewitz failed to resolve this problem. In his classic work *On War* he argued that the balance between opponents in battle usually shifts slowly and inexorably, establishing a trend that can rarely be reversed. "Battles in which one unexpected factor has a major effect on the course of the whole," he wrote, "usually exist only in the stories told by people who want to explain away their defeats."[53] In wars, however, he thought that a single accident might produce quite different results, and whole campaigns might be changed if a victory were won here or a different kind of defeat sustained there. He took this as proof that success in war was not simply due to general causes, and that particular factors could be decisive.[54]

Instead of thinking in aggregate terms and adding up causes to explain major setbacks, or—following Clausewitz—looking for one cardinal factor that is "really" responsible for disaster, we shall identify different types of military failure. Some result from falling victim to one type of error or short-coming. As a matter of convenience these can be termed "simple failure," although this does not mean that they are easy to foretell or to avoid. This allows us to postulate the existence of "complex failures," in which more than one kind of error is involved. Only by thinking in these terms can we explain different degrees of military disaster satisfactorily. And this will also enable us to present a typology of military misfortune that can be used to explain many different individual examples of failure.

"Simple" Failures

As everyday life proves over and over again, some people never learn. Having experienced a disaster once, they continue to indulge in exactly the same patterns of foolhardy behavior until they are visited by disaster once more.[55] Although we expect individuals to fall ready victims to this syndrome, whether because of mental inadequacy or blind carelessness, we do not expect sophisticated organizations to do the same. For one thing, they have vast intellectual resources at their disposal; for another, we expect them to be aware of the need to amass vicarious experience by observing and analyzing the fate of others in order to maximize their efficiency. And yet this is just what happens. Like people and businesses, armed forces suffer misfortune when they fail to learn obvious lessons.

Some environments are predictably hazardous, and yet disaster strikes them at frequent intervals. Hotels are notoriously liable to fires, and yet they repeatedly fail to implement known safety features in order to diminish the possibility of disaster.[56] In such circumstances, disaster is the consequence of a failure to anticipate predictable situations. As far as individuals are concerned, we can offer a convincing psychological explanation of why such short-sighted behavior occurs. Most of us enjoy a strong sense of personal immunity which is seldom if ever rationalized; the threat of a danger hitherto not experienced is simply disbelieved; and we all try to inconvenience ourselves as little as possible.[57] All of which is understandable for individuals—even if it may be unwise—but ought not to operate for armed forces facing war, a known "disaster environment." And yet it does.

The world of civil disaster also provides us with examples of our third type of "simple" failure—failure to adapt to new and unexpected circumstances. Hurricanes and floods can be unpredictable and are effectively unpreventable in many cases; explosions and earthquakes may occur without any warning at all. In such cases, foresight and planning can minimize the degree of damage suffered once disaster has occurred and hasten recovery. Specialist agencies come into action to cope with the aftermath, but the disaster-struck community also has to cope—organizing itself, evolving patterns of cooperation and mutual self-help, sharing out unexpected tasks and resolving competing individual demands. The importance of such activity is so great that Form and Nosow maintain that "organizational integration is the most crucial dimension in disaster performance."[58] The parallels with the military world are obvious. Units which—for whatever reason—are good at responding to unexpected setbacks in a coordinated and effective manner will be more likely to avoid disaster than those that fail to rise to the challenge.

"Complex" Failure

In the military world a failure to learn, anticipate, or adapt will not necessarily bring total defeat in its train. Recovery is possible in theory and occurs in practice. Such a recovery will be more difficult—and perhaps more unlikely—when two failures occur in combination. We call these aggregate failures, for they present complicated characteristics and are therefore somewhat more difficult to explain. Catastrophic failure occurs when a military organization experiences all three kinds of failure simultaneously or consecutively. When this happens, there is often no escape from absolute disaster without outside assistance. Total defeat and political collapse are likely to be the consequences of catastrophic failure.

THE TAXONOMY OF MISFORTUNE

There are three basic kinds of failure: failure to learn, failure to anticipate, and failure to adapt. Each has its own characteristics and consequences, as well as its own parallels in the world of everyday life. Sometimes, two types of failure occur simultaneously; and on occasion all three combine. By separating them out and identifying their essential features, we can provide ourselves with a simple typology with which to distinguish one military failure from another.

The failure to absorb readily accessible lessons from recent history is in many ways the most puzzling of all military misfortunes. There are numerous examples of it in modern military history: the decision to launch the Passchendaele offensive in 1917 in apparent defiance of the previous two years' experience of trench warfare; the persistent belief of the United States Air Force in the ability of fighter-bombers to isolate the battlefield, attempted in two operations during the Second World War and the Korean War, both confidently named STRANGLE; and the decision by the United States Army that there were no tactically and operationally relevant lessons to be learned from the French experience in Indochina all fall into this category of military misfortune. There are many others.

The inability to foresee and take appropriate measures to deal with an enemy's move, or a likely response to a move of one's own, produces a second type of military misfortune. In some cases, to be sure, an opponent may conceal his intentions and abilities with such skill and success that a failure to predict in the narrow sense is eminently understandable. But this is not always so; and in some cases reasonable precautions are not taken. Among many notable predictive failures we may single out two that illustrate the phenomenon: the failure to predict the Vichy French response to Operation MENACE, the attempted seizure of Dakar; and the extraordinary myopia of Hitler and his generals in assuming that the defeat of Russia could be achieved in a matter of weeks in the summer of 1941.

A military institution may have learned what it can reasonably be expected to have learned, and anticipated what it could reasonably be expected to anticipate, and yet still suffer a misfortune. This happens because of an inability to cope with unfolding events. Where learning failures have their roots in the past, and anticipatory failures look to the future, adaptive failures suggest an inability to handle the changing present. Every campaign presents some unforeseen challenge or circumstance. Not all military organizations find themselves able to adjust in a timely and effective fashion to those challenges. The escape of the *Scharnhorst* and the *Gneisenau* from Brest on February 12, 1942, and their successful passage up the Channel and into the North Sea produced exactly that sense of shock and bewilderment that denotes true misfortune. Although the Royal Navy had been able to predict that such a move was likely, neither it nor the Royal Air Force was able to prevent it.

When two kinds of misfortune occur together we are in the presence of aggregate failure. Examples of such failure include the second American air attack on Schweinfurt in October 1943, and the Anglo-French Suez expedition, Operation MUSKETEER, in 1956. Aggregate failures most commonly combine learning failure and anticipatory failure. They are not necessarily likely to be mortal, since an ability to cope can make it possible to redeem error.

When all three kinds of failure occur together, catastrophe results. Such a compound failure carries with it the risk of bringing about a complete national collapse. This is not necessarily the inevitable result of such a failure: it is possible to identify cases of catastrophic failure from which a country has subsequently recovered—the Italian defeat at Caporetto in 1917 for example, or the British antisubmarine campaign between January and April of the same year—but in such cases escape from disaster will be only by a narrow margin. Unless outside forces come to the aid of the sufferer, or unless the ability to cope can be rekindled or reawakened, recovery will be impossible.

In the pages that follow, we shall explore in more detail some components of our theory, before using the theory itself to analyze five case studies that illustrate the different causes of military misfortune we have identified.

3

Analyzing Failure

INTRODUCTION

THIS CHAPTER EXAMINES the ways in which contemporaries and historians misdiagnose military misfortunes, the former because of political and institutional imperatives, the latter because of scholarly traditions and habits of mind. For a variety of reasons military failure does not often receive sound analytical treatment from contemporaries; what is more striking and more perverse is the absence of sound analysis by military historians and one of the chief consumers of military history—military organizations themselves. Only by clearing away this undergrowth of a priori misconceptions about military failure can we begin a useful study of it.

Following this discussion we turn to an analytic approach that offers some guidelines for the investigation of military misfortune, Clausewitz's concept of *Kritik*, or critical analysis. Although the great Prussian theorist of war offered no formulas for diagnosing all failures, let alone preventing them, he spoke to our central analytic problem. In the final section of the chapter we will lay out our method for studying failure—one we will follow in five succeeding cases. To illustrate some basic points we will look at perhaps the most famous of American military misfortunes, the Japanese surprise attack on Pearl Harbor on December 7, 1941.

WHY MILITARY MISFORTUNE
IS MISUNDERSTOOD CLOSE-UP

The Politics of Failure

No defeat in American History has had quite the impact of the Japanese air raid on Pearl Harbor on December 7, 1941. Within two hours eight American battleships had been sunk or badly damaged, nearly 2,400 men had perished or received mortal wounds, and the opponent had escaped virtually untouched. The commanders on the spot—Admiral Husband E. Kimmel, commander of the Pacific Fleet, and Lieutenant General Walter C. Short, commander of U.S. Army forces on Hawaii, were relieved of their commands within a fortnight. The justice of those decisions remains hotly disputed, and a vocal community of historians and officers insists that Kimmel in particular was made the scapegoat for the successful Japanese surprise attack.[1]

By all accounts Kimmel was an able and industrious officer who helped ready the Pacific Fleet for the challenges of the war that soon emerged; by all accounts, too, his command had suffered from having been denied access to certain critical cryptological sources of intelligence (in particular, decrypted messages to and from the Japanese consulate in Honolulu asking for precise information concerning the location of American naval shipping in Pearl Harbor). Kimmel and his apologists insist that, had he received such messages, he would have taken measures that could have averted the worst of the damage. Moreover, as naval officers in particular have pointed out, whereas the government quickly cashiered Kimmel, it did no such thing to General Douglas MacArthur, whose air force was smashed on the ground by the Japanese attack a good eight hours *after* the attack on Pearl Harbor. The result, many have claimed, was political scapegoating pure and simple.

Now, interestingly enough, although scapegoating sometimes occurs in the wake of natural or even man-made disasters, it is less widespread than one might think.[2] A diffuse cloud of suspicion may settle over an organization (NASA in the wake of the explosion of the space shuttle *Challenger*, for example, or Union Carbide in the aftermath of the poison gas accident in Bhopal, India), but rarely do particular individuals come in for minute scrutiny and public disgrace in quite this way. When they do, middle managers or operators are criticized more often than chief executives. In the case of military failure, the tendency is for criticism and responsibility to fall most heavily on the highest level of management and to be less forgiving. A chief executive of a railroad, for example, rarely loses his job over a train derailment, although the operator of the train involved most probably will. Moreover, as the case of MacArthur suggests, the spotlight will frequently miss other commanders at fault.

This phenomenon of the erratic spotlight is less arbitrary than it might appear, for two reasons. First, the politics of military failure are quite different from the politics of disaster. Military failures often cost more in terms of human life (at least in advanced countries) than do civil disasters. Moreover, except in rare cases natural and even manmade disasters rarely threaten national self-esteem or core values. Whereas a Pearl Harbor calls into question the efficiency of the most essential institutions of government, a landslide, an earthquake, or even an airplane crash rarely does so. The explosion of the space shuttle *Challenger* in 1986 is the exception that proves the rule: Americans had viewed their prowess in space exploration as a demonstration of unique American capabilities, and the conquest of space as a national adventure. That NASA, the organization that had put men on the moon, could have allowed such a *seemingly* routine event to fail so catastrophically shook Americans far more deeply than the failure of, for example, the Nuclear Regulatory Commission to prevent the Three Mile Island nuclear reactor failure.

Of course, the launch of a space shuttle was only *apparently* a routine kind of event—in point of fact, it remained a hazardous undertaking, as those within NASA knew very well. In a variety of ways, however, NASA officials had given precisely the opposite impression to the American public by putting nonprofessionals (from a U.S. senator to a high school science teacher) on spacecraft. This misleading appearance of security and safety contributed to the public reaction to the disaster. It should additionally be noted that those in charge also, to some extent, deceived themselves ("NASA and Thiokol accepted escalating risk apparently because they 'got away with it last time'").[3] The same holds true for many military misfortunes as well. The inflated reputation of the fortress of Singapore in 1942 contributed to the calamity of its fall—not only to public distress, but to the reactions of statesmen and commanders groping for strategic responses to the Japanese onslaught. The confidence of the American government and Far East Command in November 1950 that Chinese Communist forces would not oppose in strength a U.S.–Republic of Korea advance to the Yalu contributed not only to public disbelief over the rout of the Eighth Army in the hills of North Korea, but to the collapse itself.

Military organizations overall, and even particular installations, embody

national pride and self-esteem. When they fail, and in particular when
they fail catastrophically, confidence in government itself is shaken, for
the first duty of government is national defense. In some cases, moreover,
the blow lands not only on a nation's self-esteem but on its cities and
population. As a direct consequence of Pearl Harbor, American residents
on the West Coast believed themselves in imminent danger of enemy
attack, perhaps even invasion. Similarly, the sight of blazing shipping up
and down the East and Gulf coasts in 1942 stimulated fears of sabotage
and even air attacks by the German enemy. Military misfortune, then,
because of its scope, its practical implications, and even more deeply felt
threats to national self-esteem, evokes a far different response than does
a "normal" disaster. Political authorities often have no choice but to respond by dismissing a senior military commander and replacing him with
another, in effect creating a scapegoat. They do this not out of pusillanim-
ity, but because the aftermath of military misfortunes differs from other
disasters. Once a natural or man-made disaster has occurred, it is over;
a time of recovery begins. In the case of military failure, however, the
crisis has only begun, and recuperation from the immediate consequences
of defeat—in the case of Pearl Harbor, tending to the wounded and sal-
vaging the blasted hulks littering the bay—can be less important than
coping with its larger consequences, namely a loss of confidence in and
of the armed forces. To indulge in the kinds of complicated explanations
of failure that we essay in this book runs counter to the immediate and
pressing requirements of national emergency: Public men immersed in
the here and now may well judge that such efforts, which require intro-
spection and intricate argumentation, will do more damage than good.

The Dogma of Responsibility

Political necessity, therefore, impels contemporaries, particularly politicians, to focus on the senior commander. So too does what one might
call "the dogma of responsibility," the tradition, dominant in virtually all
military organizations, that the commander bears full responsibility for all
that happens to his command. This is expressed perhaps most powerfully
in the naval semitradition of a captain going down with his ship; it is seen
more frequently in the practice of sacking captains whose ships run
aground or into other ships, even if the proximate cause of the failure is
the error of a junior officer. Thus, one of the intelligence officers at Pearl
Harbor who believed (together with many officers) that Admiral Kimmel
was badly, indeed shamefully, treated reluctantly agreed with the imperative that he be relieved:

> A decision to relieve a defeated commander is not a question of justice. There is no justice in a war that sends one man to safe duty in a basement while thousands of his comrades are dying in desperate battle within a mile of where he sits. Kimmel should have been relieved, but not in disgrace.[4]

The decision to relieve a defeated commander, even if the fault is not his in a narrow historical or legal sense, rests on a number of grounds. One is that a military commander's responsibility far exceeds that of an executive in business or other government agencies because his power and authority equally exceed theirs. He can order men to their deaths; he can control their activities twenty-four hours a day and seven days a week; he can and must insist on obedience and formal deference incomparable with those in the civilian world. The code of responsibility is drummed into officers from their first days as subalterns. Their right to command rests, ultimately, not only on their acceptance of greater risk and hardship than those under their command but on their willingness to accept responsibility. To say that a spectacular failure is either nobody's fault, or everybody's, or indeed the consequence of a complicated chain of events and decisions, is to undermine the moral order an army requires in order to be able to fight.

Because of the grip of the dogma of responsibility, a defeat, even if not a commander's fault, can shatter his nerve, and a commander whose will has been shaken is worse than useless. This can be true of the most experienced and successful of military leaders as well as those not previously tested in war. When the Egyptian-Syrian onslaught against Israel began on Yom Kippur (October 6) 1973, the Israeli Minister of Defense, Moshe Dayan, suffered a collapse in confidence that rendered him ineffectual throughout much of the war.[5] Even if a leader's self-confidence remains intact, the psychological scar tissue resulting from having presided over disaster may deprive him of good judgment. Admiral Kimmel's obsessive refusal to admit oversights and errors in the wake of the Pearl Harbor attack indicates that defeat had precisely that effect on him.

One final reason peculiar to military organizations contributes to the dogma of responsibility: the apparently vast ability of commanders to influence the forces under them. A general or admiral can, if he chooses, control *certain kinds* of events far more easily than can executives in other organizations. Should he order an army to attack or a fleet to sail, it will happen, and fairly quickly, if physically possible. In business, by way of contrast, except in the most autocratic of corporations, decisions are taken in a far slower and more collective fashion. To be sure, operational military decisions are often far more constrained by a host of considerations—enemy abilities and actions, logistics, political directives, and so on—than they appear outwardly. Nonetheless, what counts is the appearance, and frequently the reality, of enormous abilities to influence events. In addition, a senior commander can radically change everyday matters, which, though seemingly petty, can drastically alter the lives of those under him. By doubling the amount of physical training required every morning, for example, or by reducing or increasing parade ground drill, a commander can change the tone and morale of hundreds of thousands of men. Thus, General Matthew Ridgway, on assuming command of the Eighth Army in Korea in 1950, recalls not only his attempts to improve the tactics and training of his beaten command, but minor details of how it lived:

> I concerned myself with petty matters too, some of which may seem at a distance to be trifling in the extreme but all of which have a cumulative value in building esprit. For instance, when I first took a meal at the Eighth Army Main, I was shocked at the state of the linen and tableware—bedsheet muslin on the tables, cheap ten-cent-store crockery to serve the food in. Not that I personally fretted over whether I ate off linen or linoleum. But this sort of thing, at the mess where VIPs from all over the world were sure to visit, struck me as reflecting a total lack of pride in the whole operation—a confirmation that this was indeed what it was sometimes called at home: the Forgotten War. I promptly got that dreary muslin swapped for serviceable linen and that crockery changed for presentable chinaware.[6]

Ridgway, it should be noted, was widely and correctly known as a fighting man's general, indifferent to his personal comforts.

This concentration of despotic power in a single individual, however, is often deceptive. Obviously, what the enemy can and does do forms the greatest constraint on a military leader—one which he cannot ignore. But a commander can be, and often is, also at the mercy of organizations not under his control, of organizational subcultures so deeply ingrained that they are oblivious to his influence, of political pressures he cannot counteract, of military technologies he cannot change, of allocations of human and material resources he cannot affect. He can be a prisoner of assumptions he shares and of earlier decisions he cannot unmake. Kimmel made his defense on just these grounds, and they have some, though not exclusive merit. It is precisely in these gray regions that a commander cannot control (or can do so only with great difficulty) that military misfortune develops.

WHY MILITARY MISFORTUNE IS MISUNDERSTOOD
FROM A DISTANCE

Military History and the Study of Defeat

The politics of failure and the dogma of responsibility combine to focus
attention on the commander, for understandable and indeed often laud-
able reasons. It is harder to understand, perhaps, why those who study
military history—including the armed forces themselves—have not come
up with satisfactory methods for analyzing it. In fact, military historians,
amateur and professional, have probably done more to obscure than to
reveal the reasons for military misfortune. In order to develop a useful
method for analyzing military misfortune—a method that must perforce
be historical—we have to look at how the peculiarities of military history,
as it has been written for the past century, have obstructed a coherent
study of military failure. Two particularly striking paradoxes immediately
confront the student of military historiography. The first is that although
military history is one of the oldest branches of history (think back on
Thucydides' *Peloponnesian War*), and perhaps the most popular with the
literate public, it is one of the least respectable among academic historians.
The second is that although the military profession has few of the intellectual pretensions of, say, law and medicine, it is far more disposed than
are those professions to turn to historical study, albeit in odd ways.

This latter fact helps account for the variety of purposes military history
can serve. All history, of course, plays a role in sustaining a community's
sense of purpose; all individuals, consciously or not, make use of history.[7]
In the case of military organizations, however, this is more true than
others: History serves as a monument to past achievements, an inspiration
to newly inducted members, a database for operational analysis, a training
ground for prospective commanders, an institutional memory, and as a
source of recreation.[8] In few other areas (diplomatic history may be one)
do governments make such efforts to produce official histories, which
influence historical writing and reasoning for decades thereafter. At the
same time, the historical writings of scholars in this field compete with
the writings of popular historians, journalists, serving and retired officers,
and the occasional autodidact. Military history is often written in horizontal layers: either as battle history, campaign history, or the history of
strategy making. Sometimes (Pearl Harbor is a case in point) it is written
about everything leading up to the clash of arms, and sometimes about
nothing but. In the words of one distinguished military historian, "Mili-

tary history is prey to problems and pressures that are involved far less often in the writing of other kinds of history."[9]

This plethora of purposes and forms has had a deleterious effect on the analysis of campaigns, and particularly those campaigns involving failure. This is most notable in the case of utilitarian military history—that is, the kind of history by and for military organizations desiring to train men, and officers in particular, for war. A belief in the utility of historical study for this purpose first took root in the same country that provided many of the pioneers of historical method—Germany.[10] In the view of the German General Staff, and particularly its greatest chief, Helmuth von Moltke, a rigorous study of military history offered one of the best substitutes for direct experience of war available to a peacetime army.[11] Moltke himself, a writer of some note and ability, wrote a number of campaign studies, and personally supervised the production of the General Staff's histories of the campaigns of 1864, 1866, and 1870, which led directly to the unification of Germany under Prussian hegemony. The General Staff's historical section invariably included officers of high intellectual and leadership quality; where an assignment to serve as an official historian in the United States military today usually signifies a career coming to an end, it meant just the reverse in the German Army.

At the heart of the German army lay its General Staff, at the heart of the General Staff the *Kriegsakademie*, or War College; and at the heart of the curriculum there lay military history, which absorbed as much time as tactics.[12] History was taught according to the applicatory method, first introduced in the 1820s. This method of historical study involved the extremely detailed study of a battle *from the point of view of the commander*. It required the preparation of special narratives interrupted periodically by questions to the reader asking him to judge whether the commander's action was the correct one, given what he knew at the time.[13] As one practitioner of the method put it, the student's

> study of the campaigns of his famous predecessors must be active and not passive; he must put himself in their place, not content with merely reading a lively narrative, but working out every step of the operation with map and compass; investigating the reasons of each movement; tracing cause and effect, ascertaining the relative importance of the moral and the physical, and deducing for himself the principles on which the generals acted.[14]

The applicatory method was not confined to Germany: G. F. R. Henderson, a British colonel and a writer of great skill applied it at the turn of the century to his biography of Stonewall Jackson, a far livelier and more rewarding tome than the scores of studies cranked out by the laborious methods of the German General Staff. But whether their works were dry or vivid, the authors of applicatory history could not but distort reality, for they focused all their attention on the commander. Given what we have said above concerning "the dogma of responsibility," this comes as no surprise.

Formal applicatory history faded in the early twentieth century, although it continued to do well in the field of small-unit tactics.[15] But the legacy of applicatory history remains in the tendency of readers of military history, and particularly military students of the subject, to see battles and campaigns as a clash between two commanders—a duel in which the wits and moral qualities of a single leader determine the outcome of battle. While there is some accuracy in this view, it lends credence to the fallacy of homogeneity—the habit of speaking of a large organization as a unitary whole rather than as a collection of suborganizations with definable subcultures, routines, and modes of operation.

A second type of utilitarian military history, related to the first, is that which seeks to use experience to demonstrate or validate certain principles or procedures. As even Admiral Herbert Richmond, a thoughtful writer and capable naval war planner, wrote:

> War consists of several elements, and into all of these enter principles. Those principles are permanent, and those who study history find a wealth of instruction in the application of those principles.[16]

Frequently, however, the search for immutable principles of war is but a lazy approach to the applicatory method. Where the latter attempts to train a commander's judgment by giving him vicarious experience, the former leads to a reckless ransacking of history for evidence to support *a priori* positions.[17] At best, the attempt to write or read military history as a vindication of principles leads to mechanistic and rigid simplification.

The final utilitarian purpose of military history inheres in its myth-making and morale-building functions. These are, one hastens to point out, necessary functions. Pride in one's service or one's regiment contribute to military effectiveness, and help integrate officers, particularly new officers, into their organizations. Particularly important—and dangerous—in this regard is what one might call "monumental history," official history written to record for posterity the armed forces' achievements in a particular war. Even official history written with the most honest of intentions can fall into the trap of being overly solicitous of reputations, excessively unwilling to criticize high-level decisions and policies.[18]

This is not to suggest that official history is necessarily biased or dishonest, that it shuns a critical examination of failure in order to celebrate success. Much official history has won high praise even from private scholars inclined to suspect its quality. The remarkably candid British official history of the strategic bombing offensive against Germany comes to mind, as does virtually the whole of the United States Army's history of World War II and the recently published German history of the same conflict. The danger resides more in the uses of officially produced history, in an unwillingness to go beyond it, than in official history itself. Indeed, from time to time military organizations have looked to official history to rescue themselves from the artificial optimism of most war games and exercises. A U.S. army educational review in 1971 commented:

> One of the most consistent student comments about curriculum content is that the synthetic operational problems are generally euphoric in nature–the U.S. Army always wins with relative ease.
> . . . A strong element of every curriculum should be historical studies which frankly analyze unsuccessful American military efforts. This should not be a "head-hunting expedition" or invidious to any individual, but it should involve an objective discussion of what we did, what went wrong, and why. This single action would do more to establish credibility for our instruction than any other known to me.[19]

The three varieties of utilitarian military history—applicatory history, history in support of principles, and history as monument—all have justifiable if sometimes unattainable purposes. The point is that all three kinds of history turn one's attention away from the dissection of military misfortune, and particularly from its study as organizational rather than individual failure.

Academic historians have done little better in this regard, largely because military history has, even to the present day, gained little respectability in academic circles. Even in Wilhelmine Germany military history was never a well-established branch of the discipline, being viewed instead as a subject suitable only for the technical experts of the Great General Staff. Thus, in the 1880s, the faculty of the University of Berlin stoutly opposed the appointment of the greatest nineteenth-century military historian, Hans Delbrück, to a chair of military history.[20] Similarly, the handful of British nineteenth and early-twentieth-century military historians, chiefly at Oxford, found themselves contending with a widespread prejudice against their subject matter. This took a variety of forms: In part, it came as a reaction against what has come to be known as "the drum and trumpet" school of military history—the flashy and stereotyped battle pieces of popular military historians. In some cases (in England, at any rate) it reflected a simple disbelief in the importance of war itself; in others a suspicion (not altogether gone on today's American campuses either) that an interest in military history indicated an unhealthy bellicosity out of keeping with the pacific traditions of scholarship. This last complaint led the holder of the Chichele Professorship at Oxford (until recently the only endowed chair devoted to the study of war) to remark to his colleagues, "You are no more likely to become a militarist or a jingo through addiction to military history than an ornithologist is likely to feed his children on gobbets of raw flesh, still warm, because he has become fascinated by the behavior of birds of prey."[21]

The suspicions with which academic historians have viewed military history is, however, a chronic source of resentment, not necessarily a block to creative scholarship. More serious for the writing of military history since World War II have been the critiques offered by military historians themselves, or at any rate those sympathetic to them. By the 1950s, Walter Millis, an American military historian of some note, was writing that "military history as a specialty has largely lost its function. There is a panache about military history which has kept it alive since the days of Homer and presumably will always do so," but, he continued, it had become irrelevant to modern war: Its only hope is to become "less military and more civilian," to merge itself into the general study of social history.[22] Many other military historians, including some of the most talented practitioners of what had until the 1960s been conventional military history (narrative accounts of campaigns, in particular) took up this refrain. Peter Paret declared in the early 1970s, "Far too much military history is being written in America," most of it "descriptive history, centering on leading figures, campaigns, and climactic battles."[23] Agreeing with this criticism, many military historians turned instead to the study of "War and Society," a resolute attempt to place military institutions and events in ever broadening contexts. Instead of studying battles, historians (often equipped with the latest statistical techniques and computer databases) examined patterns of recruitment, the relationship between arms industries and economic development, the daily life of soldiers, or the relationship between group interests and the emergence of military doctrines.[24] This new kind of military history gained impetus from the more general rise and dominance of social history in the post-1945 period, and in particular the so-called *annales* school of social history.

What all this did was to leave the original, core subject of military history—war itself—in a state of extraordinary neglect. John Keegan's remarkable book, *The Face of Battle* did a brilliant job of resurrecting "the battle piece," showing just how well a historian could do in recreating the facts of battle.[25] Keegan opened a door onto the academic study of combat—but no one followed him through. This is all the more astonishing in view of the fact that one of the most striking methodological innovations in the study of military history—S. L. A. Marshall's system for the collective interviewing of units immediately after battle—offered an opportunity to capture the essence of contemporary warfare in a way not possible by more conventional methods.[26]

Although by the 1980s signs of a return swing of the pendulum had become visible, it was nonetheless the case that many academic historians had allowed themselves to become curiously remote from the central fact of war—combat.[27] Whatever the merits of the "War and Society" approach, it steered attention toward one explanation of victory and defeat (insofar as one was interested in such questions at all): the view that war was a test of a whole society's resources and abilities, and that success in battle stemmed directly therefrom. This view shunned a close analysis of military organizations in war; it inhibited the writing of a military history relevant to the concerns of professional soldiers; and, above all, it drew interest away from the close study of battle necessary to understand failure in war.

Social Science and the Study of Surprise

As some historians have ruefully noted, in the postwar period social scientists have taken the lead in the study of military matters.[28] From sociological studies of the American soldiers in World War II, to general works on civil-military relations, to studies of the theory of strategy, social scientists have set the scholarly agenda. This has included the study of military failure, or rather one kind of failure: surprise attack or, more broadly, intelligence failure.

Beginning in 1962 with Roberta Wohlsetter's book *Pearl Harbor: Warning and Decision,* political scientists have mulled over how it is that large and sophisticated intelligence organizations have missed the clues of an impending attack. The conundrum was particularly acute in the case of Pearl Harbor, because that was one of the first cases in which it was publicly acknowledged how far modern decryption of radio messages had gone. The central puzzle that social scientists found—or set for themselves—recurred in a number of cases, including Pearl Harbor, the German invasion of the Soviet Union in 1941, the Chinese intervention in Korea, and the Egyptian and Syrian attacks on Israel in October 1973.

According to the social scientists a number of causes accounted for the failure of intelligence. One of these was "noise"—the difficulty of sifting out the correct and important from the irrelevant or the false; the problem was not, as had been thought, that organizations had too little information at their disposal but too much. Others focused on the importance of deception, and of the surprising ease with which one country could mislead another about its intention to attack.[29] While some analysts made the case that institutional arrangements such as having competing analytical groups could reduce surprise, the consensus seems to be just the reverse. In the words of the most persuasive student of surprise:

> Intelligence failures are not only inevitable, they are natural. . . .
> Scholars cannot legitimately view intelligence mistakes as bizarre,
> because they are no more common and no less excusable than
> academic errors. . . . My survey of the intractability of the
> inadequacy of intelligence, and its inseparability from mistakes in
> decision, suggests one final conclusion that is perhaps most
> outrageously fatalistic of all: tolerance for disaster.[30]

Although the "no-fault" view of intelligence surprise has been challenged, it remains the reigning one among scholars. When surprise does occur, and when culpability can be assigned, it belongs at the level of the highest civilian decision maker: "The principal cause of surprise is not the failure of intelligence but the unwillingness of political leaders to believe intelligence or to react to it with sufficient dispatch."[31] The analysts of failure repeatedly warn their readers about "the silly certainty of hindsight," saving their criticisms for the political misjudgments at the very top, which either mislead intelligence analysts or cause them to be ignored, usually with dire results.[32]

The problem with most studies of intelligence failure stems at once from their excessive claims and from their incompleteness. If every failure—be it of any army, a corporation, or a government—which results from not taking appropriate action based on "clear," "timely," "reliable," "valid," "adequate," and "wide-ranging" information,[33] is an *intelligence* failure, the term becomes meaningless. Conversely, if inadequate intelligence is the norm, there can be no standards for judging good or adequate intelligence at all. It is interesting that few of the students of intelligence failure have also discussed at length the nature of successful intelligence work. Part of the reason lies in the fact that sound intelligence (or sound use of it) frequently causes the opponent to change or even cancel the course of action he intended: A study of surprise attacks predicted is usually a study of nonevents. Of course, intelligence has, on a number of occasions (the Battle of Midway, for example, or the Battle of Alăm Halfa) enabled one side to anticipate another's actions. But chiefly it is the narrow definition of intelligence as the foretelling of the future that inhibits a more realistic understanding of the role and limits of intelligence.

If some students of surprise claim too much, others bound their studies too narrowly. Typically, case studies of intelligence failure look at two different kinds of organization: the organs of supreme command—a president or prime minister and his military advisers, for example—and intelligence organizations. Rarely do surprise attack theorists study the operational commands on whom the blows of a surprise attack fall, and when they do so it is only in order to trace their reactions to warning in the fatal few hours immediately before an onslaught. The reason for this self-limiting study is simple: Most investigations of intelligence failure stop their investigations at the point of combat. Their interest lies in why surprise occurred, not in what its consequences were.

In some cases these consequences may seem self-evident, though even here appearances may be misleading. The Japanese success at Pearl Harbor, for example, had only negligible strategic consequences, since the sunk or damaged battleships would prove irrelevant to the ensuing battles of Coral Sea, Midway, and the Solomons. As we shall see in some of the case studies below, it is an error to think that surprise by itself determines more than the outcome of the first engagement: Thereafter other factors—the quality of command, prewar doctrine, quantitative elements, and others—come into play. In Clausewitz's words,

> But while the wish to achieve surprise is common, and, indeed, indispensable, and while it is true that it will never be completely ineffective, it is equally true that by its very nature surprise can rarely be *outstandingly* successful. It would be a mistake, therefore, to regard surprise as a key element of success in war. The principle is highly attractive in theory, but in practice it is often held up by the friction of the whole machine.[34]

The overvaluation of surprise by some analysts of intelligence failure stems from an exaggerated picture of what intelligence is and can be. By implication, at any rate, many of them would appear to conceive of it as an ability to see into the future, to know today the likely outcome of the interactions of military forces locked in combat a week, a month, or a year from now. In truth, however, military intelligence can do two more limited, if still necessary, things: it can try to answer the question, Where is the enemy now? and, equally important, What is the enemy like? In some cases it can even suggest answers to the question, What is the enemy likely to do? At its best, intelligence can provide the bounds for strategic calculation, but it is asking too much to expect it to look into the future.

In addition—and this is the most serious deficiency in their arguments—the theorists of surprise treat failure as a homogeneous entity. They do so because they do not explore the operational consequences of surprise, that is, the battlefield outcomes of the intelligence failures whose genesis they have traced with such care. As we shall see in many of the following case studies, however, failure is rarely if ever homogeneous. When the Chinese intervened in force in Korea in late November 1950, they routed some American forces but not others: where the Second Division of the United States Army soon crumbled into small groups of desperate men, the First Marine Division conducted an orderly retreat, inflicting extremely heavy losses on its opponents and remaining intact to the end as an effective fighting force. If all American units had suffered the fate of the Second Division, the UN Command might well have had to evacuate the Korean Peninsula; if all had fought and endured as hardily as the First Marine Division, the rebound might have come well before UN forces had fallen back behind the 38th Parallel. When the Japanese lashed out at American and British forces in the Pacific in 1942 they achieved partial surprise in both the Philippines and the Malay Peninsula, and in the end forced garrisons in both areas to capitulate. But whereas the British forces collapsed quickly—by February 1942—the Americans were able to hold out until April; one defeat was a humiliation with dangerous political (and hence strategic) consequences at home and in the theater, the other was a "forlorn hope" that became an inspiration, not a disgrace. When Egyptian and Syrian forces attacked Israel in 1973 the campaigns went quite differently on the southern and the northern fronts. In the south the Egyptians managed to overpower a fortified line named for an Israeli chief of staff, seize terrain from which they were never dislodged and beat back a major Israeli counterattack. In the north, with one minor and temporary exception, the Syrians achieved no such gains and were soon repelled, albeit with much hard fighting. Once again, the psychological and political repercussions—particularly the consequences for peacemaking—were immense.

Like academic military historians, surprise attack theorists have fallen into the habit of ignoring the central element of war—the fighting. Like some of the utilitarian historians, and many contemporary observers, they tend to focus on only one level of command, usually the very highest civilian authority, such as a president or prime minister. It is therefore to other analytic traditions or approaches that we must turn in order to learn how to dissect military misfortune.

IN SEARCH OF METHOD: CLAUSEWITZIAN KRITIK

Let it be clear at the outset that the analytic task faced by the student of military misfortune is formidable in the extreme. He or she faces the usual difficulty of military history, rendering some sense out of the chaos that is a battlefield. There is an addition the problem one astute general called

> the tendency of all ranks to combine and recast the story of their achievements into a shape which shall satisfy the susceptibilities of national and regimental vain-glory. . . . On the actual day of battle naked truths may be picked up for the asking; by the following morning they have already begun to get into their uniforms.[35]

Despite the plethora of documentation generated by soldiers and their organizations—memoirs, regimental histories, not to mention war diaries and after-action reports—the reality of battle is often obscure, and the forces for dissimulation, be they conscious or unintended, potent. This is, of course, trebly true when speaking of disaster, when the urge for bureaucratic self-protection by means of the creation of spurious or misleading documents can be overwhelming.

But quite apart from the problem of evidence—eyewitnesses who either forget spontaneously or choose to do so, war diaries written months after the event by harried junior officers, reports concealed for reasons of security—is the problem of procedure. Even in cases where the historian's normal methods of evaluating and cross-checking sources can work, how should we set about thinking through particular military failures? Perhaps the best guide for the analysis of military misfortune comes from the greatest of all students of war, Carl von Clausewitz, and particularly from book 2 of his masterwork, *On War*. In this section of *On War*, Clausewitz discusses his concept of "critical analysis," or *Kritik*, which forms the basis for his approach to the study of war. *Kritik* supports the development of military theory, which is the subject of his book.

Clausewitz begins with a notion of theory quite different from that of the contemporary social sciences. Rather than seeking to develop an axiomatic set of hypotheses to reduce the world to formulas—an enterprise Clausewitz views as futile at best, pernicious at worst—the critic attempts to develop his understanding of "the relationship between phenomena," a sense of how wars unfold, and an ability to judge. It is "a guide to anyone who wants to learn about war from books. . . . It is meant to guide him in his self-education, not to accompany him to the battlefield."[36] His approach has more in common with that of the well-schooled art critic than with that of the physical scientist, for where the scientist seeks to set forth propositions verifiable by experiments that can be duplicated, the critic seeks to understand unique events. "Just as some plants bear fruit only if they don't shoot up too high, so in the practical arts the leaves and flowers of theory must be pruned and the plant kept close to its proper soil—experience."[37]

Kritik has three steps: the discovery of facts, the tracing of effects to causes, and the investigation and evaluation of means.[38] Clausewitz argued against what we have called horizontal history—the study of war at only one level, be it that of tactics, strategy, technology, or whatever. Rather, he believed that military questions must be studied at all levels because of the interaction among them. Thus, "a means may be evaluated not merely with respect to its immediate end: that end itself should be appraised as a means for the next and highest one. . . . Every stage in this progression obviously implies a new basis for judgment. That which seems correct when looked at from one level may, when viewed from a higher one, appear objectionable."[39]

Clausewitz advocated the study of military history in support of the study of war, and indeed, some three-quarters of his writings dealt directly with military history, not theory. Yet his approach diverged from that of the academic historian as well. He believed in the systematic study not only of what actually occurred in a battle or a war, but in the investigation of what *might have happened,* the study not only of the means that were used, but the means that *might have been used.* In addition, he accepted some of the premises of applicatory history. For the most part, the critic should look at war from the point of view of the commander. Clausewitz rejected, however, the rigid adherence to this method that characterized the utilitarian historians we discussed earlier.[40]

Finally, Clausewitz believed in the utility of studying a few relatively recent military episodes in detail rather than studying dozens in a more superficial way. In war facts and motives "may be intentionally concealed by those in command, or, if they happen to be transitory and accidental, history may not have recorded them at all. That is why critical narrative must usually go hand in hand with historical research."[41] Moreover, in war effects "seldom result from a single cause; there are usual several concurrent causes," each of which must be pursued to the end.[42] Only by a close study of relatively few cases can one hope to get to the truth of what war is about.

Clausewitz suggested a method: intensive historical case study, a willingness to think through hypothetical actions systematically and multilevel analysis. Equally, and perhaps more important, he offered a mental approach, a cast of mind conducive to the study of military misfortune. In war, he wrote, "criticism exists only to recognize the truth, not to act as judge."[43] We may legitimately criticize a general's decision without implying that we ourselves would have done better in the same way that an art critic can point to a flaw in a sculpture without meaning to suggest that the artist was anything other than a skilled craftsman.[44] Thus, although *On War* is written for future commanders, it succeeds in avoiding the pitfalls of what we have called "the dogma of responsibility." Clausewitz helps us realize that our chief concern is not the awarding of demerits or prizes to defeated or successful commanders, not deciding whether a decision to relieve them from or retain them in their positions was just, but to discover why events took the turn they did.

MAPPING OUT MILITARY MISFORTUNE

Having seen how failure may be misunderstood, and having looked at approaches that may help us in uncovering its sources, we turn to the method of studying military misfortune we will use in the cases studied below. It involves five steps. First we must ask, What was the failure? To do this we must be willing to make a serious use of counterfactual analysis. More simply put, we must ask, What would have been required to transform failure into something less, a mere setback perhaps? Proceeding from this, our second question is, What were the critical tasks that went incomplete or unfulfilled? We look, in other words, at the key failures that determined the eventual outcome. Third, we conduct "layered analysis," examining the behavior of different levels of organization and their relative contributions to military misfortune. This procedure culminates in the fourth step, the drawing of an "analytical matrix," a simplified chart of failures that presents graphically the key problems leading to military misfortune. From this chart, finally, we derive our "pathways to misfortune"—the larger cause of the failure in question.

To illustrate how this process works, we return to the story of Pearl Harbor, already noting one very large difference between our approach and that of most of the literature on it. Most writers—from the authors of the congressional report on the attack to historians and social scientists discussing it a generation later—have concentrated on the question, Who was to blame? Various men have paraded through our imaginary dock, including the local commanders (Kimmel and Short), the professional heads of the armed services (Stark and Marshall), their civilian superiors

(Knox and Stimson), and even the president himself. Some have argued that the dock should be empty, or that all Americans should be in it. Without denying the practical importance of allocating responsibility and blame—a task both distasteful and essential during the war—we leave it aside entirely. Having satisfied ourselves that none of the principals were outright incompetents (and no one, including the harshest critics of Kimmel and Short, has said that), we turn to a study of the failure proper.

WHAT WAS THE FAILURE?

The first and most important task confronting the student of military misfortune is figuring out what, precisely, constitutes the failure under discussion. A satisfactory answer to this question requires more thought than may be apparent. As the case of Pearl Harbor illustrates, it is not simply the fact of being attacked and suffering heavy losses: The same occurred in the Philippines, yet the Japanese onslaught there had nothing like the psychological or indeed the material impact of the assault on Hawaii. Some (particularly Kimmel's partisans) ascribe this to the superior capacities of General MacArthur for self-promotion and concealment of mistakes, as well as civilian inclination to pillory the navy rather than the army for the failure. But there are simpler and more powerful reasons for Pearl Harbor's peculiar status as a failure.

First and foremost is the discrepancy between the losses suffered by the United States and those experienced by the Japanese. At the cost of only twenty-nine aircraft the Japanese had managed not only to virtually eliminate American airpower in Hawaii but to sink most of the battle fleet and to inflict losses that would have been heavy for a nation accustomed to war and that were stunning for a nation thinking itself at peace. At Pearl Harbor 2,400 men died, a number only somewhat smaller than those who fell on the first day of the invasion of Europe in 1944.[45] Second, the Pearl Harbor attack clearly came as a surprise to all concerned—a fact immediately noted with dismay not only by the newspapers but by Secretary of the Navy Frank Knox (who arrived in Hawaii two days after the attack) and by an investigatory committee that arrived a few weeks later. Even at the time this jarred sharply with the sense that American authorities knew very well that war with Japan was imminent; after the war was over, and the fact of the decryption of some Japanese ciphers could be revealed, the element of surprise seemed even more astonishing. In the words of the Joint Congressional Committee that investigated the attack: "The Committee has been intrigued throughout the Pearl Harbor proceedings by one enigmatical and paramount question: *Why, with some of the finest intelligence available in our history, with the almost certain knowledge that war was at hand, with plans that contemplated the precise type of attack that was executed by Japan on the morning of December 7—Why was it possible for a Pearl Harbor to occur?"*[46]

The failure was *not* that American soil had been attacked—that was an eventuality expected by many Americans including the armed forces; the failure was *not* that American forces were roughly handled—that happened in the Philippines, at Wake, and at Guam and would happen again at the Kasserine Pass in North Africa. The failure was not even that the Japanese achieved a certain amount of operational surprise—that their ships and planes were not detected until they were an hour or two from Hawaii. Surprise is endemic in all warfare, and American intelligence was not, in fact, effective. It had temporarily lost its insight into Japanese movements by virtue of improved Japanese communications security, and that too was reasonable to expect.[47] No, the shock of Pearl Harbor lay in the failure to inflict heavy losses on, or simply put up a stiff resistance to, an enemy who was expected to get in the first blow. Had the Kido Butai (the Japanese task force) lost a hundred airplanes and perhaps one or two ships, and had American losses been smaller—say, the loss of only one or two battleships rather than eight—the Pearl Harbor attack would have no greater status as a military failure than the attack on the Philippines.

There was, in addition, a latent failure more perilous than that which occurred. The sunken and battered battleships of the Pacific Fleet would soon prove largely irrelevant to the strategic balance in the Pacific Fleet would soon prove largely irrelevant to the strategic balance in the Pacific: The age of the aircraft carrier had arrived, and the battleship soon found itself relegated to a secondary (if still important) role in shore bombardment, antiaircraft protection, and limited surface engagements. The extraordinary operational and tactical success of the Japanese had, in the end, virtually no strategic significance, save insofar as it enraged the American people and strengthened their will to win. But the Japanese *could* have changed the conduct of the Pacific war very greatly by attacking not the battleships but the supporting facilities at Pearl Harbor, particularly the Pacific Fleet's vulnerable oil supplies. As Admiral Nimitz remarked after the war: "All of the oil for the Fleet was in surface tanks at the time of Pearl Harbor. We had about four and a half million barrels of oil out there and all of it was vulnerable to .50 caliber bullets. Had the Japanese destroyed the oil it would have prolonged the war another two years."[48]

In point of fact the Japanese commander, Admiral Chuichi Nagumo, urged by his subordinates, considered a third air attack on Pearl Harbor aimed against just these targets but decided against it.

The failure at Pearl Harbor was a failure of vulnerabilities and an absence of precautions, an operational failure, not solely or even primarily an intelligence failure. "The disaster of Pearl Harbor lies in the failure of the Army and Navy in Hawaii to make their fight with the equipment at hand—it was not that they had no equipment, for they did, but they did not utilize what they had."[49] That a marginally higher level of alertness, an ability to take advantage of the tactical warning provided by radar or improved patrolling would have made a difference can be seen by comparing the impact of the two waves of Japanese aircraft, which hit Pearl Harbor a bit less than an hour apart, at 0755 and 0850 respectively. The greatest damage—including the mortal blows to the battleships *Oklahoma* and *Arizona*—was done by the first wave, which launched its torpedoes, dropped its bombs, and strafed with its machine guns for a precious five minutes before return fire was encountered in quantity. The second wave came in for much rougher treatment, even though American sailors, marines, and soldiers were frantically busy succoring the wounded and battling the blazes set by the first attacks. This second wave lost twenty planes (versus nine from the first), and its participants reported a far heavier volume of fire directed against them.[50]

CRITICAL TASKS, CRITICAL LAPSES

Having established the nature of a failure—in this case, the absence of a stout defense—we begin to look for the critical tasks that were not fulfilled, the critical lapses or mistaken assumptions that led to that failure. After Pearl Harbor, everything from American immigration legislation to the attitude of professional soldiers to national guardsmen came under review as "causes" of the failure. Accompanying this tendency to find a plethora of weaknesses on the defeated side was, as always, an inclination to overlook fragilities on that of the victors. To overcome these natural predispositions we must define the critical junctures at which a scheme of attack or defense broke down.

One way to find out the nature of critical tasks is to look at ways in which the defeated forces actually came close to achieving their objective, in this case the vigorous defense of Oahu against air attack. As we argued above, failure is never homogeneous, and two aspects of the Pearl Harbor attack bring this point out particularly clearly. First, two of the twenty or thirty army air force pilots who got off the ground that day attacked a swarm of Japanese airplanes over Haleiwa airfield: they had little success, but Haleiwa became the only field to escape serious Japanese attack. Even relatively limited air action by fighter aircraft showed that the assault could be disrupted. Second, and more striking, is the discrepancy between the performance between navy and army antiaircraft fire. Whereas the batteries on all navy warships were in action between five and seven minutes after the first attack had begun, only four out of the army's thirty-one batteries engaged the Japanese at all, many of the remainder not coming on line until noon, several hours after the raid had ended.[51] These discrepancies are not only puzzles that call for a solution, they indicate something of what might have been achieved by way of a successful defense of Pearl Harbor.

Once guns were manned and airplanes aloft, the Americans managed to disrupt or at least sharply diminish the force of the second Japanese attack. Neither the quality nor the quantity of American weaponry or skills was grossly deficient: A vigorous defense was entirely possible. One critical failure, then, was that of alertness of the active defenses of Pearl Harbor, and by alertness in this case we mean the ability to come into play within minutes, or perhaps as much as a half hour of warning. A second critical failure was passive in nature—the absence of certain measures that might not have increased Japanese losses but that would have limited the damage that the raiders could have done. This includes the dispersal of aircraft (which were lined up wing tip to wing tip in order to enable protection against sabotage) and the burial of the vulnerable oil tanks, which luckily were never hit. Two measures in particular were missing: barrage balloons (sausage-shaped balloons tethered to long wires) and antitorpedo nets to shield important warships. The former would have complicated immensely the task of low-flying Japanese airplanes; the latter would have rendered useless one of their most lethal weapons, the torpedo. Interestingly enough, to the end Japanese intelligence agents in Hawaii received insistent queries concerning the presence of either of these defensive measures—and for good reason.

The success of the Japanese attack depended on their ability to use torpedoes launched by aircraft in shallow waters and accurately to drop bombs on "point" (as opposed to "area") targets. Given the nature of air-launched torpedoes, the limitations of contemporary aiming devices, and the relatively small bomb loads of Japanese aircraft, this could only be achieved by low-level flying, with all its many hazards. The chief vulnerability of the Japanese plan lay not in the danger of discovery, which the Japanese understood and accepted, Admiral Isoruku Yamamoto warning task force officers that they might have to fight their way into Pearl Harbor.[52] Rather, the danger lay in the possibility that American defenses would force them to operate in such a way that the combined carrier task force would do little harm to its chosen targets and lose its scarcest resource of all—the crack pilots of the Japanese Naval Air Force.

The critical American failures—to maintain an adequate level of alertness and to have in place an appropriate air defense—were intimately linked. It was not a matter of simply having patrols out, although it certainly was a major failing of Admiral Kimmel's not to have ordered limited reconnaissance to the north and northwest of the islands—an area long recognized as one vulnerable to an enemy approach. Rather, Pearl Harbor lacked an effective air defense system, even if most of the component pieces of machinery (antiaircraft batteries, fighter planes, radar, and so on) were in place. No central operations room controlled the air space over Oahu, for example. Thus, when the radar operators at Opana Point detected the approaching Japanese at 0702 on the morning of December 7, their report to the virtually unmanned information center was interpreted as a flight of B-17s coming in for refueling on the way to the Philippines. Had the radar plot been appropriately interpreted, however, only the fighter planes of the Fourteenth Pursuit Wing would probably have been alerted—and they were on a mere four-hour alert. The information center had no responsibility for alerting the navy afloat or ashore.

The subsequent Pearl Harbor investigations revealed that the army depended for its information primarily on navy long-range reconnaissance for warning, radar being regarded as a new and unreliable device. Yet the army had no idea what kind of reconnaissance the navy had or would implement. At the same time, the navy, whose installations were to be protected by army fighter planes and antiaircraft guns, did not control the army's level of alert or even understand that General Short had chosen the lowest level of alert, which only covered antisabotage precautions. The navy was supposed to control air operations against enemy ships heading toward Pearl Harbor, the army air force to coordinate air operations overland—using airplanes allocated by separate commanders more or less as they saw fit.[53] This lack of communication and coordination *within* Hawaii has not received the same attention as the lack of communication between Washington and Hawaii, yet in the end it proved the more dangerous.

LAYERED ANALYSIS

Having identified the critical failures we can begin analyzing the behavior
of different layers of organization and command. We look for the interactions between these organizations, as well as assess how well they performed their proper tasks and missions. By so doing we help avoid the
pitfall of "horizontal history" and lay the groundwork for the concluding
part of our study. There is no formula for selecting the right levels to
examine; that depends on the case at hand. Echelons of command or
organization have varying importance depending on their military mission
and chiefly on the nature of the war in question. A guerrilla conflict, for
example, may give no scope to the middle echelons (battalion or brigade):
Instead, the actions of small-unit leaders and regional commanders may
be the most important. In more conventional forms of warfare, however,
these middle echelons may prove the critical ones.

In the case of Pearl Harbor four levels stand out, the first two of which
can be subdivided in turn. The first of these is the high command in
Washington, which can be broken down into the civilian echelon (the
president and the secretaries of navy and war) on the one hand and the
military echelon (the chief of naval operations and the chief of staff of
the army) on the other. The chief responsibilities of these echelons were
to provide adequate resources to the Hawaiian commands, which they
did. The chief question raised over their performance has to do with their
effort to warn the local commanders of the impending Japanese attack.

The question of warning at Pearl Harbor is an extremely tangled one,
about which many books could be and have been written. The following
points, however, are central. First, Washington had no timely and unambiguous warning of a Japanese attack on Pearl Harbor, although, like
some of the local commanders, it had worried about just such a surprise
attack for over a year and had communicated those concerns to Kimmel
and Short. Chief of Staff George C. Marshall, for example, had written
the following to Short on the day the latter took over his command:

> My impression of the Hawaiian problem has been that if no serious
> harm is done us during the first six hours of known hostilities,
> thereafter the existing defenses would discourage an enemy against
> the hazard of an attack. The risk of sabotage and the risk involved in
> a surprise raid by Air and by submarine, constitute the real perils of
> the situation.[54]

On the other hand, in the weeks before December 7 both Stark's and
Marshall's offices withheld, for a variety of reasons, certain important in-

telligence items from Hawaii (most notably a Japanese request to its local agents for detailed descriptions of where American warships were moored in Pearl Harbor). However, on November 27 Kimmel was alerted with a warning that began, "this dispatch is to be considered a war warning," and Short received a similar message from General Marshall. In addition, both commanders were generally apprised of the collapse of negotiations with the Japanese and the official view that a major Japanese aggressive move was in the works. The evidence suggests that thereafter neither Marshall nor Stark monitored closely the defensive measures undertaken by local commanders.

The second echelon is that of the major commands in Hawaii, which may again be subdivided. In one category is the commander in chief, Pacific Fleet, who was also the commander in chief, U.S. Fleet, who had overall control of navy forces in the vicinity of Pearl Harbor. In the second category was Rear Admiral Claude C. Bloch, Commandant of the Fourteenth Naval District (COM 14 in navy jargon), who had responsibility for all shore installations in Hawaii, and the commanding general of the Hawaiian department, Lieutenant General Walter Short. This subdivision indicates already some of the problems under which American forces in Hawaii labored: although Short's nominal counterpart was Admiral Bloch, he worked more closely with Admiral Kimmel, who had the real authority over the deployment of naval forces. It is at this level that decisions were made concerning the nature of military alerts to be adopted in peacetime—both the structure of such alerts and their actual implementation. The critical decision here was Short's decision to order a level one alert (against sabotage only) rather than a level two (all measures in one, plus precautions against enemy air, surface, and submarine action) or three (all-out attack). Kimmel had placed the navy on what was known as a "modified level 3 alert," which required partial manning of antiaircraft weapons and was the lowest of the navy's three alert levels.[55] It should be noted that not only did the navy and army have different alert procedures: Kimmel did not even know that the army had more than one kind of alert.

Below the level of the higher commanders in Hawaii were the component commands there, and in particular those of the Army: the Hawaiian army air force and the Hawaiian coast artillery, which controlled most of the fighter planes and antiaircraft artillery respectively devoted to the defense of the base. These commands, which might have been expected to provide the bulk of the coordinated defense of the island—the vectoring in of fighters to intercept the Japanese, the activation and supply of antiaircraft batteries, and on the navy side, the sustained reconnaissance by long-range patrol aircraft of the commander, Naval Base Defense Air Force—exhibited the most spectacular failures in the attack, as we have already discussed.

Fourth, and finally, we have the units at the sharp end, the battleships and fighter squadrons, the antiaircraft batteries and support units that most keenly felt the effects of the air raids. Here it should be noted that the critical failure was that of alertness. Within these units, particularly on board ship, the response to the attack was remarkably fast and, within the limits of practicality, effective.

THE ANALYTICAL MATRIX

Having described the critical failures, and selected the chief layers of command, we can now represent the problem graphically as in Figure 3–1.

PATHWAYS TO MISFORTUNE

An exercise such as this, though it may oversimplify some of the relationships between failures, is a handy device for analyzing military misfortunes. If, after looking at the chart, we draw arrows indicating relationships between various failures, we can define pathways to misfortune. We notice several things about the resulting picture. First, the critical pathway to misfortune comes in the column headed Coordination—it is through the failure of coordination at levels three through five that American forces found themselves at such low levels of military alert. Then we note a secondary pathway from box 2.1 through box 3.1 to box 4.2—the misleading nature of the warning sent out at a rather higher level, and its liability to misinterpretation by the rather literal-minded commanders on the scene.

It is in the first pathway—that stemming from failure of coordination, however—that we may find the most important explanation of the Pearl Harbor disaster. Reflected in that disaster is not simply the unpreparedness of a pacific people, or the narrowness of inflexible commanders, though both elements were present in some degree. Far more serious and dangerous was the absence of a harmonious garrison on the island of Oahu, organized and directed by a single unifying scheme, under a single commander. Had all of the forces in Hawaii been under the vigorous

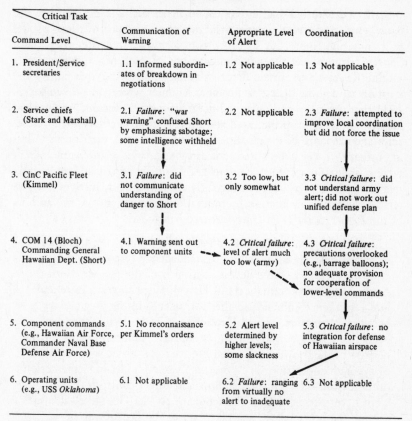

Critical Task Command Level	Communication of Warning	Appropriate Level of Alert	Coordination
1. President/Service secretaries	1.1 Informed subordinates of breakdown in negotiations	1.2 Not applicable	1.3 Not applicable
2. Service chiefs (Stark and Marshall)	2.1 *Failure*: "war warning" confused Short by emphasizing sabotage; some intelligence withheld	2.2 Not applicable	2.3 *Failure*: attempted to improve local coordination but did not force the issue
3. CinC Pacific Fleet (Kimmel)	3.1 *Failure*: did not communicate understanding of danger to Short	3.2 Too low, but only somewhat	3.3 *Critical failure*: did not understand army alert; did not work out unified defense plan
4. COM 14 (Bloch) Commanding General Hawaiian Dept. (Short)	4.1 Warning sent out to component units	4.2 *Critical failure*: level of alert much too low (army)	4.3 *Critical failure*: precautions overlooked (e.g., barrage balloons); no adequate provision for cooperation of lower-level commands
5. Component commands (e.g., Hawaiian Air Force, Commander Naval Base Defense Air Force)	5.1 No reconnaissance per Kimmel's orders	5.2 Alert level determined by higher levels; some slackness	5.3 *Critical failure*: no integration for defense of Hawaiian airspace
6. Operating units (e.g., USS *Oklahoma*)	6.1 Not applicable	6.2 *Failure*: ranging from virtually no alert to inadequate	6.3 Not applicable

Arrows indicate causal links. Solid lines indicate primary pathways; dashed lines, secondary pathways.

FIGURE 3–1. Matrix of Failure

operational control of a single commander—most likely the commander in chief, Pacific Fleet—it is unlikely (though not inconceivable) that multiple alert system would have existed side by side, that the air above the islands would not have had a single center controlling it, or that Oahu's fighter defenses would have assumed that long-range patrols would give them four hours' warning of an enemy's approach. In fact, within weeks of the debacle at Pearl Harbor the chief of staff of the army and the chief of naval operations ordered the establishment of joint commands and joint operations centers in all areas where navy and army had to work side by side.[56]

Stark and Marshall had attempted to make such arrangements in the days before Pearl Harbor, but they met the resistance of those on the spot, not only there but in other commands as well. Rejecting (with Short's concurrence) the recommendations of both his superiors and a visiting Royal Navy captain (later Admiral), Louis Mountbatten, for the creation of a joint operations center, Kimmel wrote on November 3, 1941 that the army and navy had different tasks. "Strategic, rather than tactical cooperation, is indicated and therefore the necessity for rapid receipt and exchange of information and arrival at quick decisions is of less importance."[57] Let it be noted that army and navy relations on Hawaii were nothing if not cordial: Kimmel and Short, in particular, had friendly relations, playing golf together regularly and pledging themselves to a system of military coordination by mutual cooperation. But as the authors of the *Report on the Pearl Harbor Attack* concluded,

> The evidence adduced in the course of the various Pearl Harbor
> investigations reveals the complete inadequacy of command by
> *mutual cooperation* where decisive action is of the essence. Both the
> Army and Navy commanders in Hawaii failed to coordinate and
> integrate their combined facilities for defense in the crucial days
> between November 27 and December 7, 1941. While they had
> been able over a period of time to conceive admirable plans for the
> defense of the Hawaiian Coastal Frontier consistent with the system
> of mutual cooperation when the time came for the implementation
> of these plans they remained hollow and empty contracts that
> were never executed. . . . The tendency to "let George do it," to
> assume the other fellow will take care of the situation is an
> inseparable part of command by mutual cooperation.[58]

The result, the congressional committee found, was the conduct of operations in a "state of joint oblivion."

THE MISSING DIMENSION OF STRATEGY

The congressional committee investigating the Pearl Harbor disaster was, perhaps, closest to the mark of all the studies before or since in its focus on the fragility—and in some cases, the absence—of army/navy communication and cooperation on Oahu in the months before the Japanese attack. By dissecting military misfortune in the way demonstrated in this chapter, we find our attention drawn repeatedly to what one might call "the organizational dimension of strategy." Military organizations, and the states that develop them, periodically assess their own ability to handle military threats.[59] When they do so they tend to look at that which can be quantified: the number of troops, the quantities of ammunition, the readiness rates of key equipment, the amount of transport, and so on. Rarely, however, do they look at the adequacy of their organization as such, and particularly high level organization, to handle these challenges. Yet as Pearl Harbor and other cases suggest, it is in the deficiency of organizations that the embryo of misfortune develops. And it is to the varieties of organizational disfunction in war that we now turn.

4

Failure to Learn
American Antisubmarine Warfare in 1942

ONSLAUGHT

IN THE LATTER HALF OF JANUARY 1942, more than a month after the beginning of World War II, German U-boats began an assault on coastal shipping in the immediate vicinity of the United States. During the next nine months, an unparalleled massacre of American shipping took place within a few hundred miles of the coast and often within sight of the American waterfronts. Shipping in the coastal zones (referred to as Sea Frontiers by the United States Navy) suffered far heavier losses than did the main North Atlantic convoy routes—which, indeed, were successfully guarded throughout most of this time. For the first and indeed the only time in the war, Grand Admiral Karl Doenitz, commander of the German submarine force, came within appreciable range of achieving the gross tonnage losses—some 700,000 tons a month—he believed would make it impossible for Britain, and hence the Allies, to prosecute the war actively.[1] During the period January–September 1942, in fact, the Allies and neutral nations lost to all causes an average of 650,000 tons of shipping monthly—more than twice the monthly average in the earlier phases of the war.[2] During this time, as indeed during the earlier stages of the war, sinkings continued to outrun new merchant ship construction by something like 200,000 tons a month, despite steady increases in American shipbuilding capacity.

59

Of the 650,000 gross tons of losses mentioned, half or more occurred in waters nominally under the control of American forces. In March 1942, for example, the Eastern and Caribbean Sea Frontiers, together with the Bermuda area (where the United States had naval and air bases), witnessed losses of over 380,000 tons of merchant shipping—this during a month when total Allied and neutral shipping lost 840,000 tons to *all* causes (including accidents, mines, surface raids, and so on) in *all* theaters of the war, including the Pacific. And when we look at losses to German U-boats in the Atlantic alone the statistics become even more dramatic: From mid-January until September 1942 losses in American coastal waters accounted for more than half of total shipping losses in the Atlantic, and often far more. In May, for example, more than 85 percent of the merchant shipping losses suffered by the Allies occurred in American eastern and southern coastal waters. We can judge the magnitude of these losses by comparing them with the heaviest attacks on the North Atlantic convoys, which occurred in March 1943. During that month U-boats sent nearly 300,000 tons of Allied shipping to the bottom; during most of 1942, however, losses in American coastal areas exceeded this figure month after month.

Even these statistics do not fully capture the shock that this "merry massacre," as Samuel Eliot Morison has called it, exerted on those who witnessed it—bathers on southern beaches watching as tankers burned within sight of shore, merchant crews fleeing their sinking ships or perishing in the cold Atlantic waters, frustrated and baffled sailors and airmen able to rescue survivors but unable to smite their assailants. U-boat skippers looked through their periscopes at the brightly lighted skylines of American cities, and this is what they saw: "Before this sea of light, against this footlight glare of a carefree new world, were passing the silhouettes of ships recognisable in every detail and sharp as the outlines in a sales catalogue. Here they were formally presented to us on a plate: please help yourselves! All we had to do was press the button."[3] Small wonder that they would call this their second "happy time"—the first (and lesser) one having occurred in the summer and fall of 1940.

Winston Churchill, hardly a man given to panic, wrote to Harry Hopkins in early March 1942, "The situation is so serious that drastic action of some kind is necessary . . ." particularly in view of the slaughter of tankers in the Caribbean.[4] The problem was as much—even more—a British as an American one: As an irate British intelligence officer told Rear Admiral Richard S. Edward, Admiral Ernest J. King's chief of staff, "The trouble is, Admiral, it's not only your bloody ships you are losing. A lot of them are ours."[5] Nor were responsible American officers any more

Merchant Ships Sunk by U-boats in the Atlantic, December 7, 1941 to July 31, 1942

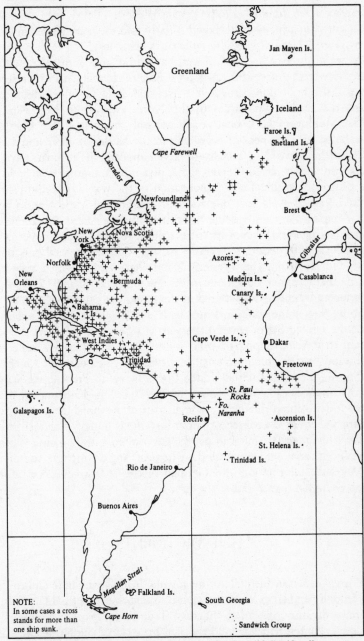

NOTE:
In some cases a cross
stands for more than
one ship sunk.

SOURCE: Adapted from Samuel Eliot Morison, *The Two-Ocean War: A Short History of the United States Navy in the Second World War* (Boston: Little, Brown, 1963), p. 112.

complacent. On June 24, 1942, Captain Wilder D. Baker, the U.S. navy's chief antisubmarine warfare expert bluntly told the commander in chief, U.S. Fleet, "The Battle of the Atlantic is being lost."[6]

As we shall see below, most American, British, and German contemporaries viewed the successful attack on American shipping in 1942 as something different in kind from—less explicable and far more disgraceful than—the hard-fought battles of the North Atlantic in 1940–41 and 1943. Moreover, the U-boat attack not only humiliated the Allies but threatened their chances of prevailing in the battles of 1942 and 1943. In Churchill's words, "For six or seven months the U-boats ravaged American waters almost uncontrolled, and in fact almost brought us to the disaster of an indefinite prolongation of the war."[7] The shortage of tankers (caused by U-boat operations in the Gulf of Mexico and Caribbean) caused particularly acute difficulties for the Allies, imperiling the impending invasion of North Africa. Although the U-boats never came close, during this period, to severing Britain's lifeline—its vital imports of food and fuel from the Western Hemisphere—there was a very real chance that offensive operations in Europe in late 1942 and 1943 would be crippled by the losses suffered in the American campaign.

To be sure, some additional merchant ship losses were to be expected once the United States entered the war as a belligerent. Yet no one expected that Allied shipping would suffer losses on so large a scale and for so long a time (nine months). In retrospect, the failure of American authorities, in particular the United States Navy, to prepare adequately for this attack became more rather than less puzzling. Knowing what we know today—about the relatively small scale of the initial German attack, (a bare half dozen U-boats took part at first) the U.S. navy's correct anticipation of large-scale American participation in an antisubmarine warfare (ASW) campaign, and above all the extent of Anglo-American sharing of ASW-related information—the German success at first appears even less comprehensible than it did at the time.

THE INDICTMENTS

The assessments of this military misfortune made at the time and to this day tend, by and large, to fit the kind of categorization of military failure we have discussed in earlier chapters. True to the pattern discussed in chapter 2, contemporaries and historians have placed the blame either on an individual—Admiral Ernest J. King, commander in chief, U.S. Fleet—

or on an entire institution—the United States Navy. In both cases, they have resorted either to accusations of sheer incompetence ("man in the dock" theories) or psychological diagnoses ("man on the couch" theories) to explain this military failure.

In both cases critics properly identify the critical failure as one of *learning*. Although a shortage of resources (convoy escorts in particular) helps account for the U-boat success of 1942, virtually all observers point to other, seemingly more important sources of failure. We shall discuss these below, but for the moment we shall merely point out the central problem: the failure to learn readily accessible lessons from the British experience of antisubmarine warfare. To take only the most glaring of examples: The British recognized even before the outbreak of World War II, that a convoy system would be required to protect merchant shipping against the depredations of the U-boats. Royal Navy officers repeatedly told their American counterparts about the value of convoys, and they in turn saw its effectiveness in action. Yet it was not until May 1942, nearly six months after the U.S. entry into World War II that coastal convoys were established along the American East Coast. Along the Gulf Coast it took several more months for such convoys to be arranged, and it was not until September 1942 that the complex Interlocking Convoy System was finally in place.[8]

One school of thought places blame squarely on the shoulders of one man: Admiral Ernest J. King.[9] In the aftermath of Pearl Harbor, President Roosevelt made King, hitherto commander of America's Atlantic Fleet, commander in chief, U.S. Fleet, or COMINCH (the abbreviation CINCUS being considered unpropitious!). In this capacity he held supreme command of U.S. naval forces throughout the world, subject only to the authority of the secretary of the navy and the president of the United States. On March 26, 1942, he received a second responsibility as chief of naval operations, charged with the "preparation, readiness, and logistic support" of these same naval forces.

King, who is reputed to have remarked in early 1942 that "when the war starts they bring on the sons-of-bitches," was a difficult man. Demanding and ruthless in his treatment of staff and subordinates, brusque to the point of rudeness with American and foreign colleagues, his character had no soft edges. President Roosevelt remarked that King was so tough that he shaved with a blowtorch and trimmed his toenails with torpedo net cutters.[10] His intelligence, energy, and organizational abilities won the respect of all those who worked with him; unlike his Army counterpart, George C. Marshall, however, he never gained their reverence or affection. His jealous protection of the independence of the U.S.

navy from the army and the embryonic air force were well known; so too was what struck many observers as an instinctive antipathy to the British.

Thus, it is not surprising that many writers, particularly Englishmen writing about the failure of American antisubmarine operations in 1942, see the problem as the fault of King and King alone. The following passage is typical:

> This officer, of such determined character, showed on many occasions two facets of his thinking—that he regarded the Pacific as the prime theatre of operations for the United States, despite the joint Allied decision that victory over Germany should take priority over the Pacific war, and that, in fighting the U-boat, he was not willing to follow British experience hard-won in more than three years of war at the same time as he retained personal control over his navy's antisubmarine operations.[11]

These twin indictments—that King ignored the Atlantic because he had no interest in the European war, despite his government's policy, and that he hated the British so ferociously that he refused on principle to learn from them—do not, however, hold up to a careful examination.

King did not, either before or after the American entry into the war, disregard Atlantic operations. An active proponent of the invasion of Europe in 1943, he agreed with Marshall and the army in their ultimately unsuccessful opposition to British desires to delay the full-fledged return to Europe. More important, a survey of the officers that King appointed to various commands in the Atlantic suggests that he spread his scarcest resource—capable captains and admirals—around in both hemispheres. Low (chief of staff of Tenth Fleet), H. Kent Hewitt, Royal E. Ingersoll, Richard L. Conolly—all were men of whom King thought well and who contributed greatly to the success of Allied operations in North Africa, the Mediterranean, and Northwest Europe.

In addition, although King certainly saw the main challenge to the United States Navy in the Pacific, throughout 1940–43 he concerned himself with the problems of securing adequate resources to fight properly in the Atlantic. For example, when asked by the General Board in the summer of 1941 to provide a priority list for naval construction, he placed destroyers for the Atlantic convoy war second only to submarine building for a prospective war against Japanese sea-lanes—both ahead of additional carrier, cruiser or battleship construction.[12] Earlier, as a member of the General Board himself, King had supported construction of *Hamilton-*

class cutters in lieu of larger and more expensive destroyers, specifically in order to fight the Atlantic convoy battle.[13]

Though King did, undoubtedly, battle for resources to fight the war in the Pacific, he had a strategic rationale for this. First, he argued that it would be enormously costly to allow the Japanese to dig in on the defensive perimeter they had seized in the first months of 1942. Only by engaging in an immediate counterattack could the United States prevent the Japanese from consolidating their gains and developing the bases and fortifications that would make an eventual American offensive extremely costly. In this he was right: It was not until September 1943 that the Japanese began in earnest the fortification of the island chains they had seized so swiftly in the first four months of the war. Moreover, by forcing the Japanese to fight (particularly for Guadalcanal), American forces could begin the long process of wearing down Japanese strength, particularly in such critical areas as the supply of trained pilots.

Second, King appreciated the enormous logistical difficulties posed by any kind of operation in the Pacific. To cope with the vast distances involved, and the primitive infrastructure that characterized the region, the American armed forces would have to pour men and machines into the area if they were to have any hope of beating back the Japanese. And as it was, American forces in the Pacific, particularly in the early stages of the war, were often convinced that they were the last to receive modern equipment and supplies.[14]

Anglophobia did, no doubt, animate King in some measure: On a number of occasions he went out of his way to inform admirals of the Royal Navy that Britannia no longer ruled the waves and that the United States Navy was the largest and best in the world. He rejected British cooperation in the final drive on Japan (partly on logistical grounds)—a rejection later overruled, luckily for American forces in the Pacific. It is even said that he wished to change the navy uniform in an effort to eradicate any resemblance to Royal Navy uniforms. One might add that King occasionally displayed a no-less-petty attitude toward the U.S. army and above all the U.S. army air force.[15] Indeed, one school of students of the failure of American ASW in 1942 focuses on King's antipathy toward air forces, and particularly the USAAF, rather than King's hostility to the British.[16]

For all of this, however, King's undoubted antipathies and dislikes did not often overwhelm his judgment. Not all British officers who came in contact with him thought him anti-British so much as "excessively pro-American."[17] Similarly, King did not always indulge in a reflexive rejection of interservice cooperation—it was he, for example, who initially suggested that the navy share the Pentagon with the army.[18] Indeed, the larger impression one gets of King is of a bitter and choleric man who nonetheless had the intelligence and will to discipline his own unsociable character.[19] None of this should suggest that King had no responsibility for the ASW failure of 1942: As we shall argue below, he did, but in a way quite different from that often presented.

Although some authors have attempted to assess the blame for the failure of American ASW in terms of Admiral King's individual responsibility, many more have held the United States Navy as a whole accountable. Among those adhering to this view is no less a personage than Samuel Eliot Morison, the Navy's foremost historian:

> This writer cannot avoid the conclusion that the United States Navy was woefully unprepared, materially and mentally, for the U-boat blitz on the Atlantic Coast that began in January 1942. He further believes that, apart from the want of airpower which was due to prewar agreements with the Army, this unpreparedness was largely the Navy's own fault. Blame cannot justly be imputed to Congress, for Congress had never been asked to provide a fleet of subchasers and small escort vessels; nor to the people at large, because they looked to the Navy for leadership. Nor can it be shifted to President Roosevelt, who on sundry occasions prompted the Bureau of Ships and the General Board of the Navy to adopt a small-craft program; but, as he once observed, "The Navy couldn't see any vessel under a thousand tons." In the end the Navy met the challenge, applied its energy and intelligence, came through magnificently and won; but this does not alter the fact that it had no plans ready for a reasonable protection to shipping when the submarines struck, and was unable to improvise them for several months.[20]

For the most part, criticisms of this kind take the same general approach as do those leveled against King. Once again, British authors are the most bitter on the subject: "Nothing had been done either in training, routing, or command organization to take advantage of the experience the British had gained in the hardest school over three grueling years. . . . It is not realized, perhaps, how much the U.S. Navy, like the German, gained expansionary wind from jealousy of the Royal Navy. . . ."[21] Henry Stimson, the American secretary of war, sketched the most biting portrait of hidebound American admirals, adamant in their refusal to look at the experience of others or even common sense, men who "frequently seemed to retire from the realm of logic into a dim religious world in which Neptune was God, Mahan, his prophet, and the United States Navy the only true Church.''[22]

This failure to learn readily available lessons about the conduct of ASW seems all the more culpable in view of the Navy leadership's own realistic prewar assessment of the probability of having to fight an antisubmarine battle in the North Atlantic. Even before the outbreak of World War II in Europe, the forerunner of the Joint Chiefs of Staff, the Joint Board, had discussed the navy's need to be able to conduct ASW in the Atlantic.[23] By early 1941 the Navy had already begun searching for German U-boats in American and international waters. In April 1941 the chief of naval operations, Admiral Harold Stark, wrote to his principal fleet commanders, "The question as to our entry into the war now seems to be when, and not whether."[24]

Yet this institutional indictment falls into the same traps we discussed in chapter 2. A close examination of the navy's attitudes and responses to ASW reveals very different behaviors among its component organizations. Moreover, the personnel involved in ASW remained pretty much the same throughout the war; the navy's critics give scant attention to why and how the macropathology disappeared. Within a bit more than a year the navy had adapted very well to the ASW problem—including learning such lessons as the British had to offer.

THE FAILURES

All of which brings us to the central question: What was the nature of the failure in 1942? At the time, implicitly or explicitly, military authorities worked from two quite different measures of success or failure—sinkings of Allied merchant ships and sinkings of German U-boats. Whether one focused more on the former or latter determined, in part, one's reaction to the events of the first half of 1942.

The larger purpose of command of the sea in the Atlantic was to shuttle men and matériel to Great Britain for use against Germany. From that perspective it made little difference how many U-boats escaped destruction, provided that they did not do too much damage. In World War I, after all, German U-boats grew in number until the very end of the war, but the introduction of convoy and other antisubmarine measures kept their depredations under control.[25] This strategic point of view had a tactical counterpart. Often, by their mere presence, escorting ships and planes could prevent U-boats from attacking a convoy. Early in the war the appearance of American and British "scarecrow" patrols—unarmed airplanes—forced U-boats to dive. Since a submerged submarine had barely a fourth or a fifth the speed it had on the surface, and since it had a slower speed than that of even the slowest convoy, submergence usually meant that it would temporarily lose contact with its potential victims.

On the other hand (and unlike the Allied experience in World War I) the sheer numbers of U-boats available for service made a large difference in their effectiveness. Not only were the U-boats of World War II more effective than their World War I predecessors but they worked from a better operational concept. Controlled by a small-but-efficient central staff in France, the U-boats could concentrate their efforts in wolf pack attacks—and escorts found the attacks of a half dozen submarines working together far more difficult to handle than those of the same number attacking individually. Once their numbers grew large enough (particularly in late 1942, when more than a hundred a month roamed the seas), they could form patrol lines convoys could not avoid by evasive routing.

From this aspect the number of U-boat kills, not the tonnage safely transiting the Atlantic, constituted the chief measure of effectiveness. Even if the Allies protected their merchant shipping in the short run, they ran two dangers if they failed to sink large numbers of U-boats. First, the Germans would acquire a growing pool of experienced (hence more effective) skippers and crews. (As in other activities, skill in U-boat operations corresponded with increased experience.) Secondly—and perhaps more important—failure to control the numbers of U-boats threatened a catastrophic situation in 1943.

Figure 4–1 indicates the primary reason for this: the startling increase in German submarine production from mid-1940 through 1941 and the continued, though moderate, growth in production thereafter. Allowing for the delay between the completion of a U-boat and its operational deployment (that is, the months required for crew training and sea trials), these statistics foretold a grim situation in late 1942 and early 1943. And indeed, the average number of U-boats at sea rose from ten in 1940 to thirty in 1941, to nearly sixty in 1942, to over one hundred in early 1943; at the same time, the average life of U-boats at sea (their life expectancy, not the duration of particular cruises) rose from three months in 1940 to twelve in 1942.[26] In 1941 and 1942 new U-boat construction exceeded sinkings by a wide margin; the result was a steady cumulative increase in the number of operational U-boats until early 1943 (see Figures 4–2 and 4–3).

From *both* points of view, however, that of merchant ship protection

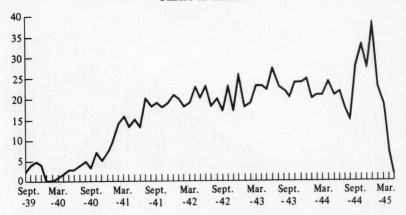

FIGURE 4–1. German U-boat Production, September 1939–April 1945 (Not including midget submarines)
SOURCE: United States Strategic Bombing Survey, *German Submarine Industry Report* (Washington, D.C.: Government Printing Office, 1947), Exhibit B-2.

and that of U-boat destruction, American ASW in the first nine months of 1942 performed very badly indeed. At the beginning of this chapter we discussed the former; an examination of Figure 4–4 reveals the latter. In the first half of 1942 American forces sank barely half a dozen U-boats—in the course of the entire year they sank only sixteen. A compari-

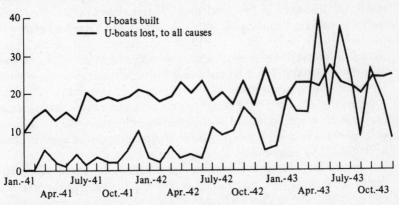

FIGURE 4–2. U-boat Construction vs. Sinkings, 1941–43
SOURCES: First Lord of the Admiralty, *German, Italian and Japanese U-Boat Casualties During the War: Particulars of Destruction* (London: HMSO, 1946), p. 35; United States Strategic Bombing Survey, *German Submarine Industry Report* (Washington, D.C.: Government Printing Office, 1947), Exhibit B-2.

The Germans began the war with some thirty oceangoing U-boats.

FIGURE 4-3. Cumulative Increase in U-boats, 1939–43 (Sum of new construction minus losses)
SOURCES: First Lord of the Admiralty, *German, Italian and Japanese U-Boat Casualties During the War: Particulars of Destruction* (London: HMSO, 1946), p. 35; United States Strategic Bombing Survey, *German Submarine Industry Report* (Washington, D.C.: Government Printing Office, 1947), Exhibit B-2.

son with British efforts at different points in the war makes these tallies particularly unflattering. First, American forces did slightly less well than the British had done in 1940, when ASW technique was far more rudimentary, and the numbers of both submarines and ships and planes to pursue them far fewer than in 1942. Second, as mentioned earlier, even though in terms of losses American areas bore the brunt of the U-boat offensive in most of 1942, British and British-controlled forces accounted for almost four times as many kills during that year as did their American counterparts. Moreover, the American contribution in 1942 looks particularly weak when compared with American efforts in the latter three years of the war, a period in which most U-boats operated again in areas of British ASW responsibility.

It should be noted that American and British forces knew with a fair degree of certainty how many U-boats they had sunk *during* the war, not just at its end: When they erred they did so on the side of caution. Thus, in 1942 they estimated some eighty U-boats sunk; postwar assessments revealed that eighty-five had been sunk.[27] The Allies knew quite well from the beginning how well (or poorly) they were doing in the U-boat war: all critical statistics—U-boat sinkings and construction, as well as their own losses and construction—seem to have been available promptly.

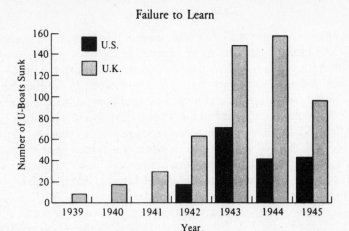

FIGURE 4-4. Sinkings of U-boats, by Nationality
SOURCE: Compiled from statistics in First Lord of the Admiralty, *German, Italian and Japanese U-Boat Casualties During the War: Particulars of Destruction* (London: HMSO, 1946), p. 4. Included under British kills are all kills achieved by British, Dominion, Imperial, and Allied (other than U.S.) forces under British operational control; included under U.S. kills are kills achieved by all U.S. and Allied (other than British, Dominion, and Imperial) forces under U.S. operational control. This report represents the consolidated statistics produced by an Anglo-American committee formed at war's end to reconcile these statistics.

On both scores, then, American ASW in early 1942 proved disastrously ineffective. The relatively small scale of the German attack made this failure more embarrassing at the time and makes it more puzzling for the historian. Operation *Paukenschlag* ("Drumbeat"), as Doenitz called it, mustered barely half a dozen U-boats at first, and he never threw more than a dozen at once at American shores.[28] Forced by the campaign in the Mediterranean to keep several dozen submarines there, required by Hitler to deploy a score to fend off an expected attack on Norway, and further constrained by the time required for refit and transit to and from patrol areas, Doenitz could not bring to bear the force his two hundred operational U-boats should have exerted on the American coasts.[29]

Finally—and making all of the above even more inexplicable—the United States Navy had had access from the beginning of the war to British information about virtually every aspect of the antisubmarine war. It is indeed this fact that makes the disaster of 1942 so peculiar. To be sure, ASW did not receive adequate resources from the navy and the government more generally (we shall discuss this further below); to be sure, some initial losses were to be expected as the navy and the country went from peace to war; nonetheless, the fact remains that with respect to critical matters of doctrine (most notably convoying, but also the use of land-based aviation and the tactics of antisubmarine attacks) and organization (with particular regard to intelligence, but also to centralized control), the navy failed to learn lessons that were readily available from the British. And, to pile paradox on paradox, we must observe that the United States Navy had in fact made strenuous efforts to learn from the British. It is, however, in answering the *how* and *why* of such learning that we shall begin to understand the enigmas of American ASW in 1942.

Anglo-American discussions about cooperation with respect to ASW began before World War II. As early as June 1939 then–Chief of Naval Operations Admiral William D. Leahy presided over a discussion with the British naval attaché in which Leahy tentatively agreed that the United States would cooperate in Atlantic ASW in the event of war.[30] The so-called ABC meeting of spring 1941 formalized these vague commitments, resulting in an agreement that American forces in the Atlantic would participate in the convoy war.[31] In the interim, American naval observers had gone to Great Britain in large numbers, headed after August 1940 by Rear Admiral Robert C. Ghormley, former director of the War Plans Division of the Office of the Chief of Naval Operations. Although previously the American naval attaché, Captain Alan G. Kirk (later head of the Office of Naval Intelligence) had had friendly relations with a number of British officers, the British had hitherto shown some restraint in sharing ASW information. Following the conjunction of the fall of France and the beginning of the first U-boat blitz, however, sources opened up.[32] The Ghormley mission inaugurated the extraordinary sharing of information that would characterize the Anglo-American war effort as a whole.

Ghormley (titled Special Naval Observer) arrived in August 1940 in time to participate in the meetings of the Bailey Committee, named after Admiral Sir Sidney Bailey of the Royal Navy, former director of planning for the Admiralty. Although nominally a British committee only, it met in the presence of the American observers to make recommendations to the British chiefs of staff and the American military on Anglo-American cooperation. The Bailey Committee ranged over a host of issues pertaining to Anglo-American strategic, operational, and tactical cooperation, and its report set the tone for the overall relationship between the two countries.

In short order a flood of information—some channeled through the Office of Naval Intelligence, some passed directly to the Chief of Naval

Operations by Ghormley—came to the United States. Even in that most sensitive of all areas, cryptography, American and British officers exchanged information with unprecedented (although not yet complete) openness—in autumn 1940 the Americans informed the British that they had broken into "Purple," the Japanese cipher; in January 1941 the British took two U.S. army and two U.S. navy observers to Bletchley Park, the home of their cryptanalytic effort.[33] In the meanwhile scores of American naval officers sailed with Royal Navy ships, toured British facilities, and interviewed British officers.[34] A steady stream of memoranda, prototypes, and visitors crossed the Atlantic—in both directions. Shortly after his arrival in Britain, Ghormley wrote back to Chief of Naval Operations Admiral Harold Stark: "I am impressed with the fact that under present conditions we are getting advantage of priceless information from actual war laboratory which will not be available to us in case of German victory."[35] Ghormley's description of the Royal Navy's experiences as a "war laboratory" recurs constantly throughout his correspondence and that of his staff. The ominous phrase, "in case of German victory," reminds us that the Americans felt a particular urgency to learn as much as possible from the British. Not only might the United States need such information if it entered the war on Britain's side, its military chiefs feared greatly that they might have to fight the war alone. At this time (autumn 1940 and through the first half of 1941) many American officers did not believe that Britain could escape invasion and ultimate subjugation by the Nazis. Even if the English could beat back such an onslaught, they might yet find themselves forced by the Luftwaffe and the U-boats—as well as their own sense of the futility of the struggle—to make a compromise peace with Hitler.

"The U.S. Navy was able to assimilate Royal Navy wartime ASW knowledge as rapidly as it was bitterly gained."[36] We shall argue below that this verdict is radically incomplete, if not in one sense profoundly wrong. Still no one can justifiably accuse the navy as a whole, or its leadership, of ignoring the British experience or dismissing it as irrelevant.

THE PROBLEMS

We have thus far sketched out the scope of the disaster of 1942 and attempted to dispel the most common broad-brush explanation for it, namely a *willful* failure to learn from the British experience of 1940–42. We can now examine what went wrong in rather greater detail. Curiously enough, few of the participants or historians who reviewed the failure of Americans ASW after mid-1942 attributed the disaster to the absence of adequate escort vessels and aircraft. Initially, however, the shortages were severe: two weeks after the beginning of war but three weeks before the U-boats arrived off the Eastern Sea Frontier, Admiral Adolphus Andrews, commander ESF, reported to the Chief of Naval Operations that he had at his disposal barely one and a half dozen escort craft, none of which could outdistance (and many of which could not outgun) submarines operating on the surface. His dour report that "should enemy submarines operate off this coast, this Command has no forces available to take adequate action against them, either offensive or defensive" proved grimly prescient.[37] In February Andrews argued that to introduce convoy he would require 64 escort vessels, which he did not have, a requirement rising in a March report to nearly 80. By May, however, over 110 vessels (many, to be sure, too small and slow to be of much use) were on hand in the Eastern Sea Frontier alone, plus 45 more under repair, plus 16 destroyers sporadically available for escort and patrol duties.[38] Similar deficiencies in numbers of aircraft disappeared equally quickly: In the Eastern Sea Frontier alone the several dozen ill-assorted army and navy patrol planes of January 1942 gave way to 165 by the end of March, and more than 300 by the end of July.[39] Overseas reinforcements also arrived speedily: By the beginning of March the Navy also had the use of 22 Royal Navy antisubmarine trawlers, complete with experienced crews, provided by the British.

Why did the early deficiencies occur? We can attribute part of the problem to the suddenness of the outbreak of war in the Pacific. The American high command stripped Atlantic naval and air forces in order to provide badly needed escorts and reinforcements for the hard-hit garrisons in the Far East.[40] Moreover, the famous agreement to transfer fifty obsolescent World War I–era destroyers to the British deprived the U.S. navy of craft which, though outmoded and excruciatingly uncomfortable for mid-Atlantic convoy work, would have made very useful coastal escorts. The reluctance of the Bureau of Ships to spend money during the naval expansion of the late 1930s on escort vessels (as opposed to multipurpose destroyers, which could help the battle fleet as well) hurt; so too did the division (about which more below) of responsibilities for antisubmarine air patrol between the navy and the army air forces.

Nonetheless, when all is said and done we cannot conclude that the first nine months of losses came about because of insufficient resources. As we see, such material deficiencies disappeared with remarkable speed—within several months of the outbreak of war—and yet losses continued at a high rate until the introduction of a complete convoy system, and submarine kills did not rise sharply until 1943. The enemy did not (as was the case in the North Atlantic convoy battles of the next winter and the spring of 1943) swamp the defenses by sheer numbers—most of the execution was done by seven or eight U-boats operating at a time, and individually rather than in wolf packs. Although air cover remained far from perfect, commanders of the sea frontiers had far more airplanes available for surveillance and escort work than did escort commanders on the main North Atlantic convoy routes. Above all, few professional observers, from Morison to the senior commanders dealing with ASW in late 1942, saw the problem chiefly in terms of resources. Thus, Captain Baker's June 24, 1942, "the Battle of the Atlantic is being lost" memorandum to Admiral King mentioned "insufficient vessels and aircraft" as the third of a list of five reasons for those losses—and even then argued that such deficiencies were aggravated by other, less tangible failings.[41] As we shall see, though, the initial professional judgment—that the problem was largely a material one—had great significance; subsequent reflection and analysis did not bear this out.

Of particular interest are the judgments made by Admiral Doenitz and his staff in Lorient—then headquarters of the German U-boat command. (Doenitz insisted on full and prompt reports from his skippers, which were then transcribed into the command's war diary.) The Germans believed that organization and doctrine, not lack of matériel, were the roots of the American problem. The war diary contains such entries as "enemy air patrols heavy but not dangerous because of inexperience."[42] "[The enemy is not] able to make allowances and adjustments according to the prevailing submarine operations."[43] "The American airmen see nothing, and the destroyers and patrol vessels proceed at too great a speed to intercept U-boats, and likewise having caught one they do not follow up with a tough enough depth charge attack."[44]

These German assessments point the way to the core issues. It is quite true that both the quantity and quality of American ASW equipment in the first few months of 1942 were poor, but as German records indicate, these were not the most important failings. Two major needs went beyond technology, and in both the United States Navy in 1942 did poorly and the Royal Navy excelled. The first was operational intelligence. In the words of a distinguished historian who observed these matters firsthand during World War II, "The war against the submarine . . . was, in one manifestation, a contest between systems of information, an intellectual exercise demanding the collection, organization, interpretation and dissemination of many different kinds of data."[45] To wage the antisubmarine war well, analysts had to bring together fragments of information—direction-finding fixes, visual sightings, decrypts, and the "flaming datum" of a U-boat attack—for use by a commander to coordinate the efforts of warships, aircraft, and convoy commanders. Such synthesis had to occur in near-"real time"—within hours, even minutes in some cases. The navy also needed intelligence of a larger if less urgent kind—study of enemy procedures and tactics, even the quirks of particular commanders. Furthermore, the Navy needed a systematic study of its own methods, their strengths and weaknesses in order to adjust one's own force composition and doctrine to the changing threat.

But analytic success, which the navy already had in some measure, could not achieve anything in the absence of organizational efficiency. A prompt and accurate intelligence assessment would mean nothing if the analysts could not communicate that assessment directly to commanders on the scene, if those commanders did not have operational control over the various air and naval assets they required to protect shipping and sink U-boats, if they saw no reason to heed that intelligence, or if they had no firm notion what to do about it. The working out of correct standard tactics required, for example, to attack a U-boat seen submerging a mile from a destroyer could have no impact if destroyer skippers did not know or would not apply them. Moreover, as the U-boats changed their tactics and equipment (and they did so often—a benefit of their centralized control by Doenitz), the antisubmarine forces needed to adopt compensating tactical changes and technological innovation.

The British antisubmarine effort, clearly the most successful of any of the participants' in World War II, succeeded in large part because of their ability to master these two requirements of ASW: efficient collection, collation, and communication of intelligence and development of appropriate doctrine. They accomplished the former in large part because of the efforts of the Royal Navy's Operational Intelligence Centre, and in particular its submarine tracking room, under a lawyer turned naval reserve officer: Rodger Winn.[46] The OIC received intelligence from all sources—decrypted radio intercepts (which it analyzed in raw form, unlike the arrangements made for land and air decrypts), land-based radio direction finding, prisoner-of-war interrogation reports, photographic intelligence, and all the many other forms of raw intelligence—which it received directly from intelligence collectors. Its small staff could not only communicate directly with field commanders: It established its credibility so fully that it received permission to disseminate not only "hard" intelligence about the location and activities of enemy units but "working fictions" as well-educated guesses, based on incomplete information and the judgment of the OIC analysts. Given the fact that OIC was a largely civilian operation, and given the jealous proclivity of naval commanders to make their own estimates of likely enemy action, this constituted a remarkable bureaucratic as well as analytic achievement. In the United States Navy, by contrast, the aggressive head of the CNO's War Plans Division, Admiral Kelly Turner, successfully battled to take responsibility for intelligence estimates away from the Office of Naval Intelligence, making it part of the office of the CNO and later the office of COMINCH.[47]

How did the OIC and naval intelligence contribute more generally to the Royal Navy's successes in ASW? First, it allowed for the diversion of convoys away from waiting wolf packs—at least until the number of U-boats grew so large that diversion became completely impossible. Second, and probably more important, it enabled the British to concentrate their scarce and overworked escort vessels and aircraft to protect the most endangered convoys. Third, it enabled the British to develop a database on the tactics and habits of U-boats and their skippers, a database useful for future analysis.

The success of British naval intelligence did not stem solely from technical accomplishments, and in particular decryption of German radio transmissions, important as those were.[48] Rather, the British system worked because it had developed an organizational structure that enabled the Royal Navy and RAF to make use of *all* of the intelligence at their disposal, to analyze it swiftly and accurately, and to disseminate it immediately to those who needed to have it. The arrangements that allowed them to do so—the creation ·of an independent OIC within the Naval Intelligence Division, allowed to communicate directly with commanders at sea and staffed largely by civilian analysts temporarily recruited for the war—came into place in 1938, well before the outbreak of war and, interestingly enough, considerably before anyone suspected that cryptography would supply the enormously valuable services that it later did.[49] All this came about because of British experiences in World War I, when the Royal Navy failed to make sufficient use of the brilliant cryptanalysts of Room 40, the forerunner of the OIC, for precisely these organizational reasons. Cut off from noncryptologic sources of intelligence, allowed to communicate only with the Admiralty in London rather than operational commanders at sea, discouraged by admirals from offering educated hypotheses about likely enemy behavior, Room 40 made a smaller contribution to that war than it might have done. The failure to deal a crippling blow to the exposed German High Seas Fleet at the Battle of Jutland stemmed directly from the bureaucratic and organizational relationships that prevented the appropriate use of intelligence.[50]

British World War II ASW doctrine evolved in almost as centralized a fashion as did operational intelligence. Two organizations—the Royal Air Force's Coastal Command and the Royal Navy's Western Approaches Command—handled air and most naval ASW respectively. Because of the original bureaucratic disposition of naval aircraft to the Royal Air Force in the interwar period, all landbased naval aviation lay in the hands of Coastal Command; because of geography, most escort groups were based in Liverpool under CINCWA. Both had close links to OIC in London: both (particularly in the latter part of the war) operated under senior commanders in constant touch with one another. Both made efforts to develop standardized tactical procedures and equipment for ASW: both were increasingly successful, particularly in 1941 and after.

In the case of Coastal Command the development of sound doctrine benefited from the early and successful use of operations research analysts, led in the summer of 1941 by P. M. S. Blackett, probably the most distinguished one of the war.[51] OR analysts studied a variety of problems, which contributed to the solution of such problems as the organization of search and patrol and the most efficient tactics for attacking surfaced submarines. By 1941 OR analysts worked directly for the head of Coastal Command, rather than as previously for the chief scientist of the Air Ministry.

Western Approaches Command took longer to apply OR to antisubmarine warfare—only in the spring of 1942, for example, did the Royal Navy ask Blackett to help organize the Royal Navy's operations research effort.[52] Western Approaches could and did, however, standardize training, in part by ensuring that new skippers would study the methods of successful commanders and in part by centralizing the various forms of classroom and open-water training.[53] The Royal Navy may have resisted the use of operations research more than did the RAF; It succeeded equally, however, at discovering which tactics worked and at making sure that such procedures were taught and applied.

Theoretically, after April 1941, Coastal Command came under the operational control of the Royal Navy for the prosecution of ASW. Not surprisingly, sailors and airmen have disputed the significance of this arrangement.[54] It is more important to note that the headquarters of CINCWA stood side by side with those of the Coastal Command's Fifteenth Group, which provided most of the antisubmarine convoy escorts, and that the two commands worked extremely closely. In addition, Western Approaches Command concentrated exclusively on the antisubmarine war, and Coastal Command largely so. Although from time to time Coastal Command aircraft raided German coastal shipping or had to provide cover for naval operations in British waters, most of its attention—and its own sense of purpose—focused on the problem of ASW.

British arrangements were far from perfect, to be sure. The friction between the Royal Navy and the RAF over control of Coastal Command and, more importantly, allocation of resources to it, flared up throughout the war. More could probably have been done earlier to develop the tactical doctrine required for the prosecution of ASW. Nonetheless, British antisubmarine warfare worked remarkably well throughout the war, and largely because of the organizational arrangements that supported it. As we shall see, in late 1942 and early 1943 the United States Navy duplicated these arrangements—thereby dramatically improving its antisubmarine effectiveness. Proper organization constituted the critical problem for the conduct of antisubmarine warfare. While individual decisions and disputes had short-term impacts on the conduct of the American antisubmarine war, none had anything like the cumulative impact of the larger organizational disfunctions we shall discuss below.

To demonstrate, let us take four of the most frequently offered "single-problem" explanations of the failures of 1942, beginning with the infamous absence of a coastal blackout until April 1942.[55] Heinous as this failure was, it cannot account for the continued heavy rates of sinking after the imposition of a blackout, nor does it account in any way for the second kind of failure—the low kill rates of 1942 compared with 1943 and 1944. It came about in part because of divided command (the coastal blackout was the concern of the army, not the naval Sea Frontier commanders), but dramatic as it was it cannot explain why British ships and planes could find and destroy U-boats and American ships and planes could not. The same holds true of convoy (or rather the absence of convoy), probably the single most important mistake made by the United States Navy in 1942: It too does not account for low kill rates following sub contacts. More important, the decision not to introduce convoy was not simply a thoughtless blunder but an agonizing decision made with full awareness of the possible cost. The Eastern Sea Frontier war diarist wrote in the entry for February 1942:

To defend merchant shipping against submarine attacks there is one classic procedure. The history of the first world war demonstrated that ships, men and weapons, could be brought into most successful combination against the U-boats through the operation of the convoy system. British experience in the early years of this war has served only to confirm this lesson of the past.[56]

Yet various factors—above all, the number of ships requiring protection and the number and quality of airplanes available for escort work—seemed to argue against immediate introduction of convoy. The issue did not focus on the abstract merits of convoy; Everyone agreed on that. The difficult questions were: Under what conditions? How large? With what kinds of escort? These issues did not go away in 1942 for either American or British naval authorities: the size of convoys, the appropriateness of allowing very fast merchant ships to sail independently, and the distribution of warships between escort and supporting hunter groups remained contentious from 1939 through 1945.[57]

A third "single-problem" analysis—more common at the time perhaps than now—looks at critical weapons, which might have tipped the ASW balance either way. The secretary of war, for example, believed that airborne radar (which could detect submarines on the surface) would enable the Allies to turn the tide against the U-boats.[58] In this view, the failure to introduce a critical system—airborne radar—promptly accounts for the failure of 1942. Yet *particularly* in the Battle of the North Atlantic, no weapon ever proved decisive. Before the war the Royal Navy thought that sonar had virtually eliminated the submarine threat: Surface attacks and adroit tactics negated much of its value. The Germans thought that torpedoes that homed on a ship's propeller noises would turn the war around: The Allies developed a device to spoof it. So too for airborne radar. The Germans managed to acquire or develop radar-warning receivers enabling U-boats to submerge before the airplane arrived, and by developing the snorkel (an air funnel which allows a submarine to recharge its batteries without surfacing completely) they were able to reduce greatly the time U-boats had to spend on the surface. Each technological advance was necessary, and without unremitting technical competition the Allies could not have won the Battle of the North Atlantic. But no single weapon or family of weapons proved fatal to the U-boats.

This brings us to the fourth "single-problem" explanation of the disaster of 1942—the dispute over the use of land-based naval aviation. One cannot say that aircraft proved the most effective enemies of U-boats, although they may have accounted for marginally more kills than surface vessels operating alone (see Figure 4–5). As mentioned above, no single weapon system turned that U-boat threat around, and ship sinkings of U-boats continued to rise until the last year of the war, when all destruction

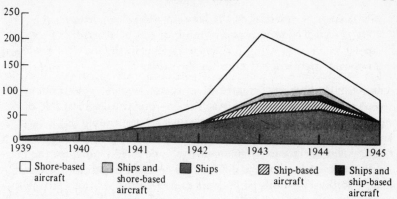

FIGURE 4-5. Sinkings of U-boats at Sea, by Cause *
*This table excludes sinkings by bombing raids, naval mines, submarines, and other or unknown causes. Bombing did not account for any substantial destruction until late 1944 and early 1945, when 22 and 40 U-boats, respectively, were destroyed from the air. During the last three years of the war submarines accounted for barely half a dozen U-boats a year. Mines (laid by ship and by plane) accounted for a dozen U-boats each in 1944 and 1945, but only several a year before then. In 1944 large numbers of U-boats (some 40 in all) were lost to unknown causes, which from 1940–1942 accounted for some half a dozen U-boats a year.
SOURCE: First Lord of the Admiralty, *German, Italian and Japanese U-Boat Casualties During the War: Particulars of Destruction* (London: HMSO, 1946), p.4.

of U-boats fell off. The sheer presence of escort vessels could force U-boats to act in ways that would subsequently make them vulnerable to air power. Nonetheless, air power exerted a major influence on the outcome of the Battle of the North Atlantic: Airplanes operating from ships and shore accounted for a bit less than half of the U-boats sunk by Allied forces; others located U-boats or by their sheer presence forced them to operate inefficiently. Given the promise and the reality of the aerial contribution to ASW, it is not surprising that serious disputes arose between the organizations responsible for handling it.

In 1942 the United States Navy and the Army Air Force (which controlled most, but by no means all, of the aircraft useful for long-range antisubmarine warfare) had very different views about the proper role of aircraft. As the Army Air Force official historians put it:

Naval doctrine emphasized the basically defensive functions of convoy escort and the patrol of more or less fixed sectors of the coastal waters ... Army Air Force students of the problem expressed an equally marked preference for the offensive.[59]

This dispute, however, mirrored an equally violent disagreement between sailors and airmen in Great Britain– one equally incapable of resolution. In point of fact, aircraft, whether based on shore or on carriers, and warships as well, participated in both escort of convoy *and* so-called hunter-killer operations. While convoys undoubtedly provided the magnet that attracted U-boats and hence provided the targets for the antisubmarine forces, at various points pure hunter-killer operations proved successful as well—the 1943 Bay of Biscay offensive, for example, which interdicted U-boats attempting to break into the Atlantic from their French bases. Despite the extreme language on both sides, neither sailors nor airmen practiced purely offensive or purely defensive operational concepts. Moreover, disruptive as these disputes were, they did not (in the British case, at any rate) spill over into the day to day functioning of antisubmarine warfare: working relationships between operational commanders, and in particular CINCWA and the commander of the Fifteenth Group remained close. In the United States in 1942, however, abstract doctrinal disputes folded into a much more serious absence of working cooperation in the field—which returns us to our central thesis.

THE MATRIX

Figure 4–6 presents the failure matrix for this chapter. In it we have broken down the functions which the Navy (and the Army Air Forces, in some measure) into four: resource allocation, coordination and communication, control and command, and doctrine and technique. Along the vertical axis we have four levels of command responsibility. In the first row we have the highest civilian and military authorities, plus the support agencies (e.g., the Bureau of Ships or the Office of Naval Intelligence). In the second, we have the operational commanders such as the commander of the Eastern Sea Frontier and First Bomber Command (the army air force units responsible for ASW). In the third row we have an intermediate level of command, represented by the commanders of the naval districts, who had charge of escort units in the major ports, plus control of shipping in and around those ports; and in the fourth row, the

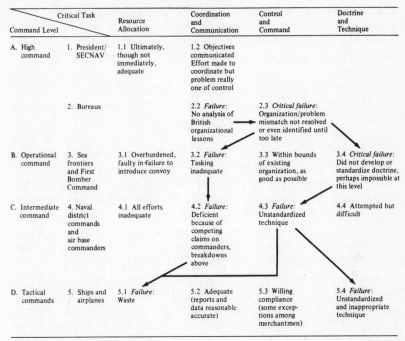

Arrows indicate causal links.

FIGURE 4–6. Matrix of Failure

actual operators—the skippers and crews of the ships and airplanes that went out to attack enemy submarines.

We can begin our analysis in the usual fashion, by looking at the sharp end of the organization—the forces actually in contact with the enemy. At this level we find neither failure of communication (that is, ships not communicating adequately with one another) nor of command (ships or airplanes failing to do as they were told). Rather, we find ships and airplanes improperly distributed, fruitlessly patrolling sea-lanes in search of submarines, for example. As mentioned above, we also find doctrine and technique inadequately standardized and developed. Air crews, for instance, which had only one or two chances of actually attacking a submarine in the course of their operational experience, had few opportunities to learn by doing: They needed sound doctrine the first time because they might never have more than one chance to apply their knowledge.[60]

The next level of command, that of Naval District Command, ostensibly controlled local escort operations through the spring of 1942, when the commander Eastern Sea Frontier recommended a reorganization of the ESF that would have reduced their operational responsibilities considerably.[61] The naval district commanders occupied an impossible position, in which they had to juggle responsibility for harbor security (no mean task), administrative control of naval shore facilities in their areas plus the local defense forces used to hunt submarines. Moreover, they rarely had any direct liaison with the army air force (which insisted on working directly with ESF, if not indeed altogether independently), at least through official channels. As a result, these intermediate commanders failed to coordinate their efforts or to use what assets they had effectively.

Ironically, the operational level of command, that of the Eastern Sea Frontier and its counterparts (Gulf Sea Frontier, and so on) had been designed expressly to forestall some of the problems that later emerged. Created in early 1941 in order to unify the splintered peacetime organizational arrangements (which divided the seaboard into naval district commands, usually based on major ports), ESF in particular grew steadily, encompassing more and more of the Atlantic Coast all the way down to Florida. The Sea Frontiers had prime responsibility for the conduct of coastal ASW in 1942. The most notable failures at this level occurred in the areas of doctrine and technique (in particular, the decision not to go with weak convoys sooner, rather than wait for stronger escorts) and in the communication of prompt and reliable intelligence to local commands.

It is at the highest level that the source of failure becomes most explicable, or at least most readily apparent. Two central problems set up the difficulties under which all three lower levels of command operated. These were first and foremost the failure to understand and act on the mismatch between the organizational structure for conducting ASW and the nature of the problem itself and second, the failure to learn from the British experience how to rectify that mismatch.

THE CAUSES

Every war brings to the surface areas of warfare that may form an intelligible whole but that do not—for a variety of reasons—come under the purview of a preexisting military organization. One test of the high command in any war lies in its ability to perceive (and if possible anticipate) such "problem-organization mismatches" and attempt to resolve them.

Immense obstacles to recognizing and coping with such mismatches always exist. The drive for organizational autonomy—a more potent force than any other, including the drive for organizational aggrandizement—may make organizations willing to abandon certain missions rather than dilute their independence. This in fact occurred in the case of the army air forces, which concluded their running dispute with the navy over control of land-based naval aviation by relinquishing it in the summer of 1943 rather than submit to navy operational control over AAF units.[62] Moreover, this problem did not simply operate between services: Its effects were felt within the navy as well.

In World War II naval officers maintained (as they do today) their belief in systematic decentralization, hence their resistance to command arrangements that tended to reduce the autonomy of local commanders. Although this is largely true, it does not capture the full reality, which is that the navy simply centralizes *differently* than do land or air forces; that is, at the level of the ship, a far-more-centrally-controlled military unit in combat than a battalion or even a fighter squadron.[63] Admiral King, in particular, believed strongly (though with some exceptions) in the virtues of delegation. He began a famous order (issued in January 1941, when he was commander in chief of the Atlantic Fleet) with the lines:

> I have been concerned for many years over the increasing
> tendency—now grown almost to "standard practice"—of flag officers
> and other group commanders to issue orders and instructions in
> which their subordinates are told "how" as well as "what" to
> do. . . . It is essential to extend the knowledge and the practice of
> "initiative of the subordinate" until they are universal in the exercise
> of command throughout all the echelons of command.[64]

King had a particular horror (again, one commonly shared in the navy, though perhaps with less vigor than his) of entrenched central staffs, to which end as COMINCH he kept his own staff remarkably small—barely three hundred officers and as many enlisted personnel.[65] He also made a point of rotating officers through Washington, trying not to keep any there much longer than a year, except in extraordinary cases.

This insistence on decentralization, so much a function of the traditions and the requirements of command at sea as well as King's own personality, did not always square with the military problems that the U.S. navy faced. Indeed, the president and the secretary of the navy had recognized this in King's dual appointment as chief of naval operations (CNO) and commander in chief, U.S. Fleet (COMINCH). In the latter position he had operational command over all U.S. naval forces—authority never granted General George C. Marshall vis-à-vis army forces. As the Royal Navy had discovered as early as World War I, the age of radio communications meant that both intelligence and command would, in many cases, thereafter be centrally controlled. This was every bit as painful a reversal of traditional attitudes for the Royal Navy as for the U.S. navy, both of which shared a reverence for the autonomy of the man on the spot. Henceforth, shore-based commanders would have to coordinate the actions of ships and planes operating hundreds of miles away: Admirals could no longer direct all operations from their flagships. Neither the United States Navy nor the Imperial Japanese Navy had adjusted to this fact by late 1941—indeed, King maintained a cruiser to act as his flagship and insisted that his staff be small enough to sail aboard it. Admiral Yamamoto sailed as commander in chief with the Japanese Combined Fleet to participate in the Battle of Midway and proved unable to control the fleet adequately there; his American counterpart, Admiral Chester W. Nimitz, however, remained at Pearl Harbor and helped shape its successful outcome.

Nimitz's behavior at Midway suggests that the U.S. navy did not simply refuse to change its traditional attitudes to command, painful as that might prove. The creation of the Sea Frontiers in 1941 provides some evidence along these lines as well, and so too, does the early use of civilian operations research analysts in support of antisubmarine warfare. As early as April 1942 the navy took some first steps toward centralization of ASW—the handing over of the operational research unit to COMINCH from the Atlantic Fleet, for example, although training doctrine remained ("of course," as the directive put it) in the hands of local commanders.[66] Within a year and a half of American entry into the war, a highly suitable organization for ASW had evolved, as we shall see. But why did this not happen sooner?

One partial answer has to do with what one might call the "55/95 problem"—the tendency to see that element of military difficulty that bulks largest (55 percent of your problem) as the whole of it (95 percent). In this case the *initial* shortages of escort vessels and aircraft made such an impression that they made it difficult to understand the nature of the organizational challenge facing the navy. As the Eastern Sea Frontier war diarist wrote in January, 1942,

> The heart of the problem of anti-submarine warfare can perhaps best be stated in terms of mathematics. Effective application of the methods and efficient use of the weapons depends directly upon the numerical strength of the forces involved. The solution of this

problem, therefore, must be arrived at primarily in terms of mathematics. Changes in principle or redesign of instruments will accomplish little if it is impossible to increase the numerical strength of ships and planes to the amount required.[67]

Five months later, however, the same war diarist would record that "a far more important factor in our present losses long hidden by the obvious fact of our great material weakness, is now, in the days of our material strength, becoming discernible. *It is the factor of human error.*"[68] Through the first three months of 1942 one could reasonably attribute failure to lack of resources, although as a number of contemporary observers pointed out, the problem lay deeper. Later, by the early fall of 1942, Doenitz had shifted the focus of his attacks once again, striking now at the North Atlantic convoy areas, which in September experienced half the merchant ship losses suffered in the Atlantic.[69]

The undeniable resource shortages of early 1942 helped conceal the underlying problems of American ASW; the swelling tide of Allied ship production thereafter further obscured them. By August 1942 construction of new shipping had begun to exceed losses: With one brief exception in November of 1942, it would continue to do so for the rest of the war. Even in the terrible month of March 1943, new merchant vessel construction would exceed sinkings by 300,000 gross tons.[70] Moreover, the ships lost to the U-boats were older and for the most part slower, smaller, and less efficient than the new Liberty and Victory ships that replenished the fleet. Finally, as time went on, more destroyers, destroyer escorts, and long-range patrol airplanes would come to the fleet: These too could not fail to have an impact insofar as the preservation of shipping went.

The above analysis might suffice to explain why it took the United States Navy until the spring of 1943 to evolve the appropriate organization and procedures for the conduct of antisubmarine warfare—had it not been for the issue of British experience. British antisubmarine organization in 1942 was by no means perfect, and it had not yet reached the high efficiency of 1943, when a participant could call it "a streamlined job, a smooth essay in destruction."[71] Nonetheless, the basic arrangements were in place, and the more-acute American observers had some sense of their value.[72] We have seen, moreover, that the United States Navy made a serious and protracted effort to learn from British experience. Why did they fail in such a striking way?

The answer seems to lie in how the United States Navy defined learning, particularly in the context of preparation for war. In a nutshell, *the navy's leadership defined its problem as that of acquiring technical information, not assimilating new forms of organization.* From the Ghormley mission in the fall of 1940 to the American entry into the war, the emphasis in all American reporting from Britain fell on technical matters—the performance of sonars, new types of depth-charge throwers, attack trainers, and the like.[73] Within this narrow sphere the United States Navy stood remarkably open to foreign ideas and contrivances: In October 1941, for example, it conducted a careful study of how the British had refurbished an American four-stacker destroyer acquired under Land-Lease—with a view to following suit.[74] Later in the war, it would adopt British ship designs for the construction of destroyer escorts and landing ships. Neither did a few broad-spirited officers monopolize this openness: The General Board of the Navy had no hesitation about recommending that the United States acquire and learn to operate from the British such basic equipment as sonar.[75]

All this occurred, however, within this oddly narrow definition of learning, which in turn stemmed from the navy's own definition of readiness, which was largely technical in nature. In three remarkable reports prepared in 1939, 1940, and 1941, entitled "Are We Ready?" the General Board of the Navy (a small group of senior admirals who reported to the chief of naval operations and the secretary of the navy), attempted, with remarkable honesty, to answer that question. Yet although the General Board discussed organization at the very highest level, calling for the creation of a joint general staff in order to coordinate national defense planning, it did not look at organizational requirements within the navy for war. Rather it focused its attention on numbers and quality of ships, planes, munitions, and supplies; although it addressed in a cursory fashion the adequacy of war plans, it did not ask whether the *organization* of the navy's forces matched wartime requirements.

We can understand this predisposition to see readiness (and hence the lessons to be learned about readiness) in terms of technology if we consider the nature of navies in general, and the problems of navies in the mid-twentieth century in particular. A variety of technical innovations— radar, radio communication, and naval aviation in particular—had begun to force fundamental changes in the way the navy operated and planned. Under such conditions a fixation on technical rather than organizational-operational questions becomes understandable. But another factor as well affected the U.S. navy in learning from the British. In the one area in which the United States Navy knew about the impact of British organization on operations, the lesson had only a cautionary import.

One report that came back from London in January 1941 included an unambiguous suggestion: "Strongly recommend that we never entrust designing of construction of our Fleet aircraft to any but naval personnel."[76] British naval personnel, including the Fifth Sea Lord, had expressed their deep discontent with the quality of British naval aviation, which was controlled (in their view, neglected) until the late 1930s by the Royal Air Force.[77] As a result, although new British aircraft carriers often had innovative features such as armored decks (which the United States Navy would later imitate), British naval aircraft could not compete with the basic land-based fighters of the Germans and the carrier-based aircraft of the Japanese. The basic torpedo plane of the Royal Navy, for example, was the Swordfish biplane, a suicidally slow aircraft of a design more appropriate to the First World War than the Second.

In addition, American officers knew about the Royal Navy's dissatisfaction over the autonomy of RAF Coastal Command, and its relatively low priority compared with Bomber Command when it came to the allocation of long-range aircraft. Although the British ultimately overcame both problems, they did not do so until 1942–1943: Before that time British admirals chaffed under the arrangements that gave the RAF a great deal of say over the disposition of air power in the war against the submarine.[78] Small wonder that Admiral King, worried about the aggrandizement of an embryonic American air force that had little interest in antisubmarine warfare, would growl to General Marshall that the model of a Coastal Command had nothing to offer the United States Navy.[79] What the United States Navy knew about the impact of British organization on the success or failure of British operations, then, suggested that the British had little to teach on that score, save a host of cautionary lessons.

Finally, if the United States Navy had thought seriously about adapting its organization to the challenges of ASW in a fashion similar to that chosen by the British, it would have required major changes in how existing organizations operated, and in no case would this have been more true than that of intelligence. The Office of Naval Intelligence (ONI), the counterpart of Britain's Naval Intelligence Division (NID), had nothing like its purview. Traditionally, ONI served a number of useful functions, primarily involving the collection of static intelligence (order-of-battle information, that is, the numbers and characteristics of enemy ships), serving as a "post office" for naval attachés, and providing domestic security services.[80] In one bruising bureaucratic battle for turf after another it lost responsibility for the making of strategic estimates to the CNO's War Plans Division under the aggressive Admiral "Kelly" Turner, and lost control of communications intelligence to the Office of Naval Communications.[81] ONI's own administrative historian came to the conclusion that

ONI had, during the interwar years, forgotten the words of Franklin Roosevelt as assistant secretary of the navy in 1919: "[The first duty of intelligence is] the collection and compilation of prompt, reliable, and accurate information concerning the approach, arrival, movements, and position of enemy naval forces."[82] As a result, ONI had no responsibility for, or interest in, operational intelligence. Whereas the Royal Navy had an organization to analyze and communicate operational intelligence promptly—an organization in close touch with the agencies that actually fought the war, and treated by them as an equal—the United States Navy did not. Instead, COMINCH and his subordinates had small combat intelligence units, which maintained map rooms and current intelligence files but had no organizational base in naval intelligence. Hopeless as ONI had become by 1942, it could not be resuscitated: A different solution had to be found.

Three factors, then—a predisposition to define learning and readiness in technical terms, a reinforcing belief in the inadequacy of critical British organization, and the fact that an attempt to mirror British organization would have required transformation of existing institutions—explain the navy's stubbornly schizophrenic attitude toward learning from the British. Eager to acquire and assimilate technology and low-level tactics, it did so; unfortunately, these alone could not make American ASW efficient.

ADAPTATION AND SUCCESS

Nonetheless, the navy did eventually adapt organizationally to the challenges of ASW. While so doing, in some measure it not only adopted but surpassed some British practices. This process culminated in the creation in May 1943 of a unique organization: Tenth Fleet.[83] Nominally headed by Admiral King himself, it bore the imprint of the man who had served since April as his Assistant Chief of Staff for Anti-Submarine Measures, Rear Admiral Francis S. Low. He supervised directly only three small divisions, formed from pre-existing organizations: an operations unit, the Convoy and Routing Section, and Anti-Submarine Measures (this latter including the civilian scientists of the Anti-Submarine Warfare Operations Research Group, or ASWORG). In all, Tenth Fleet included directly fewer than a hundred officers, plus supporting enlisted and civilian personnel. At the same time, Commander Tenth Fleet had responsibility not only for ASW training (including the use of the various training establishments as Tenth Fleet's "laboratories"), but for the direction of operations at sea as well:

> The Commander, Tenth Fleet, is to exercise direct command over all Atlantic Sea Frontiers, using sea frontier commanders as task force commanders. He is to control allocations of anti-submarine forces to all commands in the Atlantic, including the Atlantic Fleet, and is to reallocate forces from time to time as the situation requires. In order to insure quick and effective action to meet the needs of the changing A/S situation, the Commander, Tenth Fleet, is to be given control of all LR (Long Range) and VLR (Very Long Range) aircraft and certain groups or units of auxiliary carriers, escort ships, and submarines which he is to allocate to reinforce task forces that need help, or to employment as "killer groups"—under his operational direction in appropriate circumstances.[84]

In effect, Commander Tenth Fleet could override the dispositions of any naval commander in the Atlantic in the conduct of antisubmarine operations. Although King envisaged appointing someone else as Commander Tenth Fleet, he soon saw that it would be best to have it remain one of his functions, with day to day operations conducted by Low. In practice, Tenth Fleet staff refrained from issuing orders to local commanders, relying instead on carefully phrased "recommendations"—which were rarely if ever ignored.[85]

This arrangement, which fused operational intelligence, the control of convoys, the allocation of all antisubmarine units, and the direction of all establishments charged with the development of doctrine and technology, had no parallel elsewhere. At the end of the war the British commander in chief of the Western Approaches, who most closely approached this level of control, would write unhappily in his final report: "I am more than ever convinced that my original conception was correct, and that there was a pressing need for the appointment of a Chief of Anti-U-Boat Warfare with scope analogous to that of Admiral Doenitz."[86]

This concentration of power in one organization, though occasionally proposed in England, never received official approval there.[87] In the United States, however, it quickly brought results. As Farago points out, in the eighteen months before the creation of Tenth Fleet the United States Navy sank thirty-six U-boats; in the six months after, it sank seventy-five. This could not have occurred, to be sure, without the advent of the new antisubmarine aircraft carriers and the general improvement of men and matériel for the antisubmarine war. Nonetheless, the organizational framework of Tenth Fleet allowed the navy not only to create a uniform tactical doctrine but to see to it that commanders applied it; it also enabled the navy to adjust that doctrine to changing circumstances. The work of ASWORG, in particular, which had existed in various forms since early 1942, benefited greatly from the Tenth Fleet arrangement.[88] Only when the diverse data generated by the antisubmarine war could be centrally processed, disseminated, and acted upon could the efficiency of American antisubmarine operations increase.[89]

Tenth Fleet did not create any large new organization. Rather, it brought together smaller units that evolved slowly: The Antisubmarine Warfare Unit of Atlantic Fleet, for example, had come into being in March 1942 at the suggestion of the commander of American escort forces in the North Atlantic, Rear Admiral Arthur LeR. Bristol, Jr. Gradually it began the development of standardized doctrine, incorporating the work of the embryonic operations research group. Its pronouncements carried no weight, however, because they came from what was technically no more than a research-and-analysis arm of a fleet command.

The creation of Tenth Fleet did *not* bring more talented individuals into the field of ASW than had previous organizations. Dr. Philip Morse of MIT continued to direct ASWORG's main activities, and the same held true, by and large, of the other sections incorporated into Tenth Fleet. What Tenth Fleet did allow, by virtue of its organization and mandate, was for these individuals to become far more effective than previously.

Interestingly enough, the Germans throughout the war failed to establish a correspondingly efficient organization to conduct anti-merchant-shipping operations. The Luftwaffe and the chief of U-boats, for example, notoriously failed to cooperate with one another, although in some instances (in the Arctic and certain phases of the Battle of the Bay of Biscay) exceptions occurred. Even Doenitz's own organization, however, despite the centralization that enabled him to deploy the U-boats as part of one fleet, remained amateurishly small and incomplete. Doenitz had a staff of fewer than two dozen officers and no organic scientific research unit until the end of 1943. One opponent would describe it, perhaps too harshly, as "an eighteenth century way of war in a twentieth century age of technology."[90]

Yet tiny, undeveloped, and unsystematic as this centralized command was, it gave Doenitz enormous strengths, which his opponents recognized. In addition Doenitz's remarkable ability to train and inspire his U-boat crews gave him a weapon of exceptional strength and resiliency. The German submariners fought bravely and with extraordinary determination against overwhelming odds, suffering probably the highest casualties of any branch of the German armed services in the war. Aided by a small but efficient signal intelligence organization (which benefited, in turn, from Allied carelessness about the security of merchant ciphers), they not only inflicted heavy losses upon the Allies but seemed to threaten their very ability to continue the war.[91] As Churchill would put it: "The U-boat attack was our worst evil," and, "The only thing that ever really frightened me during the war was the U-boat peril."[92]

Later historians would cast doubt upon Churchill's sense of threat, arguing that had the Germans improved the efficiency and increased the weight of the U-boat attack, the Allies would have reacted earlier, with greater strength and more ample resources.[93] To this one can only respond with the words of a great historian of an earlier conflict: "To us of this day, the result of [this] part of the war seems a foregone conclusion. It was far from being so; and very far from being so regarded by our forefathers."[94] Certainly, those who fought in the Battle of the Atlantic did not consider it won until the very last moment, and the authors of a secret postwar report warned, "Today we are technologically unprepared to cope with the U-boats which the Nazis had on the point of readiness for operational use in 1945."[95] One can, at the very least, insist that if the Allies had not won the Battle of the Atlantic they could not have won the war, and that the winning of that battle required enormous efforts, resources, and ingenuity on quite the same scale as any of the other campaigns of the war. Furthermore, had it simply taken another year to win the Battle of the Atlantic—victory in 1944 rather than 1943—the war would have looked quite different.

In the winning of that battle, it must be conceded that the United States Navy played a subordinate role to the Royal Navy. Of those U-boats we know to have been destroyed by hostile action (as opposed to accidents of various kinds), during World War II, only a quarter fell to American or American-controlled forces. Consider, however, that in 1942 only a fifth of all U-boats met their fate at American hands, although the most destructive U-boat campaign took place in American-controlled waters. In 1943, 30 percent of all U-boats sunk by the Allies fell prey to the Americans. Although this percentage declined somewhat in 1944, this largely reflects the fact that the U-boat war had moved well away from the ocean areas for which the United States held responsibility. By mid-1943, in other words, the humiliations of the bitter spring of 1942 were well on their way to being avenged.

CONCLUSION

We should not conclude that learning failure was the particular province of the United States Navy. In the interwar period the Royal Navy itself failed dismally to study systematically the lessons of the antisubmarine operations of World War I. Although the Royal Navy accepted the biggest lesson—the imperative of convoy—in principle, the many questions of detail (How large a convoy? How fast? Under what conditions should ships be allowed to sail independently? How should air power operate against the submarine?) were not raised, much less resolved, until the onset of the Second World War.[96]

The United States Navy's learning failure of 1940–1942 did not prove fatal for two reasons—the fact that the navy did not bear the full or even the largest part of the responsibility for the conduct of Allied antisubmarine warfare, and its own ability to adapt quickly to its environment. Indeed, the ability to adapt is probably most useful to any military organization and most characteristic of successful ones, for with it, it is possible to overcome both learning and predictive failures. In the interim, however, the cost of such failures will be—and in this case was—high, in terms of blood, treasure, and time.

5

Failure to Anticipate
Israel Defense Forces on the Suez Front and the Golan Heights, 1973

THE YOM KIPPUR WAR—
COURSE AND CONSEQUENCES

A FEW MOMENTS BEFORE 2:00 P.M. on Saturday, October 6, 1973, the armies of Syria and Egypt simultaneously attacked Israeli forces on the Golan Heights in the north and along the Suez Canal in the south. Before the war it had been universally expected—in Jerusalem, Washington, Moscow, and, to a large extent, even in Cairo and Damascus—that a future Middle East conflict would be a short and bloody affair of a few days, leading to a clear Israeli victory. More to the point, however, most Israeli and American decision makers thought that war would not come to the Middle East in 1973; the Arabs, having no serious military option, would not attempt something so clearly beyond their strength.

These expectations proved wrong: The war lasted two and a half weeks, not one, and inflicted on the Israelis at least 2,569 dead and 7,500 wounded.[1] When the fighting ceased, the Israelis had pushed the Syrian Army back some 20 kilometers toward Damascus, which now lay almost within range of Israeli artillery. On the Suez front, however, Egyptian forces retained control of a narrow strip of land on the East bank of the

95

Suez Canal. True enough, the Israelis who had crossed the canal to the west had encircled one of the two Egyptian armies (actually, corps-size formations) on the east bank of the canal. Nonetheless, the Israelis had proved unable to win the quick and elegant victory expected by so many and had endured traumatic losses to boot. One senior general describes the onset of the war as "the most shattering experience in the history of Israel," and in her memoirs Golda Meir refers to the war as something that came very close to an utter disaster—and she uses the word *shoah*, which in modern Hebrew also refers to the annihilation of six million Jews by the Nazis.[2]

The Israelis had, moreover, suffered strategic surprise, an astonishing turn of events given the deserved reputation for excellence of Israeli intelligence. In the wake of the war, students of intelligence failure and surprise turned to the study of the Yom Kippur War in search of lessons about the nature of such calamities and in order to test hypotheses on their origins. We will examine the Yom Kippur War, and particularly the actions on the southern (Sinai) front, as a study in failure of anticipation. What was shocking in 1973 was not simply that the Arabs attacked Israel but that the Israelis seemed so poorly prepared for that attack. They did not merely fail to predict the onslaught until the very last moment, they had failed to take reasonable precautions to avoid or blunt it.

THE ORIGINS OF THE WAR AND ARAB STRATEGY

The roots of the 1973 war lie in the smashing defeat suffered by the Arab states in June 1967, when in six days the IDF occupied the Sinai Peninsula, the areas west of the Jordan River, and the Golan Heights. In the aftermath of the Six-Day War, Israeli decision makers expected that Arab states would sue for peace.[3] This did not happen; rather, in October 1968, President Gamal Abdel Nasser of Egypt resumed the contest as a "War of Attrition" (formerly announced in March 1969) along the Suez Canal; at the same time Palestinian terrorist organizations increased their activities.

The War of Attrition ended on the Suez front in August 1970 with an uneasy but surprisingly durable cease-fire. The trickle of casualties borne by the Israelis along the Suez Canal had inflicted acute pain in a country of some three million, where a black-bordered picture of every soldier killed would appear in the nation's newspapers immediately after his death. Yet the War of Attrition proved more costly to the Egyptians,

Deployment of Forces on Suez Front, 1400 Hours, Saturday, October 6, 1973

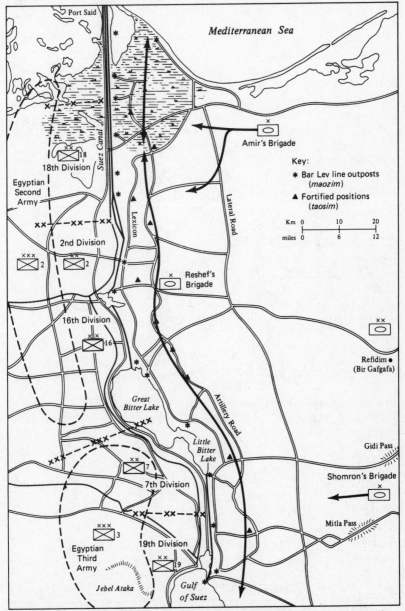

SOURCE: From *The Arab-Israeli Wars*, by Chaim Herzog. Maps and typography copyright © 1982 by Lionel Leventhal, Ltd. Reprinted by permission of Random House, Inc., and Arms and Armour Press, Ltd.

Deployment of Forces on the Golan Heights, 1400 Hours, Saturday, October 6, 1973

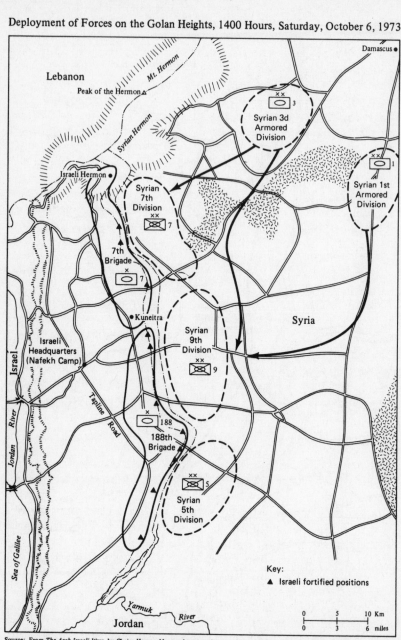

Source: From *The Arab-Israeli Wars*, by Chaim Herzog. Maps and typography copyright © 1982 by Lionel Levanthal, Ltd. Reprinted by permission of Random House, Inc., and Arms and Armour Press, Ltd.

who in the end considered it a defeat. Deep penetration raids by Israeli Phantom jets demolished factories and power plants; the war made the cities along the canal uninhabitable; and Israeli raiders scored humiliating coups in daring hit-and-run attacks. In the air, neither Egyptian nor Soviet pilots could match the Israelis, and the Israeli Air Force (IAF) managed to prevent the orderly emplacement of Soviet SAMs near the canal, albeit at a loss of twenty planes in the last six months of the war, including the loss of five Phantom jets in the last month or so of fighting. In the wake of the cease-fire, however, and despite its provisions, the Egyptian armed forces deployed a thick belt of SAMs along the canal zone—a move that would prove of immense operational importance three years later.

Egypt's new President, Anwar el-Sadat, believed that the situation was unendurable. The Suez cities were vacant shells, their populations crowding an overburdened Egypt; the presence of thousands of contemptuous but seemingly necessary Soviet advisers exasperated Egyptians, who had to put up with open-ended compulsory military service, a deteriorating economy, and a galling sense of having been humiliated by the Israelis. Sadat's first resort, in February 1971, was a peace overture, albeit one that to many Israelis seemed suspiciously like a call for unilateral withdrawal from the Sinai. When Sadat met an Israeli rebuff (despite the misgivings of Minister of Defense Moshe Dayan, who had opposed approaching the canal in 1967 and favored withdrawal thereafter), he threatened war in 1971 and again in 1972. Frustrated by the Soviet Union's refusal to supply his forces the wherewithal for war, and hoping for an opening to the United States, he suddenly announced the expulsion of Soviet advisers from Egypt on July 18, 1972.[4] But despite a flurry of diplomatic activity the situation remained stalemated.

In November 1972, Sadat decided to go to war—an option long prepared and studied by the Egyptian military but one in which many officers lacked confidence.[5] Finding Minister of War Muhammed Sadek opposed to war, Sadat dismissed him in January 1973, replacing him with a more willing general, Ahmed Ismail Ali.[6] Syria, always one of Israel's most bitter foes, would gladly join in; the other frontline Arab states, Lebanon and Jordan, had neither the military resources nor the inclination to risk another confrontation with the Jewish state. In December 1972, Sadat restored relations with the Soviets: The Soviets received renewed access to Egyptian ports, and the Egyptians began to get vast Soviet arms shipments. By March 1973, preliminary planning had been completed. In a secret April 1973 meeting with President Hafaz Assad of Syria, the leaders and planning staffs had identified May, late August–early September, and October as possible dates for war. In early May,

Syrian and Egyptian planners met to coordinate their attacks, and later that month Egyptian and Syrian forces began large scale mobilizations.[7]

Although Israeli military intelligence—AMAN, in its Hebrew acronym—deprecated the possibility of war, Chief of Staff David Elazar alerted Israeli forces and conducted preparations for war, although not a large-scale mobilization of the reserves.[8] War did not break out. In October it did.

Syria had simple objectives in the Yom Kippur War: regaining a large chunk of the occupied Golan Heights, and with luck all of it. Egyptian objectives—or more accurately, President Sadat's objectives—were far more subtle and complicated. First and foremost, Sadat thought it essential to break a diplomatic stalemate intolerable for Egypt (and his own position as president); by the very act of opening fire the deadlock would break, and fluidity would return to Middle Eastern politics.[9] Anything short of a catastrophic Arab failure, and perhaps even that, would force the United States and the Soviet Union to renew the quest for a Middle East settlement. Sadat's second set of objectives emerged from his reading of Arab and Israeli psychology. Egypt had to purge itself of those complexes—"whether defeatist 'inferiority' ones or those born of suspicion and hate"[10]—brought about by mortifying Israeli victories. If Egypt could seize and retain even a morsel of Sinai, Sadat thought, its self-confidence and self-respect would return and its honor be redeemed.[11] The preconditions on the Egyptian side for a settlement with Israel would then exist.

But Sadat thought it equally or more important to destroy through war what he termed the "Israeli Security Theory." In the Egyptian view, this theory consisted of five propositions: Israeli military and technological superiority must convince the Arabs that they could not achieve their objectives by force; in the event of war Israeli mobility and internal lines, coupled with Arab disunity, would allow Israel to concentrate her forces against one opponent at a time; Israel must immediately move a war into Arab territories; a war could not be permitted to last more than a week; Israel could not tolerate high losses.[12] Sadat believed that the breaking of this theory required that the Arabs convince their opponent that "continued occupation of our land exacts a price that is too high for him to pay, and that consequently his theory of security—based as it is on psychological, political, and military intimidation—is not an impregnable shield of steel which could protect him today or in the future."[13] This could be achieved only by *"inflicting the heaviest losses on the enemy."*[14] Thus, neither the mere fact of opening fire nor the seizure of land would suffice; Israel had to suffer heavy losses in a protracted (by Middle Eastern standards) war.[15] Sadat had shrewdly formulated intangible war objectives—the smashing of an enemy's theory, the resurrection of Egyptian pride, and the alarming of the superpowers—although they could require, as he well knew, massive blood shed. He did not command his armed forces to seize all or even most of the Sinai by force: Indeed, he would content himself with very limited territorial gains, provided Israel suffered enough in battle.

The Arab plans reflected careful, and in some respects unprecedented, studies of their own strengths and weaknesses and those of their opponents. They judged Israeli advantages to lie in the superiority of its air force, IDF skill in conducting mobile operations with large armored forces in open terrain, its high technological level, the quality of IDF training overall, and its support from the United States. Israeli weaknesses, they thought, stemmed from relatively long lines of communication in Sinai after 1967, limited manpower and sensitivity to losses, the fragility of its economy during a long war, and its excessive self-confidence. The key to Arab strategy would lie in launching a simultaneous two-front war, begun under conditions of strategic surprise, which would be gained by rigorous security and a program of deception at many levels. At the operational level, the plans called for a broad-front crossing of the Suez Canal by five infantry divisions and the seizure of a strip of land 10 kilometers deep. Following a pause to absorb Israeli counterattacks, Egyptian forces—reinforced by two armored and up to three mechanized divisions—would attack into Sinai in hopes of gaining the key passes leading from the canal area to central Sinai. On the Golan Heights, the Syrians planned an initial assault by three mechanized divisions to seize approximately half of the heights, with a follow-up attack by two armored divisions to complete the operation and consolidate the Syrian position on the heights, preparing in the event of unexpected success to cross into Israel proper.

The attack plans required at least a fifteen-day period of preparation, yet the beginning of the countdown was known to very few.[16] Planning staffs agreed on the date for war in a highly secret meeting on August 22, 1973, yet according to the Egyptian chief of staff, the commanders of Egypt's Second and Third Armies, tasked with the crossing of the canal, learned of the war only on October 1; divisional commanders on the third; and battalion and company commanders on the fifth.[17] According to Israeli sources, the Arab high commands held information even more tightly.[18] The Egyptians did not plan to give the Soviets much warning, nor did they; they gave broad hints to Moscow on October 1 and an explicit warning on October 3, only three days before war actually broke out on the sixth.[19] The Egyptians did not set the actual hour of the attack (shortly after 2:00 P.M.) until October 3, when War Minister

Ali visited Syria.[20] Nonetheless, despite their extraordinary security precautions, the Egyptians appear to have expected that Israeli intelligence would know of the attack at least five days before it occurred.[21] For that reason, the Egyptian (and one would assume, the Syrian) plans contemplated taking very heavy losses—26,000 men in the crossing of the canal alone.[22]

ISRAELI PLANS AND THE CORRELATION OF FORCES

Following the May 1973 crisis, when some in the Israeli defense establishment (although not the head of AMAN and his analysts) thought war likely, Israeli leaders relaxed. In the wake of the June 1973 summit meeting between American President Richard Nixon and Soviet leader Leonid Brezhnev they believed that neither superpower wanted a war in the Middle East. Chief of Staff David Elazar felt comfortable enough to overhaul the Israeli high command, rotating in new commanders for the IAF, Southern Command (that is, the Sinai front), and lower levels as well.[23] There was talk of reducing the period of obligatory military service from three years to two and a half, and an air of optimism pervaded the general staff and the ministry of defense. War might break out in 1975 or 1976, thought the head of AMAN, Major General Eliyahu Zeira, once the Arabs had acquired the ability to blunt the IAF's threat to their rear areas with surface-to-surface missiles and long-range bombers capable of striking pre-1967 Israel.[24] Until then, however, war appeared highly unlikely.

Israeli military planning before 1973 assumed that the IDF would anticipate the onset of war by two days, more or less. This would give Israel time to mobilize its reserve forces and to strike a preemptive blow with its air force, bringing the war to a favorable conclusion in four or five days—ten or twelve days if warning was very short or preemption forbidden.[25] Yet—and this is a key point—even with shorter periods of warning Israeli commanders believed they could hold their defensive positions along the Canal and on the Golan Heights. In June 1972 the head of AMAN warned the deputy chief of staff, Major General Israel Tal, that warning might be as brief as thirty-six hours on the Egyptian front, and less than that on the Syrian front.[26]

In normal times Israel kept one armored brigade—fewer than one hundred tanks—on the Golan Heights and three brigades (nearly three hundred tanks) in Sinai. These forces would require reinforcement by Israel's very large reserve forces, which constituted the bulk of its armed forces.

In the event that Israel had to begin the war on the defensive, even with short warning, the Israelis had no intention of giving up ground. In the south, Plan Dovecote (*shovach yonim*) would take effect.[27] The fortifications along the canal—known as the Bar Lev line—would be stripped of their garrison of four or five hundred reservists, who would be replaced by crack paratroops. These outposts (sixteen, down from thirty-one constructed during the War of Attrition) each held between sixteen and sixty men, and occupied the 160-kilometer length of the canal, as well as 20 kilometers of the Mediterranean coast. Just behind a ridge line some 10 to 12 kilometers east of the canal the Israelis had built a road ("Artillery Road") on which they could deploy self-propelled artillery to cover the canal area. Near the road lay another line of eleven strong points (*taozim*), which were only partially occupied. Along a second and higher ridge line some 20 to 30 kilometers east of the Artillery Road the Israelis had built another road, the so-called Lateral Road. Yet another 30 kilometers to the east lay the passes to central Sinai, the Mitla and Gidi Passes that covered the large Israeli bases in central Sinai, particularly that at Refidim. "Dovecote" required the deployment of two armored brigades close to the front: twenty-four tanks in eight platoons actually on the canal along the high sand ramp and firing positions constructed by the Israelis, with eight companies (some eighty tanks) and three battalions (another ninety tanks) deployed farther back along the two roads parallel to the canal. A third armored brigade was to be deployed near the Refidim base on the eastern side of the passes, as a reserve force. The armor school brigade in the Negev served as an emergency reserve.

The Golan Heights spread over a length (some 60 kilometers) one-third that of the canal front and were defended in peacetime, as noted, by one armored brigade as well as by small infantry and artillery units. In addition, the Israelis had built some seventeen strong points, mainly in small volcanic hills along the length of the post-1967 cease-fire line; these small forts, manned by some fifteen men apiece, would normally be supported by a platoon of three tanks each, firing from prepared positions. The Golan differed from the Suez front in several ways. Where the canal served as a formidable antitank obstacle, no such major water obstacle blocked a Syrian advance; conversely, the Israeli observation posts on Mount Hermon had a far better view of Syrian positions than did their counterparts in the Sinai. Most important, the Golan had little operational depth (15 kilometers to the Golan escarpment, versus 70 kilometers from the canal to the Mitla and Gidi passes—themselves well over 100 kilometers as the crow flies from Israel proper).

In both north and south, the IDF believed that the standing forces,

Table 5-1. The Arab-Israeli Military Balance, October 1973

	Egypt	Syria	Other Arab*	Israel	Arabs:Israel
Medium tanks	2,200	1,820	820	2,000	2.4:1
Anti-tank missiles	850	350	?	280	4.3:1
Anti-tank rockets	2,500	2,800	?	650	8.2:1
Anti-tank guns	1,300	900	?	0	—
Armored personnel carriers	2,400	1,300	620	4,000	1:1(−)
Artillery (over 100 MM)	1,210	655	190	570	3.6:1
Fighter-bombers	400	282	?	358	1.9:1
SAM batteries	146	34	?	10	18:1

*Includes forces that actually participated in the Yom Kippur War.
SOURCE: Taken from Dupuy, *Elusive Victory*, p. 608, and Adan, "Eichut v'kamut," p. 255. See also Anthony H. Cordesman, *The Arab-Israeli Military Balance and the Art of Operations* (Washington, D.C.: American Enterprise Institute, 1987), pp. 37–53.

composed chiefly of conscripts, could hold the line with a modicum of warning until the reserves had completed their mobilization.[28] What accounted for this confidence? In the view of the IDF's leaders, after 1967 the qualitative discrepancy between the Arabs and Israel had grown, while the quantitative balance had remained stable (see Table 5-1).[29]

This table does not, of course, fully sum up the military balance. In particular, it omits additional Arab forces that had the potential to enter the war, although, on the other hand, it includes some forces (for example, the Iraqi expeditionary force) that did not enter the war until a week or so after it had begun. Moreover, it does not capture the qualitative balance, in terms either of manpower or technology. The IAF had aircraft—particularly the F-4 Phantom—with ranges and payloads far superior to their Soviet counterparts on the other side; furthermore, most Israeli artillery was self-propelled, and hence more mobile, even under fire, than the towed guns and howitzers of the Arabs. At the same time, it should be noted that the Israeli stock of APCs consisted chiefly of obsolete World War II–type half-tracks—the IDF had barely five hundred modern American M-113s, and even those did not have the fighting potential of the Soviet APCs in Arab hands. With respect to quantity and in some cases quality of SAMs and antitank missiles, the Israelis were grossly inferior. Moreover, the Arabs (particularly the Syrians) had a distinct edge in night-fighting equipment for their tanks.[30] Finally, it should be noted that a good technical net assessment requires comparison of dissimilar weapon systems—SAMs vs. airplanes, for example, or antitank missiles vs. tanks. The Arab states had invested heavily in weapons designed to nullify Israeli advantages in air power and tanks, and not only by building up their arsenals with similar weapons.

The Egyptians disposed of five infantry, three mechanized, and two armored divisions; the Syrians of three mechanized and two armored divisions. Both countries had, in addition, large commando units, numbering more than thirty battalions between them.[31] Israeli organizational strength remains vague, reflecting a deliberate Israeli policy of concealing such statistics. Nonetheless, it is known that the Israelis ultimately deployed a total of seven *ugdot*, which are more or less the equivalent of western armored or mechanized divisions, during the war. Of these, however, only five appear to have been full-strength armored divisions, the decision to form the other two having been taken the previous summer. The seventh *ugda*, in fact, was an improvised force assembled in the course of the war. In addition, Israel had as many as eighteen independent brigades, including some four paratroop and nine infantry brigades for use in mobile operations.

THE PREWAR CRISIS

On September 13 an air battle erupted north of Israel's border when Syrian fighters attempted to attack an Israeli reconnaissance plane: One Israeli plane fell, as did twelve Syrian planes. The Israelis thought the Syrians might attempt some retaliation for this humiliating skirmish, possibly even a raid on the Golan Heights. It was in this light that Israel intelligence viewed the Syrian forward deployment of their forces. When similar developments appeared on the Egyptian front two explanations took hold: first, that the Egyptians were merely preparing for an exercise (Tahrir 41) that would begin on October 1; second, that the Egyptians feared that war might break out as a result of tensions in the north. Within AMAN there was little doubt about this view, at least at the level of Zeira and the head of AMAN's research department, Brigadier General Aryeh Shalev. As early as September 25, however, Zvi Zamir, the head of the Mossad (Israel's foreign espionage organization), may have suggested that war could erupt.[32] Zamir did not, however, press this view. The Mossad had neither the responsibility nor the resources to conduct alternative analyses: Throughout the prewar crisis AMAN would provide virtually all the finished intelligence to decision makers.

The first alarm expressed outside the Israeli intelligence community came from the commander of the northern front, Major General Yitzhak Hofi ("Chaka"), who expressed concern about the possibility of war as early as September 24; as a result Minister of Defense Dayan visited the Golan Heights.[33] On September 28 Hofi met with the chief of staff (Lieutenant General David Elazar), his deputy (Major General Israel Tal), the head of AMAN (Major General Eliyahu Zeira), his deputy (Brigadier General Aryeh Shalev), and the commander of the IAF (Major General Benjamin Peled) to discuss the situation in the north. Elazar decided to dispatch elements of an additional armored brigade (including twenty-five tank crews) to the north, remarking, "We'll have one hundred tanks against eight hundred—that's enough."[34]

On the next day, Saturday, September 29, a group of Palestinian terrorists controlled by Syria hijacked a train in Austria carrying Jewish émigrés from the Soviet Union. Many in Israeli intelligence now believe that this episode was part of the Arab deception program, although they disagree about its impact. Prime Minister Golda Meir, in Europe on other business, flew to Vienna for a difficult interview with Chancellor Bruno Kreisky concerning the proposed closing of Austrian transit facilities for Soviet Jews.[35] But AMAN continued to monitor the Arab buildup. By September 30 Israeli intelligence noticed developments in Egypt that could not be attributed to the exercise Tahrir 41, and the Syrians continued unprecedented activities, including the deployment of fighter aircraft to forward airfields. Hofi continued to press for reinforcement, and Tal, the deputy chief of staff, declared, "This means war," but Zeira, the head of AMAN agreed with those of his assistants who insisted that "the probability of war is low."[36]

On Monday, October 1, signs continued to accumulate of trouble building on both north and south: Egyptian officer exams had been cancelled, and a particularly good intelligence source warned of war. Nonetheless, the regular meeting of the general staff on that day dealt with the threat in 1975–76, not an impending war in 1973. Throughout this period it appears that Zeira decided to refrain until quite late from opening a special source (or sources) of intelligence, which was (or were) expected to deliver additional and perhaps unambiguous knowledge of Arab intentions. Although Israeli writings (and interview subjects) speak of this subject only guardedly, one may say the following: (1) The senior political and military leadership expected unambiguous warning of war, in part because of their knowledge of the sources of Israeli intelligence; (2) there were delays, caused by operational difficulties and by late decisions to activate a source or sources that might deliver this unambiguous warning; (3) senior Israeli leaders, including Dayan and Elazar, claim to have been misled—accidentally, perhaps—by Zeira into thinking that all collection assets were operating. In fact, as the Agranat Commission reported, they were not. By 5:00 P.M. on Friday, October 5, Zeira had substantial indications of an impending war but was awaiting confirmation from an extremely important source, which only came through in the very early hours of October 6.[37]

By Wednesday, October 3, doubts had spread to Moshe Dayan, the minister of defense. The Syrian buildup on the Golan had no precedent— where in May 1973 only 250 tanks had appeared on the front line, now 850 had moved into jump-off positions.[38] Over the next two days much of the rest of a reinforcing Israeli armored brigade (the Seventh, a crack unit) was sent north; instead of the 70 tanks in place two weeks earlier, the total now reached 188; moreover, Hofi was authorized to continue preparing the terrain for war.[39]

On October 3 Golda Meir convened a meeting of her kitchen cabinet, including Dayan, several other ministers and confidantes, Elazar, and Zeira's deputy, Aryeh Shalev (Zeira was sick). Although Shalev presented worrying information—for example, that the Syrians had concentrated their SAM batteries at the front rather than around Damascus and that live ammunition had been issued to Egyptian forces—no one drew the correct conclusion.[40] All present accepted Shalev's view that the Egyptians did not believe themselves to be ready for war. A cabinet meeting was convened for October 7, the day after Yom Kippur, to discuss the situation on the Golan Heights, where a limited Syrian operation seemed a distinct possibility.

On Thursday, October 4, however, two alarming pieces of information caused the first faint doubts among Zeira, the research branch of AMAN, and the chief of staff. First, the Israelis learned that the Soviets had begun evacuating the families of their advisers from Egypt and Syria; second, aerial photography of the canal zone—hitherto delayed several days by mechanical malfunctions of the reconnaissance planes and their equipment—revealed an unprecedented buildup of Egyptian forces. Fully 1,100 artillery pieces were poised on the canal's west bank, as were five forward-deployed infantry divisions. At a meeting that took up the morning of Friday, October 5, Elazar, with Dayan's support, undertook several important measures. He raised the IDF to Alert Level C; this canceled all leaves, required soldiers in front-line units to prepare for war, and readied the call-up system for instant operation. According to some, this was the first time the IDF had gone to this level of alert since 1967.[41] Elazar sent the remainder of the Seventh Armored Brigade to the Golan and ordered another brigade to the Sinai. Zeira still doubted that war would break out, but he stopped using the term *low probability*, to which he had clung until then. Later that day Dayan received permission from the prime minister to call up the reserves without the usual cabinet meeting, if that should prove necessary.[42] Yet the atmosphere was not a tense one. Golda Meir recalled later:

> I was promised that we would receive adequate warning in time to deal with any real emergency, and in any case we were sending reinforcements to the fronts adequate to conduct any containing operations for which there would be a need. Everything that was required was done, and the Army stood on high alert, particularly the air force and the armored corps.[43]

Thus, although there was some doubt in the minds of the minister of defense, the prime minister, the chief of staff, and senior officers, no national-level leader thought that war was imminent, or even a sufficiently large and dangerous possibility to merit a call-up. No matter what, Chief of Staff Elazar thought, he would get, at a bare minimum, twelve to twenty-four hours' absolutely firm warning of the outbreak of war; and if a war began soon Israel would cope well.[44]

Yom Kippur, the Day of Atonement or the Day of Judgment, is the holiest day of the Jewish calendar on which even many nonobservant Israeli Jews attend synagogue; those who do not usually stay at home. From the Israeli point of view this was a blessing: Mobilization went remarkably smoothly because there was no traffic on the street, and re-servists were known to be in one of two places—at home or in the syna-gogue. At approximately four in the morning of Yom Kippur, Saturday, October 6, the military aide to the prime minister, as well as the chief of staff and the minister of defense, were awoken with the news that war was imminent and would break out by sunset that day. The news was regarded as definitive—a curious fact, which we will consider further be-low. The message was interpreted to mean that war would break out at or near sunset—at 6:00 P.M. In fact, on October 3 the Egyptians had agreed to set the attack time at 2:00 P.M., although they had preferred a later time in order to attack with the sun at their backs and in the eyes of the defending Israelis.[45]

Israeli leaders convened a series of hasty meetings. At 6:00 A.M. Elazar and Dayan met, the former wanting an instantaneous mobilization of four *ugdot*, the latter thinking it sufficient to mobilize two, one for each front, in order to secure the borders. Interestingly, Elazar wanted the two additional *ugdot* for a swift counterattack, not for defense. They agreed to defer the decision until a later meeting with the prime minister who, at 9:00 A.M., decided in Elazar's favor. A rump cabinet meeting at 9:30 A.M. decided to communicate immediately with the American ambassador in order to avert war at the last moment. There was further deliberation about a preemptive air strike, discussion of which was postponed until a noontime meeting. The meeting was still in progress when word came that the attack had begun.

THE WAR

It is not our purpose here to trace in detail the events of the war.[46] At approximately 2:00 P.M. the air forces of Egypt and Syria struck Israeli airfields in Sinai, plus some command posts and supply areas, but did not launch serious attacks against Israel proper. On both fronts a massive artillery bombardment—comparable in weight to those of the great offensives of World War II—supported assaults across the canal and into the Golan Heights. On the southern front the Egyptians managed to bridge the waterway on a broad front on the first two days, penetrating up to 10 kilometers inland (to the so-called Artillery Road) and digging in for the inevitable counterattack. This came on October 8 and 9, in the form of an attack by an Israeli reserve armored division led by Major General Avraham ("Bren") Adan. The attacks failed, with heavy losses, and the Israelis reverted to a defensive posture, broken only by sporadic and limited counterattacks to relieve the besieged posts on the Bar Lev line, all but one of which were evacuated or surrendered within the first few days of the war. The Israelis smashed an Egyptian armored attack on October 14, launched across the front with the aim of reaching the line of the passes and, while so doing, relieving pressure on the Syrians. On the night of October 15–16, small Israeli forces crossed the canal in the vicinity of the Great Bitter Lake at Deversoir; despite fierce battles on the sixteenth through the eighteenth, the Israelis maintained their bridgehead on the west bank of the Canal, and prevented the Egyptians from cutting it off on the east. By October 22 they managed to encircle most of the Egyptian Third Army on the west bank of the canal, and following the breakdown of a UN cease-fire that night, completed the encirclement of the Third Army on October 24.

On the northern front the Syrians came very close to breaking through Israeli defenses in the southern sector on October 7. Indeed, for a short period of time—from approximately 5:30 A.M. to 10:30 A.M. on that day—only a handful of tanks and a stream of successful air attacks by the IAF stood between attacking Syrian forces and the pre-1967 border. By October 8, however, the situation had improved as the Israelis began to concentrate three *ugdot* (divisions) on the Golan Heights; by the tenth they had restored almost all of the pre–October 6 border, and by the eleventh had begun to penetrate further into Syria, approaching, during the next three days, to within 43 kilometers of Damascus. The advent of a large Iraqi expeditionary force made the weary Israelis pause but did not push them back. From the fourteenth to the end of the war the Israelis reverted to the defensive, beating off continuing, though weakening, Syrian counterattacks.

Given the disadvantages under which they had begun the war, the Israelis had recovered magnificently. Nonetheless, the war's course and outcome exceeded their most pessimistic prewar calculations. The war lasted two or three times as long and cost far more in human terms than the Israelis had expected. In matériel as well as in lives the Israelis took heavy losses, for results that were less than expected. By October 7, for example, the regular armored *ugda* in Sinai under the command of Albert Mendler had lost fully two-thirds of its tanks—fewer than a hundred were left in commission.[47] Similarly, in the first twenty-seven hours of the war the Israelis lost thirty aircraft, or 8 percent of their front-line strength; this compared with forty lost on the first day of the Six-Day War. In that war, as the commander of the IAF pointed out, they lost only six more on the remaining five days, but such was not the case in 1973.[48] In the course of the Yom Kippur War the Israelis lost more than one hundred airplanes, or better than a quarter of their total force.[49] Despite this, they did not succeed in smashing the Syrian air defense system. The IAF did far better against the Egyptians, who lost most of their SAM batteries, but only fairly late in the war. Whereas the IAF had expected, before the war, to eliminate Egyptian air defenses within two days, it was not until the very end of the war that the IAF could operate with impunity on the west bank of the canal.

Indeed, Israeli losses were so heavy, particularly in the first few days of the war, that it appears from several sources that they might have accepted a cease-fire on the tenth or even as late as the twelfth of October.[50] To be sure, many of the losses were recovered. The Israelis are reported to have lost more than eight hundred tanks, or over 40 percent of their prewar total; yet by dint of wartime and postwar repair they recovered fully half of those, in addition to three hundred or more usable Egyptian and Syrian tanks captured during the war.[51] The American airlift of supplies to Israel could not have made good these kinds of losses in so short a time.

The Arabs had suffered even more grievously, as Table 5-2 indicates. Yet at no point did the major Arab armed forces collapse, as they had in earlier conflicts. To the end the Syrians and Egyptians put up a dogged resistance, even after losing two-thirds of their armored force (in the case of the Syrians) or most of their front-line surface-to-air-missile (SAM) batteries (in the case of the Egyptians).

Moreover, Israeli military performance was, in some cases, unsatisfactory. The disjointed attacks of October 8 and 9 on the southern front, for example, temporarily reduced the strengths of Adan's and Sharon's divisions to between a half and a third of their normal size.[52] In these attacks masses of tanks, largely unsupported by infantry or artillery, attempted to clear the canal by frontal assaults and suffered heavy losses to Egyptian infantry armed with antitank missiles and rocket-propelled grenades, as well as to Egyptian tanks.[53] After the war Israeli observers would criticize the IDF's failure to fight at night (a traditional Israeli strength) and its largely frontal counters to enemy attacks. Some commentators—including reserve generals—argued after the war that Israel failed to make adequate strategic choices, for example, by massing ground forces for a counteroffensive in the north while contenting itself with defensive operations in the south.[54] The brilliant adaptive capacities of Israeli commanders and the skill and raw courage of their men redeemed the initial defeats of the first few days leaving Israel master of most of the battlefields by October 24. All this notwithstanding, Israel emerged from

Table 5-2. Arab Losses—1973 War

	Egypt			Syria		
	Prewar	Losses	%	Prewar	Losses	%
Tanks	2,200	1,000	45	1,650	1,100	67
APCs	2,925	450	15	1,500	400	27
Artillery	2,220	300	14	1,200	250	21
Fighter planes	653	222	34	388	117	30
SAM batteries	146	44	30	34	3	9

SOURCE: Figures taken from Gazit, "Arab Forces," pp. 188–90. Prewar numbers of tanks count only those tanks in units, not total numbers of tanks in inventory, which are higher. The Arabs did not recover anything like the quantity of captured or their own repairable equipment that the Israelis did. Moreover, aside from tanks and airplanes, Israeli losses in other kinds of equipment were relatively light—only 10 percent of APCs for example, negligible artillery, and no SAM batteries.

the Yom Kippur War shaken and its Arab enemies if not triumphant, at least content.

FAILURE TO ANTICIPATE—
SOME PRELIMINARY VERDICTS

The Agranat Commission

In 1974 and 1975 a high-level Israeli commission, chaired by the chief justice of Israeli's Supreme Court, Shimon Agranat, and consisting of another justice, the comptroller general of the Israeli government, and two former chiefs of staff of the IDF published three portions of a long and detailed critique of the initial surprise and the conduct of the war to the Israeli government. Very brief excerpts of that report have been published; further portions will be released early in the twenty-first century, and others may never be released.[55] The three partial reports had, however, an immediate impact in Israel and continue to influence students of the 1973 surprise. The Agranat Commission undertook the thankless task of assigning blame for the surprise and initial failures of the Yom Kippur War. It was cautious in passing judgment on political-strategic decisions during the war and the period leading up to it—a critical though perhaps an understandable flaw.[56] Although it enquired into many aspects of the preparation for war and its actual conduct and made recommendations for changes in various areas, the Agranat Commission came to two sets of conclusions.

First and foremost, the commission, particularly in its first partial report (issued April 1974), took a hard look at the individual responsibility of particular individuals. The chief of staff; the head of AMAN; and his deputy for research, the head of the Egyptian desk at AMAN; the commander of the southern front (Shmuel Gonen); and his chief intelligence officer came in for severe criticism. In this section of their report (omitted in some of the English translations) the commission concluded that none of these officers should continue to serve in their current positions. In some cases—particularly those of David Elazar and Eliyahu Zeira—the commission came to its conclusion with evident regret. These two men had brilliant records as operational commanders: Elazar had conducted the one-day blitz on the Golan Heights in 1967; Zeira had served as a paratroop brigade commander and former head of the operations branch of the general staff. Both had done much good for the IDF, before as well as after the 1973 war had broken out: Elazar, in particular, had been a pillar of strength throughout its darkest moments.

There are a number of points of interest in the personal indictments. The commission criticized Elazar sharply for his unquestioning faith in AMAN before the war, for his handling of the armed forces in the week of muted warnings before Yom Kippur (including refraining from requesting a full mobilization on the morning of Friday, October 5), for his failure to plan for attacks without benefit of warning (which was not strictly true), and for failing to adopt the original Dovecote plan of distributing two armored brigades forward along the Suez Canal and one back. The commission criticized Zeira for his unflinching adherence to the erroneous intelligence "concept" that the Egyptians would not attack (about which more below), and for his insistence, until October 5, on saying that the probability of war was low. It argued in addition that he assured the IDF of several days' advance warning of any attack, when he could not guarantee it, and that he failed to activate special intelligence sources that could have gained additional information.

The first partial report quoted Zeira's testimony before the commission in a passage that reveals a personality less than comfortable with ambiguity:

> The Chief of Staff has to make decisions, and his decisions must be clear. The best support that the head of AMAN can give the Chief of Staff is to give a clear and unambiguous estimate, provided that it is done in an objective fashion. To be sure, the clearer and sharper the estimate, the clearer and sharper the mistake—but this is a professional hazard for the head of AMAN. . . .
>
> I served most of my time in the IDF not as a staff officer but as a commander. My nature does not lead me to pass responsibility to my superiors, if that is at all avoidable. . . . To take the course that you have suggested [that is, to have indicated at the beginning of October that the intelligence was ambiguous] would be in effect to say [to the Chief of Staff], "we have a complicated situation here: you make a decision." So I was not inclined to do that kind of thing, and have done so very rarely. In general, I do not bring to my superiors matters that fall in my area of responsibility, saying, "even though these matters are my responsibility I am passing them on to you—you settle them."[57]

Zeira's self-confidence comes across equally clearly in an interview with American military journalists very shortly before the war: "The biggest problem Israeli intelligence faces? 'To underestimate what we're up against,' Zeira says. 'But an equally big risk is that we would *over*-esti-mate.'"[58] It is said that when Zeira became head of AMAN, an Israeli reserve general remarked: "Now we are heading for a catastrophe: there are three men at the top [Dayan, Elazar, and Zeira] who do not know what it means to be afraid."[59]

Lower-level officers—with the exception of a lieutenant in the southern command, whose reports were suppressed by the southern command intelligence officer—received even harsher judgments from the Agranat Commission. Lieutenant Colonel Yonah Bandman, the head of the Egyptian desk at AMAN, received particularly sharp criticism for adding to an intelligence assessment of October 5, prepared at 1:15 P.M., the following paragraph:

> Even though the evidence of deployments along the Canal would appear to indicate an intention to attack, according to our best estimates there has been no change in the Egyptian assessment of the balance of forces between themselves and the IDF. Therefore, the probability that the Egyptians intend to renew warfare is low. . . .

Bandman added this paragraph to the thirty-nine preceding it, which described the massive Egyptian deployments that indicated war. When asked why he did so, he gave this response:

> I wrote the first version of the intelligence digest without paragraph 40 [quoted above], and I felt before I wrote it that I did not have to add it. . . . [after completing the first draft, however,] I thought that if I did not add paragraph 40 I would not have fulfilled my obligations. Because it was not enough that I simply presented the information: I was obligated to evaluate it as well. My assessment was that from a purely military point of view there were all the signs you could ask for of a design to attack; from the point of view of real intent there remained, in my view, the fact that they did not think of themselves as prepared for an offensive. They attacked twenty-four hours later, but that is a different matter.[60]

Bandman's assessment, the commission believed, played a large role in the Israeli failure to mobilize until the morning of October 6.

What drove Bandman, as well as others in the Israeli military establishment, was what the Agranat Commission stigmatized as "the Concept." The Concept had two parts: first, that Egypt would not attack Israel without the means (long-range bombers or surface-to-surface missiles) to strike at Israel proper, and particularly its airfields. This would enable the Egyptians to pin down the IAF and to deter the painful blows to Egypt's heartland that had characterized the War of Attrition. Second, the Concept had it that Syria would only launch an all-out attack on Israel in cooperation and simultaneously with Egypt. (This second part held true.) AMAN did not, however, reassess the first and critical part of the Concept in accordance with changing political considerations and deliveries of hardware (including SSMs and improved air defense weapons) to Egypt.[61] Because of the Concept, AMAN, and the IDF more generally, worried more about the years 1975–76, when the Egyptians were expected to have purchased long-range bombers and SSMs from the Soviets.[62] Indeed, even midmorning of October 6, Major General Mordechai Hod, the former commander of the IAF who had just come to IDF headquarters in Tel Aviv, expressed his disbelief that war would break out: "The Egyptians don't have an air force!" he exclaimed.[63]

A second implicit theory was reflected in the Agranat Commission's recommendation that more diversity be created in the Israeli intelligence community. In this view, AMAN's virtual monopoly on intelligence assessments precluded the emergence of alternative explanations of Arab troop movements. The Agranat Commission urged the appointment of a special intelligence adviser to the prime minister, complete with a small staff; the strengthening of the foreign ministry's research department; the creation of an office in the Mossad for evaluating the information it produced; and the improved dissemination of raw intelligence reports to the various assessment bodies *and* the prime minister and the minister of defense.

Two theories—individual responsibility and the lack of organizational diversity—appear to have explained, in the Agranat Commission's view, the intelligence failure. Their verdicts, however, have received sharp criticism, and not only from those most directly affected. The "failure by organizational monopoly" explanation, for example, runs afoul of two facts. First, even the highly pluralistic American intelligence community did not predict the Egyptian and Syrian attack, despite its access to overhead reconnaissance from spy satellites, as well as other sources.[64] Second, the Israeli intelligence community *did* have some limited elements of pluralism. The navy and the air force each had its analytical staff; and in fact the Israeli Navy mobilized fully on the strength of its internal analyses.[65] Moreover, the separate commands had their own intelligence staffs. Unfortunately, the southern command intelligence officer, Lieutenant Colonel David Gedaliah failed to pass on assessments by his order-of-battle officer, Lieutenant Binyamin Siman-Tov, prepared on October 1 and 3, which argued that Egyptian deployments reflected not an exercise but preparation for an attack. Gedaliah, like his superiors, adhered to the

Concept.[66] There is evidence that others in AMAN were alarmed by Syrian and Egyptian moves in the two weeks before the crisis, and sought to intensify collection efforts as well as disseminate dissenting views. These efforts were rejected or blocked, however, by AMAN's senior leadership, which dominated the analytical process.[67]

The "man in the dock" theory, although far from irrelevant to the surprise, cannot fully account for it either. Zeira was, no doubt, a very different man from his predecessor, Major General Aharon Yariv. One Israeli official who knew both men recalled that the more-cautious Yariv would always ask about a large-scale exercise (which, as all in AMAN realized, could cover preparation for war), "But are you sure? And what if it is not just an exercise?"[68] And it must be noted that the Arabs viewed the 1972 retirement of Yariv—described by Mohamed Heikal as "an exceptionally astute officer"—with relief.[69] On the other hand, Zeira had, and to this day retains, a reputation not only for bravery and leadership but intellectual brilliance as well. Furthermore, despite the Gedaliah episode and Zeira's apparent failure to activate certain intelligence sources, it should be noted that the Israeli intelligence and security community tends to distribute information very rapidly. Any incident—a hostage taking, a raid, even a cross-border exchange of fire—immediately attracts the attention of senior leaders, and the same holds true, by and large, for raw intelligence reports as well.[70] Bandman's stubbornly obtuse paragraph forty, quoted above, followed thirty-nine paragraphs of detailed reporting of Egyptian deployments.

What, then, of the Concept? Some have taken the Agranat Commission's Report to criticize the very notion of having a concept, and not just that of 1973. The sheer existence of a theory of this kind, some believe, blinded intelligence officials to the reality suggested by the data flowing into AMAN. As many commentators have pointed out, however, it is impossible to conduct intelligence analysis without concepts or hypotheses: A stream of raw data will simply overwhelm decision makers, who will, in any event, apply their own hypotheses to such information.[71] *More important, however, the Concept was not the product of Israeli analysis of logical Egyptian options; the Israeli Concept was in fact the Egyptian Concept, up through the beginning of 1973.*[72] Based on good—indeed, superb—sources, the Israelis understood Egyptian thinking about the initiation of war very well indeed. It was, for example, very largely because Muhammed Sadek adhered to the Concept that Sadat dismissed him as minister of war in late 1972, choosing as his replacement a man who would be willing to launch a war without long-range air power. Thus, it is incorrect to suggest that the Israelis had a priori hypothesis which they then tested against the evidence. Rather, AMAN started with information and then confirmed it with the analysis of operational experts in the various branches of the IDF, whose analyses confirmed the military soundness of the Egyptian views.[73]

Deception, Noise, and the Inevitability of Failure

Critics of the Agranat Commission generally offer two alternative assessments of the intelligence failure of 1973. First, they suggest that Arab deception efforts successfully masked the Egyptian and Syrian buildup, a view strongly supported by Arab sources who take considerable pride in those efforts.[74] The deception efforts actually took three forms—*concealment*, the hiding of preparatory moves; *deception* proper, an attempt to mislead the Israelis about the purpose of such activities as were observed, and about Arab capabilities in general; and *misdirection*, an attempt to direct Israeli attention to misleading or irrelevant data. The maneuvers along the canal, the ostentatious release of 20,000 Egyptian reservists on October 4 and the dispatch of soldiers on the pilgrimage to Mecca on October 5, the raid on the Austrian train, a studious refraining from bellicose rhetoric in Sadat's prewar speeches—all, in this view, prevented the Israelis from foreseeing the onset of war.

No former or current Israeli intelligence official interviews for this chapter attributed much importance to Arab deception efforts, however. Even those most critical of AMAN's activities in September and October 1973, and most impressed by Arab military performance, rejected the notion that deception played an important role in the intelligence failure. One should not accept these arguments without looking at the evidence, for capable members of a competent intelligence service are hardly likely to admit that their opponent has fooled them. In most respects, however, the evidence bears them out. Consider for example the news stories that appeared shortly before the war concerning the breakdown of Egyptian equipment following the departure of thousands of Soviet military advisers in 1972; Israeli officials warned American journalists that such reports were "a very big exaggeration."[75]

Nor is it true that the changed borders after 1967 allowed the Arabs to station large units on the border, thereby depriving the Israelis of warning time. A great deal of forward deployment of men and matériel occurred, and the Israelis noticed it. By September 30 it was quite clear that the Syrians had massed forces in unprecedented quantity along the Golan Heights; and as soon as the aerial photography of the canal became available late on October 4, there too it was obvious that a buildup inexplicable by maneuvers alone had taken place. Poor weather and malfunctioning cameras had prevented aerial photography from the first through the fourth, yet even on the first enough evidence existed to lead Lieutenant Siman-Tov to draft his first warning report and to make Major General Tal wary that war might break out. When the war did break out, the Israelis knew the nature and location of all units, as well as the plan for the initial crossing, although their understanding of subsequent stages in the planned operation were hazier.[76] By way of contrast, Allied deception operations against German forces in France before the Normandy landings successfully misled the Germans about the Allied order of battle, the concept of operations, and above all, the location of the main landings.

Nor did the IDF meet unanticipated Arab weapons. Israeli technical intelligence knew about the existence of anti-tank and surface-to-air missiles, and understood both their technical parameters and the quantities in which the Egyptians and Syrians had them—as even a cursory glance at the 1970–73 issues of the Israeli general staff journal, *Ma'arachot*, reveals. Finally, it is a cardinal principle of deception that the deceiver succeeds by reinforcing his opponent's misconceptions. In this case, there is no evidence that the Arabs knew of the Israeli Concept, or that they structured their deception efforts to support it.

Egyptian and Syrian operational and tactical deception efforts alone, therefore, do not account for the surprise. On the strategic level, however, they had slightly better success. Perhaps the raid on the Austrian train did distract the attention of senior decision-makers, who might otherwise have had more time to reflect on the stream of intelligence reports, and to quiz the producers of intelligence more closely. The use of an exercise to cover forward deployments, although a ruse foreseen by AMAN, did provide an excuse, however flimsy, for AMAN's misreading of those moves. Yet even had Sadat announced on national radio and television that he intended to launch a war, he would not have been believed by the Israelis, because he had made similar declarations in the past. And even when Egyptian and Syrian security slipped—when, for example, Egyptair canceled all its flights early on October 4 and began dispersing its airplanes—the Israelis did not pay attention.[77]

Following from this, a second school emerges, which argues that intelligence failures are inevitable by virtue of the sheer intractability of the intelligence task. The future is not predetermined, so intelligence cannot be the same as prophecy; although intelligence agencies can guess at capabilities—the product of "hard" information—they cannot read intentions, which follow from "soft" and often unobtainable sources. Moreover, it is argued, in this particular case oversensitivity to Arab military mobilizations would have exposed Israel to unacceptably high costs. Reserve mobilizations bring Israel's economy and society to a standstill, and to respond to every Arab gesture of this kind would be to give Israel's enemies extraordinary leverage over Israel's daily life. Furthermore, in this view, the Arabs could have responded to counterpreparations by calling off a war; the result would be the discrediting of an intelligence agency that had always cried wolf. Finally, it should be noted, during a similar period of Arab mobilization in May 1973 AMAN's skepticism about Arab intentions had proved correct: War did not break out despite the concerns of Chief of Staff Elazar, who was criticized for the thirty-million dollar "Blue White" counterpreparations by the IDF. Thus, the surprise of Yom Kippur becomes a tragedy without villains and without faults.

With reference to this particular case, however, the "no fault" school of intelligence in unconvincing. We find no direct evidence, for example, that IDF Chief of Staff Elazar refrained from soliciting a mobilization on October 5 merely because he feared a repeat of the May experience or subsequent criticism of taking unnecessary precautions. Indeed, the measures implemented on October 5 were, in some respects, similar to those that began April 10, 1973, and lasted through August 15, 1973, and were at their most intense in May.[78] In May the IDF deployed nearly two hundred tanks on the Golan Heights and three hundred in Sinai; reserve training exercises took place in Sinai, but although the IDF recalled a few reservists it refrained from a general call-up, even a limited two-division reserve mobilization of the kind envisioned by Moshe Dayan on the morning of October 6. Rather, the Israelis (as on October 6) redeployed some active forces and put the rest on a higher state of readiness. In addition, they undertook construction projects which would facilitate rapid mobilization then or at any later point.[79] And, in fact, many of these longer-term investments paid their dividends in October.

Was the May alert a false alarm? Based on classified research in their own files, a number of prominent members of the Israeli intelligence community no longer think so.[80] In their view, the May crisis involved an actual countdown for war, stopped by the Soviets, who did not want the June 1973 Brezhnev-Nixon summit aborted. Much collateral evidence supports this view: Brezhnev's seemingly spontaneous and highly irregular late-night meeting with Nixon on June 25, after the summit had officially concluded, to insist on a Middle East settlement lest war break out, for example.[81] Evidence from the Egyptian side—including the selection of May as one of three possible occasions in 1973 for a war, and the secret high-level meetings with the Syrians in April of that month—also point in this direction. Thus, in May 1973, AMAN may well have been right for the wrong reasons: The Arabs called off the war under Soviet pressure, not because they still adhered to the Concept. In October, according to this view, the Soviets, though unhappy about the onset of war, felt they could no longer defer it without provoking a complete rupture with Sadat. Nonetheless, according to some IDF officers, they deliberately launched the airlift of dependents from the region on October 4 to signal to the United States the onset of war, and their lack of involvement in it.[82]

The no-fault theory relies, in part, on the assumption that statesmen ignore intelligence agencies that "cry wolf." Yet here again, no evidence suggests that fear of crying wolf provoked Israeli analysts to be overly cautious in their assessments in September and early October 1973. Moreover, the costs of false alarms cut both ways. Preparations for real war have real costs, both physical and psychological, costs that would cut into the Egyptian budget and psyche every bit as much, and probably more, than the corresponding costs of Israeli preparedness. Sadat confided to Mohamed Heikal that he considered war in October to be his last chance; both his domestic and his international prestige rode on the war beginning then.[83]

Finally, the "intentions-capabilities" distinction neither excuses intelligence agencies from failure nor, indeed, serves a useful purpose in understanding the tasks they face. "Capabilities" are not necessarily the reflections of quantifiable, easily measured data: They include include such intangibles as morale, training, and the quality of leadership of an opposing force. Insofar as an intelligence agency looks (as it must) at tactical and operational doctrine, it must consider "intentions." To catalogue only "capabilities"—including suicidal assaults, for example—would be to make the rendering of any informed decision by statesmen and generals impossible. Israeli intelligence did no small service to the IDF by understanding the Egyptian crossing plan—and what is a plan but an intention? Nor is the notion of a "hard" evidentiary base for capabilities and a "soft" one for "intentions" sustainable. Some data on capabilities will be very soft—"hard" information on the tactical skill of an untested commander is rare, and even data on technical matters (for example, the impact of masses of antitank missiles) can be unobtainable. At the same time, some hard data can depict intentions quite accurately—an intercepted order to begin an attack, for example. Thus, the distinction between capabilities and intentions separates what is in human affairs mixed, and inextricably so. In the words of William James, it is "an insane logic" that ignores the relationship between purpose and belief on the one hand, and physical capacity on the other.[84]

HOW TO THINK ABOUT FAILURE TO ANTICIPATE

Alternative Outcomes

How, then, should we think through the problem of the Israeli failure to anticipate the Yom Kippur War? As mentioned in chapter 2, the essence of a failure to anticipate is *not* ignorance of the future, for that is inherently unknowable. It is, rather, the failure to take reasonable precautions against a known hazard. One might open the issue by asking what other kinds of outcomes were possible in 1973. What would have happened, for example, if the chief of staff and minister of defense had become convinced of the imminence of war earlier than the morning of October 6?[85] This is, of course, the question that agitates Israelis to this day. Many would agree with the judgment of Chaim Bar Lev, the former chief of staff who became *de facto* commander of the southern front several days into the war, that the surprise attack accounts for virtually all of the setbacks suffered by the IDF.[86] Bar Lev and others believe that had Israeli leaders received the expected forty-eight hours' warning they would have authorized a reserve mobilization and perhaps a preemptive attack against the Egyptians and Syrians. Certainly, there would have been a *démarche* to the United States in the hopes of preventing war from breaking out.

Whether a preemptive attack would actually have taken place, however, is quite another matter. The debates of the morning of October 6 suggest that in fact the Israeli government would not have permitted a preemptive attack unless they could expect American support, and it is hard to imagine that Washington would have gone along with such a move. Before the war the Israelis had become increasingly confident about their ability to avoid premature mobilization, which suggests that a full-scale call-up might also not have occurred, even with greater warning.[87] More likely would have been a limited reserve mobilization of the kind authorized by Dayan early on the morning of October 6—that is, one *ugda* for each front and the implementation of the basic defensive plans. Whether or not such deployments would have sufficed is an interesting question. The force ratios in the south, in particular, would have remained against the Israelis, and the heavy use of antitank missiles would still have told against massed Israeli armor. The Egyptian crossing might have been beaten back in several areas and suffered far heavier losses, but it is quite conceivable that they might have held on to one or two bridgeheads and inflicted heavy losses on Israeli armor. In the north the story might have been different, since there the battle was much more a classic armor-on-armor clash; the presence of an additional *ugda* might have prevented the Syrians' first-day gains and enabled an earlier counteroffensive, although again it is hard to see how casualties would have been light. An early mobilization might, however, have enabled the IDF to concentrate its forces against one front, rather than split them in a 3:4 ratio between north and south. Nor would a preemptive air strike have bought much more than psychological gains. In point of fact, on the morning of the sixth the IAF could prepare only for an air strike against Syria and, because of weather conditions, only against targets in the Syrian heartland.[88]

In any case, though, the IDF should have understood that political considerations would probably prevent Israel from opening the war in its preferred fashion– that is, by preemption. There was a striking disjunction here between Israel's strategic doctrine—the assumptions driving much, though not all, of the prewar planning—and political reality. On the whole, the IDF expected that it would begin any large war with a preemptive blow, and yet the combination of confidence in Israel's armed forces, the distance of the new borders, and increased dependence on the United States made political authorization for such an a blow unlikely.[89] This was but one respect in which IDF thought appears not to have adjusted to the strategic realities of the early 1970s.[90]

Although Israelis have tended to look at favorable alternative outcomes—prompt warning leading to early mobilization—one should also consider less-favorable outcomes. Suppose, for example, that the special source of intelligence had not come through on the morning of October 6, for technical or other reasons? In that case at least one senior decision maker believes that Israel would not have mobilized until *after* the attack began at 2:00 P.M.[91] Moshe Dayan's account reinforces this view:

> The source of the intelligence was trustworthy. This was information on a decision for war, not information describing physical events along the fronts. We had received this intelligence in the past; afterwards, when the Arabs had not attacked, came the explanation that "at the last minute" Sadat had changed his mind. This time as well the source said that if it would be clear to Sadat that we understood the situation, and that hence he had lost the advantages of surprise, there was a chance that he would defer the time of attack. But this information and other information—particularly on the exodus of Russian families from Syria and Egypt—appeared firm. It was clear that we had to work with the assumption that Egypt and Syria were about to begin the war.[92]

Even a five- or six-hour delay in mobilization could have worsened the situation on the Golan Heights, where reinforcing reserve units arrived barely in time to contain the Syrian forces that had occupied the southern portion of the heights. Without this warning, and with only slightly more aggressive Syrian action, one can imagine the Israelis permanently losing a portion of the Golan Heights—conceivably even all of it. In this scenario, as in the real war, it is not hard to imagine the Syrians and Egyptians choosing to bring about a truce earlier than they did—on October 12, for example, rather than a week and a half later.

Indeed, the more one reflects on the Yom Kippur War the luckier the Israelis appear to have been. Had the Soviets not evacuated their dependents from Egypt or Syria, or refrained from doing so in such a blatant manner, one wonders how much less the sense of threat on Friday, October 5, would have been. Israel might not have stood in danger of literal annihilation during the Yom Kippur War, as Dayan, for a moment at least, seems to have feared; but it most certainly stood in danger of losing many of the gains of the Six-Day War, and emerging even more badly battered at war's end than it did. To look at the war only in light of better outcomes for the Israelis is, in fact, to misread the magnitude of the IDF's calamity in 1973.

A Failure of Intelligence Alone?

There *was* a failure of intelligence in 1973. The culpable failure of AMAN's leaders in September and October 1973 lay not in their belief that Egypt would not attack but in their supreme confidence, which dazzled decision makers, and the dogmatism with which they clung to the Concept. Rather than impress upon the prime minister, the chief of staff, and the minister of defense the ambiguity of the situation, they insisted—until the last day—that there would be no war, period. Even a partial mobilization, for example, a two-*ugda* call-up, would have foreclosed the possibilities of real disaster that opened up on October 6 and 7. But it would be unfair to lay exclusive blame on the stubbornness of a few intelligence officers. On the whole, Elazar, Dayan, and others had at their disposal—or could have demanded access to—the facts in the hands of AMAN, and although they relied on AMAN for analysis, they had shown themselves ready in the past (particularly in May) to make up their own minds. Intellectual docility is, among statesmen and generals, a grievous failing.

The failure of intelligence went beyond a misreading of facts to a misunderstanding of the strategic conceptions of Israel's chief antagonist, Anwar Sadat. On the whole, Israeli statesmen and commanders, even after the war, saw Arab war aims in territorial terms; the far more subtle purposes

of Sadat have, until recently, been misunderstood.[93] Very shortly before
the war then Major General Ariel Sharon, who had recently completed
a tour as commander of the southern front told American journalists:
"Maybe the Canal is not a line of peace. But the Canal is a line on which
you can avoid war. The only reason nations go to war is if you are
attacked, or think you can win. On this line, Egypt has no chance to
win."[94] A stark distinction between winning and losing makes sense in
tactics, but not strategy: as we have seen, winning, for Egypt, meant
achieving intangible, political goals through the use of force.

Even if one discounts as excessive some of the Israeli self-criticism after
the war it becomes clear that the failure of 1973 was, in some respects,
greater than that of Pearl Harbor.[95] In December 1941 the United States
(including the Hawaii garrison) knew of the imminence of war with Japan
more than a week before the attack on Pearl Harbor. The same could
not be said of Israel and the IDF until eight hours before the onset of
war in 1973. But the failure was not a failure of intelligence alone. The
extreme and unwarranted self-confidence of the IDF, its reliance on an
unbalanced "all-tank" doctrine, its failure to understand the enemy's strategic purposes, and its own inability to rethink its strategy in the light of
the new conditions of 1970–73 suggest a more complicated and intercon-
nected kind of failure than that suggested by most accounts, which focus
on the intelligence failure alone.

THE MATRIX

To deal with the problem of surprise attack, which it understood to be a
real one, the Israeli security establishment had three central tasks in 1973:
intelligence collection and reporting; effective net assessment, or weighing
of relative strengths; appropriate levels of alert and preparedness. The
resulting failure matrix looks as shown in Figure 5–1.

The critical failures of the Israelis in 1973 lay at the heart of the Israeli
military establishment, in the general staff, including AMAN, but above
it there lay failures of political supervision. In Israel in 1973 the IDF, and
in particular the general staff, had a monopoly on military advice—the
minister of defense, for example, had no independent staff, but had to
rely on the general staff. More important, however, was an aura of prestige gained in 1967 and indeed throughout twenty-five years of state-
hood, which made the breezy self-confidence of the IDF's leaders at once
contagious and beyond criticism. Moshe Dayan, himself a former chief

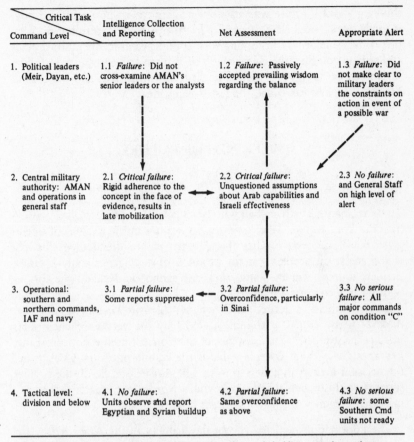

Critical Task / Command Level	Intelligence Collection and Reporting	Net Assessment	Appropriate Alert
1. Political leaders (Meir, Dayan, etc.)	1.1 *Failure*: Did not cross-examine AMAN's senior leaders or the analysts	1.2 *Failure*: Passively accepted prevailing wisdom regarding the balance	1.3 *Failure*: Did not make clear to military leaders the constraints on action in event of a possible war
2. Central military authority: AMAN and operations in general staff	2.1 *Critical failure*: Rigid adherence to the concept in the face of evidence, results in late mobilization	2.2 *Critical failure*: Unquestioned assumptions about Arab capabilities and Israeli effectiveness	2.3 *No failure*: and General Staff on high level of alert
3. Operational: southern and northern commands, IAF and navy	3.1 *Partial failure*: Some reports suppressed	3.2 *Partial failure*: Overconfidence, particularly in Sinai	3.3 *No serious failure*: All major commands on condition "C"
4. Tactical level: division and below	4.1 *No failure*: Units observe and report Egyptian and Syrian buildup	4.2 *Partial failure*: Same overconfidence as above	4.3 *No serious failure*: some Southern Cmd units not ready

Arrows indicate causal links. Solid lines indicate primary pathways; dashed lines, secondary pathways.

FIGURE 5-1. Matrix of Failure

of staff, partook of that confidence, and indeed fostered it. Golda Meir—who remarked, perhaps facetiously, that she had no idea what a division was—had little inclination to probe the professional judgments of her military advisers.

At the same time, our matrix suggests as well a failure of communication by civil and military leadership. The cabinet, and in particular the prime minister, had no intention of allowing military leaders to make politically important decisions on such matters as mobilization or preemption, yet it appears that soldiers and civilians never harmonized their thinking about a future war, its strategic context, its purposes, and how it might break out. Israel began its fourth (or fifth, depending on how one counts) major war brimming with confidence in its operational plans and tactical doctrine, the effectiveness of its intelligence organizations, and the mettle of its fighting men. The first was misplaced, and the second excessive; luckily for Israel, the last was justified.

TWO KINDS OF FAILURE

Intelligence Addictions

Two explanations help explain why Israel failed, in several ways, to antici-pate the Yom Kippur War. One reason lies not in the *analysis* of intelli-gence but in its *sources*. Studies of intelligence failure often look exclusively at the analytical problem, at the products of intelligence analysis rather than its sources. Yet in many cases one cannot understand the former without reflecting on the latter.

In two articles a retired IDF general, Aharon Levran, argues that AMAN was "struck . . . blind" in 1973 by the very excellence of its intelligence sources.[96] The existence of the Concept itself is not surprising, Levran argues: What is remarkable is the stubbornness of AMAN and the decision makers in adhering to it. The explanation lies in the sources supporting this belief, which, in Levran's words, was "material that any intelligence agency would long to get hold of";

> The information depicted clearly the inability of the Arabs to
> consider war with Israel at that time. This information explained
> completely and clearly all developments in the area, and the false
> warnings during most of the time preceding the Yom Kippur War.
> This information struck analysts blind because it supported their
> conceptual estimates, and also because it passed various practical tests
> as well.[97]

Confidence in their sources of intelligence misled the Israelis in two ways. First, AMAN had complete insight into Egyptian thinking about the timing of a future war until January 1973; it then lost that insight simply because its source did not continue to provide information about it. Secondly, the Israeli high command, with very few exceptions, believed that they would receive from another very special source two days' warning (or better) of the onset of war: That source did come through, but later than expected.

To be sure, AMAN, like any large, modern intelligence agency, collected intelligence data in many ways—we have already noted, for example, the importance of aerial photography and intercepted communications during the Soviet airlift. But some sources carry more weight than others, and one plausible explanation, at least, of the intelligence failure was that AMAN let itself be bewitched by sources that were indeed reliable and remarkably good, but incomplete in one case and tardy in another. One might note, in the same vein, that the surprise of the German Ardennes offensive in 1944 owed something to the comparable reliance of Anglo-American forces on signal intelligence. In that case ULTRA failed to provide detailed warning of the attack because of German use of land lines rather than radio transmissions. There, too, overreliance on an unimpeachable and copious source "struck analysts blind."[98]

Implicit Net Assessments

The obsession with a particular source of intelligence explains, perhaps, the immediate failure of Israeli intelligence in 1973—the faith that war would not come, which remained unshakable until two days before war came and which crumbled only on the morning of October 6. But a deeper cause was also at work: a failure of net assessment. Net assessment, the formal and explicit weighing of opposing military forces in the context of political objectives and conditions, is a relatively recent addition to Western military thought. Where the Soviet military has long had the notion of the "correlation of forces"—a systematic and, indeed, quantifiable measurement of power—only in 1973 did the United States create an Office of Net Assessment in the Office of the Secretary of Defense. Similarly, Israel seems to have had no formal net assessment system in 1973; rather the general staff performed this task in its annual assessment of the situation in the Middle East. At other times decision makers or their staffs made judgments about the adequacy of Israeli forces to handle particular threats. But even when a separate machinery for weighing the two sides is lacking, net assessments occur; and herein lies another explanation for the Israeli debacle of the first part of the October War.

Individuals and organizations perform net assessments all the time; the only issue is whether they do so explicitly or implicitly, on the basis of hunch and instinct or analysis. In the case of the Yom Kippur War one finds that the Israelis made a host of implicit net assessments that shaped their behavior in the weeks leading up to the conflict. A retired general in Israeli military intelligence recalls that

> At the end of 1973 I asked an important intelligence officer who had played a major role in the failure, 'Didn't you think for a moment what would happen if your optimistic estimates were incorrect' He replied to me: 'I thought—in fact, I knew—that we had a large and powerful air force, in terms of readiness and capabilities. We had 300 tanks in the Sinai. We had doubled our tank force in the Golan Heights, after we released to them the 7th Brigade. I knew that in any case no catastrophe could occur.'[99]

Zeira made similar remarks to the Agranat Commission, and it is evident that such thinking pervaded the IDF, including AMAN, in 1973. The notion that the IDF refrained from an alert along the lines of May 1973 is false; by the evening of October 5, 1973, the Israelis had raised their forces to roughly the same level of readiness (or higher) that they had achieved six months earlier. The problem lay not in the absence of a decision to institute standard alert procedures so much as in an altogether too optimistic picture of what the balance of forces would look like should war break out. After the war Major General Gonen, the disgraced commander of the southern front, explained the essence of the failure by quoting from the prayer book of the Day of Atonement, a passage repeated frequently in synagogue services that day: "For the sin that we have sinned before You through lightheadedness. . . ."[100] The IDF's net assessment was, in fact, shaped by a reckless overconfidence. The mistakes included a brash faith in the capabilities of large all-tank formations to smash Arab armies, no matter what the odds, and in spite of the well-established importance of combined arms operations in modern warfare.

Intelligence officials sometimes say that, precisely because of situations such as that of 1973, they should refrain from making any kind of net assessment. And indeed, there are sound bureaucratic reasons for having net assessment organizations separate from regular intelligence agencies. But *implicit* net assessments will always go on. One former Israeli intelligence officer observed, in an interview conducted for this chapter, that one could not help but be influenced by the tremendous confidence of commanders on the prewar fronts. Because of the intimacy with which Israeli intelligence officers knew their own forces' dispositions, their knowledge of the commanders and of terrain preparation and fortification, they drifted into complacent readings of the enemy. The overweening optimism of the IDF contaminated its readings of Arab capabilities.

The problem is an old one, and not likely to be resolved by isolating intelligence officers from commanders or from detailed knowledge of their own forces. This is, first and foremost, impractical, particularly in a small country like Israel, but even in a large one like the United States. Intelligence officers participate in planning and exercises, war games, and maneuvers, and cannot help but absorb the temper of their own forces and share some of the worldview of their commanders. Nor would it be a desirable thing to isolate intelligence from operations: Often intelligence officers need a knowledge of their own side's activities and dispositions in order to make sense of how an opponent is reacting to it. In World War II the Royal Navy's Operational Intelligence Centre gained access to current operational information concerning the movement of British convoys and the progress of antisubmarine warfare. Without such information it would have been unable to understand as thoroughly as it did the dispositions and tactics of the German U-boat force.

In October 1973 AMAN possessed reliable order-of-battle information about the Arab armies and it monitored accurately the forward deployment of Syrian and Egyptian forces during the weeks leading up to the onset of war. Where it and the IDF more generally failed was in the area of comparative assessment of doctrine and effectiveness. In particular, the IDF's implicit net assessment failed with respect to two tactical-operational judgments—the effectiveness of a dense SAM–antiaircraft artillery belt along the canal, and the impact of hand-held antitank missiles against tanks operating alone. But more important were the failures of the political and organizational dimensions of Israel's net assessment. Israeli expectations of a relatively quick and relatively cheap victory might have been justified had Israel been able to launch a preemptive attack; political considerations forebade such an attack, and this could have been expected well before 1973. The failure to understand that in a future war the enemy was virtually certain to throw the first punch had many implications for operational planning, which appears to have slighted the problem of fighting containment battles, concentrating rather on the task of launching a prompt counteroffensive.

Moreover, the IDF underestimated the import of substantial improvements in the quality of Arab (and above all, Egyptian) training and coordination since 1967. Because of intensive Soviet advice and, more important, their own efforts, the Egyptian and Syrian armed forces had improved considerably since that war, at virtually every level. To be sure, the IDF had also made tremendous strides in this period, and hence many IDF officers then and since have argued that the relative gap remained the same or had even opened slightly in Israel's favor. The Israeli conception of relative advantage, however, oversimplified the changing relationship between the two sides. In particular, the higher quality of Egyptian junior officers and the vastly increased strategic sophistication of the Egyptian high command meant that no matter how great the disparity in, let us say, tank crew performance or the maneuver capacity of armored battalions, the Israelis faced a far more serious challenge in 1967. One Israeli officer described the problem with an educational metaphor:

> Before 1973 we thought they had gone from being in a poor
> elementary school [in 1967] to a good one. In fact, they had come
> much further—they were now at the university level. Now, there are
> good universities and bad universities and on the whole theirs was
> still a poor one. Intelligence agencies can identify revolutionary
> change when they see it; they can also monitor gradual change.
> What we did poorly was to understand the *cumulative effects* of
> evolutionary change; in fact, I doubt that we ever posed that sort of
> question to ourselves [before 1973].[101]

In 1973, as in previous Arab-Israeli wars, the IDF clearly had the upper hand in terms of the skill of individual weapons crews and in the overall adaptability of its larger units. Yet this advantage—which may indeed have grown in the period 1967–73—could not compensate for changes at other levels of warfare. The tenacity of the individual Arab fighter had increased greatly and at the higher strategic level of war the opposing high command had improved beyond all recognition. There was not one gap between the Arab and Israeli defense forces but several, and comparisons needed to be drawn along all of them.

In the end the surprise and operational failures of October 6–9, 1973, are best understood not as accidents created by an indecisive political leadership or as the result of unavoidable pathologies of intelligence. Rather, they were, at the deepest level, the products of a failure to think through the many dimensions of a changing strategic challenge. By confining their implicit net assessment to only one level of military effectiveness—essentially, the tactical dimension of warfare—and by failing to gauge the cumulative impact of change, the IDF set itself up for a calamity.[102] The operational *and* the intelligence brains of the IDF had failed, and had done so together. It is a tribute to the IDF's resilience and professional skill, and to the raw courage of its soldiers, that it redeemed that defeat and ended the Yom Kippur War with its forces in striking range of Cairo and Damascus. But that military achievement did not eliminate or even diminish the fact that, in strategic terms—that is, in terms of the political objectives for which it fought—Sadat's Egypt emerged the victor from the Yom Kippur War. Ironically, both Israel and Egypt would eventually benefit from this—the most important measure of victory—for the Yom Kippur War paved the way for the peace that followed.

6

Failure to Adapt
The British at Gallipoli,
August 1915

THE GREAT CHANCE

IN APRIL 1915, when the Allied armies in France and Flanders were already experiencing the frustrations of trench warfare that were to render them practically immobile for the next three years, some 70,00 British, Australian, New Zealand, and French troops were launched against Turkey in an attempt to circumvent the bloody deadlock on the Western Front. Their destination was the Gallipoli Peninsula, where they were to help the Royal Navy force a passage through the Dardanelles against Turkish guns; the prize was Constantinople and, beyond it, access to the West's beleaguered ally, Russia. As well as knocking Turkey out of the war and unlocking a supply route to the massive but underequipped Russian armies, the Gallipoli campaign, if successful, also seemed to offer the chance of gathering useful allies from among the Balkan states and so, in Lloyd George's celebrated phrase, "knocking the props from beneath Austria-Hungary." Two years later, during the post mortem into the failure at Gallipoli, the former prime minister H. H. Asquith lamented a lost opportunity. "If we had succeeded . . . in my judgment it would have produced a far greater effect upon the whole conduct of the war than anything that has been done in any other sphere of the war."[1]

After the venture had ended in failure, the disgraced commander of the expedition, General Sir Ian Hamilton, opined that the fate of his force had always hung in the balance. "No man in Europe could have foretold whether the landing of April 25th was to be a success or a dreadful disaster," he wrote. "Too many of the factors were unprecedented under modern conditions for any forecast to be made."[2] The poet John Masefield, who saw action at Gallipoli, took a somewhat different view of the failure at Suvla Bay in August 1915. He believed that success had been almost within the Allies' grasp but that, in the words of the nursery rhyme, "for want of a nail, a battle was lost." "In war, as in life," he wrote, "the unusual thing, however little, betrays the unusual thing, however great." In this case what could have turned a defeat into a victory were "two fresh battalions and a ton of water."[3]

Hamilton's somewhat gloomy assessment contrasts strongly, however, with the mood of buoyant optimism that predominated at all levels before the first landings took place, a mood that owed much to a failure to consider exactly what an amphibious operation might entail and not a little to a deeply entrenched attitude of racist superiority toward the Turkish people in general and the Turkish army in particular. The notion that British troops—any British troops—must be superior to their Turkish opponents was the counterpart of the notion of prestige as the basis of British imperial rule.[4] It was widespread throughout all levels of British society, and the expedition's commander was deeply impregnated with it. "Let me bring my lads face to face with Turks in the open field," he begged his diary some three weeks before Suvla Bay. "We must beat them every time because British volunteer soldiers are superior individuals to Anatolians, Syrians or Arabs and are animated with a superior ideal and an equal joy in battle."[5] Hamilton valued each British soldier as worth several dozen Turks; at Suvla Bay the cold statistics suggest that every Turk was the equal of ten Britons.

At its outset the Gallipoli campaign lacked a clear operational design. Adopted to solve a variety of diplomatic and strategic problems and launched largely as a result of the passionate advocacy of Winston Churchill, then First Lord of the Admiralty and political head of the navy, it was first to be an attempt by battleships to rush the narrows at Gallipoli and break into the Sea of Marmora. When the admiral on the spot was asked his advice, however, he recommended a longer-drawn-out operation to force the straits by means of methodical bombardment and minesweeping combined.

Overwhelmed by Churchill's persuasive oratory, and imprisoned by a concept of service that made them passive instruments of naval adminis-

The Gallipoli Peninsula

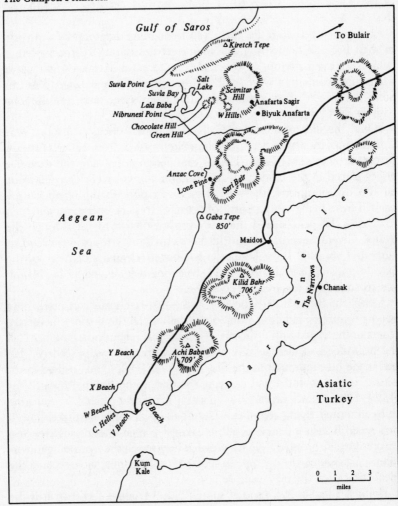

tration rather than active participants in naval policy, the senior admirals in Whitehall endorsed the plan although the serving head of the Royal Navy, Admiral Sir John Fisher, had gone on record ten years earlier opposing any such venture. "Any naval officer who engages a fort worthy of the name fort deserves to be shot!" he had declared. "Nelson said this!"[6]

Attempts to demolish the Turkish forts guarding the straits by a mixture of shell fire and demolition by landing parties during February were a failure; a second attempt to knock out the forts on March 18 was halted when three battleships were sunk and three more badly damaged.[7] At this point the weight of the operation shifted from sea to land, and the long path to Suvla Bay began to open up.

When the idea of attacking Gallipoli was first discussed by the War Council on January 8, Kitchener intimated that at least 150,000 troops would be necessary.[8] Gradually, as the weeks passed and the excessive hopes placed in the efficacy of naval bombardment were revealed to be far too overoptimistic, the role of ground troops in the operation expanded from being "in support" of the navy to joint operations and then to seizing the peninsula if the navy proved unable to get through the straits. Given the situation on the Western Front, troops were hard to come by, but after some hesitation Kitchener released a division for the expedition, and on March 12, 1915, he appointed General Sir Ian Hamilton to command the military forces.

A brilliant commander who was also a first-rate trainer of men and a good organizer, Hamilton seemed to combine all the qualities necessary to make the expedition a success. Although an infantryman, he had "all the brilliance and dash usually associated with the cavalry leader."[9] He had made his reputation in the first Boer War (1880) and on the Northwest Frontier of India and cemented it during the South African War (1899–1902), which he ended as an acting lieutenant general coordinating thirteen mobile flying columns.[10] During the years of peace that followed he revised British infantry tactics, breaking up rigid lines of advance into smaller flexible groupings; in his writings he stressed the overriding importance of attacking the enemy. In short, Hamilton must have seemed the ideal choice for the new venture.

Hamilton had at his disposal some 70,000 troops—less than half the number Kitchener had thought necessary, but the demands of the Western Front made it impossible to release any more. They also meant that the Gallipoli expedition went short of artillery and ammunition; British divisions should have had 304 guns but Hamilton's had only 118, and there was an almost total lack of howitzers, trench mortars, grenades, and high-explosive ammunition. Had he landed his force on the peninsula in mid-March, it would have faced perhaps 25,000 Turks.[11] But on March 26, alarmed by the second British attempt to force the narrows, the Turks had given the German general Liman von Sanders overall responsibility for the defense of the peninsula and some 60,000 troops. Liman split his forces into three equal parts. One, at Besika Bay, protected the Asiatic shore; a second guarded the Bulair Lines; and the third was posted on the Gallipoli Peninsula.[12] On the eve of the landing, Hamilton reckoned that he faced 40,000 Turks.[13]

Lacking adequate resources, Hamilton also lacked adequate guidance and even up-to-date information. No general plan of operations was worked out by the general staff in London, on the assumption that Hamilton and his naval opposite number, Vice Admiral Sackville Hamilton Carden, would do that on the spot, thereby leaving much to extemporization between staffs which were uncoordinated. When Hamilton's chief of staff, General Walter Pipon Braithwaite, asked the War Office for information about his foes and his destination, the Intelligence Department gave him "an out-of-date textbook on the Turkish army and two small guidebooks on western Turkey."[14] Later Hamilton bewailed both the lack of a plan of operations and the lack of lucidity in Kitchener's orders; but at the time he accepted the situation uncomplainingly.[15]

The Gallipoli landings took place on April 25, 1915. A successful deception operation in the Gulf of Saros, involving a naval bombardment of the coast and the presence of transports loaded with troops, kept Liman's attention away from the southern end of the peninsula for twenty-four hours—though the Turks later claimed that only one of the three Allied landings (by the Australians, at what became known as Anzac landing) took them by surprise.[16]

Due to the narrowness of the beaches, a shortage of boats from which to land the troops (primitive landing craft had been constructed but were not available), and the lack of room to maneuver troops from a single point, Hamilton chose to attack the peninsula at three different points near its southwestern tip. The attack was based on two assumptions, both of which turned out to be unwise: that the only really difficult part of the operation would be getting ashore, after which the Turks could easily be pushed off the peninsula; and that the main obstacles to a happy landing would be provided by the enemy.

When the day dawned, and the sun shone straight into the eyes of the attacking troops, dazzling them and thereby giving the Turks a small but important advantage, British inexperience and Turkish resilience confounded both these expectations. Ships lost their way; troops were landed in the wrong place; arrangements for soldiers to land by way of improvised temporary wharves failed; and supporting firepower proved either

inadequate or nonexistent. The enemy posed yet more obstacles. The
Turks defended and counterattacked with unexpected ferocity. Against
the Anzac landing, which they estimated at 12,000, the Turks launched
regiments totaling 4,000 men. After twenty-four hours they had suffered
50 percent casualties.[17]

Fierce Turkish resistance stopped the Anzacs' progress; and it also put
up what proved to be an impenetrable barrier in the south, where general
Hunter-Weston had put the 29th division ashore at four different landing
places. But at the third landing site—"Y" beach—2,000 men embarked
without a hitch, meeting no opposition. What happened next was—with
hindsight—a pointer to the fate of the whole expedition, for a golden
opportunity went begging. Aylmer Hunter-Weston, preoccupied with
the stiff fight going on at the toe of the peninsula, ignored "Y" beach.
The troops there, lacking any order to press forward at all costs, first dug
themselves in and then, next morning, began to drift back down to the
beaches. Hamilton saw what was happening, but did not intervene.[18] His
passivity—so great a contrast with his reputation for boldness—resulted
from his conception of command, which we shall explore later. The consequence was a minor tragedy: Bereft of any clear orders, and discovering
that an extemporized embarkation had already begun, the local commander permitted it to gather pace. After twenty-nine hours of unfettered
freedom, during which they could have carved a sizable hole in the improvised Turkish line, the British troops pulled out.

When the first day at Gallipoli ended, the Allies had toeholds in three
places on the peninsula and faced the task of expelling a ferocious opponent from one of the finest natural fortresses in the world. Hamilton,
showing the mixture of overoptimism and misunderstanding characteristic
of his entire period of command, cabled the Anzac commander on the
evening of April 25, "You have got through the difficult business, now
you have only to dig, dig, dig until you are safe."[19] Short of sufficient
strength from the outset, his forces had suffered some 12 percent casualties in the first three days. The deficiency could not immediately be made
good because Kitchener had refused to supply the extra troops normally
allotted for wastage. Over the next three months the Allied troops strug-
gled to enlarge their foothold against the opposition of Turkish machine
guns and the difficulties of the terrain, while their commander telegraphed
home for more divisions and more artillery ammunition. Men were easier
to find than shells, and with them Hamilton planned to make a major
effort at the start of August to surge to the crests of the hills which dominated the Gallipoli peninsula. Once held, they would put the Allies in a
commanding position from which to bombard the Turkish positions, sup-

port the navy against Turkish batteries strung out along the narrows, and clear the peninsula. All that would remain would be a triumphant advance on Constantinople, already terrorized by the appearance of Allied battleships off the Golden Horn. Excitement at the prospects offered by success, and frustration at the failure of the April landings, added a heavy burden of hopes to the new venture.

A LOST OPPORTUNITY

The battle that took place on the peninsula from August 6–9, 1915, provides one of the most striking examples in modern military history of the failure of an organization to seize and secure a success that, to both contemporaries and subsequent historians, looked to be there for the taking. Confronted by what seems to have been a golden opportunity to achieve a local success of major dimensions, the result of taking the Turks completely by surprise at Suvla Bay, British troops failed to see and to take full advantage of an opportunity presented to them by considerable enemy weakness. Thus the Suvla Bay landing presents exactly those major characteristics we have identified as indicative of true military misfortune: the failure of one party to do what might have been reasonably expected of it, and widespread shock at the outcome once the true scale of the lost opportunity became known. Winston Churchill, deeply involved in the genesis of the campaign and with much to justify—as well as much to conceal—allowed his pen free rein when he came to write his personal account of the war.

> The long and varied annals of the British Army contain no more heartbreaking episode than that of the battle of Suvla Bay. The greatness of the prize in view, the narrowness by which it was missed, the extremes of valiant skill and of incompetence, of effort and inertia, which were equally presented, the malevolent fortune which played about the field, are features not easily to be matched in our history.[20]

Though they lacked his magisterial powers of self-expression, others shared Churchill's view. One officer who was present at the battle held that Suvla Bay "will always remain one of the great failures of the war, and a black page in the history of the British Army."[21] And Alan Moorehead, a later historian, set out very clearly the two sides of the puzzle to be solved:

Somewhere, one feels, there must be some missing factor which has not been brought to light—some element of luck neglected, some supernatural accident, some evil chain of coincidence that nobody could have anticipated. And yet it was quite unlike the April landing. One does not have the feeling that it was touch and go at Suvla, that some slight shifting of pattern would have put things right again. There is instead a strong sense of inevitability; each event leads on quite inexorably to the next. . . . [22]

To understand what went wrong, and to be able to chart the pathways to misfortune such historians as Moorehead have perceived, we shall first examine what was expected to happen and then test the contemporary explanations for the failure. Only then shall we be in a position to construct our matrix and identify the root causes of the failure to cope with a golden opportunity.

Suvla Bay is a long, curved stretch of sand backed by a flat plain from which rise several low hills. Some four and a half miles north of the main Allied positions, it lies at the end of the chain of mountains that command the center of the Gallipoli Peninsula. It was for the possession of this chain, and particularly of the heights of Sari Bair, that Hamilton was about to launch his main attack from the Anzac landing. Until the beginning of August, Suvla Bay had escaped the fury of battle, neither side perceiving its importance in the struggle to escape from the fringes of the peninsula and gain control of the commanding high ground. The idea of operating in the bay area was first raised at the end of July when General Sir William Riddell Birdwood, commanding the Anzac landing, proposed attacking Sari Bair with two divisions and added that if he had a third he would send it to Suvla Bay.[23] Herein lay the first seed of failure: Always perceived as a secondary operation, Suvla Bay never got the full attention it merited from Hamilton's headquarters staff.[24]

The difficulties inherent in the kind of operation Lieutenant General Sir Frederick William Stopford was about to undertake were sadly underrated. On the eve of the April 25 landing, Hamilton had been forcibly struck by "the amount of original thinking and improvisation demanded by a landing operation."[25] Twenty-seven years later, when American marines landed on Guadalcanal on August 7, 1942, they had expected six months' grace to train for their first Pacific operation but were given only six weeks. However, unlike Stopford's men, they had the benefit of such prewar innovations as combat loading to ease their task.[26] Stopford's force lacked any such body of doctrine and technique; it lacked experience; and it lacked time.

To command IX Corps, which was to be entrusted with the landing, Hamilton asked for an experienced general from France. He requested General Sir Julian Byng or General Sir Henry Rawlinson, but was denied either by Kitchener and left with a choice between two senior but retired generals—"dug-outs," in the parlance of the day. His choice fell on Stopford. The novelist Compton Mackenzie, meeting Stopford shortly before the attack, was forcibly struck by his shortcomings:

> He was deprecating, courteous, fatherly, anything except the commander of an Army Corps which had been entrusted with a major operation that might change the whole course of the war in twenty-four hours.[27]

This assessment of Stopford may well have benefited from the wisdom of hindsight; but the new corps commander certainly did not have a high reputation inside the army, where he had made his career chiefly as an administrator, and Hamilton chose him only because he had the necessary seniority over one of the divisional generals he would have to command, Lieutenant General Sir Bryan Mahon. A less passive commander might have pressed harder for an officer he felt suited to the difficult task at hand; but Hamilton can certainly be faulted for failing to take steps to keep a close watchful eye on a general he suspected was not up to the job.

Stopford first learned of the Suvla Bay plan on July 22, fifteen days before he was scheduled to carry it out.[28] His orders laid down the main objective as the "capture and retention of Suvla Bay as a base of operations for the northern army"; to do this he was to capture the low hills in the basin behind the bay quickly and then take the heights on its northern and eastern sides. Subsequent moves would "depend upon circumstances which cannot at present be gauged," but it was "hoped" that Stopford's troops would then be able to move southeastward to give flanking assistance to Birdwood's main attack on the heights of Sari Bair.[29] These instructions were faulty in that they insufficiently emphasized the primary importance of cooperating with the offensive on Sari Bair; nor did they alert the commander to the vital need to take every advantage of opportunity. A more aggressive commander might not have needed to be told so bluntly what to do—but Stopford was not such a commander, and Hamilton had good reason to suspect as much. As the task of planning passed down the chain of command, Stopford now began to take a personal hand, yet further closing down the opportunities to profit from surprise and success.

Within four days of receiving his orders, Stopford began to emphasize nonexistent difficulties. Leaning heavily on current experience in France—which bore little resemblance to Gallipoli—he argued that without a large number of howitzers, troops could not be expected to attack an organized system of trenches.[30] Hamilton did not have the howitzers—but neither did the Turks in the bay area enjoy the luxury of a Western Front–style organized trench system. Rather than point out what aerial photographs showed to be the weak positions occupied by the few Turks in the area, Hamilton's staff officers left IX Corps to discover for itself that these fears were groundless. Revised instructions issued by Hamilton on July 29 emphasized that the primary objective of Stopford's force was to secure Suvla Bay as a supply base for all forces operating in the northern part of the peninsula; this might require all the troops at Stopford's disposal, but if he had troops to spare they should be used to help the main Anzac attack.[31]

In view of all the charges subsequently leveled at Hamilton, Stopford, and others for failing to capitalize on a golden opportunity, we may pause to note that the commander in chief—the source of all direction and authority—apparently never perceived the Suvla Bay landing as playing any more than a subordinate role in the push for Sari Bair and made no provision to expand it if circumstances favored such a course. For him, the greatest possibility held out by possession of the bay was that a light railway could be run up to the troops on Sari Bair more effectively from there than from the narrow and crowded beaches at Anzac Landing.[32] Looking further ahead to operations in 1916, he saw Suvla Bay as an ideal winter base for the troops on the northern part of the peninsula.[33] Hamilton had failed to develop a scheme that accommodated the idea of capitalizing on local success, thereby putting a heavy burden on the troops when opportunities later presented themselves.

Hamilton's failure to perceive and emphasize the broader possibilities inherent in the operation encouraged Stopford to give further vent to his naturally pessimistic frame of mind. Writing to his commander on July 31, he warned that attaining "security" in the bay was likely to be so demanding a task as to make it "improbable" that he would be able to give Birdwood any assistance; if, however, the opposition was sufficiently slight as to allow him to free some of his troops, "you may rely upon my giving him [Birdwood] every assistance in my power."[34] This attitude bespoke a reluctance or inability to perceive opportunities that boded ill. It was magnified as orders were passed down from general headquarters through corps and divisional staffs to the brigades that would do the fighting. The urgency of seizing key positions quickly was watered down; the lack of precision in the orders was magnified; and what were perceived as important geographical positions simply disappeared from the orders put out to the fighting units as they filtered down the chain of command.[35] A combination of pessimism in command and deficient staff work—evident in the chaotic arrangements for unloading water, stores and equipment on the beaches—resulted in Stopford's taking command of a battle for which his troops were inadequately prepared.

The landings on the shore of Suvla Bay, which began just before dawn on August 7, quickly bogged down in confusion. Mistaking the shoreline in the dark, the navy landed one brigade in the wrong place; the direction of attack was altered by one of the divisional commanders not once but several times; and men began to pile up on or near the beaches in confused masses. The early omens looked good; one member of the naval landing party recorded hearing

intermittent firing accompanied by some cheering going on ashore, so that already some of our troops were in action and judging by the slackness of the fire, it looked as if we had taken the Turks by surprise.[36]

More ominously, the same eyewitness noticed that troops met little opposition until they had penetrated about a mile inland, where they began to be held up by snipers. The demoralizing effect on the troops of a handful of Turkish sharpshooters was exacerbated by the growing heat of the day; eventually temperatures mounted until they stood at 90°F. in the shade. Over the next forty-eight hours thirst began to determine the attitudes and then the actions of many of the troops.

During the first day Stopford put some 20,000 men ashore. His force enjoyed a massive ten-to-one superiority, for it faced an opposition that amounted to no more than 2,000 Turks under the command of a determined Bavarian, Major Willmer, backed by eleven guns. Willmer's men fought well, using to full effect the advantage of defending ground that was clothed in dense, thorny ilex scrub. The odds were heavily against them; the outcome of the battle depended on one commander reacting faster and more effectively than the other to the unexpected.

A general Allied attack on the enemy line, which had started the previous day, distracted the Turks' attention from Suvla for a while, but on August 7 Liman von Sanders decided—wrongly—that Suvla Bay was the main British objective. By misunderstanding his enemy's plan, he put himself in a position to snuff out the unexpected opportunity offered to Stopford. But his quick mental reaction was not matched by physical action: Turkish reinforcements were 30 miles away at Bulair, and the local commander, Feizi Bey, was listless and incompetent. On August 8,

Liman replaced him with the energetic but as-yet-unknown Mustafa Kemal (later, as Kemal Atatürk, the father of modern Turkey) and ordered an attack the following morning. Reinforcements were ordered up on the double, and meanwhile Kemal prepared to defend to the last. For forty-eight hours, though, the way to the heart of the Gallipoli peninsula was there for the taking, barred only by a handful of resolute Turks.[37]

On August 7, the British lines should have been alive with movement and activity. Instead, they were a picture of tranquility. An anonymous artillery officer recorded being "struck by the restfulness of all around. There appeared to be little going on, a good many infantrymen sitting about or having a bathe."[38] Stopford lay off shore on board the *Jonquil* and there he stayed throughout the day. He sent one telegram to Hamilton at 7:30 A.M. reporting that one of the hills in the plain behind the bay—Hill 10—had not yet been captured, ending his message "As you see, we have been able to advance little beyond the edge of the beach." Hamilton—one hour's steaming away on the island of Imbros—received this message about noon; some four and a half hours later his chief of staff replied to Stopford: "Chief glad to hear enemy opposition weakening, and knows you will take advantage of this to push on rapidly. . . . take every advantage before you are forestalled."[39] At the front, his commanders were getting into a hopeless tangle. Major General Frederick Hammersley of the Eleventh Division ordered one of his brigadiers, W. H. Sitwell, to support an attack on another of the objectives that had originally been labeled vital—Chocolate Hill—by Brigadier General Hill. Sitwell promptly began to dig in. Hill arrived and failed to get any support from Sitwell for his attack. After a dispute between the two brigadiers over Hammersley's orders, Hill began the weary trudge back through the sand to divisional headquarters in search of a ruling.[40] When, at length, an attack was launched on Chocolate Hill, none of the three units involved was accompanied by its brigadier.

On the evening of August 7 Stopford wanted to press on but was told by his two divisional commanders that their men were exhausted and short of water and that any further movement was impossible for the time being. Accordingly, he postponed any further attack for twenty-four hours. His troops, far from being in a position to seize the hills surrounding the bay, were barely masters of the plain. Stopford lacked the resolution to push them forward. His first priority was the safety of the landing place, and he issued orders early the following morning to select and entrench the best possible covering positions; his intentions were first to consolidate his position and then to land much-needed stores and supplies.[41] Later that same morning he urged his troops to "push on as far as possible" but not to launch frontal attacks on positions held in strength.[42] As yet, no enemy position confronting him was held in any strength.

On the second day of the Suvla Bay landing, after first dispatching an unjustifiably optimistic congratulatory telegram to the *Jonquil,* Hamilton began to grow perturbed at the lack of progress and sent a staff officer— later to become the official historian of the campaign—to find out what was going on. The scene that met Colonel Aspinall's eyes was later summed up by Churchill thus:

> the placid, prudent, elderly English gentleman with his 20,000 men spread around the beaches, the front lines sitting on the tops of shallow trenches, smoking and cooking, with here and there an occasional rifle shot, others bathing by hundreds in the bright blue bay where, disturbed hardly by a single shell, floated the great ships of war. . . . [43]

Seeing Stopford still aboard the *Jonquil* and little happening on shore, Aspinall sent an urgent wireless message to GHQ: "Feel confident that golden opportunities are being lost and look upon the situation as serious."[44] At last Hamilton decided to go and see for himself, but by one of the many malevolent twists of fate that seemed to scar the face of this battle, the ship the navy had allotted him had to put out her boilers to make repairs and was unable to take the commander in chief anywhere.

At 4:30 P.M., after a five-hour wait, Hamilton finally found a ship to take him to Stopford. Once there, he learned that Stopford planned to attack the following day but felt unable to get his troops moving any sooner due to a lack of water and of artillery. Pressed by Hamilton to attack that day, he demurred. Hamilton then went ashore—unaccompanied by Stopford, who excused himself on the grounds that he had a bad knee.[45] Once there, Hamilton heard the divisional commander, Hammersley, report that no advance was possible until the next day; his troops were too scattered, the ground in front of them was unreconnoitered and bad, and orders could not be passed around in time for junior officers to be able to study them. "Hammersley's points," Hamilton recorded,

> were made in a proper and soldierly manner. Every general of experience would be with him in each of them, but there was one huge danger rapidly approaching us . . . we might have the hills at the cost of walking up them today; the Lord only knew what would be the price of them tomorrow.[46]

In a belated attempt to impose a sense of drive and purpose on a battle that had so far been conducted without either, Hamilton ordered Hammersley to attack the heights of Tekke Tepe that night with one of his brigades. No one told Stopford of this change of plan. In the event, it took the brigade selected for the task most of the night to sort itself out, and when it finally launched its assault on the hill early on the morning of August 9, it was too late; Kemal, reinforced by troops who had carried out an exhausting forced march, attacked first. Seizing the heights, he caught the advancing British troops spread out below him on the steepest part of the hillside. The British attack was easily broken, and with it went all hopes of levering the Turks off the commanding heights of the peninsula. A major attack at Suvla launched twelve days later in an attempt to redeem the situation proved totally fruitless. The "outstanding opportunity of the whole campaign," which had presented itself on August 7 and 8, had been wasted.[47]

THE MATRIX

In the failure matrix for this chapter (Fig. 6–1) the horizontal axis identifies the three functions of paramount importance that fell to army commanders: supplying the means of combat, identifying goals, and control and coordination. Along the vertical axis we have five levels of command activity. The first level comprises the high command in London, embodied in the person of the secretary of state for war, Lord Kitchener. On the second level we have the expedition's military commander, General Sir Ian Hamilton. At the third level we have the commander charged with overall responsibility for land operations at Suvla Bay, General Sir Frederick Stopford; at the fourth level, the division and brigade commanders who directed the fighting on the ground; and finally at the fifth level we have the fighting troops.

Although errors were made at the highest command level, the matrix shows that none of them contributed directly to the failure we are analyzing; indeed, their indirect contribution is not enough to make them the source of any secondary pathways to misfortune. Nor, contrary to what we might expect, are the critical failures to be found where eyewitnesses commonly sighted them: in the shortcomings of the troops themselves. Failures certainly occurred at this lowest level, but they contribute only secondary pathways to misfortune.

The matrix shows that the primary pathways to misfortune originated at two separate levels: with the expedition and operation commanders. Hamilton's failures to identify goals comprehensively enough and to exercise full control over his subordinate contributed directly to Stopford's

Critical Task Command Level	Supply of Means	Identification of Goals	Control and Coordination
1. High command	1.1 Insufficient troops and equipment; inadequate senior commanders	1.2 Shift from assisting naval breakthrough to major land operation to clear Gallipoli peninsula	1.3 Failure to support expedition commander vs. regional military authorities
2. Expedition commanders	2.1 Reluctance to press for forces adequate for allotted task	2.2 *Critical failure*: failure to perceive major opportunity offered by Suvla Bay operation	2.3 *Critical failure*: reluctance to push subordinates even after necessity to do so has become obvious
3. Operational command	3.1 *Failure*: underestimation of own resources relative to those of the enemy	3.2 *Failure*: allows progressive dilution of aggression in orders	3.3 *Failure*: complete absence of control and supervision of subordinates
4. Division and brigade commands	4.1 Exaggeration of local difficulties (strength of enemy, lack of water, etc.)	4.2 *Critical failure*: concern to hold limited ground rather than take as much as possible	4.3 Unresolved conflicts between subordinates absorb time and energy
5. Units	5.1 Undertrained and inexperienced	5.2 No clear understanding of local or general objectives	5.3 Bad ground puts a premium on low-level initiative

Arrows indicate causal links. Solid lines indicate primary pathways; dashed lines, secondary pathways.

FIGURE 6–1. Matrix of Failure

147

own failures. Had Hamilton applied a corrective force to overcome his subordinate's excessive caution, two of Stopford's failures would have been less significant and might have been eradicated entirely. A second feature of the matrix is that it reveals how failures can cross boundaries to have a malign influence on a subordinate in a different functional area. Hamilton's failure to perceive the opportunity offered by the Suvla Bay venture meant that Stopford was not impelled—or *compelled*—to alter his policy of leaving his subordinates an entirely free hand. Finally, we may note that the weight of failure in this case does not lie in an inadequate supply of means—a reasonable commonsense supposition—but in the realm of goal identification and control and coordination.

PROBLEMS

Shortage of Water

Both at the time and afterward the commanders actively involved in the Suvla Bay landings laid great stress on the shortage of water as a major cause—some tried to suggest *the* major cause—of the failure to take the heights before the Turks occupied them in force. An eyewitness recorded on the second day of the battle:

> The water question is acute, the whole corps having to be supplied from lighters and the arrangements are at present hopelessly inadequate and it is most pathetic to see men down from the firing line having to wait in the sun for sometimes as long as four hours before they can get their water bottles filled. Everything has to be improvised and why it wasn't thought of before, I don't know.[48]

The scenes that occurred at the beaches certainly suggest that lack of water was a major factor in determining the fate of the battle: Troops rushed into the sea and cut the hoses from the water lighters to the shore in order to slake their thirst, while further inland some units undoubtedly went very short of water. Stopford believed that want of adequate water supplies was severely restricting his troops' capacity to fight; on August 8, as has been seen, he accepted without demur his divisional commanders' reports that their men were too exhausted by fighting and thirst to push on that day, and afterward he claimed that the want of water was so bad that men were reduced to drinking their own urine.[49]

After the campaign Hamilton held that shortage of water had not been a problem, and his view was backed up by evidence from Hammersley and his two brigade commanders, Sitwell and Haggard. Sitwell, who had lived in Rhodesia, pointed out that there were Turkish wells in the area and that with a little effort water could be found. However, no proper arrangements had been made to look for it.[50] To some extent the shortage of water suffered by the troops was their own fault; it is unlikely that Australian or New Zealand troops would have allowed such conditions to develop without doing something. One of the witnesses to the Dardanelles Commission of Inquiry, Lieutenant Colonel A. J. A. Hore-Ruthven, V.C., put the contrast in attitudes between the two armies well:

> if there is any water to be got anywhere they [the Anzacs] will get it. The English soldier, till he has had a bit of experience on active service rather waits till the water is brought to him, and if it is not he says "I have no water." It is just those little things that make the difference.[51]

Behind the disagreements over the significance of the water shortage for the outcome of the battle lay a failure to exercise command responsibility adequately. Stopford assumed that his responsibility for water supply only began once water had been landed on the beach, as did Deputy Assistant Quartermaster General Major-General Poett.[52] Until then, the two saw the problem as one to be solved jointly by Hamilton's headquarters and the navy. Delays in landing the mules that were to carry the water to the front line, an inadequate supply of water lighters, a lack of receptacles to receive water once it had been landed on the beach, and the absence of any alternative arrangements in case the mules failed to arrive all bespeak a failure of foresight and coordination. Hamilton and Stopford failed to sort out the issue in advance, and at the front Hammersley took no steps to secure or even to ascertain the source of his supply.[53] A cavalier attitude and incompetence combined to make the water problem appear much more serious than it really was—with unhappy consequences.

The way Birdwood prepared for the Anzac landing on April 25 shows how differently things could have been managed. He began to make arrangements to secure his water supplies nearly two months before the attack, buying 2,000 kerosene tins and a number of donkeys to carry them. He also ensured that special parties of field engineers were detailed to search the gullies for water as soon as the landing had taken place; the result was that within forty-eight hours twenty wells had been sunk and were providing 2,000 gallons a day.[54] In his general plan for the attack on Sari Bair in August, Birdwood made equally careful provision to secure his water supply.[55] His example could easily have been followed and his experience utilized, but his advice was never sought. British generals preferred to rely on their own blinkered interpretations of administrative responsibility at different levels in the military hierarchy. As a result, a difficulty was magnified until it assumed the proportions of a major setback—and, later, an explanation for failure.

Shortage of Artillery

In March and May 1915, British attempts to break the German lines on the western front at Neuve Chapelle and Aubers Ridge failed. The official explanation for both of these failures was that the necessary quantities of heavy guns and high-explosive ammunition with which to pound the German trenches to pieces had been lacking.[56] This experience produced an "artillery fixation" in the minds of British generals, who became convinced that success or failure—at Gallipoli and elsewhere—hinged on the possession and use of large amounts of artillery. In fact, conditions at Gallipoli did not demand a "Western Front" style of operations: This was a different theater, with different problems. But a preoccupation with the need for lots of guns and heavy preliminary bombardments to soften up enemy trenches blinkered local commanders so that they were unable to perceive and then follow up an opportunity when it occurred. In its analysis of the causes for the failure at Gallipoli, the Dardanelles Commission concluded that the absence of artillery "must have materially contributed to the failure at Suvla."[57] This conclusion reflected the opinions of many of their witnesses—and, no doubt, their own prejudices. Brigadier General R. P. Maxwell, commanding a brigade in Hammersley's division, told the commission, "Even at the end I think if we had had enough howitzers we should have forced the Turks out."[58] In fact the shortage of artillery was probably not a critical factor on August 7 and 8; Stopford had more guns than the Turks who opposed him, but in any case the broken ground, thick cover, and scattered position of the enemy (whose lone snipers did much damage) suggest conditions artillery could have done little to ameliorate. However, the critical fact is that Stopford's self-confidence—such as it was—was sapped by the belief that the means allotted to him were inadequate to the job.

From the moment of his arrival off the peninsula Stopford was afflicted by a tendency to compare conditions at Gallipoli with those on the Western Front, where it was believed that with heavier artillery bombardments the German line could be broken. Visiting Birdwood at the Anzac landing, Stopford was inclined to consider that a preliminary bombardment was necessary before any attack and disregarded his host's suggestion that he trust to surprise.[59] His orders of July 22 reflected a concern over the likely role of enemy artillery, which he believed was emplaced on the hills overlooking Suvla Bay; and his preternatural caution was fully evident in a letter he wrote to Hamilton on July 26, which led to a revision in his orders three days later. "The whole teaching of the campaign in France," he wrote, "proves that troops cannot be expected to attack an organized system of trenches without the assistance of a large number of howitzers."[60]

Stopord's conviction that the success of his attack required a massive artillery barrage was given more support by his chief of staff, Brigadier General H. L. Reed, V. C. Reed had been attached to the Turkish army in the Turco-Bulgarian war and had formed a very favorable view of the resistance that Turkish troops could put up on the defensive; and he came to Gallipoli from France, where he had been imbued with the artillery ethos being built up there.[61] Aspinall later described Reed as

> obsessed with the difficulty of fighting without lots of howitzers . . . he gave me the impression that he did not think the plan could succeed. He never said so, but he had the whole air of a man who does not think he is going to perform his task.[62]

With such half-heartedness at the top, it is scarcely surprising that negative forces triumphed over positive ones during those hot August days at Suvla Bay.

Once again, however, as in the case of the water shortage, a minor problem—though one that exercised a strong psychological effect—conceals a different but related problem that posed a major threat to the chances of success. The real difficulty was summed up by a New Zealand soldier some three weeks before the attack on Suvla Bay; lamenting a failed attack, he added, "With a stock of mills bombs and trench mortars we could have gone to Constantinople."[63] What was desperately needed in the hand-to-hand combat amid the scrub, thorns, gullies, and ravines, were infantry weapons that could suppress local opposition quickly and accurately without needing a sighting. For this task rifles were all but useless and grenades essential, yet the troops were always short of them. At the end of May there were only twelve grenades per company, and in June only four trench mortars in the whole of the Anzac position. The mortar problem was never solved, and not until August 29 were there enough grenades to supply attacking troops with two per man. A week before this, one regiment had been ordered to attack "with bomb and bayonet" even though its commanders knew it possessed no bombs at all.

To enable the troops to do their job, the high command needed to equip them with the necessary means. The full value of bombs and mortars was not yet recognized by the generals—though it was by the troops themselves—but instead Hamilton took comfort from the fact that Stopford would have naval artillery to support his attack. In common with Vice Admiral John de Robeck, Stopford seems to have felt that naval guns were completely ineffective against deep trenches. The weapon he favored to crack this nonexistent nut—for there were no such lines of trenches facing his troops at Suvla Bay—was not available. Even more corps artillery might not have turned failure into success. A year later the real requisite was more readily apparent. "Had we had half the mortars (I mean trench mortars) we have here," wrote Major General Sir A. H. Russell from France, "I am sure we could have won our way across the Peninsula without difficulty and the whole history of the war been altered."[64] Yet even without the missing weaponry Stopford and his men might have done better. The gap between success and failure was not one that only a particular item of equipment could have bridged.

Natural Obstacles

It is difficult now to grasp the extent to which contemporaries were ignorant of the physical problems the Gallipoli expedition would have to overcome. Maps of the peninsula were few and poor, were only gradually improved as better ones were obtained from Turkish prisoners,[65] and marked only the main spurs across which the troops would have to fight. New Zealand troops expected to find "good grazing" land confronting them; but when the Australian war correspondent C. E. W. Bean saw the peninsula at firsthand on the morning of April 25, he realized at once how misleading the maps had been.

> The place is like a sand-pit on a huge scale—raw sandslopes and precipices alternating with steep slopes covered with low scrub—the scrub where it exists is pretty dense.[66]

Facing what seemed to be an endless series of ravines and knife-edged ridges that often bisected each other like a maze and were clothed with scrub so thick that a man standing 5 yards away was invisible, the Anzacs' attack halted at the end of the first day in "country which would have been well-nigh impassable even in peace manoeuvres."[67]

The hills surrounding Suvla Bay—up which Hamilto launch a night attack on August 8–9—were equally forbi

> . . . rough stony ground, cut up into a tangled success ravines. Everywhere there was a strong growth of dwar ⎯⎯ ⎯⎯ ⎯⎯ ancient growth, with limbs frequently as thick as a man's arm, and with foliage through which it was impossible to force one's way. Here and there were narrow winding openings forming natural paths, only broad enough to allow one man to pass at a time.[68]

In country such as this a few determined snipers could put up serious resistance against attacking troops who could all too easily lose their way and wander out of reach of support: On August 12 the commanding officer of a battalion of the Norfolk Regiment together with sixteen officers and 230 men disappeared into this bush in an attack, and none of them were ever seen again.

Hamilton argued afterward that steep, broken ground such as that facing the troops at Suvla Bay was no easier to defend and no more difficult to attack than flat ground in France.[69] He certainly did little to help his troops overcome these obstacles. Reconnaissance was ruled out because he wished to keep the Turks in the dark;[70] and an excessive concern for secrecy meant that maps of Suvla Bay were only handed out after midday on August 6. As a result, on the night of the landing "many officers of the 11th Division had never seen a map of the area in which they suddenly found themselves."[71] This failure to provide the best possible information and intelligence was the more inexcusable because Hamilton knew well by then that maps were misleading, that mere visual reconnaissance from the bridge of a passing warship was inadequate, and that actual physical features often turned out to be quite different from the results of either.[72]

Like Stopford and Reed, Hamilton saw the problems presented by the physical features of the Gallipoli Peninsula in terms of trench warfare. Despite the superficial similarities between the two theaters, attacking on the Gallipoli Peninsula was often more akin to hill warfare, and it is noticeable that the units that did best were those, such as the Gurkhas, who had combat experience in similar conditions and knew, for example, that attacking troops should avoid the apparent safety of the ravines and instead pick their way up the spurs, retaining control of the high ground.[73] To do this successfully, the troops needed the most accurate knowledge they could get about the kind of ground over which they had to fight. This was denied them by their commanders, who thereby made a further contribution to the likelihood of disaster.

TRAINING AND INITIATIVE

Shortly after he had been sent out to Gallipoli by the prime minister and had witnessed the Suvla Bay attack, Lieutenant Colonel Maurice Hankey telegraphed a brief and pithy explanation of the failure to Asquith: "Troops lately sent from England unfortunately failed completely, owing partly to water difficulty, but mainly to bad staff work and want of dash and drive."[74] The latter feeling—that they had been let down by the quality—or lack of it—of the troops allotted to them was shared by a number of senior commanders. Stopford was very disillusioned with the territorial divisions he had been given; "they not only showed no dash in attack but went back at slight provocation, and went back a long way."[75] Hamilton shared the view that the troops, rather than their commanders, were at fault:

> It was general want of experience and the youth of the men. The New Army were fine men but there was a want of savvy about the whole proceedings. They were all raw; there was no one to show them the way.[76]

In his opinion, an Indian division or one with experience in France would have "walked on to the hills at once."

Hamilton had been persuaded to use troops fresh from England for the attack—not the seasoned Twenty-ninth Division, which had taken part in the original landings on April 25—on the grounds that little opposition was likely, and that even if stiff resistance was encountered, a new division was likely to give as good an account of itself as one weakened by the effects of three months' continuous fighting. This reasoning was mistaken; and the error was compounded by inadequate training and preparation, the ineptness of the timetabling for the landing, and the failure to pay sufficient attention to the need for good leadership by junior officers.

With no previous experience of amphibious landings against opposition, troop training in Britain in 1915 had no fund of experience on which to build. Divisions were trained with a view to fighting in France; in Hamilton's opinion this predisposed them to dig in at the first opportunity.[77] In any case peacetime training lessened the very sense of individual initiative that conditions on the Gallipoli Peninsula put at such a high premium.[78] This imposed an extra burden on commanders, which, as we shall see, was not recognized and catered to. Training in Egypt would probably have done little to improve matters, being "frankly admitted to be Boer War stuff."[79] In any case, in the novel conditions of warfare on the peninsula, lack of training was compounded by lack of a prior taste of battle. "It was experience, not training, which we lacked," remarked one of the Eleventh Division's colonels. In France, newly arrived divisions were introduced to the rigors of the front gradually and were given time to accustom themselves to their task before being called upon to undertake a major offensive. At Suvla Bay, Hamilton committed raw troops to a task that required especially effective leadership if underlying deficiencies were not to prove insuperable. Such leadership was not forthcoming.

The likelihood that Stopford's force would be able to cope successfully with the task confronting them was further diminished by the mismanagement that preceded the attack. Some troops had been kept on board ship since July 11 and had been given little opportunity to exercise and regain their full level of fitness. Other units were not rested before the attack; instead, normal duties were carried out until nearly midday on August 6, when the men were informed that they were about to take part in a major operation. Marched to the boats during a hot afternoon, they were unable to gather their strength for the task ahead; when the first troops reached the beach some had already been on their feet for seventeen hours. By the second day of the battle, besides being short of water and food, many of the men had had no sleep for fifty-two hours.[80] In these circumstances even seasoned regulars might have found it difficult to summon up the reserves of energy and determination necessary to push forward. Stopford's men found it impossible.

The problem of lack of training and experience was exacerbated by the fact that the new divisions lacked effective leadership at the lower levels of the chain of command as well as higher up. On the first day Turkish snipers took a heavy toll of officers. Losses among senior officers and company commanders were particularly heavy, and as a consequence, command fell on the shoulders of very young junior officers who often had less than a year's military experience. As a result of the excessive secrecy of the high command, many junior officers found themselves leading attacks without knowing what their objectives were and unable to take the kind of elementary precautions that seasoned fighters would have. Some unwisely disdained to take cover under fire, adding to the scale of losses.

Lack of experience, coupled with the lack of energy and drive that command should have supplied, magnified the troops' natural tendencies to sit down and wait for orders rather than using what initiative they had. Hore-Ruthven noticed this phenomenon: "An Australian, even if he did not get the order, if he thought it good business to go on, would go on."[81] Many contemporaries noted the combination of willingness and passivity that seemed to characterize the troops of the New Armies raised by Kitchener in 1914, and that contrasted so markedly with the Anzacs' enterprise and boldness. The Australian official historian believed that his countryman was "half a soldier before the war." Driving bullocks, gathering sheep for shearing, and particularly fighting bush fires had prepared him for combat; "fighting bush fires, more than any other human experience, resembles the fighting of a pitched battle."[82] By no means all the Anzacs were products of the Outback; but the social attitudes of the Australian soldier made him much better at overcoming the hostility of the battlefield than his inexperienced and undertrained British companion-in-arms.

EXPLANATIONS

Having examined the actual course of events and the reasons most frequently given for the failure at Suvla Bay, we are now in a position to return to our matrix and explore the "pathways" to this particular misfortune. The first thing to note is that errors made by the highest authorities, although important in general terms, had no direct role to play in contributing to disaster. Kitchener allowed Hamilton only half the number of men generally reckoned to be necessary to carry out the operation and denied him the customary 10 percent extra for wastage on the grounds that doing so would lock up troops needed in France.[83] In practice this was irrelevant, because at Suvla Bay for some 48 hours Stopford enjoyed a ten-to-one advantage over his local opponent—ample time to have brought off what might have been one of the major victories of the war. Kitchener's refusal to allow Hamilton the corps commanders he wanted probably did have a significant, but indirect, effect on the battle. However, once Hamilton knew they were not going to be released to him, it was his responsibility to take steps to compensate for this deficiency. He failed dismally to rise to this task.

As the matrix makes clear, critical failures by the expedition's commander in chief contributed directly to the subsequent failure of the troops in combat. Hamilton's failure to perceive the possibilities inherent in the operation, and his failure to insist that primacy of place in the action be given to the attack on the hills rather than the occupation of the bay area, magnified the unaggressive tendencies of his local subordinate, which in turn percolated down through the chain of command on the ground. The explanation for this lies in Hamilton's hands-off concept of military command. The view that the commander's role was to set the general objectives and then leave his subordinates and their staffs to work out all the details was well established in the upper echelons of the British army, and Douglas Haig adopted it throughout his period as commander in chief in France.[84] Hamilton did show some inclination to intervene on the spot when he realized that things were not progressing as fast as he wished them to: At "Y" beach on the second day of the Gallipoli landing he felt "inclined" to take a hand when he saw troops drifting off the crest of a hill but was talked out of doing so by his chief of staff, Lieutenant General Sir Walter Braithwaite.[85] Thereafter, following both his natural inclinations and the decided views of his staff, he lapsed back into quiescence. At the time of the Suvla Bay landing, his headquarters was located on the island of Imbros, some distance from the mainland. In a very revealing comment to the commissioners who conducted the inquiry into the Dardenelles venture, Hamilton justified the distance he had put between himself and his subordinate by explaining that "General Stopford was within an hour's run of me and knew perfectly well that I should be delighted to see him at any time."[86]

"Many a general has been saved by his subordinates," remarks Robert Rhodes James in his study of the campaign. "In the Gallipoli campaign, Hamilton was often badly let down by them."[87] While this judgment undoubtedly contains a deal of truth, it fails to emphasize the cardinal fact that the failings of Stopford and others were not simply their own responsibility but also their commander's. Hamilton believed that the Suvla Bay venture needed an energetic and experienced commander. When he failed to secure one and settled instead for a "dug-out" of pre–First World War vintage, he did nothing to alter his command arrangement to compensate for that fact.

Stopford's restful conception of command—staying on board the *Jonquil* during the better part of the battle and leaving his divisional commanders to get on with things and his brigadiers to squabble—was the counterpart of Hamilton's aloofness. Yet this was by no means the ruling pattern of behavior on the peninsula. Hunter-Weston, the general in command on the southern tip of the peninsula, also left his subordinates to get on with things, but Birdwood at Anzac Landing was conspicuous by his eagerness to get out and about among his troops.[88] Had Stopford been instructed or encouraged to do the same, some of the problems that bedeviled his troops might at least have been diminished, if not resolved.

The problems facing the troops were further magnified by the muddles surrounding the orders issued to divisional and brigade commanders, and by the misconceptions that flowed from them. Hammersley, entirely misunderstanding the intentions of the high command, believed that the attack launched by Birdwood's troops at Anzac was intended merely as a distraction to divert the Turks' attention from the main operation at Suvla Bay.[89] His natural combativeness was watered down by Stopford and impeded by his brigadiers. Hill's brigade knew nothing of the ground or the task facing them until the last minute, and twenty-four hours before the battle started they were encamped on the island of Mytilene in an elaborate attempt to deceive the pro-Turkish ruler of the island that the forthcoming attack would be launched against the Asiatic mainland.[90] Sitwell's inertia meant that his brigade completely lacked proper direction.

With control weakening progressively from general headquarters down through corps and divisional commanders and their staffs, there was no force to counteract the personal deficiencies of elderly and flustered brigadiers—one of whom had had a nervous breakdown before the war—as they tried to divine the enemy's strength and interpret the high command's intentions. It was at this level that personalities had their greatest effect in making an already difficult task even more difficult for the troops on the ground. One participant, referring to the two brigadiers most directly involved, put the matter with perceptive simplicity: "Sitwell was incapable of giving an order, and Hill was incapable of obeying one."[91] In circumstances such as these, command culpability rises above the level of the two individuals mentioned to embrace divisional, corps, and ultimately expeditionary force commanders.

There is no doubt that the troops called upon to carry out the Suvla Bay attack suffered from certain significant weaknesses. Countless contemporary observers remarked on their inexperience, lack of initiative, and dependence on their leaders. Though some of these observers were hostile to the British army as they saw it at Gallipoli, others were sympathetic. General Sir Charles Monro, who arrived at the end of October to examine the feasibility and desirability of evacuation, reported that the troops on the peninsula, "with the exception of the Australian and New Zealand Corps, are not equal to a sustained effort owing to the inexperience of the officers, the want of training of the men and the depleted condition of many of the units."[92] Although two more months of grinding combat had passed since August, and although his comments were not directed at the troops involved in the Suvla Bay episode, at least two of his critical comments apply to them.

Given the weaknesses of the instrument to hand, the staff could have taken a number of steps to fit the troops more adequately for the task at hand. An excessive concern for secrecy diminished the volume of information and intelligence available when it should have had the highest priority. The inexperience of the troops placed a premium on effective command at all levels; in the circumstances, since new company commanders could not simply be manufactured out of thin air, and once Hamilton had taken the decision not to exploit the seasoned Twenty-ninth Division, unity of conception, absolute clarity of orders, and the close monitoring of progress on the ground became vital. As we have seen, no steps were taken to secure or improve any of these requirements. Nothing was done to counteract the tendency of troops to stop halfway before objectives were reached, as "excitement and surprise at being there and alive . . . drowned all other feelings at the moment."[93] Perhaps most extraordinary of all, given the acknowledged reputation of the Anzacs as the best fighting troops on the peninsula, is the fact that Birdwood's advice on the Suvla Bay enterprise was never sought; offered once, it was brushed off.[94]

An efficient communications system is of the greatest importance in directing and controlling raw or inexperienced troops in combat. For most of the battle, Hamilton was on an island an hour distant. Stopford was offshore on one ship with his administrative staff on another, and apparently he was quite content with a situation in which staff came and went from the shore in motorboats to deliver instructions and bring back reports. The trip, he later remarked complacently, took only five minutes.[95] What he overlooked—or ignored—was the fact that, unless his staff were continuously bustling to and fro (a slow and imperfect way to transmit orders and receive information, and one that would divert them from other tasks), his ability to communicate could be only limited at best. Communications were in fact so poor that, as one commentator has suggested, "it is tempting at times to ascribe almost the whole cause of the fiasco to the absence of any efficient form of combat net radio."[96]

While a modern radio net would certainly have put into the commanders' hands the means to exercise direct tactical control over small units and receive time-urgent intelligence about the state of enemy resistance, it is a mistake to lay too much weight on its absence as an explanatory excuse for the fiasco at Suvla Bay, for the means existed to do far more in this regard than was actually done. For decades, the British army had been using heliographs as an effective means of communication in colonial wars; no thought seems to have been given to their use at Gallipoli—which is particularly surprising, given Hamilton's vast experience of such campaigns. In addition, scientific developments had made a new medium available. Ever since 1910 the Royal Navy had been equipping its ships with wireless telegraphy, an almost instantaneous means of communication, and indeed this was the means used to pass Hamilton's messages to Stopford on board the *Jonquil*.[97] Had the commander in chief been inclined to send more messages to Stopford, more messages would have reached him. The major obstacle was psychological, not technical.

From the *Jonquil* a cable was laid to the shore, and from there field engineers ran telephone lines forward to subordinate headquarters. However, this important facility was never fully utilized. When Hill and Sitwell quarreled about whether their divisional commander had or had not ordered an attack, Hill had to trudge back on foot through the sand to Hammersley because neither of the brigadiers had brought out their telephones.[98] Cables and land lines were a prey to frequent interruption; however, with much less enemy artillery in action than was the case on the Western Front, it is likely that they could have provided a much more continuous means of communication with the front line than happened in France and Flanders. Nor were the field commanders limited to telephone cables to communicate with one another. The instructions given to Stopford on July 29 included the information that he was to be provided by the Royal Navy with two military pack wireless-telegraphy stations and one Royal Marine base wireless-telegraphy station.[99] Their role in the battle remains a mystery.

The misuse or neglect of communications by commanders at various levels is a good illustration of the main finding of our inquiry into the Suvla Bay affair: that while the men at the front line may fail to achieve goals which seem to be well within their grasp, such failures are not solely—and frequently not even chiefly—the direct consequences only of their own innate deficiencies. Rather, the controlling intelligence which is directing them has failed to make reasonable provision to allow for the maximizing of every chance of success. Such provision is of special importance in war for, as we have seen, coping with unexpected opportunities or setbacks is many times more difficult on a battlefield where chaos, confusion and hostile action or reaction are features of the environment, than it is in the case of civil disasters. In the particular case of Suvla Bay, when the central ingredient for success was absent the likelihood of failure was greatly increased. As Lieutenant Colonel Hore-Ruthven explained to the Dardanelles commissioners: "It was essential to have energy and drive in the higher commands and the staffs with raw troops because, unless they got the energy and push from behind, they would not go on."[100]

THE ESSENCE OF ADAPTIVE FAILURE

Perhaps more than any of the other types of failure we are examining, adaptive failure is susceptible to the belief that success was denied by only a small margin. A few more resources, a single change in the chain of cause and effect that apparently led directly to disaster, and the outcome would have been entirely different. Suvla Bay has certainly attracted its share of such beliefs. Winston Churchill believed at first that a mere twist of fate had barred the way to success. "The slightest change in the fell sequence of events," he wrote, "would have been sufficient to turn the scale." Twenty years later he offered a more penetrating, though still somewhat narrow, explanation of the misfortune: "The Battle of Suvla Bay was lost because Ian Hamilton was advised by his C.G.S. to remain at a remote central point where he would know everything. Had he been on the spot he could have saved the show."[101] The Dardanelles commissioners, collectively wiser than either man, recognized that the reasons for the failure in August 1915 were more complicated.[102]

In military terms, "adapting" can be defined as identifying and taking full advantage of the opportunities offered by enemy actions or by chance combinations of circumstances to win success or to stave off failure. We have looked closely at a case of "offensive" adapting failure, but we might just as well have examined a case of "defensive" adapting failure, such as the Malayan campaign in 1942, which culminated in the humiliating surrender of Singapore and thereby, according to some historians, signaled the end of the British Empire. In both cases the requirements laid on the people directly involved are the same. Self-organization in the face of the unforeseen or the unexpected is at an especially high premium. Units and small groups must achieve levels of cooperation and mutual self-help that surpass those commonly expected of them or for which they have been prepared. Unexpected tasks must be delegated quickly and efficiently and competing demands resolved speedily and wisely.

All this may seem a lot to ask in the midst of the bloody and destructive world of combat, but it is done with a remarkable degree of success in many cases of civil disaster. People who lack any special training and are frequently unknown to one another cooperate to search for survivors, rescue victims, support the injured, and succor the homeless.[103] One of the things that best helps to explain how such untrained and inexpert amateurs can function so well and cope so effectively in these circumstances is the fact that their goals are often very clear—even, indeed, self-evident. Social ties that usually go unexamined emerge in testing circumstances and offer a clear guide to action, and often a clear set of priorities: The safety of the family is assured, neighbors are checked, friends are sought. In this way adapting builds upward from a myriad of individual actions, coordinated by the civil authorities at a more general level.

From this comparison we can draw two main conclusions about failure to adapt in the military context. The first, and perhaps the more surprising, is that it is not the strengths or weaknesses of those at the front line that are of primary importance but the proper functioning of command. To make the most of the opportunities thrown up in war, or at least not to let them slip by unnoticed, goals must be clearly and unambiguously defined, even where they may be open-ended. For at least a month before the landings on April 25, 1915, Birdwood and all his subordinates dinned into the Anzacs the instruction "Go as fast as you can—at all costs keep going."[104] Without such directions, even fit and enthusiastic troops may falter; with their aid, even ill-trained and inexperienced ones may be able to maximize their potential.

The requirements to adapt to unexpected circumstances tests both organization and system, revealing weaknesses that are partly structural and partly functional, whose full potential for disaster may not previously have been noticed. This is demonstrably true of the British army at Suvla Bay. The organization was a rigidly hierarchical one. It was structured on the basis of strict adherence to the prewar dogma of seniority as the sole determinant of appointment to particular levels of command: Because one of his divisional commanders, Mahon, was a very senior lieutenant general who guarded his status jealously and would not waive it, Hamilton, forced to look higher up the Army List, found himself accepting the unfortunate Stopford.[105] This sort of system magnified the problems associated with Suvla Bay—and may even be said to have created many of them—by forcing the task into the framework of the organization rather than readjusting the organization to meet the needs of the job at hand.

The difficulties this produced were magnified by the system through which the command structure functioned. Two aspects of this system helped produce a failure to adapt by enfeebling command. One was the compartmentalization of the planning process, which isolated parts of the organization when they should have been communicating with one another. Plans were drawn up in an idealistic vacuum since there was no consultation with the administrative and supply branches that would have to carry them out.[106] Perhaps more important regarding Suvla Bay itself was the second feature of the system: the unwritten rule that a senior commander did not interfere with his subordinates once he had set the general nature of the task they were to fulfill. The influence of his chief of staff, Braithwaite, helped ensure that Hamilton was restrained by this invisible straitjacket; and Stopford, explaining his failure to exert himself once aboard the *Jonquil*, remarked later "I should not like it, if I were a Divisional Commander, to have my orders interfered with by my corps commander."

So great is the dramatic nature of the failure at Suvla Bay that it has reached well beyond the confines of military history to find its way into the literature of systems analysis as a prime example of what not to do. "Unfortunately," says a recent author, "the operation was bedeviled by faulty staff work, an unwarranted faith in naval firepower, and failure to load ships to facilitate amphibious operations." Later, the same writer adds that whatever the motivation, the implementation was poor.[107] At Suvla Bay inadequately prepared troops were called on to carry out tasks that were not clearly defined, while being expected to rise to expectations that were not made explicit. They were inadequately led and poorly commanded, and in these circumstances the innate characteristics of the troops were magnified by the shortcomings of the military organization and the weaknesses of the system. What the example of Suvla Bay makes clear is that failure to adapt to changing military circumstances is a consequence of systemic and organizational weaknesses and not of individual shortcomings. The people at the front line certainly fail, but—contrary to what initial impressions often suggest—the more important failures occur in the rear.

7

Aggregate Failure
The Defeat of the American Eighth Army in Korea, November–December 1950

THE ROUT BEFORE THE YALU

What Happened

BY THE BEGINNING OF NOVEMBER 1950, American forces in Korea had come a very long way. Flung ashore in late June 1950 to bolster an under-armed Republic of Korea Army (ROKA) assaulted by some ten divisions of attacking North Korean People's Army (NKPA) forces, they had, at first, known only retreat. Taken from the four understrength and peacetime-soft divisions occupying Japan, they suddenly found themselves in battle with a tough, brutal, and well-equipped enemy. In the first two months of fighting American soldiers watched in disbelief as their bazooka rounds bounced off the armor of Soviet-made T-34 tanks. Men collapsed from fatigue and dysentery in the summer heat and stench of the Korean coun-tryside battling a foe whose assaults never paused. In a very short time Eighth Army had paid a heavy price to help ROK troops stop the Com-munist invaders. When the Twenty-fourth Infantry Division came out of the line on July 22 after two and a half weeks of fighting, for example, it had lost nearly a third of its initial strength.[1] By early August the American forces, now nominally under United Nations command, together with their ROK allies occupied a box of land some 75 by 40 miles around the south Korean port of Pusan. And the NKPA, despite enfeebling losses, lengthening supply lines, and American air power, stabbed by day and night at the undermanned perimeter.

By early September the tide had turned. Reinforcements streamed in from the United States and Japan; American aircraft—including propeller-driven P-51 Mustangs left over from World War II—harried the enemy; the ROK forces reorganized, and the first foreign contingents began to arrive. Under the overall command of General Douglas MacArthur, who served as commander in chief, Far East Command (CINCFE) and commander in chief, United Nations Command (CINCUNC), UN forces ground down the NKPA. The Eighth Army, which consisted of all U.S., Allied, and ROK forces in the Pusan perimeter held the enemy in check, while a new force, X Corps, spearheaded by the First Marine Division, prepared to outflank the enemy.

Despite the reservations of the Joint Chiefs of Staff and most of his subordinates, MacArthur launched X Corps at Inchon, high up the west coast of Korea, on September 15th. This bold maneuver succeeded: A formidable force of some 70,000 men, including the First Marine Division and Seventh Infantry Division, plus supporting troops and ROK marines, planted itself deep in the enemy rear. After still more bitter fighting along the Pusan perimeter, the Eighth Army broke through on September 22, scattering NKPA forces to the hills—where many would later regroup to form guerrilla bands. On September 27, X Corps linked up with the Eighth Army near Osan, South Korea.

MacArthur, with the consent of his superiors in Washington, now planned to complete the destruction of Communist forces in Korea, to cross the 38th Parallel, which had once divided South and North Korea, and to reunify Korea under President Syngman Rhee. MacArthur's Washington superiors, like CINCUNC himself, paid little attention to warnings from the newly created People's Republic of China that it would not tolerate the movement of UN forces north to the Yalu—indeed, past the 38th Parallel. Little attention, but some. The Joint Chiefs of Staff instructed MacArthur to proceed carefully, but in late September they and the secretary of defense instructed him: "We want you to feel unhampered tactically and strategically to proceed north of the 38th parallel."[2]

By the end of September UN forces had liberated Seoul and shortly thereafter began to prepare for a push north to the Yalu and the Chinese

UN Breakout and Linkup Attack and Pursuit, September 15 to October 26, 1950

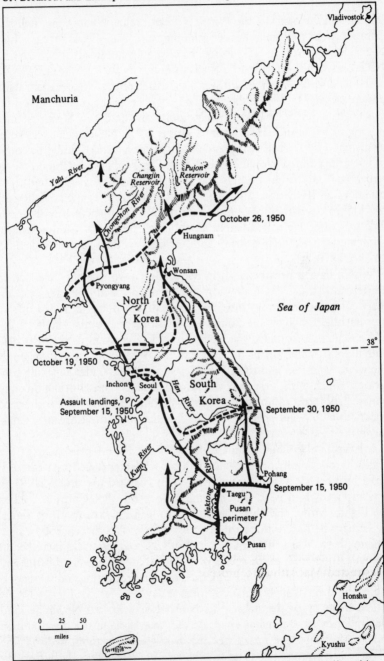

Vladivostok

Manchuria

Yalu River

Changjin Reservoir

Pujon Reservoir

Chongchon River

October 26, 1950

Hungnam

Pyongyang

Wonsan

North Korea

Sea of Japan

38°

October 19, 1950

Inchon

Seoul

Han River

South Korea

Assault landings,
September 15, 1950

September 30, 1950

Kum River

Pohang

September 15, 1950

Taegu

Naktong River

Pusan
perimeter

Pusan

Honshu

0   25   50
miles

Kyushu

SOURCE: Map from *The Korean War* by Matthew B. Ridgway. Copyright © 1967 by Matthew B. Ridgway. Reprinted by permission of Doubleday, a division of Bantam Doubleday Dell Publishing Group, Inc.

border. On October 19 the North Korean capital, Pyongyang, fell, and photographers took snapshots of grinning American officers sitting behind Kim Il Sung's massive desk. Problems of supply and steady, if weakening, NKPA resistance slowed the UN advance, but by late October US, ROK, and Allied forces prepared for a move farther north. X Corps had withdrawn through Inchon harbor and, on October 26, began landing on the east coast of Korea, after long delays caused by the heavy, Soviet-directed mining of Wonsan harbor. From October 25 to November 6, however elements of the Eighth Army and X Corps got a taste of things to come, in what the Chinese would call their First Phase Offensive. Chinese forces struck suddenly from the hills and then withdrew, after inflicting heavy casualties on ROK units and one American infantry regiment. Sobered a bit, UN forces paused once more and then began their final push north. The UN offensive ended barely a day after it began, as Chinese attacks slammed into the Eighth Army and X Corps on the night of November 26–27, 1950.

Within days it became clear, in MacArthur's words, that "we face an entirely new war."[3] ROK divisions simply disappeared from the situation maps. For the first time since the Battle of the Bulge in 1944, official reports referred to whole American divisions as "combat ineffective." Chinese units surrounded the First Marine Division and parts of the Seventh Infantry Division in the east and the Second Infantry Division in the west. American and ROK units began to retreat under appalling conditions, which in the east took the form of a sudden onset of the Siberian winter. UN forces tumbled south, and the Joint Chiefs of Staff authorized MacArthur to begin planning for the liquidation of the Korean commitment.

A letup in the Chinese attack, however, and the replacement of the Eighth Army commander, General Walton Walker (killed in a car accident) by General Matthew Ridgway, soon changed the situation. Ridgway received from MacArthur complete control of X Corps as well as the Eighth Army, and although he had to lead his men south of Seoul, by January he had restored the fighting spirit of UN forces. Following a Chinese New Year's offensive, a series of UN counterattacks increased in size and scope until, in the spring of 1951, UN forces liberated Seoul and had before them the prospect of Chinese armies retreating and surrendering in numbers as high as 10,000 men a day.

The memory of the debacle in North Korea in late November and December of 1950 remains vivid. At the time, it came as a great-enough shock: Afterward, the puzzle became even greater. It transpired that the Chinese had warned the West in a variety of ways, particularly through propaganda and messages conveyed by the Indian ambassador to Peking,

K. M. Panikkar, that they would intervene in force shou
move north.[4] Examination of Far East Command and Eigh
gence reports reveals that more direct sources of information ~~~
forces reasonably well apprised of the size of Chinese forces moving to
the Yalu border, though not over it. In addition, before the Chinese struck
in late November, the Eighth Army alone had taken nearly one hundred
Chinese prisoners of war, and these had proved remarkably cooperative
in describing the order of battle and even the plans of the Chinese armies
massing in the north.

The disaster in North Korea—which remains the largest defeat suffered
by American arms since the Battle of the Bulge—reflected a double failure. American forces failed first to anticipate the probable behavior of the
enemy. In retrospect the signs of large-scale Chinese intervention seem
unambiguous. Intelligence from a variety of sources—direct communications from the enemy, espionage, prisoner-of-war interrogation, and others—pointed to a massive Chinese intervention in the war. The American
experience suggests as well a failure of organizational learning, because
UN forces had had at least one direct experience with Chinese forces a
month before the real onslaught. Moreover, the People's Liberation
Army (PLA) had demonstrated its abilities in the course of protracted
war with both the Japanese and the government of Chiang Kai-shek: the
seeming lightheartedness with which American commanders viewed their
intervention seems all the more puzzling.

What Was the Disaster?

Although many have written about the failure of November–December
1950, few have defined it precisely. Was it the failure to anticipate any
kind of Chinese intervention, or just the kind that transpired? Was it,
more narrowly, the operational failure that ensued, the humiliating rout
of UN and, most notably, U.S. forces? Or was it the years of stalemate
that followed, in which American, ROK, and Allied forces seemed to
suffer for no purpose? No matter how they define the failure, though,
most students of the Korean War have little trouble in assigning blame
for the debacle to Douglas MacArthur.[5] Even as thorough and thoughtful
a chronicler of the Korean War as Clay Blair denounces MacArthur's
"reckless, egotistical strategy after Inchon . . . an arrogant, blind march
to disaster."[6]

MacArthur has probably attracted more praise and damnation than any
other twentieth-century American military figure. One may choose
which episodes in his career to look at—a brilliant record as a divisional
commander in World War I, the unreadiness of his forces in the Philip-

pines in 1941, the island-hopping drive from the Southwest Pacific in 1943–45, his benign dictatorship over occupied Japan, the Inchon landing, the final clash with President Truman and his relief from command—each suggests different views of him as a commander and a man. Revealingly, Matthew Ridgway concluded an unsparing discussion of MacArthur's faults with the remark "when Fate suddenly decided that I would serve directly under him in Korea I welcomed the chance to associate once again with one of the few geniuses it has been my privilege to know."[7] Wisely, perhaps, MacArthur's chief biographer decided to tell the story as straightforwardly as possible without condemnation or praise, because there is plenty of room for both.[8]

But should MacArthur be the "man in the dock"? To decide this we must examine more closely the nature of the events of early winter 1950, answering at least two questions. Did MacArthur's decisions alone, or even chiefly, provoke the large-scale Chinese intervention? Did the operational failure—the collapse of some American units (most notably the Second Infantry Division) and the subsequent retreat south—result from MacArthur's dispositions and pressure on his commanders to complete the advance to the Yalu?

The precise chain of arguments and events by which the Chinese decided to intervene in the Korean War remains unclear, although the reasons may be less obscure than they seemed at the time.[9] In October 1950 Washington intelligence agencies worried chiefly that China would intervene if American troops appeared likely to threaten Manchuria. In particular, they believed that should American (rather than ROK) troops approach the Yalu, the Chinese would react strongly out of anxiety about their hydroelectric complexes along that river and industry farther north. On the whole, the Americans believed that Chinese anxieties would take a narrow and traditional hue.[10] The Office of Chinese Affairs in the Department of State thought that the Chinese might act out of broader ideological concerns, but the views of the Central Intelligence Agency (and above all its director, General Walter Bedell Smith) predominated. These focused on the supposed importance to China of a *cordon sanitaire* south of Manchuria.[11]

The instructions the Joint Chiefs of Staff sent to MacArthur indicated that they read the situation no differently than did the CIA. They ordered MacArthur not to bomb targets within 5 miles of the Manchurian border, and to refrain from sending American troops to the Yalu. The JCS made their reasoning explicit to Secretary of Defense Marshall, arguing that although they did not know Chinese objectives, the most logical ones were the safeguarding of the Yalu border and the power complexes nearby.[12] If one accepts this view, MacArthur's violation of JCS directives (including his use of American troops in the advance to the Yalu) seemed responsible for the Chinese attack. The resulting confusion extends even to one American official historian, who writes:

> It was this suspicion of all communists everywhere which impaired the ability of American leaders to deal with the communist powers as ordinary states with interests, limitations and needs; the communist states were seen as Principalities of Darkness which could be given no quarter. . . . It was this [belief] which produced the feeling among many military leaders, most especially General MacArthur, that the war should be pursued to total victory, no matter what the cost.[13]

In fact, however, CIA and JCS assessment before November 27 reflected just the reverse—a sense that the Chinese had limited, reasonable, and indeed "ordinary" interests. But Chinese propaganda broadcasts and warnings to Ambassador Panikkar suggested that the crossing by UN forces of the 38th Parallel, and their determination to reunify Korea, constituted the *casus belli* in Chinese eyes.[14] Moreover, prisoner of war interrogation reports suggest that the Chinese expected a complete victory, as a result of which they would expel UN forces from Korea and reunify it on *their* terms.[15] All evidence indicates that the Chinese did not intend merely to restore the *status quo ante*, but to drive the UN out of Korea, and perhaps to force Western influence out of other regions of Asia as well.[16]

Why, then, did the Chinese delay their full-fledged entry in the war until late November, if UN forces made known their decision to cross the 38th Parallel almost two months earlier? The answers seem fairly simple: Before Inchon the Chinese did not expect the NKPA to fall apart and certainly not as quickly as it did, and it took time to make adequate war preparations. The Chinese politburo's decision for full-fledged intervention in the Korean War was not made until October 4, and even then, with some hesitations.[17] The Chinese had to move hundreds of thousands of troops into position; moreover, they required sophisticated civil defense, logistical, and even propaganda preparations before they began a war with a formidable foe. Even the Spartan PLA could not concentrate its forces (many deployed in the interior or opposite Taiwan) within days or weeks—months were required, and indeed, MacArthur may have been correct (if self-interested) when he declared that the final assault of late November began before the Chinese had completely prepared for battle. We cannot hold MacArthur solely or even primarily responsible for provoking the Chinese into attacking UN forces. Once the UN, and above all the American government, had adopted the goal of unifying Korea, it set in motion the Chinese intervention. MacArthur shared, no doubt, in the making of a flawed policy, but he did not initiate or determine it. We will, moreover, exclude that larger failure from our analysis here, for it is distinct from the second and equally disturbing one: the operational failure.

What, then, of MacArthur's responsibility for the costly and humiliating defeats of November–December 1950? Here the question becomes more complicated. We should note first a point raised above in chapter 3: Disasters are heterogeneous. The experiences of the First Marine Division at the Chosin Reservoir and the Second Infantry Division at Kunu-ri offer instructive contrasts. The former retreated in good order, bringing their dead and wounded and all their equipment with them. Casualties were heavy, but the Chinese forces opposite them suffered far more heavily, losing tens of thousands of men to Marine firepower and the bitter winter. When the Marines finally withdrew by sea from Hungnam on the Korean east coast they did so in the absence of enemy pressure. By dint of stout fighting a force some 25,000 strong, or barely a sixth of U.S. forces in Korea (and a twentieth of all UN forces), had disabled approximately between a quarter and a third of all Chinese forces in Korea. The Second Infantry Division, by way of contrast, suffered approximately 30 percent casualties, lost virtually all its equipment, and escaped the gauntlet, as S. L. A. Marshall described it, a collection of small, desperate groups of men.[18] Although it surely inflicted damage on its Chinese opponents, it had nothing like the success of the marines. Marshall, perhaps the greatest of all American combat historians and the author of the most important studies of combat in this phase of the Korean War, concluded that systemic—and unnecessary—differences between army and marine methods accounted for the very different outcomes.[19]

MacArthur did indeed urge his men forward in late November 1950, and thus precipitated the disaster before the Yalu. He did so despite the reservations of some of his commanders, most notably Major General Oliver P. Smith, commander of the First Marine Division. He urged the Eighth Army and X Corps forward, however, not out of sheer fecklessness but in order to gain the Yalu River before it froze, after which the Chinese would find it easier to cross and bombing of the bridges across it would be pointless. General Walker, commander of the Eighth Army, expressed some reservations about the move but nowhere nearly as forcefully as General Smith. The records of the Eighth Army, including intelligence reports, operations orders, and war diaries, reveal concern but no enormous anxiety about an (under)estimated Chinese force of some 100,000 to 150,000 men between themselves and the Yalu.[20] As late as November 27, for example, *after* the Chinese attack had begun, the G-1 (personnel) section of the Eighth Army was worried chiefly about shortages of stationery and razor blades, and about making preparations for Operation Relax, a rotation of U.S. forces to Japan for rest and recreation.[21] On the whole, the Eighth Army expected some resistance from Chinese forces but nothing overwhelming. G-2 (intelligence) at Far East Command in Tokyo took a similar view, declaring on November 26 that UN forces faced between nine and twelve Chinese divisions and the scattered remnants of NKPA forces—a maximum of 150,000 men.[22] Opposing them were some 153,000 American soldiers, 25,000 marines, 20,000 Allied forces (including 11,000 British and 5,000 Turkish troops), and some 224,000 ROK troops—a grand total of more than 422,000 combat troops, backed by ample air power.[23] With few exceptions, American commanders ordered their forces forward warily but not reluctantly: Their commander-in-chief's tempered confidence did not greatly exceed their own. Intelligence underestimated Chinese forces in Korea, but its estimates of overall Chinese strength along the border was fairly good.

After the Chinese First Phase Offensive, MacArthur curtailed the drawdown of manpower and supplies that had gone on in anticipation of an early end to the war. He pressed for special measures—above all, an intensive air campaign against the Yalu bridges and the area between the river and UN forces—to cope with the growing Chinese threat. By no means did he simply disregard disagreeable intelligence or convince subordinates to "cook" it. Moreover, MacArthur appears to have read Chinese motives better than did George Marshall, the secretary of defense, informing the latter on November 8, 1950:

> I do not believe that the hydroelectric system is the dominant consideration animating the Communist intervention in Korea. . . . they [the Chinese] now make first-class soldiers and are gradually developing competent staffs and commanders. This has produced a new and dominant power in Asia which for its own purposes is allied with Soviet Russia, but which in its own concepts and methods has become aggressively imperialistic with a lust for expansion and increased power normal to this type of imperialism.[24]

There were two quite distinct failures in Korea in the summer and fall of 1950. The first, which involved not just MacArthur but the entire American government, stemmed from the misjudgment of Chinese willingness to fight a large war to prevent unification of Korea. Whether or not this failure was a culpable one or not, it clearly concerned all who participated in the decision to allow UN forces north of the 38th Parallel. The second failure, which concerns us here, is the operational one. Why did American forces suffer so badly at the hands of the Chinese? Why did only the First Marine Division inflict on the enemy the kind of damage that, by rights, it should have suffered from the Eighth Army as well? As an exasperated Ridgway told his subordinates on January 8, 1951, "We have almost every advantage except that of numbers and it is difficult to believe that with all we have, we can't defeat the enemy."[25] Given that war with China in Korea probably became inevitable after the decision to move north of the 38th Parallel, why did most U.S. forces come off so badly in its first few months?

The problem is all the more puzzling because the Chinese forces, apparently so formidable, had glaring weaknesses that UN forces could (and in the case of the marines, did) exploit.[26] They had few if any tanks and very little field artillery: For the most part they attacked using infantry mortars, light machine guns, and hand grenades. Short of motor and even animal transport, their divisions lacked staying power. After a few days' fighting they had to return to their rear areas to replenish ammunition and food, and their wounded had little prospect of recovery save through individual resilience. The bitter cold, particularly in eastern Korea, struck at them far harder than at the well-clothed and -equipped Americans: Quilted cotton jackets were no match for Siberian winds and snows. And even under less-than-arctic conditions—wet rather than dry cold—their clothing did not shield thousands of them from death by exposure.

The second Chinese offensive, beginning on November 26–27 hurled into battle some 300,000 PLA soldiers in eighteen lightly armed infantry divisions against the Eighth Army and another dozen against X Corps. Opposing them stood seventeen Eighth Army and X Corps divisions (seven of them American) plus forces worth at least another division of fine British, Commonwealth, and Turkish troops. Counting the remaining NKPA forces, who lent some support to the Chinese, the opposing forces were roughly equal in size—some 400,000 men each. To be sure, the Chinese had enormous reserves behind them in Manchuria, and the ROK units (at this stage of the war at any rate) demonstrated a terror of the Chinese at odds with their more creditable performance against the NKPA. On the other hand, UN forces had overwhelming superiority in matériel of every kind—from artillery to food, radios to medical facilities—and air superiority only sporadically challenged by Chinese (and possibly Soviet-piloted) MIG-15s flying out of Manchuria.

UN Command and its field forces *expected* to meet stiff resistance from Chinese forces (though not a full counterattack) as they advanced. When they did so they faced no gross disparity in numbers and possessed large advantages in firepower. Nonetheless, they—and in particular the Eighth Army—suffered a costly and humiliating defeat. Herein lies the failure we will examine below.

THE ROOTS OF DISASTER

Intelligence Unaware

Students and even practitioners of intelligence often suggest that it has two chief functions: warning (predicting what an opponent is about to do) and order of battle (information about the who, what, and where of an enemy's forces).[27] In respect to both kinds of intelligence the United States fell short in November 1950. The failure to predict large-scale Chinese intervention is perhaps the more understandable, since there appears to have been some considerable debate within China about the wisdom of a full-fledged offensive in Korea.[28] American analysts devalued what appears in retrospect the best sources of intelligence—Chinese Nationalists reporting back to Taiwan. Reports from these sources warned that the Chinese Communists "intend to throw [the] book at UNO forces in Korea."[29] UN intelligence took the possibility of such an intervention seriously, and, as we have mentioned, MacArthur acted on it, most notably by ordering an intensified air campaign in North Korea.[30] Indeed, one reason for the seemingly cavalier reception accorded Panikkar's warning was that American officials believed that the Chinese already had begun to intervene in Korea—the only question was one of scale.[31]

One of the Allies' senior intelligence officers in World War II remarked that intelligence can only tell a commander that "the stage is set and that the circumstances and conditions appear to be propitious for the other side to do this or that."[32] And in fact, American intelligence, and particularly G-2, FEC, did allow that a vigorous Chinese attack could occur, but did not discuss what form it might take or what it might mean.[33] Both FEC and Eighth Army intelligence acknowledged that as UN forces neared the Yalu, warning time would decrease, and that rapid reinforcement from China remained possible. If we accept as appropriate the more modest objective of letting the commander know that "the stage is set," we must conclude that American intelligence did not fail in November 1950.

On order of battle the picture is more mixed, for FEC and Eighth Army intelligence certainly underestimated the number of Chinese troops actually in North Korea. On November 16, for example it estimated that the Chinese had twelve divisions in North Korea, although it vitiated that estimate by declaring that these units numbered only four to six thousand men each, rather than the 10,000 men per division that was their real strength. At the same time, however, intelligence took note of the enormous reserve strength in Manchuria—more than 460,000 regulars, plus 370,000 district troops.[34] Eighth Army intelligence was even more pessimistic, placing opposing Chinese forces at somewhere between 100,000 and 150,000 men. This underestimated Chinese forces by something like a factor of three, an error partly excused by the acknowledged difficulty of identifying Chinese units as they crossed the border.

The failures—or more accurately, semifailures—in warning and order of battle intelligence have received a good deal of attention from students of the Chinese surprise attack in 1950. Another more serious and generally ignored type of intelligence failure occurred, however: failure to gauge the enemy's way of war, his methods, strengths, and weaknesses.[35] It is in the picture of the enemy held by U.S. forces in the Far East that we find one of the chief sources of the failure of the winter of 1950.

The problem did not stem from a lack of basic data. Intelligence in both Tokyo and the field knew fairly well the table of organization and equipment of the average Chinese division, which it explicitly compared with that of the NKPA divisions with whom UN forces had fought for nearly half a year.[36] They noted that NKPA units had a full suite of modern Soviet equipment, where the Chinese had a meager hodgepodge of captured Japanese and American weapons. The average NKPA division, for example, had a total of forty artillery pieces—including medium-caliber howitzers—per division. The Chinese had barely nine pieces, and those were light 76-mm. howitzers. NKPA divisions had four times as many heavy machine guns and more antitank weapons than their Chinese counterparts. Chinese divisions were superior in personnel (by all of thirty men), the number of light machine guns and light (60-mm.) mortars, but drastically inferior in transport and support—the average NKPA division had some two hundred vehicles as opposed to none for the Chinese. Intelligence, therefore, came to view Chinese forces as a kind of inferior version of the North Koreans:

The quality of the Chinese Communist fighting man is probably similar to that of the well-trained Korean soldier in mid-campaign.

However, it is to be recognized that most of the CCF troops have had no significant experience in combat operations against a major combat power. In addition, their training, like that of the original North Korean forces, has been greatly handicapped by the lack of uniform equipment and assured stocks of munitions.[37]

Intelligence failed to grasp the crucial fact that UN forces faced not two varieties of the same opponent, but two completely different kinds of enemy altogether. The PLA was not simply a watered-down version of the NKPA but a *different* army, with unique strengths, weaknesses, tactics, and operational preferences. The vehicle-heavy NKPA, for example, moved and deployed like the conventional forces they were. The extreme "lightness" of Chinese divisions, on the other hand, meant that they could hide in and infiltrate through the forests and villages of North Korea, subsisting on provisions requisitioned from local peasants or carried by their own troops. No large supply trains clogged the roads in North Korea, although American aircraft did notice large movements in Manchuria.

The Soviet-equipped NKPA fought for the most part as Soviet divisions would have, using combined arms and depending on conventional means of resupply.[38] Their tactics centered on the frontal assault backed by tanks and artillery, supported by powerful flank attacks, and accompanied by infiltration behind enemy lines. Early on, at any rate, the NKPA fought by day and in the open. They maintained an unremitting offensive, even when their situation might have suggested that defense would be a more prudent posture. Even after the Eighth Army had consolidated its position in the Pusan perimeter in late August, North Korean forces continued to batter their heads against forces superior not only in firepower, but sheer numbers as well.

The Chinese did not fight this way. They attacked mainly by night, using large quantities of hand grenades, light machine gun and mortar fire (which, it will be remembered, were the weapons they had in greater supply than their North Korean counterparts) from very close ranges.[39] They usually approached from the rear, after drawing enemy fire by sniping and bugle or pipe music. Operationally, the Chinese had a more subtle approach than the North Koreans: feinting, probing, or withdrawing (as they did after the First Phase Offensive) in order to test enemy reactions or to confuse and intimidate them. They followed thereby the maxims of Sun Tzu, from whom Mao Zedong had derived much of the PLA's doctrine:

All warfare is based on deception.

Therefore, when capable, feign incapacity; when active, inactivity. When near, make it appear that you are far away; when far away, that you are near.

Offer the enemy a bait to lure him; feign disorder and strike him.

When he concentrates, prepare against him; where he is strong avoid him. . . .

Pretend inferiority and encourage his arrogance.

Keep him under a strain and wear him down.

When he is united, divide him.

Attack where he is unprepared; sally out when he does not expect you.[40]

This way of war helps us make sense of the First Phase Offensive, so often misunderstood as a diplomatic signal rather than as what it was—an important piece of campaign strategy designed to gain information, test tactics, and bewilder the opponent. As the Chinese commander later wrote, "We employed the tactics of purposely showing ourselves to be weak, increasing the arrogance of the enemy, letting him run amuck, and luring him deep into our areas."[41]

Only toward the end of December did Far East Command publish extensive discussions of Chinese tactics that suggested that the Chinese had a distinctive tactical and operational approach to war.[42] Before then such information appeared only sporadically and in odd corners of the Daily Intelligence Summaries. Far East Command did describe Chinese and North Korean guerrilla tactics, and the Eighth Army's IX Corps wrote one short note on Chinese "Hachi Shiki" (inverted-V) tactics.[43] As we have mentioned, intelligence had access to order-of-battle information from which might have been inferred (though no one did) that they might use novel tactics. Until fairly late in December 1950, however, one finds in intelligence reports no explicit consideration of what qualitative change in fighting might occur if the Chinese entered the fray. Rather, intelligence assumed that the Chinese would demonstrate (though in lesser degree) the strengths and weaknesses of the NKPA.

This latter proved to be a crucial point, because intelligence believed that it had discovered the North Koreans' critical vulnerability. Only weeks before the large-scale Chinese entry into the war, intelligence confirmed what American commanders had long believed: American airpower had paralyzed the NKPA. In-depth interviews of two thousand NKPA prisoners of war revealed that over half the NKPA's equipment losses and a third of its personnel losses stemmed from aircraft—twice as much damage to equipment and the same damage to personnel as inflicted by artillery.[44] FEC Intelligence concluded that:

> the net effect of such tactical air support was the greatest single factor contributing to the successful conduct of UN ground operations against the North Korean Communist invaders. . . . Based entirely upon PW [prisoner of war] reactions this study indicates that there can be no doubt that the impact of UN air efforts in the tactical support of UN ground forces probably has been the greatest single factor contributing to the overall success of the UN Ground Force scheme of maneuver.[45]

Air power, not the Inchon landing, had blocked the success and weakened the grip of the North Koreans investing the Pusan perimeter. General Walker, commander of the Eighth Army, put it bluntly: "I will gladly lay my cards on the table and state that if it had not been for the air support that we received from the Fifth Air Force we would not have been able to stay in Korea."[46] In proportion to its size the Eighth Army had behind it more fighter-bomber support than did Omar Bradley's Army Group storming across Europe in 1944.[47] It thought very highly of that support, and analysis proved it right to do so.

FEC Intelligence judged that UN air power would force the Chinese "to campaign under the same psychological and physical handicaps as those borne by the North Koreans."[48] American commanders judged—quite rightly—that those handicaps had been extreme and possibly decisive. Small wonder, then, that at the Wake Island conference of October 15, 1950, General MacArthur had assured President Truman that because of American air power "if the Chinese tried to get down to Pyongyang there would be the greatest slaughter."[49] Small wonder too that he fought so hard—at times almost hysterically—to get permission from the Joint Chiefs of Staff for an immediate and unrestricted air campaign right up the Yalu River and against the bridges across it.[50] MacArthur did not simply discount Chinese intervention, but he thought he had the antidote to it, in the form of broken bridges, strafed roads and tracks, and if necessary, incinerated villages and towns.

The Chinese did indeed respect American air power, but their organization and tactics allowed them to minimize its impact. By operating off the roads, at night, and close-in against UN forces, they negated much of the advantage of enemy air superiority. Their superlative camouflage and march discipline (soldiers stood stock still when an enemy airplane came into view, and officers had authority to shoot those who moved) hid them from aerial observation. In the short term, at any rate, and so long as they did not have long supply lines to maintain, the Chinese could conduct an offensive against American and ROK forces that the more conventional NKPA could not. They made of their material weakness, in other words, an operational strength.

The deficiencies of American intelligence stemmed in large part from analytical assumptions, but we cannot divorce these from the sources that helped shape those assumptions.[51] We know that prisoner-of-war interrogation yielded a great deal of information, and indeed often provided the most useful intelligence concerning the Chinese. A shortage of Chinese linguists, however, coupled with insufficient appreciation on the part of lower echelons of the importance of prompt evacuation of prisoners of war to higher levels slowed the transmissions of this kind of intelligence. Unfortunately, American intelligence treated prisoner-of-war information with reserve, failing to believe that Chinese enlisted men would possibly have as much knowledge of their organizations and overall strategy as they claimed. In this they failed again to understand the peculiar nature of their opponents, who stressed the importance of explaining their mission in great detail to their men.[52]

If it undervalued POW intelligence, G-2 overestimated the thoroughness with which aerial reconnaissance could keep track of the enemy. Desperately short not only of photo-interpreters but of photo-reconnaissance aircraft, Far East Command concentrated its resources on inspecting the bomb damage from its deep interdiction raids, particularly strikes against the Yalu bridges.[53] Virtually no careful photo-reconnaissance of other areas in North Korea occurred. S. L. A. Marshall discovered in November 1950 that as many as ten days would frequently pass between a request from the Eighth Army for aerial photographs and G-2's receipt of them—and often the Eighth Army received no more than three or four such reports a day.[54] Given Chinese abilities to move under cover and at night, and to lie up during the day, photographic intelligence, which had proved invaluable in World War II, fell short of its promise.

We know little about two other major sources of information, espionage and signals intelligence. From various sources it appears that such spy networks as UN forces had at their disposal crumpled once the North Koreans invaded the south, and despite strenuous efforts were never fully replaced. Chinese Nationalist reporting and occasional contacts through Hong Kong provided some limited but useful information on operational and strategic matters. Signal intelligence is a closed book (the army official historical monograph on the subject does not even mention it) and will remain so until National Security Agency files on the subject are opened in the year 2000. Though we may make several inferences from information in the FEC intelligence reports, these are no more than guesses. We know that the Chinese made relatively little use of radio, preferring (for good reason) to rely on intrinsically more secure land lines. At the lower levels (from regiment on down) Chinese units had no radios at all—a weakness in terms of tactical flexibility but a strength in terms of security. On the other hand, it is difficult to see how American intelligence could have tracked the movement of dozens of divisions into Manchuria and the border area during September, October, and November of 1950 if not by interception of radio signals.

Some otherwise puzzling mistakes by American intelligence—the relative rebound in confidence about Chinese intervention after the First Phase Offensive, the dramatic underestimate of Chinese divisional strengths, and the complete failure to sense Chinese preference for offensive operations—may be explicable by deliberate Chinese deception. Such efforts would be completely in character with both the Chinese style of war and Soviet practice in World War II—and the Soviets, if not the instigators of Chinese intervention, certainly aided and abetted it in a variety of ways. Signal intelligence may, therefore, have both aided and betrayed UN intelligence.

The above is, of course, pure speculation. We know for a fact that FEC and the Eighth Army ignored one valuable and freely available source of intelligence until December 1950. S. L. A. Marshall observed that G-2 had elaborate procedures to gather all kinds of intelligence, neglecting the possibility that "perhaps more is to be learned of the enemy from what has been seen, heard and felt by our own soldiers in the line."

> There is [however] no steady winnowing of this field of information. There is no machinery for adding it up, analyzing it across the board, and then deducing its lessons. . . . Infantry, being the body which under the normal situation in war maintains the most persistent contact with the fighting parts of the enemy, is the antenna of the mechanism of combat intelligence. . . . During field operations, infantry should be the *most* productive source of information pertaining to the enemy's tactics, use of weapons, combat supply system, habits and general nature.[55]

Marshall put his belief to the test, and produced the remarkable studies to which we have earlier referred, "CCF in the Attack," which quickly found their way into American Intelligence reports and thereafter into

American tactics. He gained his insight into the Chinese mode of warfare chiefly through extremely detailed interrogation of American infantry companies fresh from the winter battles. Had he, a civilian contractor (albeit a reserve lieutenant colonel) not done this, we might even today lack a coherent picture of Chinese small-unit tactics in that early period of the Korean War.

The Fragile Army

We will return later to Marshall's investigations, which have more than a passing significance. To complete our preliminary analysis of the failure in Korea, we must look at the forces on which the blows fell, at the American units, which numbered at least 175,000 all told, not counting 250,000 ROK and some 20,000 Allied troops. That the ROKA, pummeled by the North Koreans and almost superstitiously fearful of the Chinese, fell back is understandable. These were scratch forces, underequipped and hastily raised—the underofficered and ill-trained ROKA of July 1950 had doubled in size in five months, despite heavy losses. With some notable exceptions, its quality was poor. But what of the Eighth Army and X Corps, which had had over five months to shake themselves into fighting shape, which had rebounded from the calamities of June and July, endured the hard slugging of August and September, and participated in a triumphant advance in October and November? Why, with the enormous firepower ranged above and behind them—the average American infantry division had a third more artillery than its World War II predecessor— did American forces fall back? And why were some units, in particular, the Second Infantry Division in the west and parts of the Seventh Infantry Division in the east, broken by an army of peasant light infantrymen?

The Eighth Army was a hollow force. If we look behind the ample machinery of war it possessed, we find that at the sharp end, in the small fighting units at the front, its forces had suffered crippling losses. When MacArthur reviewed the first American unit to enter Pyongyang, "He asked all men in the company who had landed with it in Korea ninety-six days earlier, when it numbered nearly two hundred men, to step forward. Only five men stepped forward; three of them had been wounded."[56] As in World War II, infantry units at the lowest levels had born the brunt of the fighting; thus, a division that suffered "only" 10 percent casualties might have infantry platoons and companies at barely half strength. The Japan-based divisions that had entered the fray in June and July were a third or more understrength to begin with, and the flow of replacements did not catch up throughout this period. At the end of

November, Far East Command reported that the U.S. forces in the entire theater (including Japan), numbering 220,000 men, were fully 80,000 under authorized strength.[57] Part of the problem lay with the simultaneous expansion of the army in Europe, and the determination of the Joint Chiefs of Staff to assign equal (and in some cases higher) priority to forces there. Part of the problem, however, seems to have come from the same lack of attention to the problem of replacements that had bedeviled the army in World War II. Given the shortage of replacements (which did not begin to outnumber losses until January 1951), army planners faced a cruel dilemma. On the one hand, the heaviest losses fell in infantry units; on the other hand support units (engineers, for example) had started off with the greatest peacetime shortages. Where combat units in prewar Japan had about half their authorized strength, support units had barely a quarter.[58] By November 1950 support troops numbered less than a third of the total force in Korea, at precisely the time they were most needed to repair the damage done by heavy fighting and to maintain lengthening lines of communication.[59] UN service units reached their Korean War nadir in the month of November—31 percent of the total force, as compared with the 45 percent they would number at its end.

The U.S. army therefore sent as many service replacements as combat replacements to Korea.[60] As in World War II, the infantry replacement problem suffered not only from their scanty numbers, but from their method of handling before they entered the line. Men died under the command of lieutenants (themselves often new to the units) who had not had time to learn their names.[61] To remedy the shortage of infantry replacements, in August 1950 Far East Command instituted the practice of fleshing out American units with ROK troops. The Korean Augmentation to United States Army (KATUSA) program failed in all of its many variants, which included the use of Koreans as individual replacements or in small units such as squads or platoons. In early November the commanding general of the Second Infantry Division expressed a common view: "There has been no change in the low combat efficiency of the ROK personnel."[62] Not surprisingly, barriers of language and culture prevented the ill-trained KATUSAs from become full-fledged members of their host units. The lack of mutual trust proved disastrous, particularly in night combat, when American troops and KATUSAs had no confidence or, indeed, intelligible conversation with one another. In November 1950 the KATUSA program had reached its Korean War peak: 39,000 Korean troops served in American units.[63]

It should be noted that only one American division stood at full authorized strength and had no KATUSA: the First Marine Division. Army divisions, for the most part, were at approximately 80 percent strength, which translated into 50 percent or less strength in the infantry companies. Why did undermanning make a difference on the battlefield? The answer lies chiefly with the hilly terrain of North Korea and the tactics of the Eighth Army, which scattered isolated infantry companies in overnight positions. As the most powerful combat narrative of the war puts it: "Back of the regiment was a division, and back of the division an army, but the issue rested on how long a lone infantry company could stand unaided in defense of a solitary hill."[64] S. L. A. Marshall judged that the Army needed battalion-sized perimeters to hold off the Chinese, a practice common among the marines. A company at near full strength—some two hundred men—might have just enough strength to set up an all-around defense founded on foxholes, wire, obstacles, and well-sited automatic weapons. It could do all this and still send out patrols to link up with neighboring units and set up listening posts to detect an approaching enemy. Most of the infantry companies Marshall interviewed, however, averaged one hundred twenty-five men (one or more out of ten were flight-prone KATUSAs) when the Chinese hit.[65]

The shortage of service troops not only worsened a shortage of combat replacements but contributed to a debilitating logistical problem. The devastation wrought by hard fighting, North Korean scorched-earth tactics, and repeated U.S. air force attacks on the roads, rails, and bridges of Korea would have made it hard to keep a motorized and prodigal army on the march in the best of times. The lengthening supply lines brought about by the UN advance, the drain on American logistical support from mushrooming ROK and Allied forces, and the decision to withdraw X Corps through Inchon harbor further choked the logistical system. As a result, at the end of November 1950, the Eighth Army faced a logistical crisis: According to official records it began its advance with barely a day's worth of ammunition, one and a half day's ammunition, and only four days' food.[66] Enormous waste (the allocation of aviation gas as fuel for jeeps and trucks, for example) compounded the problem.

Laboring under manpower disadvantages they could not overcome, and subject to logistical pressures they did not fully confront, the Eighth Army commanders needed tactical skills of a high order to beat back the Chinese. Yet all the evidence suggests that despite many individual cases of courage and determined leadership, the average fell far short of what was required. A post-Korea study by the Infantry School at Fort Benning made scathing criticism of tactics in the 1950 campaign: It began by declaring that there were few new lessons to be learned—but very many to be relearned from experience in World II and before.[67] It mentioned in particular the lack of familiarity with night operations, insufficient patrolling, failure to coordinate such patrolling as did occur with artillery support, and improper use of the terrain. *The River and the Gauntlet* paints a harrowing picture of a 60-percent-strength company of the Second Infantry Division moving north on November 24, a day and a half before the Chinese onslaught:

> All but twelve men had thrown away their steel helmets; the pile cap was better insurance against frostbite and the steel helmet wouldn't fit over it. Only two men—new arrivals—carried the bayonet. The grenade load averaged less than one per man. Some rifle and carbine men carried as much as two extra bandoliers or six full clips. Others had as little as sixteen to thirty rounds on their persons. About one half of the company had dispensed with intrenching tools. . . . only a few men bothered to carry tinned rations on the march. Bedrolls and overcoats had been left behind.[68]

Throughout that chilling narrative S. L. A. Marshall describes units led in battle by men like the platoon leader who had "joined the company that morning. He didn't know the men, and he was having his first try at judging a tactical situation."[69] It is a story of units who have no cleaning supplies for their weapons, who get into their sleeping bags for the night without digging in, who give up trying to establish communications with units on their left or right because they run out of field telephone wire. Marshall tells of battalions like the one that

> had ceased issuing grenades to its individuals except as an emergency arose. When pressure slackened, the men tended to discard grenades into the unit trucks. Movement shook the pins loose, and equipment had been lost because of this carelessness.[70]

There was, as Marshall declared again and again, no lack of individual courage in army units. But, he wrote to a marine friend,

> On the other hand, I am not defending the Army—its training, disciplines, morale programs or anything else. I think we need reform until hell won't have it. The system directly contributes to the breakdown of men. . . . I think we could take over your methods and make them work in the Army on a broad scale. In fact, I have no doubt of it.
>
> Men are men. At base, the average American is still good; he wears testicles, though you would never think so, judging by what the Army does to condition him.

It isn't necessary—nor has it ever been so—to tell a Marine to have faith in his service.

But today, the average American just holds on and hopes that his Army is better than it looks—which it isn't.

Even the ranks are aware of the dry rot in the system.

You might judge from this letter that I am clean fed up. If so, you judge rightly. I had not thought it possible that we could do so many things so badly.[71]

In public Marshall leaped to the defense of the GIs and their commanders in Korea. In private—in letters and classified reports—he scourged the army he held responsible for the needless losses of November and December 1950. For Marshall, as for others who knew the full story, the rout of the Second Infantry Division, and the annihilation of Task Force Faith—over three thousand men from the Seventh Infantry Division east of the Chosin reservoir—were tales of peculiar horror. These men did not perish like Custer's Seventh Cavalry, outnumbered but at least among comrades, as a fighting unit. Rather, they died as lonely individuals or in splintered, scrabbling groups, at the hands of a cruel enemy in a frozen waste. The bitterness of men like Marshall was deepened by a sense that it need not have happened so. And it is to that part of the story we must turn next.

DISASTER REDEEMED

We have mentioned a number of times the experience of the First Marine Division. Its retreat (together with several thousand army and Allied troops) from the Chosin Reservoir was an epic of courage, endurance, and loyalty to comrades—the fighting fit brought back not only the living wounded but the frozen dead. Some 1,000 marines died or were reported missing, and 3,500 were wounded. Almost twice as many were nonbattle casualties, chiefly to frostbite. The retreat from Chosin was, however, a victory and not just a chance to live to fight again. The forces that attacked it, the twelve divisions of China's Ninth Army Group, Third Field Army, did not reappear in the field until March 1951. According to captured Chinese documents, some 25,000 men died at the hands of the Americans, another 12,000 were wounded, and tens of thousands more fell victim to the frigid weather that tortured even the well-clad and -equipped Americans.[72] When X Corps evacuated eastern Korea it did so under no significant enemy pressure: Its enemy lay prostrate in the hills to the north.

S. L. A. Marshall, working as an operations analyst for the army, obtained permission in December 1950 to study marine operations—about which, he found, the Eighth Army knew appallingly little.[73] This in turn led to other studies, including a sketch for a companion volume to *The River and the Gauntlet,* which he never completed. From these and other sources we can learn, however, why the marines did so well, both absolutely and relative to the army.

Some elements of this success have to do with certain intrinsic advantages of the Marines. They were, as we have noted, at full strength, particularly in their rifle companies. No competing buildup in Europe drained their frontline strength. They had even closer and more ample air support from their own marine air wing than the army got from the U.S. air force (which, however, provided a great deal of close air support in the retreat). Most of the marines had seen less fighting than the army divisions. Aside from one brigade introduced into the Pusan perimeter in August, most of the division took part only in the ten days' hard fighting of the Inchon landing and liberation of Seoul before being withdrawn for a repeatedly delayed landing at Wonsan on the east coast of Korea. Army divisions, by contrast, had been in the line more or less continuously since July and were feeling the strain.

All this said, the marines clearly coped far better with a challenge not too different from that which afflicted their army comrades in the west (and for that matter, in the east). They had in Major General Oliver P. Smith a commander of rare ability, who stubbornly refused to speed the northward advance (as ordered by X Corps commander Lieutenant General Edward M. Almond) until he had established adequate supply dumps and air strips along the Main Supply Route (MSR). Much of their success, however, can be attributed to very basic precautions: digging in every night, setting up barbed wire, noisemakers, and trip flares, aggressive patrolling, seizing the high ground. "[T]here was nothing radical or unorthodox. . . . It was war waged 'according to the book'; but done with such precision and power as to reilluminate the ancient truth that weapons when correctly used will invariably bring success."[74] Discipline never broke. Battalion commanders checked that troops had dug foxholes before turning in, even though they had to chip away at half a foot of frozen dirt. Company commanders watched each man perform the painful but necessary ritual of changing his sweat-soaked socks every evening despite the howling cold, in order to prevent frostbite. When the first battered units arrived at Hungnam

The men of our battalion were exhausted physically, mentally, and emotionally. We received word we were going aboard ship.
Everyone was instructed to clean weapons and all other gear before boarding. We used fish oil and rags to get the weapons in shape. This was in keeping with our basic training.[75]

By enforcing such drudgery the marines retained their fighting effectiveness.

To competent senior leadership and a solid grounding in the basics of warfare, the marines added appropriate tactics. After some initial setbacks in the Chinese First Phase Offensive at the end of October and beginning of November

the Marines established a tactical principle for coming weeks: that to nullify Chinese night tactics, regardless of large scale penetrations and infiltration, defending units had only to maintain position until daybreak. With observation restored, Marine firepower would melt down the Chinese mass to impotency.[76]

Unlike the isolated infantry companies of the Second Infantry Division, marine units did not retreat under the pressure of enemy attacks—which, contrary to newspaper accounts, did not swamp defending units by suicidal charges, but rather broke them by steadily increasing pressure. Moreover, on the whole, the marines hunkered down at night in perimeters larger than the company-size formations used by the Eighth Army. Where accounts of the fighting in army divisions usually feature the names of company and (rarely) battalion commanders, the marine histories talk more of the regimental commanders who coordinated the fight. Benefiting from carefully fostered contact with the local Korean population, marine intelligence kept the divisional commander and his subordinates aware of the Chinese buildup on their front and flanks. When the Chinese hit the marines were mentally and physically ready for them.

One further point: marine logistics kept the Marine Division fully equipped with all of the necessities of warfare, from bullets to plasma, food to warming tents, winter weather gear to barbed wire and trip flares. Much of this had to do with the easy access the marines had to navy supply ships and an operating port nearby. Logistics in the Eighth Army were, as we have noted, much more uneven. Every active duty soldier in the Eighth Army (except some hapless replacements) got a Thanksgiving dinner of turkey and trimmings, but in order to achieve this result the logistical command suspended the airlift of winter field jackets from Japan to the Second and Twenty-fifth Infantry Divisions.[77] Units found themselves running short of grenades and gasoline, barbed wire, trip flares, and antipersonnel mines—although, as Marshall noted, they rarely asked for these last three items, which would have proved useful indeed. Shortages did not lead to more careful measures of conservation at the front.

That the kind of performance turned in by the Marines rested on no mysterious formula for victory became apparent once General Matthew Ridgway took command of the Eighth Army following General Walker's death in December 1950. Ridgway immediately expressed outrage at the conditions in the Eighth Army. Finding on his initial inspection not only a lack of spirit and vigor but gross tactical deficiencies as well, he used, as he put it, "impolite language" with his subordinates.

> What I told the field commanders in essence was that their infantry ancestors would roll over in their graves could they see how roadbound this army was, how often it forgot to seize the high ground along its route, how it failed to seek and maintain contact in its front, how little it knew of the terrain and how seldom took advantage of it, how reluctant it was to get off its bloody wheels and put shoe leather to the earth, to get into the hills and among the scrub and meet the enemy where he lived. As for communications, I told them to go back to grandfather's day if they had to—to use runners if the radio and phones were out, or smoke signals if they could devise no better way.[78]

Although the official histories pass over it lightly, Ridgway purged the officer corps of the Eighth Army: "Selected superior officers took over command of regiments and battalions and soon corrected the basic weaknesses in our training."[79] He also took a ruthless attitude toward waste and tightened up the Eighth Army's poor logistical discipline.

With only marginally greater resources than had been available to Walker (some increases in replacements, and command of X Corps, which had hitherto operated independently) Ridgway turned the battle around. The Chinese New Year's offensive, following a several weeks' pause in which the Chinese resupplied themselves and replaced decimated units with fresh ones, failed to break the Eighth Army, although UN forces continued to fall back to the Han River. By May 1951, however, the Eighth Army (now under the leadership of James Van Fleet, who succeeded Ridgway after the latter became commander in chief, Far East, following MacArthur's relief), was driving north against crumbling resistance. On a single day over 10,000 Chinese and NKPA troops surrendered to UN forces, and little could have stopped American, ROK, and Allied troops from retaking Pyongyang and indeed driving back to the Yalu.[80]

Within six months Ridgway had transformed a defeat that Omar Bradley described as worse than the Battle of the Bulge into a victory as remarkable as any gained by American forces half a decade before.

THE MATRIX

Our failure matrix in this case (Figure 7–1) looks rather different from earlier ones: The failures seem more widespread, particularly at the small-unit level. Indeed, there seem to be so many different kinds of shortcoming that one must make an effort to remember what UN forces in November 1950 had going for them. To make sense of the picture that emerges from the previous analysis, we have divided the failures into clusters, and the result is two broad pathways to misfortune. The first, emerging from boxes 2.3. and 2.4. involved the unquestioning faith in air power of Far East Command and its failure to understand that the enemy properly. This linked operational and intelligence failure led to intelligence failures at the Eighth Army level, which in turn fed into the tactical unreadiness for Chinese attacks mentioned in boxes 5.3. and 5.4. A secondary pathway to failure originated at the Eighth Army level and fed directly into similar failures at the corps and even battalion levels—namely, a failure to keep a grip on the whereabouts and situation of front-line units. In both pathways, our two types of failure—failure to learn and failure to anticipate—were intertwined. When confronted with such widespread misfortune, one must ask whether a single explanation can account for such a variety of failure.

WHAT KIND OF WAR?

In the first chapter of the first book of *On War*, Clausewitz declares:

> The first, the supreme, the most far-reaching act of judgment that the statesman and commander have to make is to establish . . . the kind of war on which they are embarking; neither mistaking it for, nor trying to turn it into, something that is alien to its nature. This is the first of all strategic questions and the most comprehensive.[81]

It is in the failure of all echelons of American command, including that in Washington, but chiefly those in Japan in Korea to address that ques-

FIGURE 7-1. Matrix of Failure

Function / Command Level	Resources	Communications and Monitoring	Doctrine	Understanding the Enemy	Data on the Enemy
1. National: Washington (president, JCS, Department of the Army)	1.1 *Marginal failure*: divert replacements to Europe	1.2 *Marginal failure*: MacArthur not closely controlled	1.3 Not responsible	1.4 *Failure*: state better than CIA	1.5 Sources not much better than theater
2. Theater: Far East Command/United Nations Command	2.1 Successful "comb-out" of men and equipment	2.2 Informed JCS—more or less	2.3 *Critical failure*: excessive belief in air power as solution	2.4 *Critical failure*: G-2 interprets PLA as an inferior NKPA	2.5 Mediocre: main problem underestimation of PLA in N. Korea
3. Operational: Eighth Army/X Corps/Other subordinate commands (e.g., far East Air Forces, Naval Forces Far East)	3.1 *Marginal failure*: inadequate supplies some materials	3.2 *Failure*: little sense of situation in forward units	3.3 *Marginal failure*: (responsibility chiefly at lower levels)	3.4 *Failure*: only somewhat more anxious than FEC G-2	3.5 *Failure*: important material available (own troops, civilians) but not sought
4. Grand tactical: Corps/Division/Regiment/army units	4.1 *Failure*: no conservation	4.2 *Failure*: out of touch with frontline units	4.3 *Failure*: units dispersed	4.4 *Marginal failure*: some useful reports but not widely disseminated	4.5 *Failure*: POW info, but (except 1 Marine Division) little data from local civilians, own troops
5. Minor tactical: Battalion/company/army units	5.1 *Failure*: troops undersupplied with grenades, etc.	5.2 *Critical failure*: units out of touch with higher HQ and flanks	5.3 *Critical failure*: units poorly sited, roadbound	5.4 *Critical failure*: units not expect Chinese-style night atks	5.5 Mixed: Information there after first clashes, but no one gathers it.

Arrows indicate causal links. Circled items and arrows indicate primary pathways; dashed line, secondary pathways.

tion that we can explain the defeat that ensued. The titles or subtitles of books about Korea—*The First War We Lost, War in Peacetime, The First Limited War*—suggest the strangeness that Americans sensed in that war. The conventional wisdom has it that the peculiarity of the war stems from the fact that the United States fought for limited objectives, with limited means and limited effort. In large respect, the conventional wisdom is right. But the strangeness of the Korean War did not end here, for Korea was peculiar in the nature of the enemy and the operational and tactical patterns required to beat it. It was strange too in the flaws it revealed in the American methods and practices that had brought—or at least accompanied—victory only five years earlier. In fact, the more closely we study the failure of November–December 1950,the more it appears that it resulted from the greatest military success of American arms—the triumph of World War II. *The failure of American leaders fully to understand that the enemy's situation and their own bore little resemblance to those they had faced less than a decade before best explains the debacle in North Korea.*

This is most clear when we look at the application of air power against the North Koreans and the Chinese. As we have pointed out, close air support and interdiction of the roads and rail lines did indeed have the same effect on the North Koreans that it did on, let us say, the Germans in Italy in 1943. Constant air activity saved embattled ground units, paralyzed daytime enemy maneuvers, and inflicted steady losses on enemy vehicles and personnel. A close look at the United States Air Force in Korea reveals an extraordinary attempt to duplicate the ferocious and highly successful "strategic" and "tactical" bombing campaigns waged against Japan and Germany in 1942–45. The Joint Chiefs, and above all air force headquarters in Washington, continually urged World War II–style campaigns against North Korean industry, oil refineries, and the like.[82] By early August of 1950 Major General Emmett O'Donnell had presented to the commander of Far East Air Forces a plan prepared by Strategic Air Command that called for the air force to "go to work burning five major cities in North Korea to the ground, and to destroy completely every one of about eighteen major strategic targets."[83] And despite ROK criticism (which the official historian terms "jaundiced") the air force set about doing just that, particularly after MacArthur had ordered it on November 5, 1950, "to destroy every means of communication and every installation, factory, city and village," between advancing U.S. troops and the Yalu.[84] It was precisely this faith in air power, we have argued, which misled MacArthur and his subordinates into a drastic discounting of the Chinese threat.

This overvaluation, however, did not stem from fantasy but from experience in World War II, confirmed by recent operations against the North Koreans. In both the Atlantic and the Pacific, American air power, no matter which service administered it, did have an enormous impact on operations. It never "isolated the battlefield," as some hoped it would, but it did paralyze the movements of opponents who were conventionally armed and equipped. MacArthur in particular relied heavily on his air forces in the South Pacific campaigns he conducted so brilliantly, and air power served him very well indeed.[85] MacArthur demonstrated in his Pacific campaigns a rare ability to integrate land, air and naval forces, and like virtually all senior American commanders emerged from World War II dedicated to "triphibious" warfare. As Ridgway demonstrated, however, mastery of the narrower but essential basics of ground warfare would determine the outcome in Korea.

In other respects as well Far East Command and the Eighth Army labored under the incubus of a different war. It is noteworthy, for example, that many of the commanders in Korea were armor officers who had made their names in the European war. At the very highest level, General Walker, commander of the Eighth Army, had led XX Corps under George Patton: at the middle levels, hundreds of armored officers were made instant infantrymen and assigned positions in infantry battalions and regiments.[86] Relatively few army officers had fought the kind of infantry war in 1942–45 that fell to their lot in Korea during the winter of 1950–51, and it is no accident that it took one of the best infantrymen in the United States Army to turn the Eighth Army around.

It is again striking how different the marine experience had been. The marines—all marines—had trained for the basic infantry tasks that would be so essential for survival in the retreat from Chosin. Many had had experience in China as garrison troops in the last chaotic days of the Chinese Civil War, or in some cases as observers with Chinese forces. Indeed, the important tactical-organizational concept of dividing an infantry squad of a dozen men into three fire teams came into the Marine Corps from observers attached to Mao Zedong's Eighth Route Army in the 1930s.[87] By virtue of their organizational experience, in other words, as well as basic professionalism, the marines were far more likely than the army to assess their war correctly.

The logistical precariousness of the Eighth Army's position in November 1950 contributed to its defeat, if by no other way than undermining the self-confidence of an army used to material profligacy. Here too we see shades of World War II, in which American forces rarely, if ever, paid a severe penalty for shipping ice cream factories and PXs as well as bombs and bullets into a war zone.[88] Yet an army used to ample quantities of not only material comforts but relatively high technology found itself unprepared for the peculiar conditions of late winter 1950. Marshall's tale of the infantry company that ran out of field telephone wire and therefore failed to establish contact with the counterparts on its flanks is a symbolic one. A runner could have done the same job, but it did not occur to the commander to find a substitute for technology.

UN forces, and American units in particular, need not have suffered so severely in Korea. Despite their weaknesses and deficiencies a defensive line could have held the Chinese north of Seoul: Even a cautious probe north should not have led to the crumpling of a full infantry division and a number of lesser units. Granted the number of factors beyond their control—particularly the replacement problem and some (not all) of the logistical shortages—one can still plausibly imagine a Chinese intervention that pushed UN forces back to the 38th Parallel, perhaps, but no farther. Tightly knit divisions that followed the basic precepts on which Ridgway later insisted (and that the First Marine Division followed) would have had to yield far less to an enemy who could only fight for a week or two at a time before outrunning supplies.

Finally, at the strategic level as well, American leaders appear to have seen the Chinese onslaught in terms of World War II. The Joint Strategic Plans Committee of the JCS, for example, had concluded in August 1950 that "It is not probable that the attempts [to aid the North Koreans] will include overt Soviet or Chinese Communist aggression until the Kremlin is ready to precipitate global war."[89] The JCS found this conflict difficult to conceive of as anything but a first step toward global war, hence their willingness to consider the evacuation of the Korean Peninsula in late December 1950, in the interests of conserving forces for this larger conflict.[90]

"War has a way of masking the stage with scenery crudely daubed with fearsome apparitions."[91] When American forces confronted an enemy whose method of war differed so radically from their own, and when this enemy seemed impervious to their own way of war, fear replaced recklessness. MacArthur made, and the JCS supported, plans to liquidate the Korean commitment. By the spring of 1951, however, some of China's weaknesses—including the vulnerability of its field forces to American firepower—had become clear. American forces did indeed inflict enormous casualties on the Chinese and effectively break the forces opposing them.

Yet a crude mental picture of the enemy continued to enfeeble American strategy again. The image of an unlimited supply of trained Chinese manpower, and of unalterable will to throw it into the fray did not match the reality of the crumbling front. The "fighting hordes" had replaced the "second-rate North Koreans," in the minds of American leaders; both were caricatures. The June 1951 decision to stop at the 38th Parallel—a decision dictated not by battlefield considerations but by calculations in Washington and Tokyo—at the same time peace talks began misjudged again the character of the opponent. No longer pressed by UN forces, the Chinese dug in swiftly and took advantage of their talent for fortification and camouflage. Having nothing to gain at the negotiating table (UN forces had not occupied large chunks of North Korea with which to bargain) they settled in for a protracted war.

Wars, Michael Howard once remarked, resemble each other more than they do anything else.[92] The dangerous implication of this truth lies in the proclivity of large and successful military organizations to see all wars as pretty much the same. They are not, and what Clausewitz called "the first of all strategic tasks" requires careful consideration of the uniqueness of the individual conflict. To do so means beginning with what S. L. A. Marshall described as "the basic study in all warfare,"

> the mind and nature of the probable enemy, compared to which a technical competence in the handling of weapons and engines of destruction is of minor importance. Failing in the first, one will most likely fail in everything.[93]

One can only add that to make full use of such understanding military organizations must seek out the most difficult kind of intelligence—knowledge of themselves.

8

Catastrophic Failure
The French Army and Air Force,
May–June 1940

A GREEK TRAGEDY

WHEN HITLER LAUNCHED THE WEHRMACHT against the West on May 10, 1940, many of his senior commanders doubted whether they could repeat their Polish triumph and win another rapid victory against the much larger and better equipped French army. Their feeling that this was likely to be a long and hard campaign was shared by their opponents. Winston Churchill, who had become British prime minister on the day the German attack commenced, told Franklin D. Roosevelt on May 15, "I think myself the battle on land has only just begun."[1] Allied expectations were quickly confounded. After a mere six weeks' fighting the armies of France, Belgium, Holland, and Great Britain had been defeated and the French were suing for peace. A French defeat was entirely unexpected and the rapidity of the collapse was a shock of traumatic proportions. An impression was formed that what had occurred was a surprising failure by one side rather than a dazzling success by the other. The guns had scarcely ceased their fire before contemporaries began to try to explain the tragic puzzle.

So great were the consequences of defeat for France that it is tempting to try to find a single general cause to explain it.[2] As we have seen, this is a false lure that will easily lead us astray. Great events may have a single striking outcome—the fall of France swept away the Third Republic, which had existed ever since 1871—but their causes are generally very complex.

The speed with which France's soldiers sought to distance themselves from any responsibility for their terrible defeat did much to help to create a sense of inevitability about the fate that overwhelmed France in May and June 1940. General Maxime Weygand, who had succeeded General Maurice-Gustave Gamelin as commander-in-chief ten days after the campaign began, blamed the politicians: "We are paying for twenty years of lying and of demagoguery," he complained.[3] Marshal Henri Pétain, the aging hero of Verdun who would clamber onto the ruins of the Third Republic to hoist the flag of the Vichy regime, warned the government after only sixteen days of fighting that at no cost was the army to be blamed for whatever might go wrong as this would be "treason against the country."[4] The army's supporters claimed that it had quickly run out of men and munitions, without which it could do nothing: Even a critical soldier, while acknowledging the army's faults, felt that by 1940 there was nothing to be done since "fate had stacked the cards too heavily against us."[5]

Conservative Frenchmen who had opposed the leftward leanings of the Third Republic during the 1930s were inclined to explain the disaster as chiefly due to a moral collapse. They believed that France lacked not only material means but also "soul." Materialism and the search for the easy life had rotted the nation's moral fiber, and the decline in French patriotism meant that Frenchmen "were no longer taught the ideas for which they were to lay down their lives."[6] Even neutral observers were not immune from these ideas. After a brief tour of the battlefield William Shirer, an American radio correspondent in Berlin in 1940, concluded that France had not fought—or if it had, there was little evidence of it: "The French, as though drugged, had no will to fight, even when their soil was invaded by their most hated enemy. There was a complete collapse of French society and of the French soul."[7] France's moral and spiritual weakness, upon which the supposed activities of fifth columnists and Communist propaganda had skillfully played, appeared to be the mirror image of Germany's strength.[8]

For all its protestations of innocence, the French high command could not easily wriggle out of the accusation of military incompetence. The charge laid against it by Marc Bloch was fundamentally simple and utterly damning: that the German triumph was essentially an intellectual rather than a physical victory.[9] The Wehrmacht's leaders—youthful, energetic,

Lineup of the Allied and German Armies on the Eve of the German Invasion, May 10, 1940

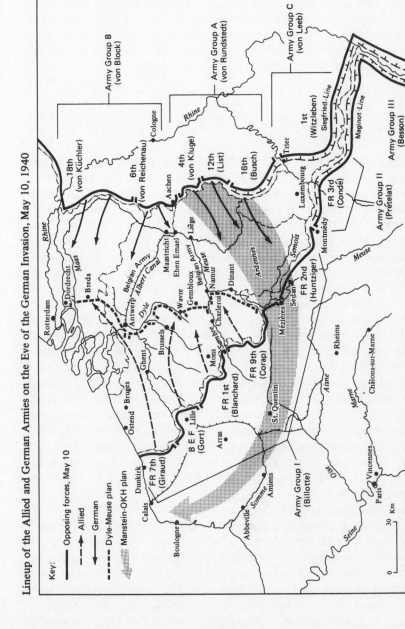

Key:

— Opposing forces, May 10

⟶ Allied

→ German

- - - - Dyle-Meuse plan

······ Manstein-OKH plan

0 ━━ 30 Km

SOURCE: Extract taken from *The End of the Affair: The Collapse of the Anglo-French Alliance* by Eleanor M. Gates, reproduced by kind permission of Unwin Hyman Ltd. Copyright © 1982 by Unwin Hyman Ltd.

and dedicated professionals—had studied modern war more closely and
had found out how to use tanks and airplanes to transform combat from a
slogging match anchored in trenches and fortifications into a fast-moving
contest whose outcome was determined by agility and daring. Meanwhile
the French high command had aged gracefully, drawing comfort and security from its successes in 1918. Its bitterest critic, Charles de Gaulle, lamented that the French army

> became stuck in a set of ideas which had had their heyday before
> the end of the previous war. It was all the more inclined that way
> because its leaders were growing old at their posts, wedded to errors
> that had once constituted their glory.[10]

The collapse of France in 1940 has been explained as being chiefly the
result of faulty decisions made long before the Germans began their war—
which largely exonerates the French army and air force from the charge
of not having fought very well once the battle started. These decisions
were themselves based on misapprehensions about the First World War.
As one American scholar has concluded, "more than being a victim of
German military excellence, France was a victim of her own historical
experience, geography and political and military institutions."[11] It is certainly true that the French high command had built up a picture of what
a future war would and should be like as a result of a selective view of
the past, and that this did restrict their capacity to understand and react
to German moves right from the start. We shall explore the nature of
these assumptions shortly. But the French were by no means condemned
to defeat solely by virtue of being shackled to the past. They also failed
to anticipate the future on the basis of available evidence that pointed
with considerable accuracy to the likely nature of a German assault. And,
along with both these handicaps, there were also moments during the
battle of France when commanders and troops failed the test of battle.
Each of the individual categories of misfortune was present; none was
solely responsible for defeat. When the same author can claim that the
French were blind to the past and to the future, complex forces were
clearly at work.[12]

The assumption that on May 10, 1940, the die was already cast—that,
as de Gaulle later put it, France was "spinning at giddy speed" down
"the fatal slope to which a fatal error had long committed us"—gives
those short summer weeks an aura of tragic grandeur.[13] Men seem to be
little more than pawns in the hands of fate, able perhaps through great
exertions to lessen the scope of misfortune but powerless to avert it entirely. But if we accept this seductive imagery in its entirety, we are in
danger of losing sight of an important dimension in France's military

misfortune. Once the guns began to fire, mistakes were made
new burdens for the troubled French army, and failures in th
at headquarters loaded the dice yet further in the German's fa.

Part of the explanation for France's sudden collapse is to be found on
the field of battle itself, where "a disastrous misjudgment in the dispositions of Allied forces combined with a small but fatal error in gauging the
speed of the enemy advance gave Hitler's Wehrmacht a golden opportunity".[14] Nor was it the case that the whole French army fought poorly,
when it fought at all; there is plenty of evidence that some units put up
a stubborn and determined resistance even when the odds were hopelessly
against them. For example, it was the heroic stand by the French First
Army around Lille that made possible the British escape from Dunkirk.
In explaining why France collapsed in 1940 we have to look as closely at
the events of May 10 through June 22 as at the twenty years that preceded them. Otherwise we shall distort our understanding of the true explanation of France's defeat.

The Six Weeks War

At 4:30 A.M. on May 10, 1940, German parachute and airborne forces
dropped from the skies to seize key bridges at Rotterdam, Dordrecht, and
Moerdijk in Holland and Maastricht in Belgium, while a handful of glider-
borne troops seized the Belgian fortress of Eben Emael, which guarded
the Meuse just north of Liège. An hour later a general assault by 135
Wehrmacht divisions began.

The overall balance of forces by no means favored the Germans. A total
of some 3,740,000 Allied soldiers (including 2,240,000 French troops) in
130 divisions faced 2,760,000 Germans. As well as a manpower advantage, the Allies enjoyed a three-to-two superiority in artillery pieces and
a no-less-striking preponderance in tanks. Although the French had only
three armored divisions to throw into the scales against ten Panzer divisions (plus a fourth, created during the battle), they committed 3,254
tanks to the fighting compared to the Germans' 2,574. Only in respect
to aircraft and antiaircraft defenses did the Germans enjoy a marked superiority.[15] However, the overall picture of the theater balance of forces
concealed a crucial local advantage in the central section of the Allied line
opposite the Ardennes, where the Germans massed forty-five divisions to
launch their main thrust against only nine French divisions.

The initial German army plans had envisaged a pincer attack to encircle
the Allied forces in the middle of Belgium between Brussels and Liège,
but during the winter of 1939–40 these plans had undergone major
changes. First, on October 28, Hitler had intervened to change a limited

operation into a drive across central and northern Belgium to cut the country in half. Then, that winter, a series of war games played by General von Manstein showed that great opportunities for decisive action could be created if the weight of the German attack was directed not into central Belgium but into northern France via the Ardennes. On February 18, 1940, the plans were radically revised to shift the weight of the German attack south. The campaign's opening thrusts into Holland and northern Belgium became feints designed to draw Allied forces north while the main German attack drove through southern Belgium and Luxembourg and into northern France behind the British, French, and Belgian armies.

The French army's plans had also changed during the nine months between the outbreak of war and the German attack, but unhappily the outcome was to make the Allied armies ever more vulnerable to the blow launched against them. On October 24, 1939, the Allies agreed to advance a short distance into Belgium in the event of a German attack to occupy the line of the Scheldt River. On November 15, Gamelin suggested extending the advance to the Dyle River. The advantages of such a move were that the three Allies would then be able to cooperate more closely and would have to hold a shorter defensive line than they would otherwise have to defend; the disadvantages were that executing the plan entailed an advance of some sixty miles into Belgium to occupy unreconnoitered defensive positions which the Belgians would not allow the allies to prepare. Shortly afterward Gamelin proposed that when the fighting began, the left wing of the allied advance should travel the length of Belgium to Breda in southern Holland to link up with the Dutch army. General Alphonse Georges, commander in chief of land forces and commander of the northeastern theater, protested vigorously against committing "the major part of our reserves in this part of the theatre, in face of a German action which could be nothing more than a diversion."[16] Despite his objections, Gamelin ordered the adoption of the so-called Breda variant on March 20, 1940, and seven of Georges' best divisions, including a mechanized division he had been holding back as part of his mobile reserve, were allocated to the Seventh Army, which would make the dash through Belgium to the Dutch border.

When the Germans launched their attack on May 10 the Allied line was strong on its left and right but weak in the center, opposite the Ardennes. The leaders of the French army had repeatedly reassured parliament during the preceding decade that this region was impenetrable and that felling trees and blowing craters in roads would be enough to secure it against any serious attack. Unfortunately the Belgian Chasseurs Ardennais either failed to carry out enough of these or neglected to stay behind and defend the area. While the Seventh Army moved to Breda, taking two days to get there and suffering heavily as a result of German air superiority, and while the French high command was preoccupied with the German thrust through central Belgium from Maastricht, German Panzers carved their way through the "impenetrable" Ardennes. Then, on May 13, while General Erwin Rommel's Seventh Panzer Division crossed the Meuse at Dinant—taking quick advantage of an unguarded weir—General Heinz Guderian's XIX Armored Corps crossed the same river farther south at Sedan.

The units facing Guderian at Sedan were second-line infantry divisions composed of elderly reservists who lacked modern training and equipment. The Fifty-fifth Division, which took the brunt of the attack, had been stiffened with extra artillery to compensate for its weakness, but it was paralyzed by the unrelenting fierceness of the attacks by Stuka dive-bombers on May 13.

> The gunners stopped firing and took cover. The infantry, cowering and immobile in their trenches, dazed by the crash of bombs and the shriek of the dive-bombers, were too stunned to use their anti-aircraft guns and fire. Their only concern was to keep their heads down and not move. Five hours of this punishment shattered their nerves. They became incapable of reacting to the approaching enemy infantry.[17]

This scene was to be repeated many times during the coming weeks, as French troops faced an onslaught for which they were unprepared and that their own air force was unable to counter.

The troops facing Guderian at Sedan retreated as soon as they could, with the heavy artillery in the lead. Their action was copied at higher levels over the next three days as divisional, corps, and army commanders pulled back their headquarters and dispersed valuable armor in fruitless attempts at forming defensive positions to stem the advancing German tide. These moves totally lacked overall coordination as Gamelin left his commanders to their own devices, despite reservations about the way General Georges was conducting the battle, until it was too late. His only significant action at this time was to order a retreat from Belgium during the night of May 15/16. At last, on May 19, while panic was setting in in Paris and after Guderian's drive west across France had brought him within one day's march of Abbeville and the Channel, Gamelin bestirred himself sufficiently to issue a "secret and personal instruction" to launch an attack into the southern flank of Guderian's Panzer corps. The order was so vague that Georges, who was supposed to carry it out, said that it was not an order at all but "an umbrella."[18] The next day Gamelin was fired, to be replaced by his seventy-three year-old predecessor, General Maxime Weygand.

Weygand took over in less-than-propitious circumstances. Recalled from Syria on May 17, he arrived in France two days later, after a grueling journey and was at once catapulted into command. It therefore took him some time to get a grip on the battle. If he was to turn a tide of events that was running strongly against him, he had to coordinate a British attack from the north and a French attack from the south in the hope of "pinching off" the German corridor that now extended to the Channel but was not yet solid enough to be entirely secure. Uncoordinated attacks south of Arras by the British on May 21 and the French on May 22 were too weak to make any impression on the Germans. Meanwhile, Weygand's efforts to launch a major attack on the Germans in the Amiens-Arras-Abbeville area foundered when General Gaston-Henri-Gustave Billotte, selected to command the action (and the only man who really understood the commander in chief's intentions), was fatally injured in a car crash on May 21. His replacement was not appointed for two days, during which the opportunity to cause the German's serious difficulties disappeared.

The end was now near in the north. The British began to fall back towards the Channel ports, determined to rescue what they could from a hopeless situation. As they began to evacuate their troops, Weygand issued a general order to the French army to stand and fight, throwing back every enemy advance by "crushing him under artillery fire and aerial bombardment and by counterattacking."[19] This was a counsel of perfection: The troops were untrained for tactics of this sort, and in any case the Germans enjoyed complete aerial superiority everywhere except over the beaches of Dunkirk. On May 28, the Belgians surrendered. Seven days later, most of the British troops left the continent at Dunkirk.

On June 5, the day after General Beaufrère had surrendered the remaining French troops defending Dunkirk, the Germans began the battle for France. The odds were overwhelmingly in their favor. To resist the onslaught of six Panzer divisions and approximately one hundred infantry divisions, Weygand could muster forty-nine field divisions, one motorized division, and the debris of two armored divisions. French counterattacks went in without any aerial protection, and there were no reserves with which to conduct a battle in depth. In the circumstances it is hardly surprising that a feeling of pessimism began to set in at the summit of the politicomilitary hierarchy.

The Germans now sought to encircle Paris from the west and east, just as they had done seventy years earlier in September 1870, to trap the remaining French forces where they stood. West of Paris, General Ewald von Kleist's army group, with Rommel in the van, drove for the lower reaches of the Seine. The French fought well, but on June 7 Rommel forced their line and advanced to within 24 miles of Rouen. The next day the city fell into German hands. Switching four Panzer divisions from west of Paris to General Gerd von Rundstedt in the east, the Germans launched the other prong of their offensive on June 9. Reims fell two days later and the Germans reached Château-Thierry on the Marne, some 30 miles east of the capital. Having ordered the army to stand and fight on the Somme, Weygand now decided not to defend Paris—largely because of his fears of German air power—but to withdraw his battered and fragmented forces to a line stretching across the center of France from Caen in Normandy via Tours and Dijon to Dôle. His stated objective was to cover the heart of his country for as long as possible and to conserve the largest number of major formations.

By now resistance was possible only in isolated pockets where some determined individual was able to rally his exhausted troops—easily bypassed by the probing fingers of German armor. Everything was being extemporized, for the pace of war no longer allowed for the preparation, writing, and transmission of orders. This disoriented French commanders (at all levels), who had expected to receive—and to offer—continual written guidance during the conduct of battle. The troops suffered the effects of repeated movements and lacked regular rations, while their leaders were unable to contact superior headquarters for orders and lacked all but the vaguest knowledge of the situation.

Early on the morning of June 14 German troops entered Paris and marched in triumph down the Champs-Élysées. While they savored this symbolic act of victory, the war hastened to its end. A proposal to create a "Breton redoubt" and fight on there was contemptuously brushed aside by Weygand, who had a rather more realistic view of the capabilities of German air power than did some of his civilian colleagues. The high command now concentrated its energies not on the Germans but on defeating those civilian ministers, led by Premier Paul Reynaud, who wanted a cease-fire that would spare the government the odium of surrender. Pétain and Weygand were determined that the war must be ended by the politicians and insisted on an armistice as the only honorable course in the circumstances.

In this poisonous atmosphere Pétain took over the reins of government on June 16 and completed the work the Germans had begun five weeks earlier. Broadcasting the following day, he announced to the French people: "I tell you today that we must end the fighting."[20] Taking this as a direct instruction, many of them did so; and Weygand had to issue instructions on June 18 that the troops were not to cease fighting until an armistice had been concluded. During the evening of the nineteenth, at the urging of Weygand and over the protests of Georges, the government declared that all towns of 20,000 or more inhabitants were to be treated as open cities and not to be defended against the Germans. Since such towns guarded the principal river crossings, the keys of what was left of France were thus unceremoniously handed over to the enemy.

On June 20 Pétain again went on the air to announce that the Germans had responded to the French request for an armistice. Reviewing France's weakness in 1940 as compared with 1918, he left no doubts in the minds of his listeners as to the causes of France's humiliation:

> Less strong than we were 22 years ago, we also had fewer friends.
> Too few children, too few weapons, too few allies, there are the
> causes of our defeat.[21]

At 6:50 P.M. on June 22 General Charles Huntziger, representing the French army and thereby saving Weygand considerable embarrassment, and field marshal Keitel signed the armistice terms. Two days later a second armistice was signed with Italy, which had entered the war against France on June 10, and the war came to an ignominious end. The inquest opened almost immediately, and has continued ever since.

Defeat in the Air

Although the balance of land forces on May 10, 1940, favored the Allies, the balance in the air was heavily against them—both materially and morally. In material terms the French could put some 1,090 modern machines into the air (comprising 610 fighters, 130 bombers and 350 reconnaissance planes) to meet approximately 3,500 German aircraft.[22] Morally, the inactivity of the "phony war" had taken its toll on the French; and shortages of uniforms and weapons, the inadequate functioning of most services, poor lodgings that were often some distance from the airfields, and physical weariness among the flight crews as a result of a shortage of personnel all combined to depress morale. However, once the battle began the French fought gallantly.[23] They had alongside them two echelons of the Royal Air Force—the Advanced Air Striking Force and the Air Component of the British Expeditionary Force, which together comprised some 160 fighters and 272 bombers. During the course of the campaign the British were able to make good their fighter losses, but the French were not.

From the outset of the battle, a combination of French caution and disorganization and German fighters and anti-aircraft guns weakened the air effort. At 11:00 A.M. on May 10 General Joseph Vuillemin, head of the French air force, agreed to strike at enemy columns but not "agglomerations," which were not to be bombed "at any price."[24] Attacks on the advancing German forces soon crumbled. On May 14 the French air force lost over 40 planes in an attempt to destroy a bridge over the Meuse River, twenty-eight of them falling to Panzer antiaircraft fire. The British did little better. On May 11 eight Fairey Battle airplanes sortied against the Ardennes and only one returned. After a week, the French had only 149 fighters available in the entire northern zone of operations, and the RAF had lost 248 aircraft. French losses between May 10 and 30 totaled 660 planes.[25]

France's material deficiencies were magnified by a clumsy command structure that soon ceased to correspond to the realities of the front line, and by the absence of any practiced methods of dealing with fast-moving armored columns. Much of the French air force was parceled out to act in cooperation with the army—which was interpreted chiefly as spotting for artillery. The air commander in each aerial operations zone received his orders from his respective army group commander and from the overall commander of aerial cooperation forces, General Marcel Têtu. Soon after the battle began, zone commanders began to find themselves on the receiving end of unreconcilable orders from both these sources, while Vuillemin conducted his own air war with the general reserves under his personal control. To make matters worse, the air zones quickly ceased to correspond to army command areas as the Allied front buckled before the German attack.[26]

In tackling the Germans, the French air force lacked not only coordination but also guidance in combat techniques. By 1939—as a result of failings in the interwar years—air doctrine had got as far as defining "assault bombing" and "dive-bombing" missions, but there were no aircraft capable of carrying them out. In a desperate attempt to fill the doctrinal gap, the commander of aerial forces in the northeastern zone rushed out "provisional instructions for rapid air support of ground operations" on May 30, 1940. But by then it was too late to remedy the failures of the prewar airmen.

To compensate for their inferiority in the air, the French tried to draw on the reservoir of RAF Home Defence Squadrons stationed in England. On May 16, Churchill provided ten extra fighter squadrons—but kept six of them operating from airfields in Kent. As British losses mounted—106 Hurricanes and Spitfires fell during the week-long evacuation of Dunkirk—the British high command became increasingly determined not to squander in France fighters that would be needed for the forthcoming battle for Britain. Desperate for British fighters to shore up their vanishing air defenses, the French suggested on June 5 that the air strength of both countries be placed under a single command. The request was rejected. At the end of the first week in June, nine British fighter squadrons were still operating in France; but after June 15, when the bombers of the Advanced Air Striking Force left the continent, only five remained behind to cover the final withdrawal of British and Allied forces from Europe. By this time, the French air force had been shattered.[27]

THE MATRIX

In the case of the fall of France, our failure matrix (Fig. 8–1) has been constructed so that each of the three functions of command we identify as of major importance correlates with one of the three types of failure with which we are now familiar. The four levels of command along the vertical axis are occupied by the high command, theater command, operational commands, and tactical commands.

In order to avoid overpopulating many of the boxes it is necessary to include in each one only the most fundamental and important actions of command. Also, to avoid a plethora of secondary pathways—since almost every box in this matrix could be connected to one or more others by such pathways—it has been necessary to indicate only the most obvious connecting links.

Once again we can see how pathways of misfortune cross boundaries to affect separate command functions. Given the disastrous performance of the armies in the field, it is hardly surprising that "all roads lead to Rome" by drawing us down to the critical failure in box 4.3—the inability of tactical commanders to react quickly and effectively to the German attacks. We shall examine each of the three types of individual failure shortly; however, our matrix does suggest several general conclusions. First, more critical failures appear under the heading "Ability to React" than in either of the other two columns, suggesting that the fall of France was predominantly the result of adaptive failure. Second, more critical mistakes were made by the high command than at any other command level. Here failure is spread equally across all three categories, providing

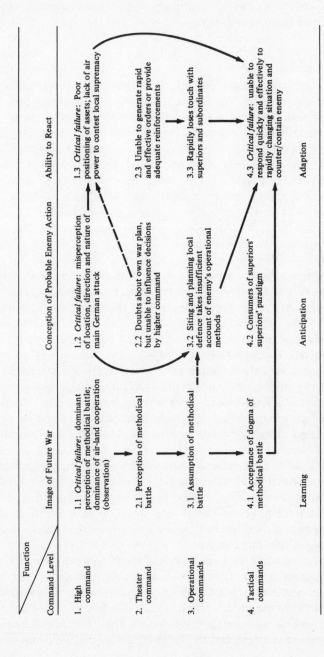

Function Command Level	Image of Future War	Conception of Probable Enemy Action	Ability to React
1. High command	1.1 *Critical failure*: dominant perception of methodical battle; dominance of air-land cooperation (observation)	1.2 *Critical failure*: misperception of location, direction and nature of main German attack	1.3 *Critical failure*: Poor positioning of assets; lack of air power to contest local supremacy
2. Theater command	2.1 Perception of methodical battle	2.2 Doubts about own war plan, but unable to influence decisions by higher command	2.3 Unable to generate rapid and effective orders or provide adequate reinforcements
3. Operational commands	3.1 Assumption of methodical battle	3.2 Siting and planning local defence takes insufficient account of enemy's operational methods	3.3 Rapidly loses touch with superiors and subordinates
4. Tactical commands	4.1 Acceptance of dogma of methodical battle	4.2 Consumers of superiors' superiors' paradigm	4.3 *Critical failure*: unable to respond quickly and effectively to rapidly changing situation and counter/contain enemy
	Learning	Anticipation	Adaption

Arrows indicate causal links. Solid lines indicate primary pathways; dashed lines, secondary pathways.

FIGURE 8–1. Matrix of Failure

clear evidence of the multiple shortcomings of the French high command both before and during the campaign.

Failure to Learn

When German forces attacked Poland on September 1, 1939, *Blitzkrieg* was an unknown quantity for all practical purposes. Although French military intelligence had paid some attention to the ideas being developed across the Rhine and had observed German maneuvers closely, neither France nor any other country appreciated the consequences of combining the power of the tank and the dive-bomber with a skillful and audacious concept of maneuver warfare. Within three short weeks the Allies were presented with apparently incontrovertible evidence of what the German war machine could do. Over the next seven months the French army had the opportunity to profit from their vicarious experience of the Wehrmacht in action in order to ready themselves to meet the challenge of the new-style war, but that opportunity was apparently squandered. "Of all the attitudes struck by the French High Command during the Phoney War," writes Alistair Horne, "none today seems more incomprehensible that its apparent refusal to take cognizance of the lessons of the Polish campaign."[28]

Strategically, the campaign in Poland differed considerably from the assault on western Europe which followed it eight months later. The Germans' aim was to encircle the Polish armies west of the Vistula and then annihilate them; and in order to achieve this, the armored and mechanized German units were held in check to keep them in touch with the advancing infantry rather than give them their head—as would happen after Guderian crossed the Meuse on May 13, 1940. But operationally the effects of German military powers were fully visible. "On the ground for the first time in modern war, the combination of armored mobile formations supported by aircraft proved devastatingly effective."[29] While the Panzers tore gaping holes in the Polish front, the Luftwaffe first paralyzed the Polish air force and then broke up Polish army columns and gave the German ground forces close air support. Within a little more than a fortnight, the war was over.

If the French failed to learn the lessons of the Polish campaign, it was not through ignorance of what those lessons were. A month after the campaign had begun the French high command circulated a detailed report by the head of the French military mission in Poland, General Paul Armengaud, which analyzed in considerable detail the new German methods. Armengaud described the German system of combining dive-bombers and tanks to break open the enemy line and penetrate deeply into the rear areas, opening the path for the infantry whose task was to clean up local pockets of resistance and occupy captured territory. He drew particular attention to the way in which the German dive-bombers had pinned the Poles to the ground, making it impossible either to get reinforcements forward or to launch counterattacks.[30] Armengaud's report was supplemented by an analysis by Colonel Maurice Gauché, head of French military intelligence, which pointed out that the Germans had aimed at destroying the Polish field army and not at capturing Warsaw.

As these reports, which were used as a basis on which to reconsider French doctrine and methods, were filtered down the chain of command, their impact was watered down. The reports that reached the lower echelons struck a more ambivalent note than Armengaud's original had done, suggesting that although the Germans would try the same methods against France, the operations would have a different appearance. War games were designed and conducted to show the superiority of the French army over the Wehrmacht and the likelihood that the French would suffer anything resembling the Polish defeat was explained away on the grounds that the defeated always exaggerated anyway, that the Poles were brave but badly led, and that they had the misfortune to live in a country that lacked natural frontiers.[31] Such actions, which may have seemed necessary in order to reinforce the morale of the mass of the French army, probably contributed to the paralysis which quickly set in after May 10 as the war took on unexpected dimensions.

At the summit of the French army, Gamelin was by no means ignorant of the true significance of the Polish campaign. At an allied conference at Vincennes on October 6, 1939, he remarked that "the chief lesson to be learned from the Polish campaign was the penetrative power of the speedy and hard-hitting German armored formations and the close cooperation of their Air Force."[32] However, he proposed to meet the new threat not by accepting the challenge of encounter battles, which would involve a major rethinking of accepted doctrine and extensive retraining, but by fighting the Germans only in previously prepared positions. Gamelin's formula for fending off a *Blitzkrieg* attack, which he defined on September 21 and reiterated on several occasions during October, involved thinning the French front to a strength able to halt a surprise attack and massing his reserves for a counterattack.[33] Unfortunately, his choice of the Breda variant would deprive him of exactly those reserves he most needed when the battle began.

The way Gamelin absorbed the lessons of the Polish campaign and incorporated them into his operational concept reflected an understandable—if unwise—reluctance to depart from the established methods of war developed by the French high command over the previous two decades. In this way predictive failure—which we shall examine shortly—helped to contribute to learning failure. However, the ink was scarcely dry on Gamelin's directives when major changes in Allied strategy forced him to reconsider both operational methods and the means to carry them out. The advance to the Scheldt and then to the Dyle, and the dash to Breda, changed the circumstances in which the French army would go into action in several important respects. While Gamelin hoped to find lines prepared by the Belgians into which his forces could settle, he had little idea of how strong and solid they would be. The one certain fact was that they would not be defensive positions carefully prepared by the French themselves long in advance, as was the case along part of the French frontier. The need for speed to get to the Dutch frontier before the enemy, and the prospect of something more like encounter battles than the French had hitherto been accustomed to, may have contributed to a change of heart by Gamelin that resulted in a partial incorporation of the major lesson of the Polish campaign into French thought and practice.

On November 11 Colonel Charles de Gaulle sent a memorandum to general headquarters urging that French tanks be gathered together in armored divisions instead of being widely dispersed as supports to the infantry. "The petrol engine knocks out our military doctrines just as it will knock out our fortifications," he wrote. "We have excellent material. We must learn how to use it as the Germans have."[34] His ideas were indignantly rejected by senior French tank specialists on the grounds that the Germans would find French lines much stronger than those in Poland, and that the traditional French doctrine of using tanks to support infantry was correct. But the notion that France must reorganize her armor on the basis of the Polish experience was taking root at a more senior level. In November Gamelin agreed to the formation of a light mechanized division and an armored division. In early December General Billotte wrote to Georges, commander in chief of land forces, pointing out that the Polish campaign had demonstrated the effects of the daring use of Panzer divisions and arguing that since the Germans might try the same thing in the West, the French must have the means to parry them. As a result of this initiative two armored divisions were created in January 1940, a third in March, and a fourth on May 15.[35] Unfortunately, these new formations had to go into action before they were either fully-equipped or completely trained.

Lessons observed at second-hand are unlikely to have quite the same impact as those experienced at firsthand: Ethnocentric ideas can lead, as we have seen, to a disparaging of the defeated party and the barrier to change which is presented by received ideas and established practice can be well-nigh impermeable. Only in the weeks before May 10, 1940, when French forces were briefly involved in the campaign in Norway, did they have any direct experience of fighting Germans. The defects revealed were immense: "no modern equipment, no ack-ack, no decisive bombing policy, no drive in the troops—except the very best—and no incisive command."[36] By then it was too late to do very much about them.

Although the French air force had no more direct experience of the Germans in April 1940 than the French army, the Spanish Civil War had provided it with an ideal opportunity to learn about modern air war in general and about the performance of German aircraft in particular. The success of Russian fighters and bombers in halting an offensive by two Italian light divisions in its tracks at the Battle of Guadalajara in March 1937, and the breakthrough at Brunete four months later by a combined Republican force of tanks and planes provided much food for thought. The French military attaché provided full reports on the demoralizing effects of dive-bombing on troops; and in February 1938 a French air mission was able to examine the main German fighter (Messerschmidt ME-109) and bomber (Heinkel HE-111) at close quarters. All this information struck a bottleneck in the Intelligence Division at Vincennes, where a lone officer had part-time responsibility for studying the war.[37] Perhaps more important—and like the army—the French air force set little store by the experience of others, preoccupied as it was in the struggle with the army over its main role in a future war.

When the Germans struck on May 10, the French armed forces were aware of some of the problems they were about to face—such as that French bombers attacking enemy ground formations would need fighter escorts, something prewar doctrine had not envisaged—but had devised no solutions to them. Learning failure was a major reason why the French found themselves forced to extemporize when battle began, and why a military organization accustomed to operate a rigid system then fell rapidly to pieces. However, the difficult task of recognizing and incorporating the lessons of Spanish and Polish experience into French military practice was itself greatly exacerbated by the long-established conviction that the next war would be similar in certain vital respects to the last.[38] Only at the eleventh hour would the French begin to modify both their ideas and their doctrine, thereby moving against the tide of interwar prediction.

Failure to Anticipate

In order to prepare themselves as effectively as possible for a German onslaught, the French had to make two sets of predictions and get them both right. Over the longer term the high command had to predict what the general nature of a future war would be and prepare the French army to fight by devising and elaborating doctrines to guide peacetime training and preparation as well as determine what types of weapons were procured. In the short term the intelligence services had to anticipate both the location and the timing of the German attack. In other words, the French had some time in which to think about how to fight, but very much less time to think about where and when they would be called on to do so. It was not sufficient, however, simply to carry out these two tasks efficiently and effectively—although in practice this was difficult enough. The two types of prediction had to marry with one another. If they did not, the French armed forces might be called on in the heat of the moment to carry out maneuvers and undertake actions in response to enemy initiatives which had not been foreseen in their peacetime preparations. This was partly what went wrong in 1940.

French experiences in the First World War had burned deep into the national psyche. By 1917 the prewar French belief in the power of the offensive had been exposed as a horrible delusion as a generation of Frenchmen were sacrificed to German machine guns. In its place Pétain, the hero of Verdun, sanctified the primacy of the defensive followed by the counterattack. At war's end he came to symbolize the new military spirit of the republic, no longer relying on republican ardor and national *élan* but putting its faith in barbed wire, artillery, and concrete fortifications.[39] The politicians of the interwar years would have found it hard to overthrow this conception of national strategy even if they had wanted to, but most of them did not.

World War I was the formative experience for the French generals who rose through the army in peacetime and reached its summit in 1940, and they based all their predictions of future land warfare on it. It was widely believed that a new era had opened in 1914 and that by dint of historical analysis all useful lessons for the future could be extracted from it. Thus, introducing a report on the army's proposals for peacetime preparation to the French chamber of deputies in 1921, Colonel Jean Fabry pointed out that what was necessary was "less a matter of innovating than of perfecting" existing practices.[40] Eighteen years later, in 1939, the French infantry journal prided itself on the fact that French tank doctrine had stayed true to the lessons of 1914–18, unlike almost all other armies.

Accordingly, influenced by their experiences in 1917 and 1918 and entirely disregarding the successful German tactics that broke the Allied lines in March 1918, the French built up a picture of future warfare based on three fundamental assumptions: the destructiveness of firepower, the strength of the defense, and the superiority of the methodically conducted battle.

The central teachings of the high command on the nature of future war were incorporated into two instruction manuals: *Provisional Instructions on the Tactical Employment of Large Units*, published in 1921, and *Instructions on the Tactical Employment of Large Units*, published in 1936. Both emphasized the preponderance of firepower in combat and underlined the importance of central command controlling the battle as it unfolded. The expectations built up in the army as a result of the latter proposition were, as we shall see, to be grievously disappointed once war actually began. Generally, both sets of regulations denied any place for initiative and stressed the overriding importance of adhering to a formulaic scheme of battle that would unfold in predetermined stages. The injunction in the 1936 *Instructions* that "audacious solutions . . . should be executed methodically" conveniently exemplifies the limitations of official thought during these years.[41]

The picture of future war built up in the various training manuals and instructions issued to the French army during most of the interwar period was one in which the measured, remorseless application of national strength would eventually grind down an opponent. The defense of prepared positions, against which the enemy's offensive strength would dissolve, was the foundation of victory. Offensives would only be carried out after careful preparation and with heavy material superiority. When they were unleashed, attacks would have a number of "phases" each consisting of two or more "bounds." Where the offensive came up against serious opposition, the French were not taught to infiltrate the weak spots but to outflank the obstacle and then destroy it.[42] This predictive scenario of future war, based heavily on a blinkered perception of the key features of World War I, catered to many national prejudices and worries but in doing so it forced the army into a mold that made if vulnerable to the techniques simultaneously being devised across the Rhine.

Although the current of official opinion flowed strongly in one direction, an occasional attempt was made to swim against the tide and suggest that France adopt a system of military organization more akin to the Germans. By far the most significant example of such heterodox thinking was Charles de Gaulle's *Vers l'armée de métier (Toward a professional army)*, published in 1934. Turning his back on France's long tradition of mobilizing huge numbers of conscripts to form mass armies of infantry, de Gaulle (who had never seen an armored division when he wrote) proposed the creation of a force of six divisions each combining tanks, mobile artillery and motorized infantry and totalling a mere 100,000 men. Such a force would be "a terrible mechanical system of fire, of shock, of speed and of camouflage" which could go into action instantaneously instead of having to go through the cumbrous process of calling-up reserves, mobilization and deployment.[43] De Gaulle's visionary ideas were treated as a blueprint, not as a speculative stimulus to fresh thinking, and were rejected on a variety of grounds that ranged from the political—such an army could easily be the instrument for a right-wing coup against the government— to the economic—that France lacked the fuel for such a force and could not be sure of maintaining the necessary supplies.

When the German army struck, France was in the worst of all possible positions: losing faith in the established predictive paradigm, it had not yet replaced it with an alternative. During the latter part of the 1930s the French army had begun cautiously to experiment with tanks operating independently of infantry. Provisional instructions for the employment of tanks in war were drawn up in December 1937 and June 1938. They envisaged large numbers of tanks being used in surprise attacks on extended fronts and foresaw operations designed to penetrate enemy positions, to counterattack, to disrupt and demoralize a retreating opponent, and to turn an enemy flank.[44] A decision taken late in 1938, after the Munich crisis, to create two armored divisions in 1940—a development hastened, as we have seen, by the onset of war—seemed to point in the direction of a new war scenario and an anticipation of the future that differed significantly from the notion of something resembling a rerun of World War I. But these developments were scarcely underway before the army was caught up in war. Hindered by the lack of productive capacity of French industry from accelerating programs of motorization and mechanization, and therefore unable to redirect the mental world of the French army toward a new style of warfare, Gamelin adopted an "equivocal stance" and prepared his army for both offensive and defensive operations.[45]

Any anticipation of the shape of future war ought logically to be based, at least in part, on how a probable enemy is likely to fight. During 1937–38, on lecture tours to French bases, Major Schlesser of the counterintelligence service took the opportunity to visit each garrison library and check up on whether anyone was reading the French translation of Guderian's book *Achtung Panzer*, which his department had distributed free. He found that not a single copy had been opened.[46] If this report accurately illustrated the ignorance of the bulk of the French officer corps about German military techniques, the same was not the case at higher levels. From the 1920s onward, the French were well aware that German doctrine was oriented towards the offensive. By 1937 French military intelligence knew, as a result of its monitoring of German maneuvers, of the war of movement being practiced on the other side of the Rhine; and a detailed analysis of Guderian's ideas on war, which was completed in May 1939, made it transparently plain that the Germans put a high premium on mobility and surprise. In terms of its general predictions of German military behavior, French military intelligence has been claimed to have been "detailed, comprehensive, and competent."[47]

The impact of German ideas on the French before September 1939 was slight partly because of the firmness of the foundations on which France had built its own doctrine. It was further diminished by the calculation that the German style of mechanized warfare might play into French hands. On the eve of the war the official view was that great advantages could well accrue to France once the enemy attack was launched:

> If our formations are well adapted to the situation and to the terrain, our flank guards vigilant, the depth [of our defense] sufficient, our antiaircraft and antitank weapons well posted at all times; if our officers demonstrate the spirit of quick decision, solid nerves and sure reactions—then it is the German who will be caught in his own trap, for he will have compromised the equilibrium of his forces for a premature action—and we will, from that moment on, have acquired over him a first and serious advantage and an indisputable moral ascendancy.[48]

This comforting conclusion both negated the value of attempting to anticipate the enemy's actions and placed a heavy responsibility on the army to cope with novel conditions when the time came. It also assumed a weapons inventory that France did not possess.

After September 1, 1939, France needed accurate intelligence about Germany's capabilities, as well as general prognostications about the broad shape of possible conflict. Three questions had to be answered: How large a force could Germany put into the field? Where would it attack? And when? French military intelligence was responsible for gathering the information upon which to answer them. Its critics have blamed it for failing on all counts[49]; its defenders have claimed that its work was the closest thing to human perfection that could ever be attained.[50] As we shall see, the intelligence services got some things right and others wrong; but as the evidence that the Germans were about to attack through the Ardennes became ever stronger, they faced the difficult task of persuading Gamelin to change his mind on the basis of inconclusive fragments of evidence that had to compete with his preferred strategy of fighting in Belgium, to which he was heavily committed.

French intelligence was most successful in predicting the order of battle of the German land forces in May 1940. It estimated that the Wehrmacht could field 110 to 115 infantry divisions and 10 to 12 Panzer divisions, whereas the actual figures were 117 and 10 respectively. However, when it came to counting tanks the French went wildly astray. Just before the battle of France opened, military intelligence predicted an attack of 4,700 German tanks, but on May 15 it raised its estimate to between 7,000 and 7,500.[51] This was three times the real size of the German tank force, which numbered 2,574. When asked why his predictions had increased so massively, the head of military intelligence was reported as replying, "It is what you call a 'covering' intelligence report, in case things go wrong."[52] French estimates of the size of the Luftwaffe were equally pessimistic. As a result of grossly overestimating the productive capacity of the peacetime German air industry, the French reckoned in June 1939 that their enemy already had over 9,000 planes. In fact, the Germans were able to put 3,500 planes into battle on May 10, 1940, somewhat more than double the numbers of French machines available but very many fewer than expected. The fact that the main French failures in "bean-counting" occurred in exactly those categories of weapons that gave the *Blitzkrieg* its awesome material and psychological force meant that morale in the higher echelons was weakened even before battle began.

In trying to forecast where the Germans would attempt to break through the Allied front, the French confronted the awkward fact that the choice was wide. The options available to Germany included attacking Holland or Belgium; assaulting the Maginot line while simultaneously carrying out flanking operations in southern Belgium and Luxembourg; breaking the neutrality of Switzerland to outflank the Maginot line from the south; and crossing the Ardennes. Even when information began to point ever more unequivocally to the Ardennes as the probable site of the German attack, the intelligence services had to convince Gamelin that their predictions outweighed his strategic preferences. This they failed to do.

The fact that the German war plans changed in February 1940 made it extremely difficult for military intelligence to gather accurate information in time to be able to persuade the high command to redirect its gaze away from central Belgium and reposition major units in the target area. However, on March 22, Colonel Paul Paillole, head of the German section of French counterintelligence, reported that the Germans had suddenly begun to study the routes from Sedan to Abbeville and were paying particular attention to roads, bridges and water obstacles. From this he concluded that "an attack through Belgium towards the Channel is imminent."[53] Warnings from the Belgians that the Germans seemed to be turning their attention to the Ardennes area were passed to the French high command early in March and repeated on April 14. Two days earlier French counterintelligence had learned from a double agent that the Germans were focusing their interest on the corridor from Sedan to Amiens. On April 13 these facts were reported not to Gamelin but to Georges, commander in chief of the northeast front.[54] This unfortunate decision, probably taken as a consequence of the deep rivalry between Gamelin and Georges, deprived the supreme commander of a vital piece of corroborative information.

In the last days of "phony war" warnings of the impending German assault began to flood in. On April 30 the French military attaché in Berne reported that the German attack was set for May 8–10 and that its focus would be Sedan. The following day French counterintelligence at Berne, relying on a Swiss source, confirmed the dates and reported that although the whole of the front would be attacked, including the Maginot Line, the main effort would come around Sedan. Also on May 1, Paul Thümmel, a member of the German military intelligence service and an agent for the Czechs, reported through The Hague that the German offensive would begin on May 10.[55] In the last week before the attack, the Dutch military attaché in Berlin received three warnings of its imminence from no less a person than General Hans Oster, second in command of the German military intelligence service, the last of them at 9:50 P.M. on the evening of May 9.[56]

Although considerable, the information which pointed to a German attack on the Ardennes was too disparate to form an incontrovertible case. It was not and never could be overwhelming; after all, the Germans were planning a simultaneous attack on Holland and Belgium as well as through the Ardennes. The best that could be said with certainty—and French military intelligence did say it—was that an attack on the Maginot Line or through Switzerland was unlikely without good warning. The scraps of information reaching the various Allied intelligence services— not all of which seem to have reached the French supreme commander— were not enough to outweigh the conglomeration of reasons that led him to focus his attentions elsewhere. The Ardennes was perceived as being extremely difficult to penetrate: An analysis undertaken in 1927 had reached the conclusion that it would take an enemy nine days to cross it, and its impenetrability was reconfirmed by Pétain in 1934 and by Gamelin himself in 1936.[57] Gamelin also had his own strategic preoccupations; the Dyle plan was proposed partly because he feared that the Germans might attack Holland only, and one of his overriding concerns seems to have been to pick a battleground where French, Belgian, Dutch, and British forces could act in combination.

The weight of evidence pointing to a German attack in the Ardennes, which Gamelin ignored, has been described as "formidable."[58] The difficulty in basing firm predictions on it was that it was far from conclusive. It also formed but one piece of a jigsaw puzzle the French were trying to piece together out of a mass of contradictions. Thus, for example, the warnings of French military intelligence that Germany was gathering its strength for an attack in the west had to be set against the report of the former French military attaché in Berlin that it would be impossible for Germany to attack in the west until autumn 1940 at the earliest.[59] France was also the victim of a skillful German campaign of deception, culminating in a speech by Goering saying that the Germans intended to attack the Maginot Line in two places between May 5 and 15.[60] Nevertheless, there were good enough grounds for Gamelin to reassess the defensibility of the Ardennes, and enough time for him to have reinforced the line with better troops than those of General André-Georges Corap's Ninth Army. In this respect the French intelligence services provided him with as much as it was reasonable to expect in the way of predictive certainties.

Failure to Adapt

For Frenchmen the most humiliating fact about the disastrous campaign of 1940 was the ease with which the Germans swept their armies aside. "This few weeks' campaign, which led to a defeat so total and so sudden," wrote General André Beaufre, "was from first to last an endless surprise exposing our inability to cope with the enemy's torrential advance or find any answer to it."[61] For the French army and air force the campaign was a total failure without even the smallest redeeming feature. Where the French were more or less a numerical match for the Germans—in men and tanks—they performed abysmally. Their national pride in tatters in June 1940, they at once began to search for scapegoats. The politicians of the interwar years were a convenient target for vilification by a regime that had supplanted them, and when the Vichy government began their trial at Riom the scope of the investigation was carefully restricted so that it excluded any examination of the military conduct of the war. In the political atmosphere of the day the need to spare the feelings of the generals and their troops had a higher priority than the search for truth.

In fact, it is impossible to explain France's collapse in 1940 without analyzing the performance of command as well as of those who obeyed its instructions. As regards the former, some judgments about the quality of the men who occupied high rank are unavoidable. It is just as important, however, to examine the organizational structure within which the generals had to operate and the systems by which they functioned. For, as we have learned, separating individuals from their working environment leaves important features of military misfortune unexplained. Judgments about the performance of French troops must be tempered by consideration of the resources available to them and the preparation they were given.

The failure of the French high command to rise to its obligations in May 1940 was itself a complex matter. In essence, it was a consequence of the personal deficiencies of a number of highly placed individuals, the defects of the structure within which they acted, and the inadequacies of the system by which they sought to operate. Failure in each of these three aspects of command was likely to be costly, though not necessarily fatal; failure in all three simultaneously put a weight of responsibility on the troops themselves that they were quite unable to bear. In large measure, the troops failed to adapt to the demands of the campaign of 1940 because their senior officers failed them.

Gamelin seems to have been acutely conscious of the weaknesses of his position and of the forces at his command from the moment the war began. Writing to Gauché of French military intelligence in September 1939, he remarked that "never in any period of her history has France been engaged in a war in conditions which are initially so unfavorable."[62] Premier Paul Reynaud, who was on the point of sacking Gamelin on May 9, 1940, called him a "nerveless philosopher" and raged at his impassivity and inertia during the Norwegian campaign: "He's a prefect, he's a bishop, but he's absolutely not a commander."[63] There is no doubt that, once the fighting began, Gamelin's inertia deprived his subordinates of the guidance they needed—a guidance that, as we have seen, the interwar regulations led them to expect. There was also a deep gulf of political suspicion between premier and supreme commander, for Gamelin was the protégé of Reynaud's predecessor and rival, Daladier, who had stayed on in the government as minister of national defense, whereas the premier was known to favor General Georges.

On the day war broke out Gamelin installed himself at Vincennes as supreme commander, appointing Georges commander in chief of land forces and of the northeastern theater. Two days later Gamelin formally gave Georges authority over the British Expeditionary Force. Having removed himself from direct control of the battle—which, in any case, he would find it hard to exercise since his headquarters at Vincennes lacked a radio—Gamelin now confused the chain of command yet further. In October, aware that he was due to retire in eleven months' time and anxious to maneuver Georges into a position that would hinder him from making a bid for the post of inspector general of the army, Gamelin demoted him and created a third headquarters organization, G.H.Q. Land Forces, under General André Doumenc.[64] Among the many unfortunate consequences of this administrative replication was the fact that the military intelligence section was split into two separate halves, one with Doumenc and the other with Georges, which did nothing to improve coordination between intelligence and planning.

When the battle for France began, the scattered locations of the headquarters for the three armies made coordinating their activities almost impossible. Gamelin was at Vincennes, just east of Paris; Georges was at La Ferté-sous-Jouarre, 40 miles east of the capital; and Doumenc was at Montry on the Marne, midway between the two. Vuillemin commanded the air force from St. Jean les deux Jumeaux, near La Ferté; and Admiral Jean Darlan was at naval headquarters at Maintenon southwest of Paris. To add further complexity to what was already a cumbrous chain of command, Georges appointed Billotte coordinator of Allied forces in the north on May 11, 1940, after the battle had started, so that he could concentrate on the Franco-German border and Switzerland, leaving operations in Belgium to his new subordinate. As well as weakening the command structure, this move diminished the prospects for Allied cooperation since neither the Belgians nor the British regarded Billotte as a person of much account.[65]

The command structure developed for the French air force was no less cumbersome, and once war began it created even greater confusion than that afflicting the army. Before the war a structure was devised according to which the commander of the air forces in the northeast theater, General H. E. Mouchard, would receive his operational orders from the commander in chief of the air force, General Vuillemin, and from Georges as the theater land commander. Then in February 1940 Mouchard was sacked, and a new cooperation air force on the northeastern front under General Têtu was created.[66] His command was in turn subdivided into a number of zones of aerial operations that corresponded to those of the army groups of the northeastern front. When the fighting started, the commanders of the zones of aerial operations found themselves having to act on orders emanating from four different sources: from their army group commander, from Têtu, from Billotte, and from Vuillemin. The air war quickly dissolved under the twin impact of the Luftwaffe and a mass of contradictory orders.

Between September 3, 1939, and May 10, 1940, Gamelin sent Georges 140 general communications. Over the next nine days he sent none, despite his reservations about how Georges was handling the battle.[67] On the morning of May 19, Doumenc telephoned the supreme commander to tell him that the moment had come for him to intervene. Gamelin then sat down and wrote out a "Secret and Personal Instruction" recommending a counterattack from north and south to slice off the columns of Panzers already nearing the Channel coast. The best that can be said for this suggestion is that it came four days too late. That same evening Reynaud sacked Gamelin and replaced him with Weygand. After first attempting to cut the German "corridor," the new supreme commander contributed to the strategic confusion by deciding to defend Paris and then changing his mind and falling back to the Caen-Dôle line.

While Gamelin was displaying such damaging inertia, his subordinates were frantically trying to repair the harm done by the advancing Germans. Communications were poor, so that commanders generally lacked up-to-date and accurate information and depended heavily on the civilian telephone net. In some cases, even this luxury was not available: at Doumenc's headquarters news arrived from all quarters by telephone, and once an hour it was relayed to supreme headquarters at Vincennes by dispatch rider.[68] In the field, divisional and army headquarters moved repeatedly, often over distances of no more than 20 to 35 kilometers. These short retirements reflected the attempt by Georges and Billotte to sew together a line of resistance as quickly as possible; however, since the Germans moved faster than the French, these moves never traded enough space to win the necessary time to organize a stand.

Under the pressure of remorseless enemy attacks the French command system broke down at all levels. At its apex Gamelin was inert, "suspended," in John Cairns' words, "between ignorance of the enemy's intention and inability to marshal a counterattack let alone a counteroffensive."[69] Generals in command of armies and army groups attempted to cope with the rapidly changing circumstances they faced and the shortage of timely and accurate information by "getting forward" to see for themselves: General Henri Giraud, having found a headquarters at Bohain with buried telephone cables, abandoned it to get forward to battalion headquarters.[70] This understandable but unfortunate response to the unforeseen broke up the command structure by removing vital portions of it at critical moments. As a result, French divisional commanders often found that they were simultaneously out of contact with their superiors and their subordinates.

One of the reasons why senior commanders acted in this apparently irresponsible way—and therefore one of the causes of their failure—was shortage of field intelligence about the enemy. Captured intelligence information was often transmitted too slowly up the chain of command to have any operational effect.[71] But in essence, field intelligence was in short supply. On May 1 the Germans changed the key settings on their Enigma ciphering machine, and the new ones took three weeks to break. Captured documents did produce some useful information, but it was generally a case of too little, too late. The Germans, in contrast, had a comprehensive knowledge of Allied dispositions, thanks to documents captured in Norway and the decryption of French military traffic.[72]

When the campaign in France is considered in the light of the dominant prewar doctrines that had shaped the French army it is possible to see how strongly these preconceived ideas influenced the actions of men who were getting little or no clear guidance from the high command. Corap's immediate response to the German penetration of his front on May 19 was to try to contain it by recreating a stable front line in order to be in a position to launch a counterattack. Jean Flavigny, the general commanding XXI Corps south of Sedan, presented with a golden opportunity on May 14 to attack the soft southern flank of Guderian's Panzers as they swung west to start their drive to the sea, instead broke up one of only four armored divisions in the French order of battle "so as to block every road and path down which the German armor might come."[73] Mistakes such as these were repeated many times as French commanders reacted to the unexpected by turning for succor to a doctrine that had deprived them of their reflexes.[74] Because the defenders' counterstrokes were so few in number and so weak in execution, the outcome of the campaign of 1940 seems to have turned largely on French military fragility. Without the remarkable imbalance between the combat performance of the two parties, it would not qualify for inclusion in our catalog of military misfortunes—even if the outcome had been the same.

Not merely did Gamelin and Weygand fail to command—they also failed to coordinate the allied armies alongside which they fought. The question of command of the Allied troops had deliberately been left unresolved, as Gamelin believed nothing would be possible until the battle actually began. The Belgians' refusal to cooperate with Britain or France until the Germans had crossed their frontier created considerable resentment. Commenting on the Dyle plan, the British chief of the imperial general staff, complained:

> We have to undertake a movement from a prepared position across a very flat plain to lines of obstacles which have in no way been prepared. All to help a country to resist invasion, and a country which is so terrified of infringing its own neutrality that it will make no preparations.[75]

The British field commander, Lord Gort, and his chief of staff, General Henry Pownall, were even more deeply prejudiced against the Belgians, from whom they anticipated the worst.[76] Nor were they much better disposed toward the French, so that both the proposed Anglo-French joint attack around Arras on May 21 and Weygand's abortive plan to get both armies to launch a simultaneous drive on Cambrai on May 24–25 failed largely through poor cooperation. Perhaps Georges might have been able to weld the Allied forces into a greater unity had he remained in command of the entire northeastern theater, though his performance under stress makes this seem unlikely. But the real fault was not that of any single individual—rather it was the consequence of an inadequate system and an imperfect organization that allowed division to triumph over cooperation.

While the failures of the generals were rapidly brushed under the carpet, those of their troops became magnified to a point at which the entire cause of the collapse was held to be the deep moral malaise that gripped the French people in 1940. "The plain truth was," writes one English author, "that the French had no stomach for another war."[77] In the aftermath of defeat, the idea that the war was lost because the bulk of the French population had lost the will to defend themselves and their country—and even that they assisted the enemy by sabotaging production in weapons factories—quickly took deep root, not least because it satisfied the need to find a general, all-embracing, and comprehensive explanation for total military failure.

The case for a failure of will and widespread moral contamination rests heavily on some major but isolated acts of industrial sabotage and on the activities of the Communist press during May and June 1940. Some cases of sabotage undoubtedly did occur at the Farman aircraft factory and the Renault tank works, where scrap iron was dumped in gearboxes and transmissions, and petrol and oil pipes were partially sawed through. More demonstrably widespread was Communist party propaganda, transmitted chiefly through its daily newspaper *L'Humanité*, which called throughout May and June 1940 for a "government of peace." However, the most recent and authoritative analysis of French public opinion has found no evidence that antimilitarism had an adverse effect on behavior in combat. Until June 1940, there were no serious cases of sabotage beside those at the Renault and Farman works. Neither peasant nor political pacifism was present in the armies during the autumn of 1939, although there was a strong sense of the preciousness of French blood. This is scarcely surprising in view of French experiences in the First World War and the decline in the birthrate during the first decades of the century. Military morale certainly fell during the early months of 1940 due to inactivity and uncertainties about the reasons for the war, and the army failed to counter this demoralization: In all units except the air force, cavalry, and motorized troops, training often took place on only one in every three days. Nonetheless, in early May morale was excellent among the cavalry, mechanized troops, tanks, and artillery and very good in almost all active units. When the fighting began French regimental commanders fully expected their men to hold firm under fire.[78]

One of the major reasons why these expectations were so dramatically disappointed was that French soldiers were taken completely by surprise by the way in which the enemy used tanks and airplanes together to create a whirlwind of fire, noise, and movement. The troops were totally unfamiliar with combat under these circumstances, having been prepared to fight a war of position.[79] In the first weeks of the war, seeking desperately to stem the onrushing German tide, the French high command issued orders that made no sense whatever to men who had not been trained for a war of movement. Weygand's general order to the troops on May 25 demanded that they meet infiltration with counterinfiltration and instructed them, if they were cut off, to form a "hedgehog" and turn themselves into breakwaters to check the advancing tide of the enemy.[80] How they were to do this was left entirely to improvisation, since no such tactics had formed part of their training. Significantly, the French units performed much better in the battles on the Somme and the Aisne in early June—before the "two-handed" attack that cut off Paris—when they were fighting a holding battle of the kind with which they were familiar from training and exercises.

The failure of the French air force to adapt to circumstances in 1940 was partly due to an inadequate command structure and system. It was also the consequence of its unresolved struggle with the army over whether it would have an independent strategic role in war or cooperate tactically with the land forces. From the early 1920s soldiers took the view that there was no such thing as independent "air war," and airmen riposted with a vision of heavy aerial strategic bombardments of military and civilian targets that alone might win a war—following the ideas of the Italian air theorist General Giulio Douhet.[81] Burdened with the tasks of cooperating with the land forces (primarily by acting as observers for the artillery), combating enemy planes, and carrying out strategic bombing by way of reprisal, in 1933 the air force made the extraordinary and ill-judged decision to develop a machine that could carry out any and all of these roles. The result was the BCR: a two-engine, eight-ton, underarmed and underpowered dinosaur. Specialized fighters, which were developed from 1936 on and were just entering service in 1940, reflected the late turn away from the BCR and were obsolescent by the time they went into combat: The Morane 445, the main French fighter, was 50 mph slower than the ME-109 and only fractionally faster than the Do17 bomber. Even the best French fighter in 1940—the American Curtiss P36—could only intercept German bombers with difficulty since they were almost as fast as it was.[82]

After its turn away from the multipurpose airplane, the French air force found itself under heavy pressure in the late 1930s to make air-land cooperation its main role. In September 1937 Air Minister Pierre Cot derided independent air action as leading to the pursuit of "uncertain objectives" and committed the air force to closer collaboration with the army.[83] Although his successor, Guy La Chambre, also insisted that the air force participate fully in the land battle, the policy was unacceptable to Vuillemin, and after a bitter dispute in 1938 the outcome was to divide the air force into two components: cooperative forces attached to land commanders, and independent reserves. In 1940, therefore, 40 percent of France's air resources were allocated for observation, and fighters were tasked with protecting spotter planes, covering troop movements, and guarding commercial routes. Thus, with its fighters scattered, it was impossible for the French air force to win local air superiority against the swarms of ME-109s. The legacy of the interwar debates and divisions was that—in the air—adaptation to meet the German threat was well-nigh impossible.

The French were seriously underequipped in a number of respects besides air power. Throughout the campaign they were chronically short of antiaircraft guns. There were also shortages of 25-mm antitank guns; munitions of all kinds, especially armor-piercing rounds; heavy artillery and tractors; and lorries.[84] One of the few weapons of which there was more than a sufficiency was the obsolete prewar "75" French field gun: in May 1940 there were still 5,667 of them left over from World War I.[85] After June 4 the material imbalance between the two sides was even greater: In the battle for France, the Germans had twice as many divisions as their opponents and nine times as much armor, as well as an even greater superiority in the air.

An old military adage says: "There are no such things as bad troops, only bad officers." This is wholly inadequate an explanation for poor combat performance, but behind it lies an important truth. In certain circumstances—and the fall of France is a quintessential example of those circumstances—soldiers can be called on to compensate for failures in pre-war and wartime leadership by fighting well. If they are to do this, clear and effective command is essential; but so are adequate preparation to meet the task at hand and sufficient modern equipment to do the job. The rank and file of the French army—and air force—lacked all three essentials in May and June 1940, and as a result they were unable to cope with the burden thrust upon them. In these circumstances their failure was hardly a dishonorable one.

CONCLUSION

A catastrophe is, as we have seen, the most complex kind of disaster to befall any military organization. It is at one and the same time the easiest to recognize and the most difficult to explain. Thus, many of the studies that have addressed the fall of France are imbued with a sense of the interplay of a number of factors whose interrelationships and relative responsibilities for the final outcome are difficult to determine.[86] The failure to provide a satisfactory analytic definition of catastrophe has resulted in a frequent retreat to oversimplification as a way out of this dilemma.

The idea that, during May and June 1940, a chain of events began to hook together that, at a certain point, became unbreakable and pointed inexorably to defeat for France, has encouraged some authors to try to identify a particular day as the "moment of defeat," after which everything the French did was to no avail.[87] There is a partial truth here. Crucial moments certainly did occur during the course of the campaign, but what makes them important is not what they were or when they occurred, but what they illustrate—that there were particular difficulties in coping with the German attack that magnified the importance of individual setbacks.

Another response to the catastrophe has been the view that things were wrong at such a deep level inside the French army that material shortages were not a fundamental issue in explaining the defeat; that—as one author has recently suggested—another thousand airplanes (which would have almost doubled the size of the active French air force) would have made no difference to the outcome.[88] This is far from being self-evident, and certainly a thousand more antiaircraft guns, skillfully sited, could have had a significant effect on the battle.

One reason why it has proved difficult to explain the fall of France in terms neither too simple nor impossibly complex is that the different types of failure that occurred shaded into one another. Learning failure was not a failure to identify and comprehend the essence of the German war machine; it was a failure to act speedily and effectively enough on that information. That in its turn can be explained, as we have seen, by the very force of the predictions made during most of the interwar period about the shape of future combat and how France should conduct its share. In turn, adaptive failure rested to a considerable degree on the shoulders of its two "partners in crime" and was magnified by earlier errors that were difficult—if not impossible—to put right at the last moment. But the individual failures themselves are every bit as important as the connections between them.

The failure to anticipate which occurred between 1939 and 1940 took place because new information that should have prompted a reconsideration of methods was not strong enough to break down existing preconceptions and presuppositions. Instead, perhaps because of the very shock of the rapid German victory over Poland, many generals clung to their faith in their established systems and anchored themselves to the rock of past experience. On May 3, 1940, Lord Gort believed that the German army was not in good fighting shape because its soldiers, although young and enthusiastic, were unsteady; eight days later the British chief of staff, General Lord Ironside, was expecting a long battle with "all the German heavy artillery coming in and pounding us."[89] Alexis Léger, secretary general of the French Foreign Office, reportedly believed in April 1940 that the German game was obvious: "They are going to await the French attack in the positions which they hold on their own soil along the Belgian frontier."[90] All these views were wrong; none accorded with the events of September 1939. But they are representative of a widespread inability to reinterpret accepted beliefs in the light of events. Perhaps the psychological cost of rising to such a challenge was too great for anyone except a de Gaulle.

To turn long-term predictive failure—the failure to anticipate the shape of the next war—into success would have required both a recognition of the new factors being introduced into warfare by the Germans, and a reorientation of doctrine to accommodate them. Clearly there was considerable knowledge of the general trend of German developments in pre-

1940 France: In 1929, to take only one example, Edouard Daladier expressed concern in parliament about Germany's motorization, mobility, and commercial aircraft.[91] And, as we have seen, changes were slowly being introduced into the French army and air force at the eleventh hour: New manuals on mechanized forces and the identification of novel tasks such as dive-bombing are examples of this. But other obstacles had to be overcome in addition to mental resistance to new ideas; an important constraint on Gamelin's capacity to update his army was the shortage of weapons-producing plants. Nonetheless, it now seems as though 1940 was a special kind of anticipatory failure. Change was afoot but unfortunately it had not had much time to take hold before the machine was put to the test.

The short-term failure of French intelligence to identify accurately the time and place of the German attack and to convince the high command that its prognostications were correct was essentially due to three factors: the ambiguity of the evidence, the lack of an established system by which to pass vital intelligence up to the top of the command chain, and the lack of readiness of commanders to take account of it. Given the reluctance of many experienced Allied field commanders to listen to their intelligence staffs in the closing stages of the Second World War, when they often had Enigma material at their disposal almost as soon as the Germans had transmitted it, Gamelin's failure to be more alert in this regard is perhaps scarcely surprising.[92]

The failure of the French army and air force to adapt to the circumstances of 1940 was largely due to lack of training, preparation, and equipment. Also, as we have seen, the rapid breakdown in the command structure and command system—which was partly self-created—added a burden of responsibility the troops in the field were unable to bear. There is, however, a special factor in this case—a particular problem in coping with *Blitzkrieg* that could turn small failures into large ones. In this campaign, due to the speed with which the Germans were able to follow up success, tactical mishaps very rapidly created the possibility for major strategic setbacks. We have seen this phenomenon occur in such incidents as Rommel's crossing of the Meuse at Houx and Guderian's forcing of the same river further south at Sedan. There are many other instances in which the same thing happened. The French had a solution to the problem, but they were unable to put it into effect because in 1940—unlike 1914—the force of the German attack did not diminish as the days went by. Failure to learn and to anticipate put a heavy premium on the need to adapt rapidly to novel circumstances in order to cope with the German attack. To do this the French needed time—the very factor denied to them by the operational virtuosity of the German Wehrmacht.

9

What Can Be Done?

THE ORGANIZATIONAL DIMENSION OF STRATEGY

MICHAEL HOWARD HAS POINTED OUT that over the last century and a half different dimensions of strategy—the operational, the logistic, the technological, and today the social—have in turn come to the fore in warfare and in the minds of those who study it.[1] To his list we would add the dimension most closely connected to military misfortune: the organizational dimension. Only through an appreciation of the ways in which military organizations work can we understand failures which have puzzled those who experience them, those who observe them, and those who try to explain them.

As we argued in chapter 3, this runs against the grain of many accounts of military failure.[2] Because military organizations are built on a strict hierarchy of rank and authority, it is entirely natural that many studies of war focus on generals and on the nature of command. Such studies are neither irrelevant or wrong-headed, for in every age, success in battle goes to the side which is well led.[3] To be sure, some military systems (the German and the Soviets most notably) have attempted to supplement or even supplant individual genius by the development of elaborate general staff systems; yet even those countries have sought military success in the prowess of a great captain, a Ludendorff or a Zhukov.

And good generals most certainly *do* make a difference. We have seen already that the recovery of the Eighth Army in Korea during the winter of 1951 owed much to the inspired generalship of Matthew B. Ridgway. Without his efforts it is quite conceivable that the United States would have withdrawn from the Korean Peninsula, accepting defeat in hopes of avoiding a larger calamity. But, as we have also seen, simply to turn the coin and explain defeats as the fault of individual commanders will not do. For although in some cases the failures of a commander are manifest, in others they are either difficult to discern or impossible to explain simply by reference to flaws of character or intellect.

The catastrophe at Pearl Harbor, as we noted at the beginning of this book, stemmed in part from the failings of several men, General Short and Admiral Kimmel among them. But neither then nor earlier in their careers did they demonstrate any particular divergence from the norms of the organizations that had educated and promoted them. Indeed, their contemporaries and superiors appear to have regarded them as exemplary officers.[4] Their failure lay not, as some have seen it, in a tragic flaw in American intelligence, or in the intelligence problem more broadly, but in their inability to weave their forces together for joint air defense of Oahu. Insofar as Short and Kimmel bear the responsibility for resisting the kinds of measures (for example, the creation of a joint air operations command post in Hawaii) that might have made the Japanese attack on Pearl Harbor a mere setback or even a draw, however, they reflected institutional proclivities and inclinations embedded in the United States Army and Navy. At Pearl Harbor, and in several of the other cases we have examined, the organizational structures and habits that commanders created, accepted, or simply could not transform failed to match immediate or expected challenges.

One can gain some perspective on military failures by comparing them to industrial accidents. The view that ascribes all fault or praise to a commander is the equivalent of concentrating only on operator error when highly complicated machines malfunction. Even if one looks beyond the individual operator to explain military misfortunes, one can conceive of broader explanations of a similar type. For example, one might argue that the fault lies in operators as a class or, in the case of military failures, the entire officer corps of a country.[5] While such a mass indictment may hold true for certain countries at certain times, it offers a greatly oversimplified view of most military calamities. We have seen that failure and success often walk side by side. The same Israeli officers corps that, through its unwarranted self-confidence, paved the way for the surprise of October 6 achieved dazzling operational successes only two weeks later. The same American naval bureaucracy—in many cases, precisely the same people—

that failed to implement an effective and coordinated antisubmarine doctrine in 1942 was enormously successful in so doing in 1943.

To continue our metaphor, one might explain failure by suggesting that highly complicated machines, even when well-designed and competently operated, require universal habits or practices to make them run smoothly. Favored all-purpose lubricants for the machinery of military organizations include such measures as forcing decision making lower down the hierarchy rather than at its summit, ensuring that information is transmitted up as well as down the chain of command, and maintaining the best communications between different components.[6] Yet it would be foolish to fall back on such axiomatic solutions—that a military organization should decentralize as much as possible, for instance. In key respects, for example, the solution to the American antisubmarine problem in 1942–43 lay in greater centralization. Likewise, the ultimate failure of Germany's offensives on the Western Front in the spring of 1918 stemmed from excessive decentralization, from a subordination of strategic considerations to purely tactical ones. The unresolved debate about whether business strategy should be created at the top or "blended incrementally and opportunistically" by suborganizations suggests that there is no universal remedy for the core problems of any complex organization.[7]

To understand why and how military organizations fail, we must abandon the temptation to focus a spotlight on any particular component to the exclusion of the rest, or to seek universal causes of failure. To understand military misfortune it is necessary first of all to understand the nature not of all organizations, but of the particular organization and above all, its critical tasks.[8] Then, and only then, we can begin to think of warding off failure. As all of our cases suggest—and as Pearl Harbor demonstrates so clearly—it is in the deficiencies of particular organizations confronted with particular tasks that the embryo of misfortune develops.

IN LIEU OF REMEDIES

Learning

One of the most obvious ways to improve performance is by learning, but failure to learn is due to far wider causes than the shortcomings of individuals who happen to find themselves in positions of command at critical moments. Part of the problem lies with the absence in many Western armed forces of an institutional locus for applied historical study. In a way, the operations research groups of World War II came into existence to fill just such a need, but their function was to look at the most recent, hence presumably the most relevant, history. Enormously useful as operations research was, it could not provide the long-term perspective required by the United States Navy in 1941, for example. Moreover, because the origins of operations research lie in the physical sciences, its practitioners have tended to look at material and procedural problems rather than managerial and organizational ones. The operations researcher instinctively looks for quantifiable data—which, as we have seen, do not always tell the full story.

Attachés and other intelligence officers might be expected to fill the learning role, but they too suffer from the necessarily narrow definitions of their tasks. Like the operations researchers, they labor under the burden of day-to-day requirements for information. Their superiors rarely want to hear from them reflections on how well their side is doing: their job is to find out what the other side (allied, neutral, or hostile) is up to. As for official historians, they concentrate on the writing of history and reflect only sporadically on its application to contemporary problems.[9] Most official history operations are small and underfunded homes for officers of an oddly scholarly bent. Rarely are such offices incorporated into the activities of a war college, much less a general staff. The main historical exceptions to this observation, the Germans and the Soviets, are instructive. In both cases military historical research has been regarded as a foundation for the development of military doctrine, and service in official institutes devoted to such work helps rather than hurts one's career.

Of course, even when they lack the wherewithal to produce high-quality official history, all military organizations study the lessons of combat to some degree. In doing so, they face the problem of deciding what in past military experience is relevant to their needs and therefore useful to them. Here they may face psychological obstacles to learning the kinds of lessons that we have discussed. It is all too easy to dismiss another decade's or another nation's experience by referring to one or two glaring differences from one's own situation—as the Royal Navy did in the 1930s by comfortably assuming that sonar had eliminated the submarine menace, or the United States Navy did by looking at the sorry state of British shipborne naval aviation.[10] This is particularly true when the lessons learned from a foreign power or from one's own historical experience suggest that one's own organization has fundamental flaws.

The problem of organizational learning, then, rests only partially on having a suborganization prepared to fulfill that function—although there is much to be said for such a unit, which might bridge the limbo of official history offices and the narrow focus of operational research sections. Equally important is the ability to tread a middle path between slavish acceptance of the superiority of a foreign model or equally unthinking rejection of it. The ill effects of the former can be seen in the United States military during the period before the Civil War, when the Napoleonic legend inspired American officers not only to immerse themselves in French doctrine but to imitate minor details of uniform and outfit as well.[11] The latter occurred in the early 1960s, when American statesmen and military leaders entered the Vietnam War in astonishing and deliberate ignorance of the French efforts there. In the words of one four-star general, "The French haven't won a war since Napoleon. What can we learn from them?"[12]

We have seen that the easiest lessons to be learned from foreign militaries concern technology and technique—gadgets that can be plugged into one's usual way of doing business. The most valuable lessons, however, may come from a study of other organizations and how they operate. Yet these are the most difficult lessons to cull, because they are the least tangible. Herbert Rosinski, a shrewd German émigré who had taught at the German Naval War College during the 1930s, recommended to the American government during World War II that the United States undertake a large scale effort to study the German general staff:

> The capture of so many German commanders and general staff officers has presented this country with a unique opportunity for the systematic study of the top-level training and organization of the German Army—which would deserve to be exploited to the utmost.
>
> That system of military training and higher organization has been studied by soldiers all over the world with the keenest attention ever since its exceptionally high level of efficiency revealed itself between 1864 and 1871, but so far with only very limited success.
>
> For the real secrets of that system—the things which "made it click"—were not to be found in the external forms of organization where the British, for example, looked for it, nor even in the detailed microscopic analysis of its strategic operations as the French did between 1871 and 1914, *but in certain almost intangible qualities of intellectual training and outlook of which even the members of the German Command and Staff System themselves were only half conscious.*[13]

Military organizations can and in many cases do learn very quickly. Sometimes this happens under the spur of defeat, as Edward Luttwak has observed.[14] But in war there is nothing like the hard school of experience, and many lessons can only be learned on the job—even by units that have devoted much care and attention in peacetime to thinking out their particular combat problems. Few organizations can have been half as well prepared for their wartime role as the United States Marine Corps in 1941: By then it had been training continuously for eight years and had put a great deal of intellectual effort into studying and practicing its role.[15] It had, in particular, studied but not been overwhelmed by the failure of the Dardanelles operation in 1915. Nonetheless, as late as 1937 its training exercises were severely criticized for having accepted unequivocally the contents of the manual on landing operations—which bore the prefix "Tentative"—and on the every eve of war it still had problems both with its matériel and with its techniques.[16] Once the war started the marines' capacity to learn had to, and on the whole did, keep pace with their mission. Robert Sherrod, a war correspondent who was present at Tarawa, noted that after two years of war they were "learning how to learn faster."[17]

What was true of the marines was no less true of some of the more distinguished commanders in World War II. In December 1942 Eisenhower noted reflectively that he was "learning many things," above all about what kind of qualities went to make a good commander.[18] And a year later, General George C. Marshall remarked that after having received an education in the First World War based on roads, rivers, and railroads, he had during the previous two years "been acquiring an education based on oceans and I've had to learn all over again."[19] Others too learned on the job. But not all commanders were as far-sighted as Marshall or as open-minded as Eisenhower, nor were all units as learning-oriented as the Marines—often quite the contrary! What both these examples suggest is that some things can be learned in peacetime, and others only in war, and that if the military are to make the most of their opportunities when war comes they must be organizationally prepared to learn.

In 1944 Field Marshal Erwin Rommel observed that on the whole American forces had shown themselves to be extraordinarily fast learners:

> In this they were assisted by their extraordinary sense for the
> practical and material and by their complete lack of regard for
> tradition and worthless theories. . . . The Americans, it is fair to say,
> profited far more than the British from their experience in Africa,
> thus confirming the axiom that education is easier than
> reeducation.[20]

Military organizations should inculcate in their members a relentless empiricism, a disdain for a priori theorizing if they are to succeed. The "learners" in military organizations must cultivate the temperament of the historian, the detective, or the journalist, rather than the theoretical bent of the social scientist or philosopher.

Anticipation

The job of anticipation is often thought of as one of the chief functions of Intelligence, which is thought to have the task of foretelling an enemy's actions. As we have seen, and as common sense would indicate, it is difficult enough for an intelligence organization to grasp the enemy's *current* state, to include his methods of operation and tactical preferences.[21] The task of predicting the future—as opposed to issuing a warning—is a wholly unreasonable one. Moreover, effective anticipation involves not only estimating the enemy's likely actions but comparing them to one's own ways of war. In the case of the Yom Kippur War, for example, the misfortune we studied was only partly driven by the stubborn refusal of Israeli military intelligence to read correctly the signs of an impending war. It went further, to the operational level of war.

Before October 1973 the IDF appears to have fought as a collection of branches rather than a coordinated, combined arms force. Shortly before the war Chief of Staff Elazar told an interviewer that:

> Israel's tankers, paratroopers and airmen share a common faith: each group is convinced it can win the next war without the help of the other . . . What results from that spirit, Lieutenant General Dado Elazar told the *Armed Forces Journal,* is that each arm develops its own 'philosophy of battle'—and he encourages the rivalry . . . 'There's no such thing as the same strategic or tactical approach between different arms of the IDF,' Elazar says.[22]

Shortly after the war, however, a chastened Elazar declared: "Combined operations and the combined task force present what I consider to be one of the major lessons to be learned on the tactical and operational level." The IDF had learned that combined arms had become "a crucial factor for success in every single battle, in every campaign, and in every war."[23]

The post-mortem analyses carried out by some Israeli officers in the aftermath of the 1973 war demonstrate the close link between the outcome of battle and the kind of internalized assumptions Elazar announced so confidently before the Yom Kippur War. In their view the IDF adhered to a rigid strategy which prevented it from yielding any ground in the Sinai, and instead committed itself to wasteful and needless counterattacks: in this view, the unsuccessful counterattacks of October 7–9 had their roots in prewar thinking. The overwhelming commitment to offensive operations not only led to inappropriate operations, but to gross overconfidence. Ya'akov Chasdai recalls one exercise before 1973 at the Israeli staff college, in which an *ugda* commander successfully pushed five Egyptian divisions back to the canal—noting bitterly that the same commander met with no such success during the 1973 war.[24] Thus, the misfortune of the Suez Front in October 1973 reflected no so much a failure to predict enemy moves—in some ways the Israelis did that quite well— as a failure mentally to match likely enemy action with the range of likely Israeli reactions. Israeli understanding of what would work and what would not, what kinds of interaction would occur between, for example, surface-to-air missiles and jet aircraft, between Israeli tank and Egyptian antitank tactics, diverged sharply from the reality of the battlefield.

The Israelis recovered magnificently at the tactical and operational levels of war. Yet consideration of their experience in 1973 points to a certain intellectual deficiency in Western military concepts. To overcome problems of anticipation, many Western armed forces have come to rely on their equivalent of "operators' rules"—manuals of military doctrine which prescribe what action to take in any combat situation. In American usage, at any rate, doctrine has meant "authoritative fundamental principles by which military forces guide their actions."[25] Shortly after the Yom Kippur War the U.S. Army attempted to absorb the doctrinal lessons of the Yom Kippur War, but did so using a stifling—and in the end unworkable—conception of doctrine. General William DePuy, commander of U.S. Army's Training and Doctrine Command:

> considered doctrine as a tool with which to coordinate the myriad activities of a complex organization. . . . Doctrine [in this view] consisted of those tactical techniques necessary for success on the modern battlefield that the schools and training centers taught and published in circulars and manuals. . . . [26]

It is interesting to contrast the Soviet definition of military doctrine as

> a system of scientifically sound guiding views which are officially adopted in one or another state and concern the essence, goals and nature of a war, the preparation of the nation and the armed forces for it and the methods of waging it. The political bases of a military doctrine disclose the sociopolitical essence of modern wars . . . The military-technical bases of the doctrine determine what the strategic nature of a future war can be like and for what sort of war and against what enemy one must be prepared to fight; what Armed

Forces are needed for such a war (their effective strength, organization and technical equipping); what the methods could be for carrying out strategic and operational-tactical missions in a future war; what forms and methods can be used to train an army and navy. . . . [27]

Ironically, despite the difference between a liberal democracy and a party dictatorship, the Soviet view is the less rigid, the richer, the more imaginative. One might say, as a kind of shorthand, that the Soviets conceive of doctrine as a picture of future war, incorporating politics and technology as well as tactics. This far more inclusive picture of war makes a great deal of sense: Failures of anticipation may be best understood as doctrinal failures, using the term in the Soviet sense. Misfortunes of anticipation stem not just—and often not even chiefly—from failing to predict the specific actions of one's enemy, but from a failure to think through the sensitive issue of how well one's own forces can react to an opponent's style of warfare. Such misfortunes result as well from a failure to think as holistically as the Soviet definition of doctrine would suggest. The Israelis, like others who have suffered such misfortunes, did not tie together the strategic (that is, politicomilitary) purposes and conditions of a future war with their understanding of enemy tactics and the interaction of new military technologies (in particular, the antitank missile and the surface-to-air missile). When military organizations look at future war they must think as hard and realistically about the politicomilitary conditions under which it will occur as about the tactics each side will adopt, and they must attempt to see how the one level of warfare will shape or direct the latter. The alternative, too often preferred by civilian policy analysts as well as military officers, is a dangerously misleading and sterile operational study, uninformed by political considerations.[28]

Adaptation

More than failure to learn or failure to anticipate, failure to adapt can be laid at the feet of command. One of Clausewitz's most-often-repeated sayings is that war is the province of chance, and chance will throw up opportunities as often as it will present adversity. (In this context it is interesting to note that the Chinese ideograph for "crisis" is made up of two characters, one meaning "catastrophe" and the other "opportunity".) By encouraging the development of initiative, troops can be trained to make the most of opportunities which present themselves on the ground—this was precisely the basis of the excellence of the German field armies in both World Wars. But in all armies, and especially in those that do not follow the German example in their training, it is the commanders' job to spot an opening and then to capitalize on it.

Failure of this type has provided a well-stocked preserve on which to hunt for scapegoats, but in truth the quarry is not merely the commander, but also *the conception of command* that prevails in a given military organization. Some systems of command made adaptation to unexpected or unforeseen circumstances relatively easy, while others make it virtually impossible. As we have seen in the case of Suvla Bay, senior officers behave in ways the system of the day encourages or expects of them. At the time, the likely consequences—and more especially, the potential drawbacks—of the system may be far from apparent, or else unquestioned because they are unquestionable without the strong possibility of official retribution. But in retrospect the way in which command is perceived in an organization, and the system by which it is exercised, can of itself greatly increase the likelihood of failure. This is especially clear when we look at the British conception of command during the First World War.

By the time World War I began, the British Army was in the grip of a personalized command system in which one or two powerful individuals at the summit of the military hierarchy were able to control selection and promotion. Higher appointments both before and during the war were a playground for favoritism and rivalry; and when Douglas Haig became commander in chief of all British troops in France in December 1915 he continued to work the system in much the same was as before. He chose or retained for his personal staff yes-men who loyally supported his ideas about the possibility of breaking the German lines and who provided him with statistical support in the form of optimistic appreciations that showed that the German army was wearing down at a faster rate than the Allies. Physically isolated at general headquarters, Haig was also intellectually isolated from any unwelcome criticism of his own strategic formula for victory.[29]

Another facet of the system of command which prevailed in the British armies between 1914 and 1918 was the explicit belief that it was not right to interfere with the initiative of subordinate commanders.[30] As a result, GHQ provided subordinate commanders with general directives on when and where to attack the enemy—laying continual stress on aggressiveness at all times—but left those same commanders to work out how to do what they were being ordered to do. Instead of reassessing goals in the light of the novel and perplexing conditions of trench warfare, Haig and his loyal coterie of staff officers disbursed reminders about age-old strategic principles and stressed general concepts. An attempt by Sir

William Robertson, who as chief of the Imperial General Staff in London had overall responsibility for the military direction of the war, to persuade Haig in 1917 that traditional principles simply did not apply any longer, fell on deaf ears. When his senior commanders recommended a cautious step-by-step approach to attacking the enemy, Haig simply selected a general with a more congenial out-and-out aggressive attitude.[31] It was not until after the near disaster in March 1918, when the German "Michael" offensive all but broke the Allied line and demonstrated beyond doubt that new techniques for launching penetration attacks led by small, heavily armed groups of stormtroops could succeed where conventional mass assaults ended in bloody setbacks, that Haig acknowledged the value of the unorthodox tactical doctrines devised by General Sir Ivor Maxse by appointing him inspector general of training.[32]

The Germans had a far different approach in World War I.[33] Their peculiar general staff system also led senior commanders to give broad orders—*Weisungsführung*, or "leadership by directive" as it was called. But balancing this was the practice of delegating to general staff members or other experts a kind of plenipotentiary power—*Vollmacht*—which short-circuited the chain of command when that proved necessary. Repeatedly during the war general staff officers of the rank of lieutenant colonel or colonel took control of situations that seemed on the brink of disaster. These interventions were not always successful—the constriction of the German left wing during the opening campaign of 1914 by Lieutenant Colonel Richard Hentsch is a particularly controversial case—but they did prevent certain kinds of failures. And the resulting flexibility enabled the Germans to score remarkable tactical successes in both the offense and defense throughout the war.

The "chateau generalship" of the British high command during the First World War, in which generals had become remote figures, glimpsed occasionally by the troops in a passing staff car, who sat in their offices like managing directors running the war like a factory enterprise, attracted the scornful and bitter criticism of Major General J. F. C. Fuller in 1933. In a book entitled *Generalship: Its Diseases and Their Cure*, Fuller castigated this style of leadership as having resulted in a neglect of the critical operational level of war. However, rather than moving on to analyze the system of command which had demonstrated so many shortcomings, Fuller concentrated his attention on leadership, or more accurately, on individual leaders, quoting with approval the judgment of the eighteenth-century French marshal, Maurice de Saxe, that a good commander needed courage, brains, and good health.[34]

In choosing to equate command with leadership, Fuller, despite his reputation as a highly unconventional soldier, lined himself up squarely alongside many of those whose performance in the Great War he so strongly criticized. Lecturing to the U.S. Army War College in 1921 on "Command," General the Earl of Cavan informed his audience that "I firmly believe, and I more believe it than ever now after the experience of two wars, that leadership is everything."[35] What leadership amounted to, as far as Cavan was concerned, was trusting one's subordinates and getting rid of any staff officer who showed himself "not capable of commanding the confidence of the men under him, and not capable of grasping what you want him to do and not capable of carrying it out." Although too wise simply to equate command with leadership and nothing else, even General George C. Marshall, about to preside over an unparalleled expansion of the United States Army, had no doubts about its paramount importance in the summer of 1940: "Command involves leadership," he wrote, and "leadership in a military emergency is, in my opinion, the most important single consideration."[36]

Fuller had accurately identified the seat of the problem as far as the British failure on the Western Front in World War I was concerned, but he failed to discern more than a single one of its facets. For—at the summit—command consists of management as well as of leadership, and although the hierarchy of rank may make it seem otherwise, it is very much a collaborative activity. This perspective was long ignored by Fuller and others. Instead, they searched for the optimum mix of qualities and attributes that make the ideal commander.[37] Only recently has the focus of attention switched to styles and functions of command, and the problem of structure has still not had the attention it deserves. Yet, as perceptive (if frustrated) leaders of military organizations have noted, changing the *concept of command* is, if anything more difficult than picking a single commander. John F. Lehman, Jr., secretary of the United States Navy from 1981 to 1987, scored an astonishing victory in purging the U.S. navy of Admiral Hyman Rickover, father of the nuclear navy. Lehman believed that despite his undeniable virtues Rickover's objective was:

> no less than the creation of a kind of new socialist man for the nuclear program. . . . In 'The Rickover Way' the age-old military paradigm 'Do not question higher authority' is raised to a higher level of purity; all the answers are to be found in the book, and the book and the checklist must be followed—a philosophy essential for nuclear safety, but grotesque when extended to every aspect of one's profession.[38]

Yet Lehman, despite his bureaucratic skills, remarkable knowledge of the U.S. navy, and sheer pluck failed in part. His account makes it quite clear that "the Rickover Way"—which he tackled head-on—survived his onslaught.[39]

"The Ghost in the Machine"

The idea that setbacks are frequently the consequence of mere bad luck is a seductive one. It is psychologically comforting to those who have not themselves experienced disaster, which may be the reason why it is so often offered as a consolation. "You have my sympathies," Admiral Nimitz remarked to Kimmel as he relieved him of command at Pearl Harbor on Christmas Day, 1941. "The same thing could have happened to anybody."[40] And Admiral Claude C. Bloch wrote (somewhat disingenuously) to a colleague some three months later: "I feel very sorry for both Kimmel and Short. . . . I think both you and I are very lucky because the same thing might well have happened to either or both of us."[41]

The kinds of misfortunes we have discussed in this book are not, however, the product of malevolent chance. Neither are they the sole responsibility of any single individual, not even the military commander. Instead, each is the consequence of the inherent fragility of an entire organization. Misfortune lurks somewhere within the bowels of every military operation: It is "the ghost in the machine" that can be conjured up by a variety of circumstances. There may be occasions when it cannot be avoided or overcome; but just as frequently it is the consequence of deficiencies in structure and function. Military misfortunes, as we have identified them, are the equivalent of the "normal accidents" described by Charles Perrow, for, as we have seen, the chain of command is often more complex than the "wiring diagrams" allow for and can operate in ways that are not immediately obvious to those who occupy those diagrams' boxes.

Sometimes a very severe deficiency in organizational structure can be easily identified even though it does not result in defeat. The fact that, in October 1944, the two naval officers in command of the major fleet units involved in the Battle of Leyte Gulf reported to different superiors meant, in the judgment of one American military historian, that "the American naval situation at Leyte was a disaster waiting to happen."[42] In this case a stroke of sheer good fortune—the loss of nerve of the Japanese naval commander, Admiral Takeo Kurita, and the consequent withdrawal of the Japanese task force at the eleventh hour, when Admiral Thomas C. Kincaid's escort carriers had all but exhausted their defensive capabilities—averted disaster. But the Battle of Leyte Gulf is most certainly a case of military failure.

When all is said and done organization and system in the military world operate at the behest of generals. If our line of argument is correct, a general or admiral who can transcend military misfortune must be willing to entertain the possibility of large flaws in how his organization operates, and be willing to risk much to correct them. But commanders cannot indulge themselves too much in reflection about potential—as opposed to present—failure, and indeed, some of the greatest commanders are those who deliberately shunt the very possibility aside. William Tecumseh Sherman once told a subordinate what made Ulysses Grant his superior in the art of war:

> Wilson, I'm a damned sight smarter than Grant; I know more about organization, supply and administration and about everything else than he does; but I'll tell you where he beats me and where he beats the world. He don't care a damn for what the enemy does out of his sight but it scares me like hell. I'm more nervous than he is. I am much more likely to change my orders or to countermarch my command than he is. He uses such information as he has according to his best judgment; he issues his orders and does his level best to carry them out without much reference to what is going on about him. . . . [43]

This relentless focus on imposing one's will on the enemy typifies the Western approach to war, and lends it much of its vigor. In the case of Grant, such apparent imperviousness to the environment paved the way for the near catastrophe of Shiloh, but it also enabled him to conduct the bloody campaigns of 1864 with a ferocity that doomed the Confederacy by the autumn of that year.

The difficulties—and indeed the dangers—of giving way to excessive reflection on potential failure have been poignantly captured by Field Marshal Sir William Slim, a defeated general who did not allow reflection to shatter his nerve following the rout of British forces in Burma in 1942.

> Defeat is bitter. Bitter to the common soldier, but trebly bitter to his general. The soldier may comfort himself with the thought that, whatever the result, he has done his duty faithfully and steadfastly, but the commander has failed in *his* duty if he has not won victory—for that *is* his duty. He has no other comparable to it. He will go over in his mind the events of the campaign. "Here," he will think, "I went wrong; here I took counsel of my fears when I should have been bold; there I should have waited to gather strength, not struck piecemeal; at such a moment I failed to grasp opportunity when it was presented to me." He will remember the soldiers whom he sent into the attack that failed and who did not

come back. He will recall the look in the eyes of men who trusted him. "I have failed them," he will say to himself, "and failed my country!" He will see himself for what he is—a defeated general. In a dark hour he will turn in upon himself and question the very foundations of his leadership and his manhood.

And then he must stop! For if he is ever to command in battle again, he must shake off these regrets, and stamp on them, as they claw at his will and his self-confidence. He must beat off these attacks he delivers against himself, and cast out the doubts born of failure. Forget them, and remember only the lessons to be learned from defeat—they are more than from victory.[44]

Slim's fortitude, strength of character, and sheer intellectual capacity allowed him to escape from the entangling coils of the paradox of command. He was able to analyze the causes of his defeat and then move forward to plan for victory on the basis of that hard-won knowledge. But if military misfortune is to be avoided, reflection must precede and preempt defeat. A general must conjure up the phantasm of disaster, as it were, encouraging it into being for the very purpose of exorcising it. This kind of activity is all too likely to bring on an attack of the very fears and anxieties engendered by the real thing, and so paralyze the will and weaken the firmness of purpose as to cause the very thing it seeks to avoid. It is old advice that generals "should not take counsel of their fears."

Shrewd intervention by senior political leaders can diminish the vulnerability of military organizations to misfortune.[45] It is, of course, one of the great responsibilities of statesmen to select the leaders of their armed forces. The judgments to be made here concern not technique but character—the variety of human types required for a balanced and effective military organization. It was by no means the smallest of Franklin Roosevelt's contributions to American success in World War II that he selected George Marshall and Ernest King to lead the U.S. army and navy. Neither was an obvious choice, and each was uniquely suited to the challenges faced by his service at the time he was appointed.

Beyond selecting senior commanders, however, the civilian heads of a military establishment must query their generals, and not merely on broad problems of strategy but about the operational plans and concepts used to meet those problems and the fitness of the organizations at their disposal to implement those plans and concepts. This was Churchill's role as a war leader in 1940–45, and although it had considerable costs, it had very great payoffs as well.[46] Yet even such a style of leadership did not and could not prevent—as Churchill warned the House of Commons in October 1940—"not only great dangers, but many more misfortunes, many shortcomings, many mistakes, many disappointments."[47]

In peacetime this cross-examination may take a different form, and concern, in particular the nature of the command systems—including the promotion and educational systems, as well as the shape of the organization charts—which govern the armed forces. The task is a delicate one, for ill-informed civilian intervention can do enormous damage, and efforts to dictate will backfire or be subverted by a recalcitrant bureaucracy. The great statesmen who have been most successful in reforming military organizations—the turn-of-the-century American Secretary of War Elihu Root, for example—worked with senior officers to overhaul command systems shown to be unsuited for the tasks before them.[48]

The causes of military misfortune are complex. For this very reason it would be foolish to proffer any antidotes to failure without first seeking to understand fully the nature of the problem of command in the age of large and complicated organizations. But command does not equate merely to the responsibilities borne by an individual, no matter how august his rank or extensive his powers. The problem of command is not universal but particular, and it is defined by the nature of each military organization and the unique strategic, operational, and tactical challenges it faces. Each commander is, as we have seen, bound by a unique set of organizational fetters. Only by understanding those bindings can he take action to make them less confining or crippling, but never can he hope to strike them, once and for all, from his wrists.

Afterword

Since this book appeared, the United States has waged two wars in Iraq, one in Afghanistan, and two in the former Yugoslavia, and conducted scores of minor operations, some quite bloody. While most of these campaigns were successful, not all were—the 1993 fighting in Mogadishu, Somalia, in which eighteen American soldiers lost their lives, was a tactical success but a strategic defeat. Shortly after the engagement (commemorated in the book and film *Blackhawk Down*) the United States withdrew from Somalia, leaving its opponent, Mohamed Farah Aideed, in control of the contested city.

Even successful operations, such as the Afghan war of 2001, or the war with Serbia in 1999, had their setbacks—the misplanned operation ANACONDA against al Qaeda and the Taliban in the Shah-i-Kot mountains, for example, was almost a disaster, as was the hapless deployment of army forces (Task Force HAWK) into Albania during the Kosovo war. Above all, the most interesting and disturbing recent "misfortune," as we have defined it here, was the insurgency waged against Coalition forces in Iraq following the swift toppling of Saddam Hussein's regime in April 2003.

Misfortune is the failure of a competent military organization to learn, anticipate, or adapt. How does that schema apply to Iraq?

When American forces began the march up from Kuwait to Baghdad they anticipated dangers aplenty. No one then knew whether the Iraqis had usable stocks of chemical and biological weapons that might be deployed against the Americans and their allies, and so American and British troops took preparations against that sort of attack very seriously indeed. On the basis of the experience of the first Gulf War, they expected a variety of Iraqi attempts to create ecological disaster or economic catastrophe by sabotaging oil wells, and so special units moved swiftly to secure key oil fields. The American high command contemplated the possibility of massive refugee flows—and therefore laid in large supplies of emergency rations and water purification equipment. These calamities did not occur, partly because Coalition actions had forestalled them, but chiefly because the Iraqis did not attempt them.

What *did* occur, however, was a vicious irregular war against Coalition supply lines, waged by units whose very existence had been either unknown or discounted by Allied commanders, as American commander Lieutenant General William Wallace freely acknowledged. But here, as elsewhere, American forces displayed that quality of adaptation that their adversaries had long noted. Shifting some infantry units to security operations along the lines of communication, and then hurling armored formations through Baghdad itself, the American-led Coalition brought down the dictatorship of Saddam Hussein and the Ba'ath party in a three-week campaign.

Most knowledgeable observers assumed that, barring the use of unconventional weapons, such would be the result; the Iraqi military, demoralized, ill-equipped, and psychologically overawed by the superpower whose forces had crushed them a decade before, could not be expected to put up much of a fight. But what happened next was a surprise. An insurgency began, not acknowledged as such by American leaders for a good half year after the overthrow of the regime. The United States stumbled repeatedly as it attempted to wage counterinsurgency warfare. Two years after the war, a force of 140,000 American troops remained in a country which, it had been anticipated, they would have long since largely evacuated. Through mid-2005 the Americans suffered approximately 10,000 casualties, a number utterly unanticipated before the conflict. Though the Americans had cleared some cities of insurgents (most notably the Sunni town of Falluja), others (Mosul, most notably) had gone from pacified if uneasy urban centers to dangerously violent centers of opposition to the Americans and the Iraqis working with them. The war was also vastly more expensive than anticipated. Far from living off its oil revenues, the fledgling Iraqi state required tens of billions of dollars of aid. Electrical power had barely returned to prewar levels of supply.

Part of what made this phase of the war so puzzling was the nature of the enemy. Unlike classic insurgencies of the past—the Algerian National Liberation Front (FLN) operating against the French in the 1950s, for example, or the Viet Cong of the 1960s, the Iraqi resistance was internally divided between Sunnis and Shi'a, former Ba'athists and foreign jihadis, criminals and tribal groups, who only periodically worked with each other. The only notable leader among them, Musab al Zarqawi, was a Jordanian, viewed with suspicion by a xenophobic population. The insurgents had no unifying message of independence or ideology, and their tactics—horrific suicide bombings of civilians—antagonized as much as they intimidated. Although their tactics improved over time, they displayed little of the battlefield competence of other insurgent movements, and they were up against a military whose advantages in every sphere of military technology and training were extraordinary.

And yet the war burned on.

Early on in the insurgency some commentators explained the difficulty simply in terms of numbers—and indeed the American military itself took this view. Using such hoary rules of thumb as that attributed to Field Marshal Sir Gerald Templer in Malaya, that it requires ten regulars to every guerrilla, the Americans would have seemed to need twice as many troops as they had. But numbers alone did not count for American missteps. When set against the historical record, much of American behavior appeared baffling.

In particular, two American failures stand out. All successful counterinsurgencies require a blending of civilian and military measures; such wars are about security, to be sure, but also about the provision of electrical power, jobs, and the basic requirements of a decent life such as sewage treatment and schools. To that end, security and civic action walk hand in hand, and successful counterinsurgency almost invariably requires unified action and unity of command, under a politically sophisticated general or a militarily knowledgeable civilian leader. In Iraq, the United States put in place an occupation structure that separated the two and, in particular, during the first critical year after the overthrow of Saddam, was headed by a civilian (Ambassador Paul Bremer) and a military commander (Lieutenant General Ricardo Sanchez) who came to loathe one another.

If unity of command escaped the Americans, so too did one of the cardinal requirements of counterinsurgency—developing local forces. Beginning with the abrupt dismissal of the Iraqi armed forces, followed by implausible schemes to develop an Iraqi military purely for external defense (rather than internal threats), and continuing with the training of security forces by contractors rather than American units, the United States did an abysmal job of developing the only kinds of units that could ultimately defeat the insurgency—units composed of Iraqis, not Americans.

These critical failures were accompanied by others, less grievous, perhaps, but serious enough. The preference for expensive, large-scale reconstruction projects run by American or European companies over smaller, local enterprises that would employ Iraqis and thereby take aggrieved and restless young men off the street, for example, meant that the insurgents could find plenty of recruits willing to take a potshot at the Americans for a modest sum of money. Botched negotiations with the Iraqi transitional government meant that a large insurgent stronghold in Falluja was allowed to develop until the spring of 2005, when United States Marines wiped it out in a bloody assault. But the two core failures—absence of unity of command at the top, and failure to develop Iraqi forces—made others more likely, and more serious.

What is peculiar is that these two failures represent in turn a dismal failure to learn from the past. Unity of command was a critical ingredient of the British counterinsurgency in Malaya in the 1950s, and an important one in the American Civil Operations Rural Development Support (CORDS) program in Vietnam in the late 1960s (despite the larger failure of that war). For that matter, unity of command was crucial for American counterinsurgency in the Philippines a century earlier. Successful American counterinsurgency in El Salvador in the 1980s rested first and foremost on the development of local forces, which had also proven indispensable at the very same time in Afghanistan.

To some extent, the story of the Iraqi insurgency represented an American failure to anticipate the chaos of a society subjected to decades of exceptionally brutal dictatorship and prolonged warfare. Having listened too much, perhaps, to Iraqi exiles, the American government failed to anticipate that once the clamps of Saddam's rule were removed, what would remain were not the structures of a fairly normal society, but a deeply fractured and distressed collection of individuals and groups, too traumatized for real self-rule and certainly for reconstruction.

The unexpected, sustained violence after the spring of 2003 represented even more a failure to learn—and this from a military that prided itself on the quality of its military educational system. Following the Vietnam war the American military self-consciously turned its back on that experience, and even as it fought small or irregular wars it attempted to define those experiences as marginal, or even in some respects illegitimate. The counterinsurgency manuals of the new century either dealt with peacekeeping, or were simply the leftovers of the Vietnam era—as if modern insurgents were still Communist-led peasants. The staff schools and war colleges focused on high intensity warfare, scanting the study of insurgency and in some ways denying its legitimacy. For many military and political leaders the lessons of Vietnam had to do not with strategy and operations—with how the United States might have succeeded, in other words—but with the parlous decision-making that took the country into that conflict. Postwar conflicts such as the El Salvador insurgency received attention only from specialists and sub-communities such as special forces officers.

The military studied its past as a set of morality plays, the failures of Vietnam set against the successes of the first Gulf War. In the former, the common civilian and military narrative had it, ill-defined objectives, a lack of public support, and timid or dishonest civilian and military leadership got us into a war which either should not have been fought or that could have been won by purely conventional means. In the latter, the narrative continued, victory came through a tightly controlled, massive application of force in pursuit of simple and limited objectives.

This narrative was at best grossly simplified, and at worst wrong. By understanding history in this way, the American defense establishment set itself up to forget much of what it had known about fighting insurgencies. It may not have been able to anticipate the problems it would face in Iraq (although some would argue that it should have), and it certainly displayed a remarkable ability to adapt, as small unit leaders reacquainted themselves with some of the lasting verities of irregular warfare, but it had failed to learn, and its men and women paid a high price for that failure.

The story of the Iraq war is not over, of course. But it is, already, a reminder that the most powerful and competent military the world has ever known can still stumble, and stumble badly. It can make large mistakes not because of stupidity or incompetence, but because it has chosen to embrace a comfortable version of history rather than an accurate one. No matter what the ultimate outcome in Iraq, it is clear that such a wishful reading of history, even if it does not yield failure, will, most assuredly, produce misfortune.

Notes

Chapter 1
WHY MISFORTUNE?

1. John Keegan, *The Face of Battle* (New York: Viking Press, 1976), p. 199.
2. Harry B. Williams, *Communication in Community Disaster*, Ph.D. dissertation, University of North Carolina at Chapel Hill, 1956, p. 69. Quoted in Charles E. Fritz, "Disaster," in Robert K. Merton and Robert A. Nisbet, eds., *Contemporary Social Problems: An Introduction to the Sociology of Deviant Behaviour and Social Disorganisation* (New York: Harcourt, Brace and World, 1961), p. 656.
3. This was the title Manstein gave to his memoirs.
4. Carl von Clausewitz, *On War*, Michael Howard and Peter Paret, eds. and trans. (Princeton: Princeton University Press, 1976), p. 85.
5. Guy Chapman, *Why France Collapsed* (London: Cassell, 1968), p. 334.
6. Marc Bloch, *L'étrange défaite* (Paris: Societé des Editions Franc-Tireur, 1946), p. 45.

Chapter 2
UNDERSTANDING DISASTER

1. For a discussion of the causes of this disaster, see John Keegan, *The Face of Battle* (New York: Viking, 1970), pp. 78–116.
2. Patrick Macrory, *Signal Catastrophe* (London: Hodder & Stoughton, 1966).
3. For an excellent account of these and other imperial misfortunes see V. G.

Kiernan, *European Empires from Conquest to Collapse 1815–1960* (London: Fontana Books, 1982).

4. Martin van Creveld, *Command in War* (Cambridge: Harvard University Press, 1985).

5. John Gooch, *The Plans of War: The General Staff and British Military Strategy, c. 1900–1916* (London: Routledge & Kegan Paul, 1974), pp. 306–7.

6. Edwin T. Layton, *And I Was There* (New York: Morrow, 1985).

7. Denis Judd, *Someone Has Blundered: Calamities of the British Army in the Victorian Age* (London: Arthur Barker, 1973) p. xx.

8. Norman F. Dixon, *On the Psychology of Military Incompetence* (London: Jonathan Cape, 1976), p. 94.

9. Ibid., p. 278 (italics in original).

10. Ibid., p. 381.

11. For a look at World War II Allied commanders from this point of view, see David Irving, *The War between the Generals* (London: Allen Lane, 1981).

12. Charles Fair, *From the Jaws of Victory* (New York: Simon & Schuster, 1971), p. 270.

13. Alan Clark, *The Donkeys* (London: Hutchinson, 1961).

14. C. S. Forester, *The General* (Harmondsworth: Penguin Books, 1956), pp. 136, 181.

15. Ibid., p. 50.

16. Jere Clemens King, ed., *The First World War* (London: Macmillan, 1972), p. xlv.

17. Winston S. Churchill, *The World Crisis 1911–1918* (London: Butterworth, abridged edition 1931), vol. 2, p. 929.

18. Leon Wolff, *In Flanders Fields* (London: Corgi, 1966), p. 276.

19. Corelli Barnett, *Britain and Her Army 1509–1970* (Harmondsworth: Penguin Books, 1974), p. 388. See also David French, "Sir Douglas Haig's Reputation 1918–1928: A Note," *Historical Journal* 28 (1985): 953–960.

20. Gerard J. De Groot, "Educated Soldier or Cavalry Officer? Contradictions in the pre-1914 career of Douglas Haig," *War and Society*, 4:2 (September 1986): 51–69. See also C. R. M. F. Cruttwell, *A History of the Great War 1914–1918* (Oxford: Clarendon Press, 1936), pp. 626–27; Sir Llewellyn Woodward, *Great Britain and the War of 1914–1918* (London: Methuen, 1967), pp. 140–42; Gerard J. De Groot, *Douglas Haig 1861–1928* (London: Unwin Hyman, 1988), passim.

21. John Terraine, *Douglas Haig: The Educated Soldier* (London: Hutchinson, 1963).

22. See Barnett, 397–98.

23. Tactical innovations are expertly summarized in Paul Kennedy, "Britain in the First World War," in Allan R. Millett and Williamson Murray, eds.,

Military Efficiency, vol. 1: *The First World War* (London: Allen and Unwin, 1988), pp. 60–72. See also S. Bidwell and D. Graham, *Firepower: British Army Weapons and Theories of War, 1905–1945* (London & Boston: Allen and Unwin, 1982), passim.

24. Tim Travers, "The Hidden Army: Structural Problems in the British Officer Corps, 1900–1918," *Journal of Contemporary History* 17:3 (July 1982): 523–38; and the same author's "A Particular Style of Command: Haig and G.H.Q. 1916–1918." *Journal of Strategic Studies* 10:3 (December 1987): 363–76.

25. Tim Travers, *The Killing Ground: The British Army, the Western Front and the Emergence of Modern Warfare, 1900–1918* (London & Boston: Allen & Unwin, 1987), p. 262.

26. Samuel R. Williamson, Jr., *The Politics of Grand Strategy: Britain and France Prepare for War, 1904–1914* (Harvard: Harvard University Press, 1969), p. 128.

27. Douglas Porch, "The French Army and the Spirit of the Offensive, 1900–14," in Brian Bond and Ian Roy, eds., *War and Society: A Yearbook of Military History* (London: Croom Helm, 1975), pp. 117–43; see also the same author's *The March to the Marne: The French Army 1871–1914* (Cambridge: Cambridge University Press, 1981).

28. Jack Snyder, *The Ideology of the Offensive: Military Decision Making and the Disasters of 1914* (Ithaca, N.Y.: Cornell University Press, 1984), pp. 17, 51, 54, 104.

29. Michael Howard, "Men against Fire: The Doctrine of the Offensive in 1914," in Peter Paret, ed., *Makers of Modern Strategy from Machiavelli to the Nuclear Age* (Princeton: Princeton University Press, 1986), pp. 510–26.

30. Walter Goerlitz, *History of the German General Staff 1657–1945* (New York: Praeger, 1959); Trevor Dupuy, *A Genius for War: The German Army and General Staff 1807–1945* (Englewood Cliffs, N.J.: Prentice Hall, 1977).

31. See Denis E. Showalter, "Army and Society in Imperial Germany: The Pains of Modernization," *Journal of Contemporary History* 18:4 (October 1983): 583–618; Martin van Creveld, *Fighting Power* (Washington, D.C.: Office of Net Assessment, 1980); David N. Spires, *Image and Reality: The Making of the German Officer 1921–1933* (Westport, Conn.: Greenwood Press, 1984); Williamson Murray, "The German Response to Victory in Poland: A Case Study in Professionalism," *Armed Forces and Society* 7:2 (Winter 1980): 285–98.

32. Hans J. Morgenthau, *Politics among Nations: The Struggle for Power and Peace* (New York: Knopf, 1964), p. 126.

33. "Italian Military Efficiency—A Debate," *Journal of Strategic Studies* 5:2 (June 1982): 248–77.

34. See Ken Booth, *Strategy and Ethnocentrism* (London: Croom Helm, 1979).

35. William H. Form and Sigmund Nosow, *Community in Disaster* (New York: Harper Bros., 1958).

36. Talcott Parsons, "Cause and Effect in Sociology," in Daniel Lerner, ed., *Cause and Effect* (New York: Free Press, 1965), pp. 51–64, 68; Irving B. Janis, "Problems of Theory in the Analysis of Stress Behavior," *Journal of Social Issues* 10 (1954): 12–25.

37. Barry A. Turner, "The Organizational and Interorganizational Development of Disasters," *Administrative Science Quarterly* 21 (1976): 385.

38. Martha Wolfenstein, *Disaster: A Psychological Essay* (London: Routledge & Kegan Paul, 1957), pp. 214–16.

39. *Chernobyl,* United Kingdom Central Electricity Generating Board, September 1986; "Chernobyl Special," *Power News,* September 1986, pp. 2–3; Julia Thornton, "Chernobyl and Soviet Energy," *Problems of Communism* (November/December 1986): 7, lists the errors.

40. *Three Mile Island: A Report to the Commissioners and to the Public* (Washington, D.C.: Nuclear Regulatory Commission, 1980), vol. 1, p. 3.

41. Ibid., p. 102.

42. Janice C. Simpson, "Business Schools—and Students—Want to Talk Only About Success," *The Wall Street Journal,* December 15, 1986, pp. 30–31. This issue of the *Journal* has an interesting set of articles about business failure. See, for example, Isadore Barmash, ed., *Great Business Disasters: Swindlers, Bunglers, and Frauds in American Industry* (Chicago: Playboy Press, 1972). A far more thoughtful—and equally entertaining—journalistic work is Paul Solman and Thomas Friedman, *Life & Death on the Corporate Battlefield: How Companies Win, Lose, Survive* (New York: Simon & Schuster, 1982).

43. See, in particular, O. P. Kharbanda and E. A. Stallworthy, *Corporate Failure: Prediction, Panacea, and Prevention* (London: McGraw-Hill, 1985), and John Argenti, *Corporate Collapse: The Causes and Symptoms* (London: McGraw-Hill, 1976).

44. On the Edsel see the odd collection of articles assembled by Jan G. Deutsch in *Selling the People's Cadillac: The Edsel* (New Haven: Yale University Press, 1976); John Brooks, *The Fate of the Edsel and Other Business Adventures* (New York: Harper & Row, 1962), and Allan Nevins and Frank Ernest Hill, *Ford: Decline and Rebirth, 1933–1962* (New York: Charles Scribner's Sons, 1962), pp. 380ff., 437ff. The account that follows is based largely on these sources.

45. Argenti, *Corporate Collapse,* pp. 128–38.

46. A metaphor developed in Bruce D. Henderson, *The Logic of Business Strategy* (Cambridge: Ballinger, 1984), pp. 1–6.

47. Charles Perrow, *Complex Organizations: A Critical Essay* (Glenview, Ill.: Scott, Foresman, 1972), p. 143.

48. See Elting E. Morison, *Men, Machines and Modern Times* (Cambridge,

Mass.: M.I.T. Press, 1966), pp. 17–44; also William H. McNeill, *The Pursuit of Power* (Oxford: Basil Blackwell, 1982), pp. 262–306.

49. Charles Perrow, *Normal Accidents: Living with High Risk Technologies* (New York: Basic Books, 1984), p. 5.

50. Ibid., pp. 72–79.

51. Ibid., p. 97.

52. Amos Perlmutter, "Military Incompetence and Failure: A Historical Comparative and Analytical Evaluation," *Journal of Strategic Studies* 1:2 (September 1978): 121.

53. Carl von Clausewitz, *On War*, Michael Howard and Peter Paret, eds. and trans. (Princeton, N.J.: Princeton University Press, 1976), p. 249.

54. Ibid., pp. 595–96. This contradiction is pointed out in Katherine Herbig, "Chance and Uncertainty in On War," *Journal of Strategic Studies*, 9:1/2 (March/June 1986): 78–79.

55. Stephen Bailey, *Fire: An International Report* (London: Hamish Hamilton, 1972), pp. 87–88, 152–55.

56. Ibid., pp. 128–29, 175.

57. Wolfenstein, *Disaster*, p. 21.

58. Form and Nosow, *Community in Disaster*, p. 244.

Chapter 3
ANALYZING FAILURE

1. Two of the more recent and interesting studies of the Pearl Harbor attack and the ensuing controversy are Gordon W. Prange, *At Dawn We Slept* (New York: McGraw Hill, 1981), and Edwin T. Layton, *And I Was There* (New York: Morrow, 1985). On the historical debate that followed Pearl Harbor see Gordon W. Prange with Donald M. Goldstein and Katherine V. Dillon, *Pearl Harbor: The Verdict of History* (New York: McGraw Hill, 1986). The best account of the disaster remains *Investigation of the Pearl Harbor Attack*, Report of the Joint Committee on the Investigation of the Pearl Harbor Attack, seventy-ninth Congress, 2nd Session (Washington, D.C.: Government Printing Office, 1946). Henceforth cited as *PHA Report*; the accompanying hearings will be cited as *PHA Hearings*.

2. See Charles E. Fritz, "Disaster," in Robert K. Merton and Robert A. Nisbet, eds., *Contemporary Social Problems* (New York: Harcourt Brace, 1961), pp. 651–94, especially pp. 657ff.

3. *Report of the Presidential Commission on the Space Shuttle Challenger Accident* (Washington, D.C.: Governmental Printing Office, 1986), p. 149.

4. W. J. Holmes, *Double Edged Secrets: U.S. Naval Intelligence Operations in the Pacific during World War II* (Annapolis, Md.: Naval Institute Press, 1979), p. 41.

5. See Chaim Herzog, *The War of Atonement* (Boston: Little, Brown, 1975), p. 280.

6. Matthew B. Ridgway, *The Korean War* (New York: Doubleday, 1967), p. 103.

7. See two wise and charming essays, Bernard Lewis, *History: Remembered, Recovered, Invented* (Princeton: Princeton University Press, 1975), and Carl Becker, "Everyman His Own Historian," in *Everyman His Own Historian: Essays on History and Politics* (1935; reprint. Chicago: Quadrangle Books, 1966), pp. 235–53.

8. See, *inter alia*, two essays by Michael Howard, "The Use and Abuse of Military History," *Journal of the Royal United Services Institute* 107:625 (February 1962): 4–10, and "The Demand for Military History," *Times Literary Supplement*, November 13, 1969, pp. 1293–95.

9. Jay Luvaas, "Military History: The Academic Historian's Point of View," in Russell F. Weigley, ed., *New Dimensions in Military History* (San Rafael, Ca.: Presidio Press, 1975), p. 34.

10. On the development of the Prussian and later German military's attitudes to military history see Heinrich Aschenbrandt, "Kriegsgeschichtschreibung und Kriegsgeschichtstudium im deutschen Heere" ["The Writing and Study of Military History in the German Army"], Historical Division, Headquarters U.S. Army Europe, Foreign Military Studies Branch, 1952. Aschenbrandt was formerly a colonel in the German General Staff's historical section.

11. Eberhard Kessel, "Moltke und die Kriegsgeschichte," ["Moltke and Military History"], *Militärwissenschaftliche Rundschau* (June 1941): 96–125.

12. The nineteenth century *Kriegsakademie* curriculum is discussed in Bernhard Poten, *Geschichte des Militär-und-Erziehungswesens in den Landen deutscher Zunge* ["History of Military and General Education in German-speaking Countries"] (Berlin: A. Hoffman, 1896), volume 4, pp. 253–307. On military history in particular see Hans H. Driftman, *Grundzüge des militärischen Erziehungs-und-Bildungswesens in der Zeit 1871–1939* ["Foundations of Military Training and Education, 1871–1939"] (Regensburg: Walhalla u. Praetoria Verlag, 1980), pp. 71, 129–35. This obsession with military history did not diminish appreciably in the twentieth century.

13. See Julius Hoppenstedt's *Wie studiert man Kriegsgeschichte* ["How to Study Military History"] (Berlin: E. S. Mittler, 1905), a primer of the applicatory method. Translations of some of the General Staff histories used to teach the applicatory method include Verdy du Vernois, *A Tactical Study Based on the Battle of Custozza, 24th of June, 1866*, G. F. R. Henderson, trans. (London: Gale and Polden, 1894).

14. G. F. R. Henderson, *The Science of War* (London: Longmans, Green, 1913), p. 49; see also p. 47.

15. See for example, *Infantry in Battle* (Washington, D.C.: The Infantry Journal,

1939), recently reissued by the U.S. Army's Command and General Staff College.

16. Herbert W. Richmond, *National Policy and Naval Strength* (London: Longmans, Green, 1934), p. 279. See his two essays in this volume, "The Place of History in Navel Education," and "The Use of History," pp. 255–93.

17. See John Gooch, "Clio and Mars: The Use and Abuse of Military History," *Journal of Strategic Studies* 3:3 (December 1980): 21–36. Regrettably, this inclination has not died out: see "General Bryce Poe Tells AFSC Historians: You Can Use History To Help Your Commanders," *Air Historian* 2 (Fall 1985): 1. General Poe urged the assembled historians to use history to help demonstrate the continuing validity and importance of the principles of war—the objective, the offensive, and so on.

18. See Kessel, "Moltke und die Kriegsgeschichte," p. 117, and John Keegan, "The Historian and Battle," *International Security* 3:3 (Winter 1978/1979): 144.

19. Major General Frank W. Norris, *Review of Army Officer Educational System* (Washington, D.C.: Department of the Army, 1971), p. 13-2. Two interesting products from Army's Command and General Staff College and the Office of the Chief of Military History, respectively, are Charles E. Hiller and William A. Stofft, eds., *America's First Battles, 1776–1965* (Lawrence: University of Kansas Press, 1986) and Charles R. Schrader, ed., "The Impact of Unsuccessful Military Campaigns on Military Institutions, 1860–1980," Proceedings of the 1982 International Military History Symposium (Washington, D.C.: U.S. Army Center of Military History, 1984).

20. Arden Bucholz, *Hans Delbrück and the German Military Establishment: War Images in Conflict* (Iowa City: University of Iowa Press, 1985), pp. 27 ff. The disdain of German academics—including the militarists—for military history is a recurring theme in this book.

21. Cyril Falls, *The Art of War From the Age of Napoleon to the Present Day* (Oxford: Oxford University Press, 1961), p. 6. For two defenses of the study of military history see his *The Place of War in History* (Oxford: Clarendon Press, 1947), and Charles Oman, "A Defence of Military History," in *Studies in the Napoleonic Wars* (London: Methuen, 1929), pp. 24–36. A similar defensive note is detectable in Louis Morton, "The Historian and the Study of War," *The Mississippi Valley Historical Review* 48:4 (March 1962): 599–613. Even in what now appears to have been a golden age of American military historiography, the general distaste of historians for military history surfaced periodically. See Arthur A. Ekirch, "Military History: A Civilian Caveat," *Military Affairs* 21 (Summer 1957): 49–54.

22. Walter Millis, "Military History," Publication #39 (Washington, D.C.: Service Center for Teachers of History, 1961), pp. 17–18.

23. Peter Paret, "The History of War," *Daedalus* (Spring 1971): 381. A similar set of complaints was offered by Walter Emil Kaegi in "The Crisis in Mili-

tary Historiography," *Armed Forces and Society* 7:2 (Winter 1980): 299–316.

24. The fullest discussion of the "War and Society" school, and some vigorous defenses of it can be found in Ursaul von Gersdorff, ed., *Geschichte und Militärgeschichte* ["History and Military History"] (Frankfurt am Main: Bernard & Graefe, 1974), and "Zielsetzung und Methode der Militärgeschichtsschreibung," ["Aims and Methods of the Writing of Military History"] *Militärgeschichtliche Mitteilungen* 20 (2/76): 9–20. The trend toward the "war and society" school goes back to before World War II. See the inaugural issue of *Revue Internationale d'Histoire Militaire* 1 (1939): 7.

25. John Keegan, *The Face of Battle* (New York: Viking Press, 1976), especially his introductory chapter on the historiography of battle, "Old, Unhappy, Far-off Things," pp. 15–78.

26. See Keegan, "The Historian and Battle," p. 145.

27. Some signs of the pendulum's return include excellent operational histories written by nonacademic historians—Max Hastings' *Overlord*, for example, as well as organizational/operational histories such as Williamson Murray's *Luftwaffe*.

28. See Kaegi, "Crisis," and Paret, "The History of War."

29. See most notably Barton Whaley, *Codeword Barbarossa* (Cambridge, Mass.: M.I.T. Press, 1973).

30. Richard K. Betts, "Analysis, War, and Decision: Why Intelligence Failures are Inevitable," in Klaus Knorr, ed., *Power, Strategy, and Security: A World Politics Reader* (Princeton: Princeton University Press, 1983), pp. 238–39.

31. Richard K. Betts, *Surprise Attack* (Washington, D.C.: Brookings Institution, 1982), p. 4.

32. See, *inter alia*, Steve Chan, "The Intelligence of Stupidity: Understanding Failures in Strategic Warning," *American Political Science Review* 73:1 (March 1979): 171–80; Gerald W. Hopple, "Intelligence and Warning: Implications and Lessons of the Falkland Islands War," *World Politics* 36:3 (April 1984): 339–61; Janice Gross Stein, "Military Deception, Strategic Surprise, and Conventional Deterrence: A Political Analysis of Egypt and Israel, 1971–73," in John Gooch and Amos Perlmutter, eds., *Military Deception and Strategic Surprise* (London: Frank Cass, 1982): 94–121, as well as the other essays in that volume.

33. Harold Wilensky, *Organizational Intelligence: Knowledge and Policy in Government and Industry* (New York: Basic Books, 1967), pp. viii–ix, 7, seems to take this view. Among other things, he asserts (pp. 24–32) that the bombing of Germany during World War II was an intelligence failure—neglecting the host of technical, tactical, organizational, and operational problems involved in conducting that effort.

34. Carl von Clausewitz, *On War*, Michael Howard and Peter Paret, eds. and trans. (Princeton: Princeton University Press, 1976), p. 198 (emphasis in

the original). See his general discussion of surprise in book 3, chap. 9 of *On War*, pp. 198–201.

35. Ian Hamilton, *A Staff Officer's Scrap-Book During the Russo-Japanese War* (1906; reprint, New York: Longmans, Green, 1912), p. v.

36. Carl von Clausewitz, *On War*, Michael Howard and Peter Paret, eds. and trans. (Princeton: Princeton University Press, 1976), p. 141.

37. Ibid., p. 61.

38. Ibid., p. 156.

39. Ibid., pp. 158–59.

40. Ibid., pp. 164–65.

41. Ibid., p. 156.

42. Ibid., p. 157.

43. Quoted in Peter Paret, *Clausewitz and the State* (New York: Oxford University Press, 1976), p. 341.

44. Clausewitz, *On War*, p. 166.

45. According to Cornelius Ryan, American forces lost some 1,500 dead, 3,200 wounded, and 1,900 missing. *The Longest Day* (New York: Simon & Schuster, 1959), p. 303.

46. *PHA Report*, p. 253 (italics in the original).

47. Ariel Levite, *Intelligence and Strategic Surprises* (New York: Columbia University Press, 1987), pp. 50–53 points out that Kido Butai's radio silence and changes in Japanese ciphers temporarily blinded American intelligence. His comparison with the battle of Midway, though flawed, is instructive.

48. Gordon W. Prange, *Pearl Harbor: The Verdict of History* (New York: McGraw Hill, 1986), p. 566.

49. *PHA Report*, p. 72.

50. Prange, *At Dawn We Slept*, p. 544.

51. *PHA Report*, pp. 66–68.

52. Prange, *Pearl Harbor: The Verdict of History*, p. 47.

53. See *PHA Hearings*, Part 14, Exhibit 44, "Defense Plans," pp. 1429–36, which includes the Joint Coastal Frontier Defense Plan dated April 11, 1941. See also pp. 1436–55, "Joint Estimate Covering Joint Army and Navy Air Action in the Event of Sudden Hostile Action Against Oahu or Fleet Units in the Hawaiian Area," dated March 31, 1941.

54. Letter to Lieutenant General Walter C. Short, February 7, 1941. Larry I. Bland, Sharon R. Ritenour, and Clarence E. Wunderlin, eds., *The Papers of George Catlett Marshall*, vol. II, *"We Cannot Delay," July 1, 1939–December 6, 1941* (Baltimore: Johns Hopkins University Press, 1986), p. 413.

55. See *PHA Report*, pp. 118–20.

56. See their joint memorandum, "Cooperation in Joint Defense; formation of

Joint Operations Centers in Coastal Frontiers," dated December 31, 1941. *PHA Hearings*, part 17, p. 2744.

57. Memorandum from CinCPACFLT to CNO, *PHA Hearings*, part 17, p. 2739. See also Short's and Bloch's memos, which take precisely the same line, pp. 2737–38.

58. *PHA Report*, p. 240. (Emphasis in the original).

59. See chapter 4, "Failure to Learn: American Antisubmarine Warfare in 1942," pp. 88–89.

Chapter 4
FAILURE TO LEARN
American Antisubmarine Warfare in 1942

1. See Peter Padfield, *Doenitz: The Last Führer* (New York: Harper & Row, 1984), pp. 239–42.

2. Statistics from earlier periods of the war also include American and other neutral shipping, hence the change in American belligerent status does not affect these figures. Statistics are taken primarily from two sources: Charles M. Sternhell and Alan M. Thorndike, *Antisubmarine Warfare in World War II* Operations Evaluation Group Report No. 51 (Washington, D.C.: Office of the Chief of Naval Operations, 1946), pp. 83–87; and Samuel Eliot Morison, *History of the United States Naval Operations in World War II*, vol. 1, *The Battle of the Atlantic, September 1939–May 1943* (Boston: Little, Brown, 1947), pp. 410–19. "*Gross tonnage* is the entire internal cubic capacity of the ship expressed in tons of 100 cubic feet each. *Net tonnage* is derived by subtracting from the gross tonnage the cubic capacity of certain internal spaces not available for carrying cargo such as machinery compartments, crew's and passengers' quarters, etc. *Deadweight tonnage* is the carrying capacity of a ship in long tons of 2240 pounds each—not, as many suppose, the avoirdupois weight of the ship itself. But the tonnage of warships *is* stated in terms of the vessel's weight, and is generally called *displacement*. Sinkings of merchant vessels in our statistics are expressed in gross tons. Deadweight tonnage (weight capacity) is roughly 50 percent more than gross (cubic capacity) in freighters, even more in the case of tankers." Morison, *Battle of the Atlantic*, p. 292.

3. Peter Cremer, *U-Boat Commander: A Periscope View of the Battle of the Atlantic*. Lawrence Wilson, trans. (Annapolis, Md.: Naval Institute Press, 1984), p. 69.

4. Winston S. Churchill, *The Second World War*, vol. 4, *The Hinge of Fate* (Boston: Houghton Mifflin, 1950), p. 119.

5. Patrick Beesly, *Very Special Intelligence* (London: Hamish Hamilton, 1977), p. 302. Remark attributed to Rodger Winn, the director of the submarine tracking room of the Royal Navy's Operational Intelligence Centre.

6. Tenth Fleet Records, Anti-Submarine Measures Division, Box 27, U.S. Navy Operational Archives, Washington Navy Yard.

7. Churchill, *Hinge of Fate,* p. 109.

8. See Morison, *Battle of the Atlantic,* pp. 252–65.

9. On King see William Robert Love, "Ernest Joseph King," in William Robert Love, ed., *The Chiefs of Naval Operations* (Annapolis, Md.: Naval Institute Press, 1980), pp. 137–79; King's own rather stilted memoirs also repay a close reading. Ernest J. King and Walter Muir Whitehill, *Fleet Admiral King: A Naval Record* (New York: W. W. Norton, 1952).

10. King and Whitehill, *Fleet Admiral King,* p. 413; reproductions of FDR correspondence.

11. Martin Middlebrook, *Convoy* (New York: William Morrow, 1977), p. 310.

12. Ernest J. King to chairman of the General Board, July 30, 1941. General Board Serial 420–22. Microfilm, U.S. Naval War College Historical Collection.

13. King and Whitehill, *Fleet Admiral King,* p. 298. This claim is borne out by an examination of the General Board hearings on the subject.

14. See, for example, Robert L. Eichelberger, *Jungle Road to Tokyo* (London: Odhams Press, 1951), p. 40.

15. Ladislas Farago, *The Tenth Fleet* (New York: Ivan Obolensky, 1962), pp. 90–104, recounts a number of anecdotes—some probably apocryphal—along these lines.

16. See, for example, John Slessor, *The Central Blue* (New York: Frederick A. Praeger, 1957), pp. 491–92.

17. Ibid., p. 491.

18. Henry L. Stimson and McGeorge Bundy, *On Active Service in Peace and War* (New York: Harper, 1947), p. 506.

19. See Love, "Ernest Joseph King."

20. Morison, *Battle of the Atlantic,* p. 200.

21. Padfield, *Doenitz,* p. 237. See also the British official history: S. W. Roskill, *The War at Sea,* vol. 2, *The Period of Balance* (London: HMSO, 1956), pp. 91–114.

22. Stimson, *On Active Service,* p. 506.

23. "Hemisphere Defense and Joint Army-Navy Basic War Plans: Joint Board Action and Recommendations November 1938–May 1939," *United States–British Naval Relations, 1939–1942,* COMNAVEU Historical Monograph, n.d. (1946?), section 1, part D, Chap. 4, Appendix A. U.S. Naval War College Naval Historical Collection, Newport, R. I. Juergen Rohwer points out that the Americans had already been using ULTRA intelligence to pursue U-boats in 1941. "Allied and Axis Radio-Intelligence in the Battle of the Atlantic: A Comparative Analysis," manuscript, November 1988.

24. *United States–British Naval Relations*, p. 314.

25. Arthur Marder, *From Dreadnought to Scapa Flow: The Royal Navy in the Fisher Era, 1904–1919*, vol. 5 *Victory and Aftermath* (London: Oxford University Press, 1970), pp. 77–120.

26. Sternhell and Thorndike, *Antisubmarine Warfare in World War II*, p. 84.

27. See Morison, *Battle of the Atlantic*, app. 2, "Monthly Sinkings of German and Italian Submarines," p. 415. This conservatism by the navies involved about their own effectiveness contrasts with the wild claims made by the commanders of the Allied heavy bombing forces about the effectiveness of their forces: to be fair, the intelligence problem involved was probably a simpler one. The Naval Intelligence Division of the Admiralty deserves some credit for this, particularly since their refusal to inflate kill statistics initially brought Churchill's wrath upon them. See Patrick Beesly, *Very Special Admiral: The Life of Admiral J. H. Godfrey, C.B.* (London: Hamish Hamilton, 1980), pp. 124–31. American estimates seem to have been equally stringent.

28. Cremer, *U-Boat Commander*, pp. 52–53; Morison, *Battle of the Atlantic*, pp. 126–28.

29. See Sternhell and Thorndike, *Antisubmarine Warfare in World War II*, p. 83, for numbers of operational U-boats. As a rule of thumb, normally one-third of the U-boat force at any one time was on station, one-third transiting to or from patrol areas, and one-third engaged in overhaul or training.

30. "Memorandum of informal conversation held at the residence of the Chief of Naval Operations at 17—," June 14, 1939, Strategic Plans Division Records, Series 7, Box 116, U.S. Navy Operational Archives, Washington Navy Yard.

31. See, *inter alia*, "United States–British Staff Conversations: Report," March 27, 1941, Ibid. For the following discussion I have drawn on Patrick Abbazia, *Mr. Roosevelt's Navy: The Private War of the U.S. Atlantic Fleet, 1939–1942* (Annapolis: Naval Institute Press, 1975), and James R. Leutze, *Bargaining for Supremacy: Anglo-American Naval Collaboration, 1937–1941* (Chapel Hill: University of North Carolina Press, 1977); as well as COMNAVEU, *United States–British Naval Relations, 1939–1942* and the relevant files at the Operational Archives.

32. See Leutze, *Bargaining*, pp. 57–70; and Donald McLachlan, *Room 39: A Study in Naval Intelligence* (New York: Atheneum, 1968), pp. 216–22.

33. Thomas Parrish, *The Ultra Americans: The U.S. Role in Breaking the Nazi Codes* (New York: Stein and Day, 1986), pp. 60–65. See "Report of Technical Mission to England," April 11, 1941, in "Collection of Memoranda On Operations of SIS Intercept Activities and Dissemination," SR-145, Record Group 457, Records of the National Security Agency, National Archives, Washington, D.C.

34. For the recollections of one such observer see John B. Hattendorf, ed., *On*

His Majesty's Service: Observations of the British Home Fleet from the Diary, Reports, and Letters of Joseph H. Wellings, Assistant U.S. Naval Attaché, London, 1940–1941. (Newport, R.I.: Naval War College Press, 1983).

35. Letter reproduced in COMNAVEU, *U.S.–British Naval Relations,* vol. 1, p. 215. See also Ghormley's letters to Stark in Strategic Plan Division Records, Series 7, Box 117, U.S. Navy Operational Archives, Washington Navy Yard.

36. Hamlin A. Caldwell, "Using and Fighting Submarines," *U.S. Naval Institute Proceedings* 110:8, 978 (August 1984): 62.

37. "Status of Available Surface Forces, North Atlantic Naval Coastal Frontier," December 22, 1941, *Eastern Sea Frontier War Diary,* December 1941, p. 30, U.S. Navy Operational Archives, Washington Navy Yard. (Henceforth *ESF War Diary.*) King refers to the initial shortage of escorts as well: *Fleet Admiral King,* p. 446.

38. All figures from *ESF War Diary.*

39. Morison, *Battle of the Atlantic,* p. 241.

40. This is discussed in part in Stetson Conn et al., *Guarding the United States and its Outposts* (Washington, D.C.: Office of the Chief of Military History, 1964), p. 95. The availability question is discussed at some length in Morison, *Battle of the Atlantic,* pp. 229–47.

41. Baker to King, June 24, 1942. In the course of research for this chapter the author could discover no observer, participant, or historian who claimed that the matter was *primarily* one of inadequate escort vessels and aircraft— a remarkable negative consensus, given the range of disagreement about the causes of the failure.

42. *War Diaries of the German Submarine Command, 1938–1945,* microfilm (Wilmington, Del.: Scholarly Resources, Inc., 1984), PG 30302, January 11, 1942, entry. The translation appears to have been done by the Royal Navy's Naval Intelligence Department. See also "Report of the Commanding Admiral, Submarines at Fuehrer Headquarters on 14 May 1942 in the Presence of the Commander in Chief, Navy," in *Fuehrer Conferences on Matters Dealing with the German Navy, 1942* (Washington, D.C.: Office of Naval Intelligence, 1946), pp. 82–85.

43. *War Diaries of the German Submarine Command,* PG 30305a, March 13, 1942, entry.

44. Ibid., PG 30309a, 14 May 1942 entry.

45. Elting E. Morison, *Turmoil and Tradition: A Study of the Life and Times of Henry L. Stimson* (Boston: Houghton Mifflin, 1960), pp. 567–68. Morison was the author of the *ESF War Diary,* a splendidly clear and thoughtful recounting not only of the events of 1942, but of how the navy interpreted them. *Turmoil and Tradition* is particularly interesting on the subject at hand, because although Morison is a sympathetic, indeed, an admiring biographer, he is familiar as well with the weaknesses of Stimson's argument.

46. Much of what follows is based on three books by Patrick Beesly, a member of OIC: *Very Special Intelligence, Room 40,* and *Very Special Admiral;* as well as McLachlan, *Room 39,* and the official histories edited by F. H. Hinsley, *British Intelligence in the Second World War,* 3 vols. (London: HMSO, 1979–88).

47. The turf battles (which ONI lost) are discussed in Jeffery M. Dorwart, *Conflict of Duty: The U.S. Navy's Intelligence Dilemma, 1919–1945* (Annapolis: Naval Institute Press, 1983), pp. 151–59.

48. German operational ciphers in the Atlantic were hard to crack: "Hydra" for example, which was used until February 1942 was only read promptly after August 1941. "Shark," introduced in February 1942 and used through May 1943 (through the height of the Battle of the North Atlantic, in other words), was only broken in December 1942, and thereafter was frequently broken late. Hinsley, *British Intelligence,* vol. 3, part 1, pp. 662–67.

49. See Beesly, *Very Special Intelligence,* pp. 10–16.

50. See Patrick Beesly, *Room 40: British Naval Intelligence 1914–1918* (New York: Harcourt Brace Jovanovich, 1982), pp. 151–68, 309–12.

51. See C. H. Waddington, *O.R. in World War 2: Operational Research Against the U-Boat* (London: Elek Science, 1973); see also P. M. S. Blackett, *Studies of War: Nuclear and Conventional* (New York: Hill and Wang, 1962), pp. 169–234.

52. National Defense Research Committee, *A Survey of Subsurface Warfare in World War II.* Summary Technical Report of Division 6, NDRC, vol. 1. (Washington: Government Printing Office, 1946), pp. 82–84.

53. See W. S. Chalmers, *Max Horton and the Western Approaches* (London: Hodder & Stoughton, 1954), for a description of Western Approaches through the life of its most famous commander, exsubmariner Sir Max Horton. The groundwork for Horton's efforts was laid by Sir Percy Noble, who was CINCWA from February 1941 to November 1942. For an account of the methods of the most successful escort group commander of the war, see D. E. G. Wemyss, *Walker's Groups in the Western Approaches* (Liverpool: Liverpool Daily Post and Echo, 1948).

54. See Stephen Roskill, *The War At Sea,* vol. 1, pp. 359–62, and John Slessor, *The Central Blue,* pp. 481–82 for diametrically opposed views on this score.

55. See Conn et. al., *Guarding the United States,* pp. 95ff.

56. *ESF War Diary,* February 1942, chap. 4, "The Convoy System Considered," p. 1.

57. See Roskill, *The War at Sea,* vol. 1, pp. 44–45, for a discussion of British perplexities in 1939–1940—problems unresolved at war's end, when German submarines again attacked British coastal shipping. See also John Winton, *Convoy: The Defence of Sea Trade, 1890–1990* (London: Michael Joseph, 1983).

58. See Morison, *Turmoil*, pp. 561–80; Stimson and Bundy, *On Active Service*, p. 509.

59. Wesley Frank Craven and James Lea Cate, *The Army Air Forces in World War II*, vol. 1, *Plans and Early Operations, January 1939 to August 1942* (Chicago: University of Chicago Press, 1948), pp. 545–46. The ASW dispute with the Navy is discussed in pp. 514–53. The Navy point of view is laid out in COMINCH, "Tentative Doctrine for Anti-Submarine Warfare by Aircraft," October 17, 1942, in *Tenth Fleet Records*, Anti-Submarine Measures, Box 3, U.S. Navy Operational Archives, Washington Navy Yard. It reads in part, "the primary function of an aerial escort is defensive and not offensive."

60. This was one of the discoveries of the operations research analysts. See Philip M. Morse, *In at the Beginnings: A Physicist's Life* (Cambridge: MIT Press, 1977), pp. 195–96.

61. See *ESf War Diary*, April 1942, chap. 8, "The Reorganization of the Frontier," pp. 1–5. In modified form these proposals were implemented in May 1942.

62. For two accounts of this see Morison, *Battle of the Atlantic*, pp. 237ff, and Craven and Cate, *Army Air Forces*, Vol. 1, pp. 514–53; vol. 2 pp. 377–411.

63. This is captured quite nicely in C. S. Forester's wartime novel about a brief action in a British light cruiser. See *The Ship* (Boston: Little, Brown, 1943).

64. CINCLANT Serial (053), January 21, 1941, "Subject: Exercise of Command—Excess of Detail in Orders and Instructions," reprinted in Administrative History, COMINCH HQ, p. 8.

65. Ibid., pp. 27–29.

66. Memorandum of Conference Between Representatives of the Atlantic Fleet ASW Unit and Representatives of the Commander-in-Chief, United States Fleet ASW Unit, April 28, 1942. Tenth Fleet Records, Anti-Submarine Measures Division, Box 24, U.S. Navy Operational Archives, Washington Navy Yard. This memorandum is interesting for its continual deference to local commanders. Thus, although COMINCH intends to publish an ASW manual, "This does not restrict the prerogative of any fleet commander to issue any manual, or instructions, as he may see fit."

67. *ESF War Diary*, January 1942, p. 6.

68. Ibid., June 1942, chap. 4, p. 6 (emphasis added).

69. Statistics from Morison, *Battle of the Atlantic*, p. 414.

70. Ibid., p. 404.

71. The phrase is Nicholas Monsarrat's, from *The Cruel Sea* (New York: Knopf, 1951), p. 397. This book captures the rhythm of the U-boat war better than any formal history.

72. The author of the *ESF War Diary* of May 1942, for example, notes abash-

edly that the British had one manual for the use of sonar and one manual for antisubmarine tactics—and that the United States Navy did not.

73. Of the twenty naval attaché reports from London in July 1941, for example, not one dealt with anything other than purely technical matters such as the ones listed here. Tenth Fleet Records, Anti-Submarine Measures, Box 2, U.S. Navy Operational Archives, Washington Navy Yard.

74. Ibid., Box 24. Morison, *Battle of the Atlantic,* pp. 211–16, gives an account of some of the devices copied from the British.

75. "Are We Ready—III" Report of the General Board to the Secretary of the Navy, July 14, 1941. SECNAV/CNO Files 40–41, Record Group 80, Box 243, National Archives.

76. "U.S.—British Naval Relations, 1939–1942," *COMNAVEU* Historical Monograph, Volume I, pp. 227 ff. Memorandum of January 15, 1941. This unpublished two volume history is extremely useful for this entire period.

77. This matter is discussed at some length in Stephen Roskill, *Naval Policy Between the Wars,* vol. 2, *The Period of Reluctant Rearmament, 1930–1939* (Annapolis: Naval Institute Press, 1976), especially pp. 194–212, 392–415.

78. All of this is discussed at length in Roskill, *The War at Sea,* see in particular vol. 1, pp. 29–41; vol. 2, pp. 77–90.

79. For King's account, see *Fleet Admiral King,* pp. 451–59.

80. Julius Augustus Furer, *Administration of the Navy Department in World War II* (Washington: Department of the Navy, 1959), p. 157.

81. See Dorwart, *Conflict of Duty,* pp. 157–59, 192. See also "U.S. Naval Administration in World War II: Office of Naval Intelligence," 4 vols. (Washington: Office of the Chief of Naval Operations, 1946), for an account of ONI in World War II.

82. Ibid., vol. 2, p. 826.

83. Farago, *Tenth Fleet* is a sensationalist and not entirely reliable account of that organization, redeemed in part by the author's personal participation in the organization he describes and by one's suspicion that he had access to official records in preparing it. The unpublished naval administrative history of COMINCH (who was nominal commander of Tenth Fleet) is drier but more reliable. See especially pp. 164–72.

84. Language from Admiral King's paper to the Joint Chiefs of Staff, May 1, 1943. COMINCH History, p. 167. See Furer, *Administration of the Navy Department,* pp. 160–62 for a further elaboration of Tenth Fleet's charter.

85. See Farago, *Tenth Fleet,* p. 169.

86. Chalmers, *Horton and the Western Approaches,* p. 290.

87. See Churchill, *The Second World War,* Volume 4, *The Hinge of Fate,* pp. 913–4.

88. See NDRC, *Survey of Subsurface Warfare,* pp. 92–94. The authors of this

report note (p. 92), "By the end of 1942 it had become clear that improvement in the quantity and quality of antisubmarine equipment and personnel could not by itself win the battle of the Atlantic. A centralized planning and operational authority was needed."

89. Ibid., p. 2. Tenth Fleet issued a monthly U.S. Fleet Anti-Submarine Bulletin that served as a standard authority on the entire antisubmarine situation.

90. Chalmers, *Horton and the Western Approaches*, p. 229. See also Cremer, *U-Boat Commander*, pp. 3, 163–64. Cremer served on Doenitz's staff, being one of the lucky few German submariners who survived the war—approximately 80 percent did not.

91. On the use made by both the Germans and the Allies of communications intelligence see Operations Evaluation Group Report #68, *Evaluation of the Role of Decryption Intelligence in the Operational Phase of the Battle of the Atlantic, 1952*, SRH-368, Record Group 457, Records of the National Security Agency, National Archives.

92. Churchill, *The Second World War*, vol. 4, p. 125; vol. 2, p. 598.

93. Padfield, *Doenitz*, p. 484, takes this point of view.

94. Francis Parkman, *Montcalm and Wolfe*, vol. 1 (Boston: Little, Brown, 1898), p. 3.

95. NDRC, *Survey of Subsurface Warfare*, p. 1. Beesly recounts in *Very Special Intelligence* that the members of the OIC, particularly Rodger Winn, were anxious to the last about the prospect of a major resurgence of German submarine attacks.

96. Peter W. Gretton, "Why Don't We Learn From History?" London: Naval Society, 1958 (reprinted from *Naval Review* 46); Arthur J. Marder, "The Influence of History on Sea Power: The Royal Navy and the Lessons of 1914–1918," in *From the Dardanelles to Oran: Studies of the Royal Navy in War and Peace, 1915–1940* (London: Oxford University Press, 1974), pp. 33–63.

Chapter 5
FAILURE TO ANTICIPATE
Israel Defense Forces on the Suez Front and the Golan Heights, 1973

1. Figures taken from Zeev Schiff and Eitan Haber, eds., *Lexikon l'bitachon yisroel* ["Israel, Army and Defense: A Dictionary"] (Tel Aviv: Zmora, Bitan, Modan, 1976), p. 239. Avraham Adan, "Eichut v'kamut b'milchemet yom hakippurim," ["Quality and Quantity in the Yom Kippur War"], in Zvi Offer and Avi Kober, eds., *Eichut v'kamut: dilemmot b'binyan bakoach batsva'i* ["Quality and Quantity: Dilemmas in the Development of Military Forces"] (Tel Aviv: Ma'arachot, 1985), p. 287, gives lower figures, which are not, however, generally regarded as reliable. Trevor Dupuy, *Elusive Victory: The Arab-Israeli Wars, 1947–1974* (New York: Harper & Row,

1978), p. 609, records that Arab casualties totaled some 8,500 dead, 19,500 wounded, and 8,500 prisoners or missing, in rough proportions of 3:2, Egypt:Syria. For a general discussion of the prewar crisis and the surprise, see Janice Gross Stein, "Calculation, Miscalculation, and Conventional Deterrence," in Robert Jervis, Richard Ned Lebow, and Janice Gross Stein, eds., *Psychology and Deterrence* (Baltimore: Johns Hopkins University Press, 1985), pp. 34–88.

2. Avraham Tamir, *A Soldier in Search of Peace*, Joan Comay, ed. (New York: Harper & Row, 1988), p. 190. See pp. 190–202 as well. Golda Meir, *Chayay* ["My Life"] (Tel Aviv: Ma'ariv Book Guild, 1975), pp. 305, 310. See also her account of a meeting with the distinguished British Labour party parliamentarian Richard Crossman in the winter of 1973–74, p. 328.

3. See Nadav Safran, *From War to War: The Arab-Israeli Confrontation, 1948–1967* (New York: Pegasus, 1969), p. 383. See as well Dayan's own account: Moshe Dayan, *Avnei derekh* (Jerusalem: Edanim, 1976; second edition 1982), vol. 2, pp. 487–92. An English version of these memoirs has been published as *Story of My Life*.

4. Sadat initiated secret contacts with the United States in October 1972, hoping to capitalize on the fact of the expulsion of the Soviets. See Henry A. Kissinger, *Years of Upheaval* (Boston: Little Brown, 1982), pp. 202–6. Kissinger admitted later that he found this a puzzling attempt to "get something for nothing" (see p. 482).

5. Useful sources on Egyptian planning for and conduct of the war are Anwar el-Sadat, *In Search of Identity: An Autobiography* (New York: Harper & Row, 1977); Mohamed Heikal, *The Road to Ramadan* (New York: Quadrangle, 1975); Saad el Shazly, *The Crossing of Suez* (San Francisco: American Mideast Research, 1980); and Hassan el Badri, Taha el Magdoub, and Mohammed dia el din Zohdy, *The Ramadan War, 1973* (1974; New York: Hippocrene Books, 1979). Heikal was Sadat's confidant, although he later became a critic; Shazly became Chief of Staff in May 1973 and later broke completely with Sadat. Badri and Zohdy taught at the Nasser High Military Academy and served as advisers to the Egyptian high command. Magdoub headed GHQ Operations Department in 1973. An extremely interesting study, based largely on captured documents, is Avi Shai, (pseud.?) "Mitsrayim likrat milchemet yom hakippurim: matarot hamilchama v'tochnit hamatkafa," *Ma'arachot* 250 (July 1976): 15–40. ["Egypt at the Onset of the Yom Kippur War: War Objectives and the Plan of Attack."] *Ma'arachot* is the foremost journal of Israeli military thought, and is a valuable source for work on the Yom Kippur War.

6. Kissinger recalls one of Sadat's conversations during the disengagement talks after the Yom Kippur War: "'My army!' he mused. 'First I had trouble convincing them to go to war. Now I have trouble persuading them to make peace.'" Kissinger, *Years of Upheaval*, p. 836. According to several senior Israeli officers, Israeli Military Intelligence misread the dis-

missal of Sadek as an internal political maneuver, rather than as the reflection of a serious dispute over policy—that is, the decision for war.

7. Badri, Magdoub, and Zohdy, *Ramadan War*, pp. 26ff.

8. These preparations included accelerating the transition from a five *ugda* (armored division) force to seven, terrain preparation, and forward deployment of equipment. Hanoch Bar-Tov, *Dado—48 shana v'od 20 yom* ["Dado—48 years and 20 days"], 2 vols. (Tel Aviv: Ma'ariv Book Guild, 1978), vol. 1, pp. 249–51. This biography/memoir, published after the death of David Elazar (nicknamed "Dado"), is a vital, albeit not fully reliable, source, based on the diary of Avner Shalev, the director of Elazar's office. It appears that Bar-Tov also had access, either through the diary or other sources, to transcripts of discussions during the Yom Kippur war itself. See also Yehuda Wallach, Moshe Lissak, and Arieh Itzchaki, eds. *Atlas karta l'toldot medinat yisroel: asor shlishi* ["Carta Atlas of the History of the State of Israel: The Third Decade"] (Jerusalem: Carta, 1983), p. 43.

9. See Sadat's instructions to War Minister Ali, October 5, 1973, reprinted in Sadat, *In Search of Identity*, p. 328.

10. Ibid., p. 312.

11. Ibid., p. 244.

12. Shai, "Mitsrayim likrat milchemet yom hakippurim," p. 17. See also Ibrahim Fouad Nassar, "The Israeli Doctrine of National Security," in Ahmed Ali Amer, ed., *International Symposium on the 1973 October War* (Cairo: Ministry of War, 1978), pp. 157–65. Lieutenant General Nassar was Egypt's Director of Military Intelligence at the time of the symposium in 1975.

13. Sadat, *In Search of Identity*, p. 327.

14. Ibid. Emphasis in the original. "Our objective was to shatter Israel's Doctrine of Security, to defeat the main enemy troop concentration in Sinai and inflict the heaviest losses possible to convince Israel that continuing to occupy our lands would entail a heavy price." Statement by Field Army General Mohamad al Gamasy in Amer, ed., *International Symposium*, p. 41.

15. Shai, "Mitsrayim likrat milchemet yom hakippurim," p. 16.

16. Shazly, *Crossing*, p. 208. Heikal, *Road to Ramadan*, p. 13, says that the Syrians required twenty days, including five to drain the Homs oil refineries to reduce their vulnerability to Israeli air attack.

17. Shazly, *Crossing*, p. 211.

18. Aharon Zeevi, "Tochnit hahona'a hamitsrit," ["The Egyptian Deception Plan"], in Zvi Offer and Zvi Kober, eds., *Modi'in v'bitachon leumi* ["Intelligence and National Security"] (Tel Aviv: Ma'arachot, 1987), p. 434, says that the commander of at least one Egyptian division learned of the impending war the day before the attack. See also Chaim Herzog, *The War of Atonement* (Boston: Little, Brown, 1975), p. 39.

19. Thus Heikal, *Road to Ramadan*, p. 24, and Sadat, *Search of Identity*, p. 246.

20. Shai, "Mitsrayim likrat milchemet yom hakippurim," p. 21.

21. So according to Heikal, *Road to Ramadan*, p. 14. Shazly, *Crossing*, p. 33, claims that it was estimated in early 1973 that the Israelis would know about the Arab intention to attack fifteen days before the event, which seems exaggerated.

22. Heikal, *Road to Ramadan*, p. 41. This would have been only half the staggering losses suffered by the British on the first day of the battle of the Somme in 1916.

23. Bar-Tov, *Dado*, vol. 1, pp. 274, 288.

24. Ibid., p. 287 summarizes Zeira's assessment of the situation as of 17 September 1973.

25. Ibid., pp. 264–5.

26. Zvi Lanir, *Hahafta'a habasisit* ["Fundamental Surprise"] (Tel Aviv: Kibbutz Hameuchad, 1983), p. 28; Lanir claims that before October 1973 even the self-confident General Zeira warned divisional commanders in a conference in Sinai that they had to prepare to defend even with very little warning (p. 20). Furthermore, and in contradiction to Bar-Tov (*Dado*, vol. 1, p. 278), he argues on the basis of numerous interviews that no one in the General Staff thought of a warning shorter than forty eight hours as a "catastrophe" (p. 30). Among other pieces of evidence, he notes that the IDF conducted an exercise (*ayil barzel*, or "Iron Ram") in August 1972 predicated on twenty-four hours warning: in it, the IDF repelled the Egyptian attack in two days, and began operating large forces on the other side of the canal in four (pp. 18–19). In fact, the Bar Tov book indirectly confirms this (vol. 1, p. 321) when it observes that Elazar expected as little as twelve or twenty-four hours' warning on October 5.

27. This account is based largely on Zeev Eytan, "'Shovach yonim'—tichnon u'bitsua b'mivchan ha'esh" ["'Dovecote'—Plan and Implementation Under the Test of Fire"], *Ma'arachot* 276–77 (October–November 1980): 38–46. Eytan, who has a Ph.D. in political science, is a well-known Israeli armored commander and colonel in the reserves, where he has served as a divisional chief of staff. After the war he worked in the military history office of the IDF studying the battles on the southern front.

28. Thus, even on 21 May 1973, when the Minister of Defense said to the military "We in the government say to the General Staff—Gentlemen, please prepare for war" the resulting alert (*kachol lavan* or "Blue-White," Israel's national colors) was not chiefly a reserve mobilization but intensified preparation of the infrastructure for war. Bar-Tov, *Dado*, vol. 1, pp. 269–70 describes this meeting.

29. Adan, "Eichut v'kamut," p. 260. Adan, a reserve major general, commanded an armored division in the Sinai in 1973, and had served as the head of the Israeli Armored Corps before then.

30. See Adan, "Eichut v'kamut," p. 258, and Geoffrey G. Prosch, "Israeli Defense of the Golan: An Interview with Brigadier General Avigdor Kahalani," *Military Review* 59:10 (October 1979): 3, as well as Kahalani's own memoir, *The Heights of Courage: A Tank Leader's War on the Golan.* Louis Williams, trans. (Westport, Conn.: Greenwood, 1984), p. 48.

31. See Shlomo Gazit, "Arab Forces Two Years After the Yom Kippur War," in William Louis, ed., *Military Aspects of the Israeli-Arab Conflict* (Tel Aviv: University Publishing Projects, 1975), p. 188. Gazit was then head of AMAN, and discusses Arab strengths and losses in 1973 in some detail—based on captured documents and prisoner of war interrogation.

32. Eitan Haber, *Hayom tifrotz milchama* ["Today War Will Break Out—The Reminiscences of Brigadier General Israel Lior, Aide-de-Camp to Prime Ministers Levi Eshkol and Golda Meir"] (Tel Aviv: Edanim, 1987), pp. 17–18.

33. Bar-Tov, *Dado*, vol. 1, p. 289.

34. Ibid., p. 294. Hofi also cancelled leaves for the tank crews on the heights.

35. Avraham Ayalon, "Muchanut leumit: t'shuva ikarit l'matkafat petah," ["National Preparedness: A Fundamental Answer to Surprise Attack"] in Offer and Kober, eds., *Modi'in*, p. 373.

36. Ibid., p. 297. Zeira repeated this phrase, *svirut nimucha*, until the day before the war. It has, not surprisingly, a particularly bitter connotation to Israeli students of the surprise.

37. Ibid., pp. 304, 323; *Duach va'adat Agranat* (Tel Aviv: Am Oved, 1975), p. 46; interviews with senior Israeli officers and officials. The importance of this latter source is discussed below.

38. Lanir, *Hahafta'a habasisit*, p. 24.

39. Since Sunday, September 30, Israeli forces had begun emplacing mines in the Golan. Raphael Eitan with Dov Goldstein, *Raful: sipuro shel chayal* ["Raful: The Story of A Soldier"] (Tel Aviv: Ma'ariv Book Guild, 1985), pp. 127–8. Eitan, a paratrooper, commanded forces on the Golan Heights; once additional Israeli units began arriving on October 7 and 8 he commanded one of the three *ugdot* operating there. After the war he eventually became Chief of Staff of the IDF, and played a key role in the invasion of Lebanon in 1982.

40. Moshe Dayan, however, came close. See Zeev Schiff, *October Earthquake: Yom Kippur 1973*, Louis Williams, trans. (Tel Aviv: University Publishing Projects, Ltd., 1974), pp. 16–21. Schiff, who had unparalleled access to the decision makers, has one of the best accounts of the war.

41. Bar-Tov, *Dado*, vol. 1, p. 315.

42. Dayan, *Avnei derekh* vol. 2, p. 574.

43. Meir, *Chayay*, p. 307.

44. Bar-Tov, *Dado*, vol. 1, p. 321. Meir's military aide has said that on October

5 he still expected at least twenty-four hours warning before the beginning of a war. Haber, *Hayom tifrotz milchama,* p. 23.

45. The Syrians, who were attacking from east to west, on the other hand, wanted an early morning attack for precisely the same reason.

46. Herzog, *War of Atonement,* remains a good English account, as does Dupuy, *Elusive Victory,* pp. 387–618. An excellent short account, illustrated with superb maps and tables, is Wallach, Lissak and Itzchaki, eds., *Atlas karta,* pp. 43–99. Nonetheless, the war still awaits a historian fluent in Hebrew and Arabic yet reasonably detached from both sides.

47. Bar-Tov, *Dado,* vol. 2, p. 53.

48. Ibid., p. 70.

49. Compared to 20 percent in the Six-Day War. The difference is that after the first day of the Yom Kippur War the Israelis were forced to adjust their tactics to new, and more confining, operational conditions.

50. Safran, *Israel,* pp. 480–83; Kissinger, *Years of Upheaval,* p. 498.

51. Dupuy, *Elusive Victory,* p. 609.

52. See, for example Avraham Adan's candid account in *On the Banks of Suez* (San Francisco: Presidio, 1980), pp. 95–190; see also Zeev Eytan, "Ha-8 b'oktober—hama'aracha kula charka" ["October 8: The Whole Array Creaked"] *Ma'arachot* 268 (April 1979): 5–11. Adan's *ugda* had 170 tanks at the beginning of the counterattack on the 8th; it ended it with fewer than one hundred and no noticeable gains. Sharon, who failed to support Adan's attack, lost fifty tanks the next day, similarly without countervailing gains.

53. Only a quarter of Israeli tank casualties appear to have resulted from missile or RPG attacks; these occurred chiefly in the first few days of the war on the Egyptian front, however. Moreover, the missile threat—to tanks on the ground, as to fighter-bombers in the air—constrained Israeli freedom of maneuver, even when it did not inflict heavy losses.

54. Some sharp criticism can be found in Adan, "Eichut v'kamut"; Matityahu Peled, "Eich lo hitconena yisroel lamilchama" ["How Israel Failed to Prepare for War"] *Ma'arachot* 289–290 (October 1983): 25–28; Ya'akov Chasdai, "Milchemet yom hakippurim: hafta'a? nitsachon?" ["The Yom Kippur War: Surprise? Victory?"] *Ma'arachot* 275 (August 1980): 7–13 and, by the same author, *Ha'emet b'tsel hamilchama* ["Truth in the Shadow of War"] (Tel Aviv: Zmora, Bitan, Modan, 1978); Herzog, *War of Atonement,* pp. 79, 253, and pp. 270–80; Zeev Schiff, *October Earthquake: Yom Kippur 1973,* Louis Williams, trans. (Tel Aviv: University Publishing Projects, 1974), pp. 303ff. and passim.

55. The full public version of the Agranat Report is to be found in *Duach va'adat Agranat.* Frequently cited versions that appeared in *The Jerusalem Journal of International Relations* 4:1 and 4:2 (1979), pp. 69–90 and 96–

128 have omitted some important excerpts that were published in Hebrew, chiefly critical assessments of several senior officers.

56. *Duach va'adat Agranat,* p. 74 (third report).

57. Ibid., pp. 34–35.

58. "All the Inefficiencies of Any Intelligence Service," *Armed Forces Journal International* 111:2 (October 1973): 47. Emphasis in the original. This issue of AFJI—which dealt almost exclusively with Israeli security—appeared on virtually the same day the war broke out, reflecting interviews done only weeks earlier. It is a fascinating source for the mentality of the IDF before the war broke out.

59. Alouph Hareven, "Disturbed Hierarchies: Israeli Intelligence in 1954 and 1973," *Jerusalem Quarterly* 9 (Fall 1978): 12. See also pp. 15–16.

60. *Du'ach va'adat Agranat,* p. 36.

61. In point of fact, Soviet arms supplies to Egypt increased rapidly following Sadat's (temporary) rapprochement with the Russians at the very end of 1972. Sadat, in fact, later remarked that by the spring of 1973 the Egyptians were "drowning" in Soviet weapons.

62. Bar Tov, *Dado,* Vol. I, p. 287.

63. Interview, retired IDF officer—September 1988, Tel Aviv.

64. See Richard K. Betts, *Surprise Attack* (Washington, D.C.: Brookings Institution, 1982), pp. 287–88. A former National Security Council staff member interviewed for this chapter recalled considerable scorn directed against the American intelligence community on the morning of October 7, 1973.

65. Michael I. Handel, *Perception, Deception, and Surprise: The Case of the Yom Kippur War,* Jerusalem Papers on Peace Problems, #19 (Jerusalem: Hebrew University, Leonard Davis Institute for International Relations, 1976), pp. 33–38. Admittedly, the small but efficient Israeli Navy needed no large-scale call-up to go on to a war footing.

66. *Du'ach va'adat Agranat,* pp. 37–38. It should be noted, in addition, that the head of the Mossad, Zvi Zamir, took a much graver view of the situation from late September on, although he did not press his arguments on senior decision-makers.

67. Interviews, retired IDF officers, Tel Aviv, September, 1988.

68. Interview, retired IDF officer, Tel Aviv, September, 1988.

69. Heikal, *Road to Ramadan,* p. 17.

70. This was stressed in a number of my interviews with retired IDF officers, Tel Aviv, September, 1988.

71. See, for example, Janice Gross Stein, "'Intelligence' and 'Stupidity' Reconsidered: Estimation and Decision in Israel, 1973," *Journal of Strategic Studies:* 3:1 (January 1980): 147–77, and by the same author, "The 1973 Intelligence Failure: A Reconsideration," *Jerusalem Quarterly* 24 (Summer 1982): 41–54.

72. What follows is based in large measure on several interviews with retired IDF officers, Tel Aviv, September 1988. See as well Stein, "The 1973 Intelligence Failure," p. 43.

73. Interview, retired IDF officer, Tel Aviv, September, 1988.

74. See Handel, *Perception, Deception and Surprise;* and by the same author, *Military Deception in Peace and War,* Jerusalem Papers on Peace Problems #38 (Jerusalem: Hebrew University, Leonard Davis Institute for International Relations, 1985), as well as *Intelligence and National Security* 2:3 (July 1987), particularly Handel's article, "Introduction: Strategic and Operational Deception in Historical Perspective," pp. 1–91. In addition, see Zeevi, *tochnit habona'a* and the accounts of Shazlie and Heikal.

75. "A Secret Israeli Ally: Arab Rust," *Armed Forces Journal International* 111:2 (October 1973):45. This article draws on a number of Arab and international press stories—the sole disagreements expressed with the "Arab Rust" theory came from Israeli intelligence officers interviewed for the story.

76. See Lanir, *Habafta'a babasisit,* pp. 32–34, 51–54, and passim. Order of battle information with respect to Syria was accurate, but AMAN misjudged the direction of a key Syrian thrust, which went southeast to northwest parallel to an old oil pipeline, rather than directly east-west, as expected.

77. See Heikal, *Road to Ramadan,* p. 213.

78. See the description in Wallach, Lissak, and Itzchaki, *Atlas karta,* p. 43.

79. See the discussion in Bar Tov, *Dado,* vol. 1, pp. 240–251.

80. Yoel Ben Porat, "Milchemet yom hakippurim: ta'ut b'mai v'hafta'a b'oktober," ["The Yom Kippur War: Mistake in May and Surprise in October"] *Ma'arachot* 299 (July/August 1985): 2–9. Ben Porat, a brigadier general in AMAN, was head of an important collection agency there. The article is based on a classified internal study published within AMAN in February 1985, and conducted by Dr. Ariel Levite, an intelligence officer and well-known scholar in intelligence studies. See also Yoel Ben Porat, "Ha'ara b'shulei hama'amar 'milchemet yom hakippurim: ta'ut b'mai v'hafta'a b'oktober,'" ["A Note in Connection with the Article: 'The Yom Kippur War: Mistake in May and Surprise in October'"] *Ma'arachot* 302–303 (March/April 1986):55. It should be noted that some AMAN officers fail to find Ben Porat's argument convincing. See also Aharon Levran, "Hesber acher l'hafta'a b'milchemet yom hakippurim" ["Another Explanation of the Surprise of the Yom Kippur War"], *Ha'aretz* October 12, 1986, p. 10. Levran was also a brigadier general in the IDF.

81. Kissinger, *Years of Upheaval,* p. 297. See also pp. 205–28, 294–96.

82. A remarkable, but by no means implausible assessment of an event that infuriated the Arabs and puzzled those who have studied the war. The airlift was extremely conspicuous, involving large Soviet transports, and much conversation over airplane radios in Russian—a clear tip-off, and an

important factor in shaking AMAN's confidence in its assessment of "low probability" of war.

83. See Heikal, *Road to Ramadan*, p. 20. Consideration of episodes such as the possibility of postponing D-day in June 1944 because of poor weather gives a good sense of the kinds of costs involved. Several IDF officials assured me that Sadat would probably have begun the war on October 6 even if Israel had mobilized a day or two earlier—and Heikal's assertion that the Egyptians expected 26,000 casualties in the canal crossing, supports this view.

84. William James, "The Will to Believe," in *The Will to Believe and Other Essays in Popular Philosophy* (1897; reprint New York: Dover, 1956), p. 25.

85. See Haber, *Hayom tifrotz milchama*, p. 15.

86. See Chaim Bar Lev, "Hamilchama v'mataroteha al reka milchamot tsahal" ["The War and its Objectives Against the Background of the IDF's Wars"] *Ma'arachot* 266 (October–November 1978): 2–8.

87. "Israel's Combat Arms," *Armed Forces Journal International* 111:2 (October 1973): 64.

88. Zeev Schiff, *A History of the Israeli Army: 1874 to the Present* (New York: Macmillan, 1985), p. 159.

89. Most IDF prewar planning assumed pre-emption, although senior IDF officers understood that this might not always occur. Interview, Major General Israel Tal, Tel Aviv, September 12, 1988.

90. Another is in the continuing drive for a decisive victory along the lines of June 1967. See Yoav Ben Horin and Barry Posen, *Israel's Strategic Doctrine* R-2845-NA (Santa Monica: RAND, 1981) for a good discussion of Israel's doctrine. An interesting and quite self-critical view is Israel Tal, "Israel's Doctrine of National Security: Background and Dynamics," *Jerusalem Quarterly* No. 4 (Summer 1977), pp. 44–57, updated in "Al bitachon leumi" ["On National Security"] *Ma'arachot* 286 (February 1983), pp. 3–7.

91. Interview, Major General Israel Tal, Tel Aviv, September 12, 1988.

92. Dayan, *Avnei derekh*, vol. 2, p. 575.

93. See Bar Lev, "Hamilchama," p. 7, which discusses Egyptian objectives in terms of reoccupying the Sinai.

94. "Israel's Combat Arms," p. 70. See too Dov Tamari, "Milchemet yom hakippurim: musagim, ha'arachot, miskenot," ["The Yom Kippur War: Ideas, Assessments, Conclusions"] *Ma'arachot* 276–277 (October–November 1980), pp. 12–13.

95. For a very interesting comparative analysis that takes a different position, see Ephraim Kam, *Surprise Attack: A Victim's Perspective* (Cambridge: Harvard University Press, 1988).

96. Aharon Levran, "Hafta'a v'hatra'a: iyunim b'sh'ailot y'sod" ["Surprise and Warning: Reflections on Fundamental Questions"] *Ma'aracbot* 276–277 (October/November 1980), p. 18.

97. Levran, "Hesber acher."

98. See F. H. Hinsley et al., *British Intelligence in the Second World War: Its Influence on Strategy and Operations*, vol. 3, Part 2 (New York: Cambridge University Press, 1988), pp. 429–30.

99. Yoel Ben Porat, "Milchemet yom hakippurim—knas deterministi shel ha-historiah?" ["The Yom Kippur War—An Inevitable Penalty of History?"] *Ma'aracbot* 305 (September 1986), p. 22.

100. The Hebrew *kalut rosh* connotes a grievous fecklessness.

101. Interview with retired senior IDF officer, Tel Aviv, September 1988.

102. For a sustained discussion of the many dimensions of military effectiveness, and the need to think through all of them, see Allan R. Millett and Williamson Murray, eds., *Military Effectiveness*, 3 vols. (Boston: Allen & Unwin, 1988).

Chapter 6
FAILURE TO ADAPT
The British at Gallipoli, August 1915

1. Command Paper Cd. 8490, Dardanelles Commission: *First Report*, 1917, pp. 39–40.

2. Hamilton mss., "The Gallipoli Campaign," vol. 2, p. 1. H 15/20. Liddell Hart Centre for Military Archives, King's College, London.

3. John Masefield, *Gallipoli* (London: Heinemann, 1916), p. 109.

4. David French, "The Dardanelles, Mecca and Kut: Prestige as a factor in British Eastern Strategy 1914–1916," *War and Society* 5/1 (May 1987): 45–61.

5. General Sir Ian Hamilton, *Gallipoli Diary* (London: Edward Arnold, 1920), vol. 1, p. 304 (June 15, 1915).

6. A. J. Marder, *The Anatomy of British Sea Power: A History of British Naval Policy in the Pre-Dreadnought Era* (Hamden, Conn.: Archon, 1964), p. 495.

7. A. J. Marder, *From the Dreadnought to Scapa Flow II: The War Years: To the Eve of Jutland 1914–1916* (London: Oxford University Press, 1965), pp. 233–34, 245–47.

8. PRO, Minutes of War Council, January 8, 1915, Cab. 42/1/12.

9. E. K. G. Sixsmith, *British Generalship in the Twentieth Century* (London: Arms and Armour Press, 1970), p. 148.

10. Thomas Pakenham, *The Boer War* (London: Weidenfeld and Nicolson, 1979), pp. 555–60.

11. Lloyd George Papers. Bax-Ironside to Grey, March 18, 1915. House of Lords Record Office, C/16/4/2.

12. Liman von Sanders, *Five Years in Turkey* (Annapolis, Md.: U.S. Naval Institute, 1928), pp. 56–61.

13. Cmd. 371, *The Final Report of the Dardanelles Commission*, 1919, pp. 17–18.

14. Robert Rhodes James, *Gallipoli* (London: Batsford, 1965), p. 53.

15. PRO, Dardanelles Commission: Minutes of Evidence, Qs. 4357–68. Cab. 19/33.

16. PRO, Replies to questions put by Australian Official Historian on fighting in Gallipoli (Answers by Turkish General Staff), Qs. 1–4, 5–6. Cab. 45/236.

17. Ibid., Qs. 15–17, 19.

18. C. F. Aspinall Oglander, *Military Operations: Gallipoli* (London: Heineman, 1929), vol. 1, pp. 201–15; Hamilton, *Gallipoli Diary*, vol. 1, p. 147.

19. Rhodes James, *Gallipoli*, p. 130.

20. Winston S. Churchill *The World Crisis* (New York: C. Scribner's Sons, 1923), vol. 2, p. 454.

21. PRO, "The 11th Division at Suvla Bay," Lt. Col. N. Malcolm (1919?), p. 1, Cab. 45/258.

22. Alan Moorehead, *Gallipoli* (London: New English Library, 1963), p. 250.

23. C. E. W. Bean, *Official History of Australia in the War of 1914–18* (Sydney: Angus and Robertson, 1921), vol. 2, p. 445.

24. Rhodes James, *Gallipoli*, p. 238.

25. Hamilton, *Gallipoli Diary*, vol. 1, p. 118 (April 18, 1915).

26. Eric Larrabee, *Commander in Chief: Franklin Delano Roosevelt, His Lieutenants & Their War* (New York: Harper & Row, 1987), pp. 262–66, 269; Jeter A. Isely and Philip A. Crowl, *The U.S. Marines and Amphibious War* (Princeton: Princeton University Press, 1951), pp. 109–18.

27. Compton Mackenzie, *Gallipoli Memories* (London: Panther, 1965), p. 275.

28. C. F. Aspinall Oglander, *Military Operations: Gallipoli* (London: Heinemann, 1932), vol. 2, p. 148.

29. Cmd. 371, *The Final Report*, pp. 144–45.

30. Aspinall Oglander, *Military Operations*, vol. 2, p. 149.

31. Cmd. 371, *The Final Report*, p. 34.

32. Hamilton, *Gallipoli Diary*, vol. 1, p. 331 (June 24, 1915).

33. Cmd. 371, *The Final Report*, p. 27 (despatch of December 11, 1915).

34. PRO, Minutes of Evidence, Q. 9621, Cab. 19/33.

35. Aspinall Oglander, *Military Operations*, vol. 2, pp. 151–55.

36. PRO, "Suvla Bay (The Second Landing). Extract from the diary of Lt. J. M. Heath R.N.," August 6, 1915. Cab. 45/253.

37. PRO, Answers by the Turkish General Staff, Qs. 73–76, Cab. 45/236.

38. Rhodes James, *Gallipoli*, p. 281.

39. Aspinall Oglander, *Military Operations*, vol. 2, pp. 263–64.

40. Cmd. 371, *The Final Report*, p. 38.

41. Stopford to Mahon, August 8, 1915 (7:10 A.M.); Stopford to GHQ, August 8, 1915 (10:50 A.M.); Aspinall Oglander, *Military Operations*, vol. 2, pp. 270–71.

42. Cmd. 371, *The Final Report*, p. 41.

43. Churchill, *The World Crisis*, vol. 2, p. 468.

44. Eric Wheler Bush, *Gallipoli* (London: Allen & Unwin, 1975), p. 249.

45. In his evidence to the Dardanelles Commission, Stopford flatly denied Hamilton's story. Minutes of Evidence, Qs. 9747–48. Cab. 19/33.

46. Hamilton, *Gallipoli Diary*, vol. 2, p. 66 (August 8, 1915).

47. Bean, *Official History of Australia*, vol. 2, p. 700.

48. PRO, Heath Diary, August 8, 1915, Cab. 45/253.

49. PRO, Minutes of Evidence, Qs. 8 331, 9 734, 9 740, 9 744, Cab. 19/33.

50. Ibid., Qs. 7823, 10 382, 11 112, 12 562, 12 564.

51. Ibid., Q. 14 536.

52. Cmd. 371, *The Final Report*, pp. 65, 67.

53. Ibid., p. 64.

54. Bean, *Official History of Australia*, vol. 1, pp. 465–66, 573.

55. Ibid., vol. 2, p. 446.

56. David French, "The Military Background to the 'Shell Crisis' of 1915, " *Journal of Strategic Studies* 2:2 (September 1979): 192–205.

57. Cmd. 371, *The Final Report*, p. 50.

58. PRO, Minutes of Evidence, Q. 10 632. Cab. 19/33. Cf. Mackenzie, *Gallipoli Memories*, p. 127.

59. Bean, *Official History of Australia*, vol. 2, p. 468.

60. Aspinall Oglander, *Military Operations*, vol. 2, p. 149.

61. Bush, *Gallipoli*, p. 239.

62. PRO, Minutes of Evidence, Q. 13 941, Cab. 19/33.

63. Cecil Malthus, *Anzac: A Retrospect* (Christchurch, New Zealand: Whitcombe and Tomb, 1965), p. 91.

64. Hamilton mss., Russell to Hamilton, September 24, 1916, H 17/3/1/1. Liddell Hart Centre for Military Archives, King's College, University of London.

65. PRO, Minutes of Evidence, Q. 7277, Cab. 19/33.

66. Kevin Fewster ed., *Gallipoli Correspondent: The Frontline Diary of C. E. W. Bean* (Sydney: Allen & Unwin, 1983), p. 67 (April 27, 1915).

67. Bean, *Official History of Australia*, vol. 1, p. 452.

68. PRO, "The 11th Division at Suvla Bay," p. 26, Cab. 45/258. Major-General Hammersley told the Dardanelles Commission, "I do not think anybody quite realised what the country was like before we landed there." Minutes of Evidence, Q. 10 274. Cab. 19/33.

69. PRO, Minutes of Evidence, Qs. 7641–43. Cab. 19/33.

70. Ibid., Q. 8022.

71. Aspinall Oglander, *Military Operations*, vol. 2, p. 141.

72. Hamilton, *Gallipoli Diary*, vol. 1, pp. 25, 178, 329 (March 17, April 29, and June 24, 1915).

73. Cmd. 371, *The Final Report*, pp. 50–51; Minutes of Evidence, Q. 11 757, Cab. 19/33.

74. S. W. Roskill, *Hankey: Man of Secrets* (London:Collins, 1970), vol. 1, p. 198.

75. Hamilton mss. Stopford to Hamilton, August 11, 1915, H. 17/7/32/7, KCL.

76. PRO, Minutes of Evidence, Q. 7500, Cab. 19/33.

77. Ibid., Q. 7473.

78. Ibid., Qs. 14 538, 14 542.

79. Malthus, *Anzac: A Retrospect*, p. 32.

80. Aspinall Oglander, *Military Operations*, vol. 2, pp. 236, 248, 272.

81. PRO, Minutes of Evidence, Q. 14 538, Cab. 19/33.

82. Bean, *Official History of Australia*, vol. 1, p. 46.

83. Cmd. 371, *The Final Report*, p. 22.

84. Tim Travers, "A Particular Style of Command: Haig and GHQ, 1916–18," *Journal of Strategic Studies* 10:3 (September 1987): 363–376.

85. Hamilton, *Gallipoli Diary* vol. 1, p. 147 (April 26, 1915).

86. PRO, Minutes of Evidence, Q. 7601, Cab. 19/33.

87. Rhodes James, *Gallipoli*, p. 319.

88. Bean, *The Official History of Australia*, vol. 1, pp. 120–21.

89. Moorehead, *Gallipoli*, p. 227.

90. Cmd. 371, *The Final Report*, p. 37; Mackenzie, *Gallipoli Memories*, pp. 263–64.

91. PRO, "The 11th Division at Suvla Bay," p. 16, Cab. 45/258.

92. PRO, Minutes of Evidence, Q. 36 (Telegram, October 31, 1915), Cab. 19/33.

93. Bean, *Official History of Australia*, vol. 1, p. 262.

94. Ibid., vol. 2, p. 466.

95. PRO, Minutes of Evidence, Qs. 9709–11, Cab. 19/33.

96. General Sir Hugh Beach, *Gallipoli Memorial Lecture* (London: Brassey's, 1985), p. 16.

97. PRO, Minutes of Evidence, Q. 25 278, Cab. 19/33.

98. Ibid., Qs. 8030–31.

99. Cmd. 371, *The Final Report*, p. 147.

100. PRO, Minutes of Evidence, Q. 14 538, Cab. 19/33.

101. Churchill, *The World Crisis*, vol. 2, p. 476. Churchill to Alexander, September 14, 1943. Quoted in Martin S. Gilbert, *Winston S. Churchill: Road to Victory 1941–45* (London: Heinemann, 1986), p. 503.

102. Cmd. 371, *The Final Report*, pp. 84–85.

103. William H. Form and Sigmund Nosow, *Community in Disaster* (New York: Harper Bros., 1958).

104. Bean, *Official History of Australia*, vol. 1, p. 344.

105. PRO, Minutes of Evidence, Q 12 395; Bean, *Official History of Australia*, vol. 1, p. 231.

106. PRO, Minutes of Evidence, Q. 9825, Cab. 19/33.

107. J. A. Stockfish, *The Intellectual Foundations of Systems Analysis* (Santa Monica: RAND, 1987), P. 7401–, p. 15.

Chapter 7
AGGREGATE FAILURE
The Defeat of American Eighth Army in Korea, November–December 1950

1. Roy E. Appleman, *South to the Naktong, North to the Yalu (June–November 1950)* (Washington, D.C.: Office of the Chief of Military History, 1961), p. 180; Max Hastings, *The Korean War* (New York: Simon and Schuster, 1987) is harsh but accurate on the failings of the U.S. Army in this period.

2. JCS 92985, Secretary of Defense to CINCFE, in *Foreign Relations of the United States 1950*, vol. 7. *Korea* (Washington, D.C.: Government Printing Office, 1976), p. 826. Hereafter this volume will be cited as *FRUS 1950*, 7.

3. CINCFE to JCS C69953, November 28, 1950, *FRUS, 1950*, 7, p. 1237.

4. The most thorough study of this subject remains Allen S. Whiting, *China Crosses the Yalu: The Decision to Enter the Korean War*, Rand R-356 (Santa Monica: RAND, 1960).

5. Joseph C. Goulden, *Korea: The Untold Story of the War* (New York: Times Books, 1982), chap. 14, "MacArthur Marches to Disaster," pp. 323–44, is a relatively moderate indictment.

6. Clay Blair, *The Forgotten War: America in Korea, 1950–1953* (New York:

Times Books, 1988), p. 464. Although we think that Blair exaggerates MacArthur's faults, this is an exceptionally fine and thorough book.

7. Matthew B. Ridgway, *The Korean War* (Garden City, N.Y.: Doubleday, 1967), p. 78.

8. See Clayton D. James, *The Years of MacArthur*, especially vol. 3, *Triumph and Disaster, 1945–1964* (Boston: Houghton Mifflin, 1985).

9. The best account is Mineo Nakajima, "Foreign Relations from the Korean War to the Bandung Line," in Denis Twitchett and John K. Fairbank, eds., *The Cambridge History of China*, vol. 14, *The People's Republic, Part I: The Emergence of Revolutionary China 1949–1965* (Cambridge: Cambridge University Press, 1987), pp. 270–9.

10. See, for example, a CIA assessment, "Threat of Full Chinese Communist Intervention in Korea," October 12, 1950, *FRUS, 1950, 7*, p. 933; this view reappears in National Intelligence Estimate (NIE) 2, "Chinese Communist Intervention in Korea," November 8, 1950, ibid., pp. 1101–6.

11. Memorandum DCIA to President, "Chinese Communist Intervention in Korea," November 1, 1950, ibid., pp. 1025–26.

12. Memorandum, JCS to Secretary of Defense, "Chinese Communist Intervention in Korea," November 9, 1950, ibid., pp. 1117–21.

13. Bevin Alexander, *Korea: The First War We Lost* (New York: Hippocrene Books, 1986), p. 9.

14. Whiting, *China Crosses the Yalu*, pp. 151–62. On Panikkar's warnings, see Ambassador to India to Secretary of State EMBTEL 716, September 20, 1950, and EMBTEL 828, October 3, 1950, *FRUS, 1950, 7* pp. 742, 850.

15. See Samuel B. Griffith, *The Chinese People's Liberation Army* (New York: McGraw-Hill, 1967), p. 189, and Alexander George, *The Chinese Communist Army in Action: The Korean War and its Aftermath* (New York: Columbia University Press, 1967), pp. 7ff. This book was based on extensive interviews with Chinese POWs in 1951.

16. The best discussion remains Whiting, *China Crosses the Yalu*, pp. 154–60. In his memoirs, Nikita Khrushchev recalls that the Chinese had this as their objective. Strobe Talbott, trans. and ed., *Khrushchev Remembers* (Boston: Little, Brown, 1970), pp. 372.

17. See Jürgen Domes, *Peng Te-huai, The Man and the Image* (Stanford, Calif.: Stanford University Press, 1985), p. 60, and Peng Dehuai's own memoirs, *Memoirs of a Chinese Marshal*, Zheng Longpu, trans. (Beijing: Foreign Languages Press, 1984), pp. 472–74.

18. S. L. A. Marshall, *The River and the Gauntlet: Defeat of the Eighth Army by the Chinese Communist Forces, November 1950 in the Battle of the Chongchon River, Korea* (New York: Time, 1962), pp. 267ff.

19. Letter by S. L. A. Marshall, quoted in William B. Hopkins, *One Bugle, No Drums: The Marines at Chosin Reservoir* (Chapel Hill: Algonquin Books,

1986), pp. 211–12. See also Roy E. Appleman, *East of Chosin: Entrapment and Breakout in Korea, 1950* (College Station: Texas A & M Press, 1987), pp. 336–40 for a somewhat more sympathetic comparison of army and marine forces in the Chosin Reservoir campaign.

20. See, for example, Eighth Army, G3 War Diary, November 23, 1950, which includes Operations Plan 16 for the final march north, and Periodic Intelligence Reports (PIR) 134–136, November 23–25 1950. Eighth Army records are in Record Group 407, Washington National Records Center, Suitland, Maryland.

21. Eighth Army, G-1, Daily Historical Report, November 27, 1950.

22. Far East Command, Daily Intelligence Summary #3000, November 26, 1950. FEC records are in RG 319, Washington National Records Center, Suitland, Maryland. This source hereafter cited as FEC, DIS.

23. Billy Mossman, "Ebb and Flow," chap. 2, n.d., unpublished manuscript, U.S., Army Center of Military History, Washington, D.C.

24. CINCFE to DA, November 8, 1950, Record Group 9, MacArthur Memorial Archive, Norfolk, Virginia. Marshall had been very insistent on the hydroelectric-plant theory.

25. Conference Notes, 8 January 1951, in "Korean War—Special File, December 1950—May 1952," Matthew B. Ridgway Papers, Archives, US Army Military History Institute Archives, Carlisle Barracks, Pennsylvania. Henceforth this archive cited as "USAMHI"

26. See, for example, Headquarters, EUSAK, "Enemy Tactics," 1951, Record Group 319, National Archives; S. L. A. Marshall, "CCF in the Attack," a two-part study done for the army in the winter of 1950–51 through the Johns Hopkins Operations Research Office, and reprinted in Hopkins, *One Bugle*, pp. 233–54; Griffith, *Chinese People's Liberation Army*, especially pp. 143–49.

27. The discussion that follows draws on Eliot A. Cohen, "Only Half the Battle: The Chinese Intervention in Korea, 1950," *Studies in Intelligence* (Fall 1988): 49–66

28. Mossman, "Ebb and Flow," chap. 3, pp. 14–18.

29. Chargé in China to Secretary of State #614, *FRUS, 1950*, 7, p. 1069.

30. Mossman, "Ebb and Flow," chap. 2, pp. 1–3.

31. See the discussion in Cohen, "Half the Battle," p. 57.

32. Kenneth Strong, *Intelligence at the Top: The Recollections of an Intelligence Officer* (London: Cassell, 1968), pp. 62–63. Strong was Eisenhower's intelligence officer in World War II and the first head of joint intelligence at the British Ministry of Defence.

33. Eighth Army, PIR #136, November 25, 1950; PIR #137, November 26, 1950.

34. FEC, DIS #2990, November 16, 1950. This potential had been noted earlier: see FEC, DIS #2971, October 28, 1950.

35. This conception of intelligence is discussed in Eliot A. Cohen and Stephen P. Rosen, *Thinking Strategically*, Chapter III, "Intelligence in Support of Strategy," (New York: The Free Press, forthcoming).

36. The following is based on the study "Comparison of CCF and NK Infantry Divisions," published in FEC, DIS #2976, 2 November 1950. US forces generally referred to PLA units as CCF, for Chinese Communist Forces.

37. FEC, DIS #2971, October 28, 1950. The one exception is with respect to guerrilla warfare, where American intelligence analysts noticed quite different styles of operation: FEC, DIS, #2946, October 3, 1950.

38. Contemporary North Korean organization and tactics are reviewed in FEC, DIS #3008, December 4, 1950. Discussions of North Korean artillery and signals equipment, organization, and doctrine are to be found FEC, DIS #2935, September 22, 1950, and #2971, October 28, 1950. Both branches demonstrated marked similarity to Soviet tables of organization and practice.

39. See note 21.

40. Sun Tzu, *The Art of War*, Samuel B. Griffith trans. (Oxford: Oxford University Press, 1963), pp. 66–69.

41. Peng, *Memoirs*, p. 476.

42. FEC, DIS #3025, December 21, 1950. Soon thereafter the Daily Intelligence Summary published Marshall's study of "CCF in the Attack," which he had just completed.

43. IX Corps, PIR #46, November 11, 1950, enclosure to Eighth Army PIR #124, November 13, 1950.

44. FEC, DIS #2988, November 14, 1950.

45. Ibid.

46. Appleman, *South to the Naktong*, p. 477.

47. Ibid., p. 256.

48. FEC, DIS #2971, October 28, 1950.

49. Notes compiled by General Omar N. Bradley, *FRUS, 1950, 7*, p. 953.

50. Weather intelligence estimated, on the basis of Japanese records, that the Yalu would freeze over in mid-December: in fact, in 1950 it froze before then. Far East Air Force Weather Study, November 7, 1950, enclosure to Eighth Army PIR #124, November 14, 1950.

51. Much of what follows is based on "Intelligence and Counterintelligence During the Korean Conflict," manuscript, Office of the Chief of Military History, 1955, which is available at OCMH and on microfilm from that institution. This draft study was not published. That document's conclusions are supported by review of contemporary intelligence reports.

52. George, *The Chinese Communist Army*, pp. 127–33.

53. On the photo-interpreter shortage see Marshall, *The River and the Gauntlet*, p. 5; Robert F. Futtrell, *The United States Air Force in Korea 1950–1953*,

rev. ed. (Washington, D.C.: Office of Air Force History, 1983), pp. 72 ff; on reconnaissance priorities see pp. 228–9.

54. "Basic Journal, Marshall's Notes, 2d Division," S. L. A. Marshall Papers, USAMHI.

55. S. L. A. Marshall, "Commentary on Infantry Operations and Weapons Usage in Korea, Winter of 1950–1951," ORO-R-13 (Chevy Chase, Md.: Johns Hopkins University Operations Research Office, 1952), pp. 120–21 (emphasis in the original).

56. Appleman, *South to the Naktong*, p. 653.

57. Far East Command, Command Report, November 1950, p. 29. Replacements scheduled to arrive in September numbered only half the number required.

58. Headquarters, United States Army Forces Far East and Eighth Army, "Logistics in the Korean Operations," Camp Zama, Japan, 1955, vol. 1, chap. 3, p. 2. Historical monograph prepared for the Office of the Chief of Military History, henceforth cited as "Logistics in the Korean Operations."

59. Ibid., vol. 1, chap 3, fig. 2a.

60. Far East Command, Command Report, November 1950, p. 36. In November the Army sent 8,600 combat replacements, and 9,000 support replacements to the front.

61. There are other indications of the mishandling of replacements. See Eighth Army, G-1 Daily Historical Report, November 21, 1950, for an account of replacements being left out in the open overnight without facilities to shelter them from the weather—one of a number of such reports.

62. Eighth Army, G-1 Daily Historical Report, November 6, 1950. See also "Logistics in the Korean Operations," vol. 1, chap. 3, pp. 26 ff.

63. "Logistics in the Korean Operations," vol. 1, chap. 3, p. 26.

64. Marshall, *The River and the Gauntlet*, p. 94.

65. Marshall, "Commentary on Infantry Operations," pp. 52–54.

66. "Logistics in the Korean Operations," vol. 1, pp. 2–11. See also Eighth Army, Command Report, December 1950.

67. "Lessons from Korea" (Fort Benning, Ga: The U.S. Infantry School, 1954), ms., Army Library, Pentagon.

68. *The River and the Gauntlet*, p. 17.

69. Ibid., p. 24.

70. Ibid., p. 243.

71. Quoted in Hopkins, *One Bugle, No Drums*, pp. 211–12.

72. Lynn Montross and Nicholas A. Canzona, *U.S. Marine Operations in Korea, 1950–1953*, vol. 3, *The Chosin Reservoir Campaign* (Washington: Government Printing Office, 1957), pp. 351–54.

73. S. L. A. Marshall, "Hearing it from the Marines," and "The Last Barrier," in *Battle at Best* (New York: William Morrow, 1963), p. 105.

74. S. L. A. Marshall, "CCF in the Attack," part 2, "A Study based on the Operations of 1st Marine Division in the Koto-ri, Hagaru-ri, Yodam-ni area, 20 November–10 December 1950," reprinted in Hopkins, *One Bugle, No Drums*, p. 257.

75. Hopkins, *One Bugle, No Drums*, p. 207.

76. Montross and Canzona, *Chosin Reservoir Campaign*, p. 107.

77. Eighth Army, G-4 Staff Section Report, 19 November 1950.

78. Ridgway, *The Korean War*, p. 88. See also Eighth Army, Command Report, January 1951, Commanding General section, which has some accounts of Ridgway's talks to commanders—and which more than corroborates his view that he spared no one's feelings.

79. Ridgway, *Korean War*, p. 97.

80. Griffith, *Chinese PLA*, p. 161.

81. Carl von Clausewitz, *On War*, Michael Howard and Peter Paret, eds. and trans. (Princeton: Princeton University Press, 1976), pp. 88–89.

82. Futrell, *U.S. Air Force*, pp. 71, 91.

83. Ibid., p. 186. On July 31 the Joint Chiefs told MacArthur that "mass air operations against industrial targets in North Korea were 'highly desirable.'"

84. Ibid., p. 221.

85. MacArthur's reliance on air power is captured in Charles A. Willoughby and John Chamberlain, *MacArthur, 1941–1951* (New York: McGraw-Hill, 1954), pp. 100–122.

86. Appleman, *East of Chosin*, p. 21.

87. Griffith, *Chinese PLA*, p. 73. The army later followed suit.

88. "Logistics in Korean Operations," vol. 1, chap 1, p. 4.

89. Joint Strategic Plans Committee, "Courses of Action in Korea," 23 August 1950, Folder CCS 383.21 Korea (3-19-45), Joint Chiefs of Staff Geographic File 1948–1950, Record Group 218, Modern Military Records, National Archives.

90. JCS99935, JCS to MacArthur, December 29, 1950, "Korean War—Special File," Ridgway Papers, USAMHI.

91. Clausewitz, *On War*, book 1, chap. 6, p. 118.

92. Michael Howard, "The Use and Abuse of Military History," *Parameters* 11:1(March 1981):13.

93. S. L. A. Marshall, *Sinai Victory* (New York: William Morrow, 1958), p. 6. Cf. Ridgway's assertion, "We are not adapting our tactics to the enemy and to the type of terrain encountered," conference notes, January 8, 1951.

Chapter 8
CATASTROPHIC FAILURE
The French Army and Air Force, May–June 1940

1. Churchill to Roosevelt, May 15, 1940. Quoted in Warren F. Kimball, ed., *Churchill and Roosevelt: The Complete Correspondence* (Princeton, NJ: Princeton University Press, 1984), vol. 1, p. 37.

2. William S. Shirer, *The Collapse of the Third Republic* (London: Pan, 1972), p. xxiv.

3. Sir Charles Petrie, ed., *The Private Diaries (March 1940 to January 1941) of Paul Baudouin* (London: Eyre & Spottiswoode, 1948), p. 92 (June 10, 1940).

4. Pétain to Reynaud, 26 May 1940. Quoted in J. Benoist-Méchin, *Soixante jours qui ébranlèrent l'occident* (Paris: Albin Michel, 1956), vol. 1, p. 306.

5. André Beaufre, *1940: The Fall of France* (London: Cassell, 1965), p. 213.

6. Baudouin, p. 46 (May 24, 1940).

7. William S. Shirer, *Berlin Diary: The Journal of a Foreign Correspondent 1934–1941* (New York: Alfred Knopf, 1941), pp. 437–38 (June 27, 1940).

8. Aldo Cabiati, *La guerra lampo: Polonia–Norvegia–Francia* (Milan: Corbaccio, 1940), p. 317.

9. Marc Bloch, *L'étrange défaite* (Paris: Societé des Editions Franc-Tireur, 1946), pp. 55–56.

10. Charles de Gaulle, *War Memoirs*, vol. 1: *The Call to Honour 1940–1942* (London: Weidenfeld & Nicolson, n.d., [1955]), p. 13.

11. Robert A. Doughty, *The Seeds of Disaster: The Development of French Army Doctrine 1919–1939* (Hamden, Conn.: Archon, 1985), p. 190.

12. Guy Chapman, *Why France Collapsed* (London: Cassell, 1968), pp. 331, 334.

13. De Gaulle, *War Memoirs*, p. 41.

14. Jeffrey A. Gunsberg, *Divided and Conquered: The French High Command and the Defeat of the West, 1940* (Westport, Conn.: Greenwood, 1979), p. 276.

15. Matthew Cooper, *The German Army 1933–1945* (London: MacDonald and Jane's, 1978), pp. 214–15; R. H. S. Stolfi, "Equipment for Victory in 1940," *History* 55 (1970): 1–20. For an interesting attempt to compare weapons systems on either side, see Philip A. Karber, Grant Whitley, Mark Herman, and Douglas Komer, *Assessing the Correlation of Forces: France 1940*, Washington, Office of the Secretary of Defense. DNA-001-78-C-0114.

16. Alistair Horne, *To Lose a Battle: France 1940* (London: Macmillan, 1969), pp. 108–9.

17. Gen. Edmond Ruby, quoted in Shirer, *Collapse*, pp. 737–38.

18. Quoted in Benoist-Méchin, vol. 1, p. 212.

19. General Order to the Troops, May 25, 1940. Quoted in ibid., 2, p. 11.

20. Quoted in P. M. H. Bell, *A Certain Eventuality: Britain and the Fall of France* (London: Saxon House, 1974), p. 84.

21. Benoist-Méchin, vol. 2, p. 382.

22. Luçien Robineau, "L'armée de l'air dans la bataille de France," in *Les armées françaises pendant la seconde guerre mondiale 1939-1945* (Paris: Fondation pour les études de Défense nationale, 1986), p. 42.

23. Patrice Buffotot, "Le moral dans l'armée de l'air française (de septembre 1939 à juin 1940)," in *Français et Britanniques dans la drôle de guerre* (Paris: Editions du Centre National de la Récherche Scientifique, 1979), pp. 173-96.

24. Shirer, *Collapse*, 690-91.

25. Gunsberg, 234; Eleanor M. Gates, *The End of the Affair: The Collapse of the Anglo-French Alliance, 1939-40* (London: Unwin Hyman Ltd., 1981), p. 161.

26. The contrast with German care and forethought, exemplified in Guderian's careful coordination with his *Flieger Korps* commander, Bruno Loerzer, is striking: Williamson Murray, *Strategy for Defeat: The Luftwaffe 1939-1945* (Maxwell, Ala.: Air University Press, 1983), p. 37.

27. For further details on the French air campaign, see Patrice Buffotot and Jacques Ogier, "L'armée de l'air française dans la campagne de France (10 Mai-25 Juin 1940)," *Révue historique des Armées* 2 (1975): 88-117.

28. Horne, p. 113. See also Shirer, *Berlin Diary*, pp. 140, 439.

29. Murray, *Strategy for Defeat*, p. 31.

30. Henri Dutailly, "Faiblesses et potentialités de l'armée de terre (1939-1940)," *Les armées françaises*, p. 28.

31. Michel Garder, *La guerre secrète des Services speciaux françaises 1939-1945* (Paris: Plon, 1967), pp. 153, 175-76.

32. R. Macleod and D. Kelly, eds., *The Ironside Diaries 1937-1940* (London: Constable, 1962), p. 117.

33. Gunsberg, *Divided and Conquered*, pp. 92-95.

34. Quoted in Shirer, *Collapse*, p. 601.

35. Gunsberg, *Divided and Conquered*, pp. 104-6.

36. Beaufre, *1940*, p. 175.

37. Col. J. Defrasne, "L'attitude du commandement français face aux repercussions militaires de la révolution technique et industrielle de 1919 à 1940: le facteur de 'renseignement,'" in *Le haut commandment français face au progrès technique entre les deux guerres* (Paris: Service Historique de l'Armée de l'Air, 1980), p. 41, 52-54.

38. For an uncompromising view that the French were dogged by the past, see Robert J. Young, "Preparations for Defeat: French War Doctrine in the Interwar Period," *Journal of European Studies* 2 (1972): 155-72.

39. David B. Ralston, "From Boulanger to Pétain: The Third Republic and the Republican Generals," in Brian Bond and Ian Roy, eds., *War and Society: A Yearbook of Military History* (London: Croom Helm, n.d.), pp. 178–201.

40. Ladislas Mysyrowicz, *Autopsie d'une défaite: Origines de l'effondrement militaire français de 1940* (Lausanne: L'Age d'homme, 1973), p. 20.

41. Quoted in Doughty, *The Seeds of Disaster*, p. 93.

42. See Robert J. Doughty, "The French Armed Forces, 1918–1940," in Allan R. Millett and Williamson Murray, eds., *Military Effectiveness* (London: Allen & Unwin, 1988), pp. 39–69.

43. Eugene Carrias, *La pensée militaire française* (Paris: Presses Universitaires de France, 1960), p. 331. For an excellent summary of de Gaulle's book, see Mysyrowicz, pp. 201–13.

44. Benoist-Méchin, vol. 3, pp. 266–67, 269.

45. Brian Bond and Martin Alexander, "Liddell Hart and de Gaulle: The Doctrines of Mobile Defense and Limited Liability," in Peter Paret ed., *Makers of Modern Strategy from Machiavelli to the Nuclear Age* (Princeton, N.J.: Princeton University Press, 1986), p. 620.

46. Garder, *La guerre secrète*, p. 31.

47. Robert J. Young, "French Military Intelligence and Nazi Germany, 1938–1939," in E. R. May, ed., *Knowing One's Enemies: Intelligence Assessment before the Two World Wars* (Princeton, N.J.: Princeton University Press, 1984), p. 302.

48. Gunsberg, *Divided and Conquered*, p. 269.

49. Bloch, *L'étrange défaite*, pp. 63–64.

50. Maurice Gauché, *Le deuxième bureau au travail (1935–40)* (Paris: Dumont, 1953), p. 101.

51. Garder, *La guerre secrète*, p. 185; Gauché, *Le deuxième bureau*, p. 189.

52. Quoted in Douglas Porch, "French Intelligence and the Fall of France 1930–1940," *Intelligence and National Security* 4 (1989): 42.

53. Quoted in Shirer, *Collapse*, p. 669.

54. F. H. Hinsley et al., *British Intelligence in the Second World War* (London: HMSO 1979–88), vol. 1, p. 131.

55. Shirer, *Collapse*, p. 669; Garder, *La guerre secrète*, p. 182; Hinsley et al., *British Intelligence*, p. 135.

56. Harold C. Deutsch, *The Conspiracy against Hitler in the Twilight War* (Minneapolis: University of Minnesota Press, 1968), pp. 328–29.

57. Doughty, *Seeds of Disaster*, pp. 58–59; Garder, *La guerre secrète*, pp. 178–79.

58. Brian Bond, *France and Belgium 1939–40* (London: Davis Poynter, 1975), p. 79.

59. Garder, *La guerre secrète*, pp. 146–47.

60. Horne, *To Lose a Battle*, p. 170.

61. Beaufre, *1940*, p. 179.
62. Gamelin to Gauché, September 1, 1939. Quoted in Benoist-Méchin, vol. 1, p. 51.
63. Quoted in Chapman, p. 88.
64. Elisabeth du Reau, "Haut commandement et pouvoir politique," *Les armées françaises*, pp. 77–78.
65. Gunsberg, *Divided and Conquered*, pp. 178–79.
66. Ibid., pp. 55, 135.
67. Shirer, *Collapse*, p. 809.
68. Beaufre, *1940*, p. 182.
69. John C. Cairns, "Some Recent Historians and the 'Strange Defeat' of 1940," *Journal of Modern History* 46 (1974): 81.
70. Chapman, *Why France Collapsed*, p. 160.
71. Horne, *To Lose a Battle*, p. 406.
72. Hinsley et al., *British Intelligence*, vol. 1, pp. 143–64.
73. Shirer, *Collapse*, p. 747.
74. Mysyrowicz, *Autopsie d'une défaite*, p. 43.
75. Macleod and Kelly, *Ironside Diaries*, p. 206 (January 14, 1940).
76. Bond, *France and Belgium*, pp. 146–48.
77. J. R. Colville, *Man of Valour: Field Marshal Lord Gort* (London: Colllins, 1972), p. 168.
78. Jean-Louis Crémieux-Brilhac, "L'opinion français devant la guerre," *Les armées françaises*, pp. 53–66.
79. Ibid., p. 64.
80. Benoist-Méchin, vol. 2, pp. 10–11.
81. Lt. Col. P. Le Goyet, "Evolution de la doctrine d'emploi de l'aviation française entre 1919 et 1939," *Révue d'Histoire de la deuxième guerre mondiale* 19 (1969): 3–41. For a survey of the popular literature on air war, see Robert J. Young, "The Use and Abuse of Fear: France and the Air Menace in the 1930s," *Intelligence and National Security* 2 (1987): 88–109.
82. Robert J. Young, "The Strategic Dream: French Air Doctrine in the Interwar Period, 1919–39," *Journal of Contemporary History* 9 (1974): 57–76.
83. Cot to Daladier, September 25, 1937. Cited in Patrice Buffotot, "La doctrine aerienne du haut commandement français pendant l'entre-deux guerres," in *Le haut commandement français face au progrès technique*, p. 30.
84. Dutailly, "Faiblesses," pp. 25, 27.
85. Doughty, *Seeds of Disaster*, pp. 96–97.
86. E.g., Beaufre, *1940*, p. 198.
87. Horne identifies it as the afternoon of May 15; Horne, *To Lose a Battle*, p. 516.

88. Robineau, *L'armée de l'air*, p. 44.

89. Colville, *Man of Valour*, p. 188; Macleod and Kelly, *Ironside Diaries*, p. 302.

90. Baudouin, p. 27.

91. Mysyrowicz, *Autopsie d'une défaite*, p. 236.

92. See Harold C. Deutsch, "Commanding generals and the Uses of Intelligence," *Intelligence and National Security* 3 (1988), 194–260.

Chapter 9
WHAT CAN BE DONE?

1. Michael Howard, "The Forgotten Dimension of Strategy," in *The Causes of War* (Cambridge: Harvard University Press, 1984), pp. 101–15.

2. By no means all, however. See for example Allan Millett and Williamson Murray, eds., *Military Effectiveness*, 3 vols. (Boston: Allen & Unwin, 1988). In addition, political scientists have done a great deal of work attempting to bring organization theory to bear on the study of the military, although rarely have they looked closely at battle outcomes, as opposed to prewar planning and civil-military relations, for example.

3. For two fine examples, see John Keegan, *The Mask of Command* (New York: Viking, 1987), and Eric Larrabee, *Commander in Chief: Franklin Delano Roosevelt, His Lieutenants, and Their War* (New York: Harper & Row, 1987).

4. Marshall to Lieutenant General Stanley Embick, May 1, 1940. Larry I. Bland, Sharon R. Ritenour, and Clarence E. Wunderlin, Jr., eds., *The Papers of George Catlett Marshall*, vol. II, *"We Cannot Delay" July 1, 1939–December 6, 1941* (Baltimore: Johns Hopkins University Press, 1986), pp. 205–6.

5. Richard A. Gabriel, *Military Incompetence: Why the American Military Doesn't Win* (New York: Hill & Wang, 1985), pp. 6–33, appears to take this approach.

6. Martin van Creveld, *Command in War* (Cambridge: Harvard University Press, 1985), pp. 270–73.

7. James Brian Quinn, "Strategic Change: 'Logical Incrementalism,' " *Sloan Management Review* (Fall 1978): 8. See also Richard F. Vancil, "So You're Going to Have a Planning Department!" *Harvard Business Review* (May/June 1967): 88–96; Richard F. Vancil and Peter Lorange, "Strategic Planning in Diversified Companies," *Harvard Business Review* (January/February 1975): 81–90; Robert H. Hayes, "Strategic Planning—Forward or Reverse?" *Harvard Business Review* (November/December 1985): 111–19; Daniel H. Gray, "Uses and Misuses of Strategic Planning," *Harvard Business Review* (January/February 1986): 89–97.

8. Our approach in this matter is very similar to that of James Q. Wilson in *Bureaucracy: What Government Agencies Do and Why They Do It* (New York: Basic Books, 1989), and owes a debt to his writing on the subject.

9. A point made by Peter K. Kemp, in "War Studies in the Royal Navy," *The Royal United Services Institute Journal* 111:642 (May 1966): 151–55.

10. On sonar see Arthur J. Marder, "Influence of History on Sea Power: The Royal Navy and the Lessons of 1914–1918," in *From the Dardanelles to Oran: Studies of the Royal Navy in War and Peace, 1915–1940* (London: Oxford University Press, 1974), p. 40.

11. See, *inter alia*, T. Harry Williams, "The Military Leadership of North and South," in David Donald, ed., *Why the North Won the Civil War* (New York: Macmillan, 1960), pp. 33–54. The same occurred in many militaries—in Europe even more than in the United States—following the wars of German unification, which led to a wave of imitation of Prussian organization and methods, down to the wearing of spiked helmets.

12. W. Scott Thompson and Donaldson D. E. Frizzell, eds. *The Lessons of Vietnam* (New York: Crane, Russak, 1977), p. 22.

13. Herbert Rosinski Papers, Box 7, R-132, (1943?) Naval War College Historical Collection (emphasis added).

14. See Edward Luttwak, *Strategy: The Logic of War and Peace* (Cambridge: Harvard University Press, 1987), p. 20. For a contrary view, see Stephen Peter Rosen, "New Ways of War: Understanding Military Innovation," *International Security* 13:2 (Fall 1988), p. 135.

15. See Rosen, "New Ways of War," pp. 158–66.

16. Jeter A. Isely and Philip A. Crowl, *The U.S. Marines and Amphibious War* (Princeton: Princeton University Press, 1951), pp. 33–71.

17. D. Clayton James, *A Time for Giants: Politics of the American High Command in World War II* (New York: Franklin Watts, 1987), p. 179.

18. Alfred D. Chandler, Jr., ed., *The Papers of Dwight David Eisenhower: The War Years* (Baltimore: The Johns Hopkins University Press, 1970), vol. 2, p. 824.

19. Quoted in Isely and Crowl, *U.S. Marines*, p. 3.

20. B. H. Liddell Hart, ed., *The Rommel Papers*, Paul Findlay trans. (New York: Harcourt, Brace, 1953), pp. 521, 523.

21. See Eliot A. Cohen, "Analysis," in Roy Godson, ed., *Intelligence Requirements for the 1990s* (Washington: National Security Information Center, 1989), pp. 71–96.

22. "Israel's Combat Arms," *Armed Forces Journal International* 111:2 (October 1973): 64. Rafael Eitan describes angry exchanges with the chief armored officer, Major General Avraham Adan, when he (Eitan) refused to give up his red paratrooper's beret for the black beret of the tank corps upon taking over a divisional command. See Eitan and Goldstein, *Raful*, pp. 124 ff.

23. Williams, ed., *Military Aspects of the Israeli-Arab Conflict*, p. 248.

24. Ya'akov Chasdai, "Milchemet yom hakippurim: hafta'a? nitsachon?" ["The Yom Kippur War: Surprise? Victory?"] *Ma'arachot* 275 (August 1980): 10.

Chasdai was a highly decorated paratroop colonel and historian, who taught at the IDF staff college and was a researcher for the Agranat Commission. See also Avraham Adan, "Eichut v'kamut b'milchemet yom hakippurim" ["Quality and Quantity in the Yom Kippur War"] in Zvi Offer and Avi Kober, eds., *Eichut v'kamut: dilemmot b'binyan bakoach batsva'i* ["Quality and Quantity: Dilemmas in the Development of Military Forces"] (Tel Aviv: Ma'arachot, 1985), pp. 262, 288.

25. Paul H. Herbert, *Deciding What Has to Be Done: General William E. DePuy and the 1976 Edition of FM 100-5, Operations,* Leavenworth Papers #16 (Fort Leavenworth, Kans.: US Army Command and General Staff College, 1988), p. 3.

26. *Ibid.,* p. 54. DePuy was bitterly opposed by Major General John Cushman, the head of the Army's Command and General Staff school at Fort Leavenworth. See p. 55, and also Kevin P. Sheehan, "Preparing for Imaginary War: Examining Peacetime Functions and Changes of Army Doctrine," unpublished dissertation, Harvard University, 1988.

27. M. A. Gareev, *M. V. Frunze: Military Theorist* (Washington, D.C.: Pergamon-Brassey's 1988), pp. 378–79. Colonel General Gareev was deputy chief of staff of the Soviet armed forces when he wrote this book.

28. See Eliot A. Cohen, "Toward Better Net Assessment," *International Security* 13:2 (Fall 1988): 50–89.

29. Tim Travers, "The Hidden Army: Structural Problems in the British Officer Corps, 1900–1918," *Journal of Contemporary History* 17:3 (July 1982): 523–44; Travers, *The Killing Ground: The British Army, the Western Front and the Emergence of Modern Warfare, 1900–1918* (London: Allen & Unwin, 1987), pp. 23, 107; Gerard J. De Groot, *Douglas Haig, 1861–1928* (London: Unwin Hyman, 1988), pp. 191–92.

30. E. K. G. Sixsmith, *British Generalship in the Twentieth Century* (London: Arms & Armour, 1970), p. 43.

31. De Groot, p. 333.

32. Sixsmith, pp. 110–12, 139.

33. What follows is largely based on Bradley J. Meyer, "Operational Art and the German Command System in World War I," Ph.D. dissertation, Ohio State University, 1988.

34. Brian Holden Reid, "Major General J. F. C. Fuller and the Decline of Generalship," *British Army Review* 90 (December 1988): 12–19.

35. U.S. Army Military History Institute, Carlisle: "Command," December 23, 1921, p. 6. Army War College Lectures, 1921–1922.

36. Marshall to Morris Sheppard, June 5, 1940. *Marshall Papers,* vol. 2, p. 236.

37. See, for example, Field Marshal Lord Wavell, *Generals and Generalship* (Harmondsworth: Penguin, 1941).

38. John F. Lehman, *Command of the Seas* (New York: Charles Scribner's Sons, 1988), pp. 19, 21.

39. Ibid., pp. 36–38.

40. E. B. Potter, *Nimitz* (Annapolis: Naval Institute Press, 1976), p. 17.

41. Bloch to Rear Admiral James O. Richardson. Quoted in James, *A Time for Giants*, p. 54. As we have pointed out in chapter 2, Bloch bore some measure of responsibility for the failure.

42. Ibid., p. 190.

43. Quoted in Lloyd Lewis, *Sherman: Fighting Prophet* (New York: Harcourt Brace, 1932), p. 424.

44. William Slim, *Defeat Into Victory* (New York: David McKay, 1961). pp. 98–99.

45. We reject the view expressed by Gabriel (*Military Incompetence*, p. 188) that political leaders have no responsibility for the competence of the forces under their control. Cf. Lehman, *Command of the Seas*, pp. 423–24.

46. See Eliot A. Cohen, "Churchill at War," *Commentary* 83:5 (May 1987): 40–49.

47. Speech to the House of Commons, October 8, 1940. Robert Rhodes James, ed., *Winston S. Churchill: His Complete Speeches, 1897–1963* (London: Chelsea House Publishers, 1974), vol. 6, p. 6293.

48. This point is further amplified in Rosen, "New Ways of War."

Index

ABOUT THE AUTHORS

Eliot A. Cohen is Robert E. Osgood Professor of Strategic Studies at the Paul H. Nitze School of Advanced International Studies, the Johns Hopkins University. He came to SAIS in 1990 following service on the policy planning staff of the Office of the Secretary of Defense and previous teaching posts at Harvard University and the Naval War College. He is a frequent consultant to the Department of Defense and the intelligence community and is the author of, among other books, *Supreme Command: Leadership in Wartime* (Free Press, 2002).

John Gooch is a professor of history at the University of Lancaster, England. One of Britain's leading military historians, he has also been a visiting professor at Yale and the U.S. Naval War College. The founding editor of the *Journal of Strategic Studies* and chairman of the Army Records Society, he is the author of a number of books, including *The Plans of War* and *Armies in Europe*.